SCHOOLING AND THE ACQUISITION OF KNOWLEDGE

SCHOOLING AND THE ACQUISITION OF KNOWLEDGE

Edited by

RICHARD C. ANDERSON
RAND J. SPIRO
University of Illinois at Urbana-Champaign

WILLIAM E. MONTAGUE
Navy Personnel Research and Development Center

 LAWRENCE ERLBAUM ASSOCIATES, PUBLISHERS

1977   Hillsdale, New Jersey

DISTRIBUTED BY THE HALSTED PRESS DIVISION OF

JOHN WILEY & SONS

New York   Toronto   London   Sydney

Lawrence Erlbaum Associates, Inc., Publishers
62 Maria Drive
Hillsdale, New Jersey 07642

Distributed solely by Halsted Press Division
John Wiley & Sons, Inc., New York

Library of Congress Cataloging in Publication Data

Main entry under title:

Schooling and the acquisition of knowledge.

    Includes indexes.
    1. Learning, Psychology of—Addresses, essays,
lectures.   2. Cognition—Addresses, essays,
lectures.   3. Education—Aims and objectives—
Addresses, essays, lectures.   I. Anderson, Richard C.
II. Spiro, Rand J.   III. Montague, William Edward
1931–
LB1051.S374   370.15   77-22004
ISBN 0-470-99293X

Printed in the United States of America

Contents

Preface

During the past decade and a half there has been a ferment in psychology. Fifteen years ago few psychologists would have called themselves psycholinguists, and almost none would have used the designation cognitive psychologist. Now these designations are as familiar as the traditional label—experimental psychologist. The shift in the names psychologists use to describe themselves signals important changes in areas of inquiry. Whereas in the past most research in human experimental psychology involved paired-associate learning, free recall of word lists, or the identification of arbitrary concepts from stylized geometric patterns, a larger and larger proportion of papers in the literature now deal with more natural units of human communication and understanding such as sentences, stories, and text. The whole point of view about what constitutes the proper goal of psychology has changed. Formerly it was construed to be the discovery of lawful relationships between observable stimuli and observable responses. Assumptions about what goes on under the skin were to be made cautiously, if at all. Now human experimental psychology takes as its proper goal modeling what the mind knows and how it knows.

Meanwhile, by and large, educational research workers who look to psychology for inspiration have continued their twenty-year love affair with behaviorism. Make no mistake, we would not care to question the practical benefits of contingency management techniques under certain circumstances. And, most certainly, we would not deny the important contributions of the instructional technology movement which, while behaviorist in origin, increasingly displays a cognitive coloration in the hands of its most skillful practitioners. Nonetheless, at the present time, work in cognitive psychology and related fields has had only modest impact on the thinking of educational researchers, and virtually no disciplined application to instructional practice. Given the increasing emphasis on ecological validity in cognitive psychology, this state of affairs need not persist.

So it was that a group of psychologists, educators, and philosophers convened under technicolor-blue skies on Shelter Island in San Diego harbor late in November of 1975 to reflect on schooling and the acquisition of knowledge. The group was interdisciplinary in character because of our conviction that the questions posed could be resolved only by the consolidation and integration of knowledge from diverse specialized domains. The one common thread running through all of the formal papers and dialogue was that the knowledge a person already possesses is the principal determiner of what that individual can learn from an educational experience. These questions were addressed: How is knowledge organized? How does knowledge develop? How is knowledge retrieved and used? What instructional techniques promise to facilitate the acquisition of new knowledge? The kinds of answers provided are characterized by their breadth as well as by their specificity. Accordingly, the volume should be of interest to both the generalist and the specialist.

The Conference on Schooling and the Acquisition of Knowledge was sponsored by the Navy Personnel Research and Development Center. The support of Earl I. Jones, Director of Supporting Research at the Center, enabled us to hold the conference. Walter Spencer and Robert Harrigan provided assistance in recording the proceedings. We also wish to acknowledge the assistance of Bonnie Anderson, Charity Armstrong, Paula Konoske, and Phyllis Spiro in preparing this volume.

Richard C. Anderson, *Urbana, Illinois*
Rand J. Spiro, *Urbana, Illinois*
William E. Montague, *San Diego, California*

SCHOOLING
AND THE ACQUISITION
OF KNOWLEDGE

1

Types of Knowledge
and Purposes of Education

H. S. Broudy

University of Illinois, Urbana

The physical scientist, psychologist, humanist, epistemologist, and educator all take knowledge for their domain, but it is sometimes difficult to recognize their maps, classifications, and directions as applying to a common territory. Consider, for example, a few of the classifications of knowledge that have achieved prominence in the history of philosophy. The four stages distinguished by Plato in the figure of the divided line in *The Republic* has had remarkable endurance. So have Aristotle's distinctions between the kinds of knowing involved in understanding, making, and choosing.[1] Kant's distinction between a priori and a posteriori knowledge, echoing the old division between intuitive knowledge of principle and empirical knowledge of fact, and the antagonism between the scientific search for truth and the humanistic one are other examples. Some classifications are based on the nature of the subject matter being studied; some on the methods of studying it. Some are characterized by their epistemic status, for example, the differences between opinion, belief, and knowledge; between knowledge by acquaintance and knowledge by description (Russell, 1912) or Gilbert Ryle's distinction between knowing that and knowing how (Ryle, 1949).

Compare the questions that an epistemologist, psychologist, humanist, and educator might ask of a discipline X.

Epistemologist: What is the logical structure of X? What are the entities, relations that enter into its laws or generalizations? What are its modes of inquiry, and what are the criteria for the validity of its results?

Psychologist: How does one discover the structure of X? How do people learn this structure? Are there stages in this process? What factors are involved in the success or failure of the process?

---

[1] In *Metaphysics*, 1025^b 25, Aristotle divides the sciences into the theoretical, practical, and productive, the ultimate goals of which respectively are knowledge, conduct, and the making of useful or beautiful objects.

1

Humanist: What is the import of X for human goals? What is its significance for humanity and for individual selves?

Educator: How does what the psychologist or epistemologist say about the learning of X help in the teaching of X? How does what the humanist says about X figure in the teaching of X or in deciding whether or not X should be taught and to whom?

Missing from this list of knowledge constituencies is the ordinary consumer and user of knowledge. Ever since formal schooling was established, it has been assumed that knowledge acquired in school would be used to enhance the quality of human life. The investment in schools was supposed to yield a return in the form of greater adequacy in occupational, civic, and personal development. There has never been a lack of critics who doubted the causal nexus between success in school and success in life. In spite of such skepticism, the faith and investment in formal schooling persist.

To understand this anomaly it may be instructive to look at some of the differences in types of knowledge, the interest of specialists who deal with knowledge, and the ways knowledge is used. It is suggested here that, in part, the anomaly rests on a mistaken orthodoxy concerning the relation between school learnings and their subsequent uses, an orthodoxy that ought to be reexamined.

I. TYPES OF KNOWLEDGE

How individuals came to have knowledge was once a standard philosophical topic. Descartes posited certain innate ideas; Locke denied their existence and argued for *tabula rasa* on which ideas and impressions of sense were recorded, combined, and retrieved. Plato's theory of recollection and Aristotle's theory of cognitive functions are also accounts of how knowledge is acquired. To a considerable extent the conclusions drawn by Plato and Aristotle regarding sensation, perception, imagination, memory, and reasoning of various sorts, are still used in psychology as well as in philosophy. Aristotle, Plato, Descartes, and other philosophers constructed their theories about the origin and development of knowledge by asking what processes and entities would be required to explain the existence of opinion, belief, and — if possible — certainty. Aristotle's postulate of active and passive intellect and Kant's forms of intuition are examples of this kind of philosophical-psychological theory resulting from observation and logical analysis of concepts of knowledge rather than from systematic empirical investigation.

As the empirical study of human behavior and mental functioning developed, the distinction became sharper between generalizations of the psychological processes and the structural-logical properties of knowledge. Today, it is generally recognized that psychology, in principle at least, should be able to say how men come to their beliefs, but psychologists are not expected to decide whether these beliefs are justified. These judgments are made authoritatively by specialists within the various disciplines to whom the data, the relevant evidence, and criteria of validity are familiar. Accordingly, as the special disciplines developed, the questions reserved for the epistemologist were reduced to those concerned with the justification of various types of truth claims and of the possibility of truth in general. As a result of this development, the relevance of epistemology to the empirical sciences and the humanistic studies becomes more and more attenuated. Epistemology tends to become a metadiscipline which the workers in the several disciplines think they can safely ignore. Thus, many nuclear physicists do not feel the need to study philosophy of science.

Epistemology by its classifications, distinctions, and theories draws attention of psychologists to loci of inquiry just as any system of terminology does, but not all philosophical questions are of equal interest to the psychologist or the educator. For example, the acres of philosophical arguments on whether or not there can be certainty in knowledge are of little immediate interest to psychologists, although an analytic psychologist might be interested in the motives that enable philosophers to devote their professional lives to formulating issues in a way that insures their unsolvability.

By contrast, a theory of knowledge and truth such as that propounded by William James, Charles Peirce, and latterly by John Dewey is of immediate interest to the educational psychologists because it suggests a method of teaching. Thus, if the truth (James) or meaning (Peirce) or warranted assertion (Dewey) can be achieved by traversing or reenacting the complete existential act of thought, we have a neat union between epistemology and psychology. The connection between Kantian epistemology and Piagetian genetic psychology is interesting for the same reason. Nevertheless, the tradition that there is a fundamental difference between the order of knowledge and discovery and between the logical and psychological orders of learning is a strong one.

The concreteness of particulars flowing together in the continuity of experience is never quite exhausted by the abstract categories used to analyze and describe these experiences, albeit psychology stays closer to this concreteness than do the sciences dealing with bodies, animate and inanimate. The humanistic disciplines, as will be noted, claim to stay closer to the human reality than any of the scientific ones. The educator, dealing with particulars — pupils — views all abstractions with extreme caution. Unlike the researcher, he does not see individuals as data for generalization, but as unique events. This ineluctable difference in perspective does not bode well for a science of education.

Nevertheless, the educator cannot be indifferent to the way knowledge is construed and dealt with by psychology, philosophy, and the humanities because his task is to unite the particularity of pupils with the universality of knowledge. Different types of knowledge make different claims on the curriculum, and justifying their place in the curriculum very soon takes on philosophical dimensions. The actual teaching transaction, moreover, is partly prescribed by the way the disciplines, the repositories of the different types of knowledge, are organized as conceptual systems. Setting the stage for the transaction whereby the forms of knowledge, in Aristotelian terms, become the forms of an individual mind is in the psychological-pedagogical sector. The difference between setting the stage for the act of comprehension and the structure of what is comprehended can be as great as that which obtains between the work of stage hands and that of the playwright.

Of the numerous distinctions among the types of knowledge that might be discussed, I have chosen three contrasts that persist not only as theoretical problems, but also as matters of educational policy.

A. Knowledge as Structure and Process

Knowledge as a system of statements about entities, relations, and theories in some domain of inquiry has its own logical properties and criteria. The theory explaining the existential process whereby these inquiries were instituted, carried on, and arrived at also has a structure (causal, developmental) but one not necessarily identical with the logical properties of the conceptual system being learned. How Einstein came to formulate the principle of relativity is not evident in the equations expressing that principle, just as the vicissitudes of Euclid's cogitations are not evident in the theorems bearing his name. To be sure, an accurate account of what went on in the life of Einstein and Euclid would contain references to relativity theory and geometry, even, perhaps, the statement or the equations and theorems themselves. However, it would contain much more, some of it having little relation to these statements. In other words, psychological generalizations about the thinking of scientists are not interchangeable with the product of that thinking, and this would apply to the generalizations of psychology itself as a science.

This discrepancy is important to education in several respects. For one thing, the logical structure of a discipline may not give any useful direction as to how the pupil may discover or learn it. Hence there is the pedagogical task of uniting the biography of a discipline (the history of its problems) with the results of the attempts to solve these problems. The PSSC (Physical Science Study Committee) physics curriculum is a notable example of how this can be done, but it took effort, money, and an unusual concern for the problems of schooling on the part of physicists to help bring it about.

In the second place, there is the temptation to argue that to think scientifically is more important than mastery of a body of scientific knowledge. A rivalry is thus set up between practicing the process and appropriating the product. For a bright high-school student, PSSC physics provides a good balance between the two, but often creates the impression that being scientific in spirit makes it unnecessary to study its letter. This enrages disciplinarians, who forget that many of their students who have studied the letter are not scientific in spirit.

Finally, the ability to comprehend conceptual systems is one of the most widely recognized indices of intellectual quality. Since Plato there has been a strong tradition — never without its detractors — that theory people are "better" than and certainly rarer than the practice people. A curriculum that stresses conceptual ability is highly abstract and easily outdistances the capacity and patience of many members — perhaps most — of the school population. In recent years this tradition has been challenged by at least two demands: one, that the professors (theory people) had better do something useful in coping with our social predicaments or lose financial support; and two, young people who want to go to college should not be prevented from doing so by academic standards that stress a high abstraction potential.

B. Scientific versus Humanistic Knowledge

Scientific and humanistic studies constitute another major contrast in the types of knowledge important to the psychologist and the educator. One expects from psychology scientific descriptions about the human psyche. But the human reality includes components that, in a literal sense, do not exist. Elements such as goals, aspirations, conscience, anxiety, regret, and repentance, refer to states in the past or future. What sort of science deals with phenomena that gain their significance from what is not yet or no longer is? On a positivistic theory of knowledge, we can apparently know nothing about this kind of reality.

Yet, it is precisely with phenomena that have nonexistent referents that the humanistic disciplines are primarily concerned. They purport to seek knowledge about human happiness and misery (not simply pleasure and pain). But in what sense can such conclusions be knowledge (i.e., justified true propositions)? They are neither inferred from controlled experiments nor are they statistical inductions from representative samples. On the contrary, a single experience may be taken as conclusive evidence of humanistic truth, like a religious conversion, a revelation, or the experience of a Job, Jesus, or Buddha. A particular image in a work of art may reveal a universal truth about the human condition (Macbeth, Guernica). These may be called exemplars, and they are not communicated by direct assertion (Broudy, 1961).

The evidence for the assertions "The sun is 93 million miles from the earth" and "I know that my Redeemer liveth" are not of the same order. The self-evidence of mathematical tautologies is not the same as that entailed by "Beauty is its own excuse." Humanistic truth or knowledge involves something other than logical or scientific validity. Perhaps it is authenticity. Authenticity is the property of being genuine, nonfake, as really issuing from the source that claims to originate it.

Authenticity is closely related to credibility. But while credibility is concerned with whether we should believe that P is not false or a lie, authenticity has more to do with whether the asserting Self is the real origin of an assertion or an act.

Thus, if I say that Mozart is a great composer it may be an authentic judgment that issues from my own experience, reflection, and evaluation. But it may also be an echo of a music critic who, for me, has high credibility in matters Mozartian.

Although we judge the credibility of persons by their access to the facts, this is not the sole or even the most important condition. We are really interested in grounds for believing the speaker is not lying. Sometimes this ground is provided by evidence that the speaker has no interest that would be served by deception, or because what he asserts may be contrary to his own interests. Sometimes a lack of sophistication is taken as evidence of sincerity, but more often we are convinced by a belief that So-and-So is not the sort of person who would deceive.

Authenticity is a property of an autonomous self. The evidence for the authenticity of an assertion P, therefore, is its congruence with the value system of such an autonomous self. It is the truth by which that self is willing to live or, if necessary, to die. Clearly, this kind of truth and evidence has different meanings than the same terms in science.

Do we have here a clue to the difference between scientific and humanistic knowledge? Scientific knowledge makes truth claims that can be assessed without raising the question of the credibility or authenticity of their author because, in principle at least, the assertion can be verified publicly by those who are competent and willing to give it a try. Humanistic knowledge, on the contrary, is about the value commitments of the race or the species as exemplified in the value systems of selves, real or imagined. About the only evidence we can adduce for the truth of these systems is that autonomous selves have regarded them as worthy of commitment and, indeed, of the highest commitment. This kind of knowledge we can possess in two forms; (1) as knowledge about the commitments that have been reported in this or that period by this or that person, and (2) as recognition of the claims of our own commitments, for we too are, or are trying to become, autonomous selves. Science is concerned primarily with truth; humanistic studies with authenticity.[2]

One of the earliest insights into the difference between natural science and humanistic knowledge came from Giambattista Vico (1668–1744). Vico argued that mathematics owed its success not to its correspondence with reality, but to the circumstance that its objects were constructed so as to be related logically in

---

[2] A case can be made for a cognitive mechanism that protects the integrity of a value system. If, for example, courage is a quality of behavior that has been generally admired and cultivated in the history of the race, not only will it acquire a kind of survival value, but it may become a parameter limiting the meaning of "human". In other words, those members of the group who do not interiorize the value of courage and experience no obligation to display behavior comportable with it are branded as non-human and treated accordingly, and this treatment is usually different from that meted out to those members who know the value and nature of courage but have failed to exercise that virtue.

a deductive system, once certain axioms and notions were accepted as given. Physicists, astronomers, and biologists, on the other hand, do not construct the objects of their investigations, hence they can never fully explain the "why" of physical phenomena. Only their Creator aware of His purpose and their ends could do this. If there were a kind of reality that human beings created and the purpose of which they knew and considered in the making, then one could hope to have explanatory knowledge of it. Human action (as distinguished from other kinds of behavior) is such a reality.

Two points follow from this for Vico. (1) A natural science of men treated as purely natural entities . . . rests on a cardinal error, for it gratuitously bars itself from what we can best understand. (2) We can reconstruct and recapture the collective experience of the race through their collective expressions in myth, rite, and language. Thus, according to Isaiah Berlin (1974), the methodological question for the understanding of human history is to ask ". . . what the experience of a particular society must have been for this or that myth, or method of worship, or language, or building to have been their characteristic expression" (p. 36). This, of course, undercuts the notion of a fixed human nature and a natural law that prescribes the ends of man, but it creates the possibility of a humanistic "science" of history.[3]

This difference between scientific and humanistic knowledge engenders a clash between two cultures, and occurs in every curriculum debate from elementary school through college. The guilds serving as custodians of one kind of knowledge rarely speak to the guildsmen serving the other. Only the classroom teacher in the elementary school is denied the privilege of specialization in one of these domains and the luxury of ignorance in the others.

C. Validity versus Utility

The third difference is between the noetic quality of a discipline which includes concepts, relations, theories, modes of inquiry and criteria of validity, and the individual or social usefulness of that knowledge. It is the difference between the questions: "What is good physics?" and "What is physics good for?"

Physics, mathematics, chemistry, biology, psychology, and even history and the arts can be used to further this or that human purpose, but the applications are not directly derived from the conceptual contents of these disciplines. The science of genetics, for example, tells us nothing about the human needs for hybrid corn or the desirability of preventing congenital defects in human beings. And although the problems of food and health stimulate the study of chemistry and biology, these needs do not determine the logical structure of these disciplines, the doctrines of Marx and Mao to the contrary notwithstanding. It is only

[3] For a concise account of Vico's life and doctrines see Vico (1944, 1965). The latter volume also contains a bibliography on works by Vico and about him.

when a technology does not perform properly that we ask whether some scientific principle is not being forgotten or misunderstood. As a rule, this is resorted to only after more technological inquiries fail to yield a remedy. As to the application of the humanistic studies, one need only look into these studies themselves to realize how much soul searching and reflection intervene between a moral principle and a commitment to a given act presumed to be comformable to it.

Schools are expected to be committed to teaching the contents of selected bodies of knowledge and to their social and individual utility. The teaching of chemistry is justified by its usefulness in many areas of commerce and industry; instruction in the humanities is justified by expected improvement in citizenship and a reduction in savagery of all kinds. Conversely, it is argued that if no use from a study can be demonstrated, then the subject ought not to be studied. Usefulness has at least two interpretations: (1) direct application to life tasks most frequently encountered by the average citizen, for example, driving an automobile or filling out a tax return, and (2) general application to wide ranges of phenomena, like mathematics, symbolic skills, critical thinking. The first interpretation favors a curriculum that is a sample of the cognitive and motor skills constituting the common life tasks. These are the identical elements upon which Thorndike relied for transfer. Indeed, there is a constant pressure on the schools to practice the tasks themselves and not to bother with transfer at all. The second interpretation relies heavily on Charles Judd's theory of transfer via generalization and gives support to a discipline curriculum. Because neither type of transfer seems to be as automatic or as predictable as one would wish, teaching for transfer is still a prime pedagogical task. Great reliance on transfer is regarded as one of the characteristics of education as distinguished from training. If generalizing requires a higher order of abstract intelligence than practicing a particular performance, then schooling may be polarized into reasoning for the elite and practice for the masses. This is embarrassing to a culture that is committed to abolishing this distinction.

For the professional and business elites in our society, theory and practice may very well converge. Theoretical competence is essential to a modern technological society, and very high rewards await those who can combine theory and utility. But that all members of society need to become knowledgeable about either science or technology is far less obvious, chiefly because the more developed the technology that goes into the production of automobiles, refrigerators, airplanes, and other blessings of a modern society, the less the consumer needs to understand how these products are made or why they function as they do.[4]

[4] This is related to Karl Mannheim's distinction between functional and substantial rationality of a social system. The functional rationality of a bureaucratic system diminishes the need for rationality in the citizens; indeed, if they persist in efforts to understand it,

The school, it seems to me, can straddle these dichotomies by asking how school studies can be used for vocational, civic, and personal adequacy in adult as well as in school life. The goal of the schools can then be to make school studies (and other activites) influential vehicles for its recipients in preorganizing, responding to, and reorganizing their experiences.

This could unify the diverse interests of psychologists, epistemologists, humanists, scientists, and educators at all levels of the school enterprise. For how schooling functions in the preorganization of the encountered situation, how it influences the judgments of relevance as regards the response, and how it reorganizes the situation is far from clear. Yet, as will be noted below, the difference between the cognitive processing of situations by those who have a good deal of formal schooling and those who have had very little or none at all is not hard to discern. I would argue that important as the inquiry of how learning takes place is, the modest influence such research has had upon schooling may be due to an indifference to the difference between the criteria for learning and the criteria for use of what is learned. It may be that different types of knowledge are used differently. In addition to knowings *that* and knowings *how*, there may be knowings *with*, about which our understanding is even less adequate than of the first two (Broudy, 1970a).

II. THE USES OF SCHOOLING

The two uses of schooling most frequently talked about are the replicative and the applicative. In the former, the school input is recalled pretty much as learned. Thus, one learns the multiplication table, the number facts, and the arithmetical operations in school and subsequently uses them as needed in arithmetical computation. Or, one learns to read in school and thereafter uses this skill to read newspapers, magazines, and books. Dates, names, terms, formulae are used replicatively, and although rote learning of this kind is not held in high esteem, higher and more complicated mental processes would be clumsy without the semi-automatic availability of ample stocks of such learnings. They are, so to speak, the constants of thinking. The user, of course, selects the arithmetical skill applicable in a particular task. But selecting the learning to be used can itself be made replicative if paradigm tasks are practiced in school, for example, how to do certain types of computational problems.

In the applicative use of schooling, one deduces a solution to a problem from the facts, rules, and principles he has learned. Thus, chemistry is applied to problems of agriculture, and the principles of physics to the manufacture of jet

---

they may find flaws in its rationality. Hence, the difference between conceptions of good citizenship in democratic and totalitarian governments. Cf. Broudy (1976) for a more detailed discussion of this paradox.

airplanes, etc. If one has learned the principles of the internal combustion engine, one is expected to apply this knowledge to repairing an automobile. Knowledge of history, ethics, moral philosophy, or economics are to be applied to solving problems in these domains.

These two uses of knowledge are commonly taken as the criteria for the effectiveness of schooling, but on these criteria, most schooling is a failure. For, the amount of rote learning one retains — unless there is opportunity for frequent recall — is discouragingly meager. Thus, despite having passed repeated courses in American history, few citizens can recall (directly or by recognition tests) most of the dates, names, and temporal and geographical circumstances of key historical events. Ordinary people, unlike idiot savants, recall such materials in detail only if they overlearn them to an extraordinary degree or rehearse them frequently as teachers of history do.

Similarly, if application is the criterion for the effectiveness of schooling, most of schooling is a waste of time. Applying the principles of chemistry, for example, to the energy crisis involves more than remembering what one has studied about hydrocarbons in school. Most of us do not apply our studies of physics in repairing our automobiles. There is a gap between the generalizations of science and its application to effect existential changes. The invention of a technology must intervene. A very complicated technology stands between the principles of describing the behavior of gases in Boyle's law and the application of them in a steam engine. It takes into account the purposes of men as well as the principles of gas behavior. This requires fairly intimate knowledge of the principles and of the phenomena constituting the existential situation. Taken in this sense, application of knowledge is largely confined to specialists, who learn how to do it in professional education and experience on the job.

Here we encounter a strange anomaly. If on replicative and applicative criteria, general education fails, why does the school and the public continue to expect these results from it? Why continue a heavy investment in what does not seem to pay off? We have, it seems to me, two choices. (1) to join those who counsel the abolition of general education. There is considerable pressure for this strategy manifested in diverse ways and coming from different quarters. The egalitarians believe general education to be a tool of the elitists and their upper-middle class supporters to maintain social supremacy. They say by limiting formal schooling to those who have high abstraction potentials, the poor and socially depressed groups will be kept inferior. Since the poor and disadvantaged cannot use general studies for economic advancement, they should be given more direct vocational training. Liberal Arts colleges hit by the depression in higher education would like to maintain their high abstraction clientele and curricula, but are searching for vocational skills that presumably lie latent in the general studies.

The second ploy is to challenge the replicative and applicative criteria on which general education performs so poorly. A move in this direction is to draw attention to the fact that general studies are usually used associatively and interpretively rather than replicatively and applicatively. Furthermore, one might explore the conjecture that for understanding a situation what has been studied need not be made explicit or fully conscious in order to be used, that is, much of our knowledge is, in Michael Polanyi's terms, tacit (Polanyi, 1966).

Experience, including school learnings, functions in a situation (1) to pre-organize it, that is, to set up expectations for perception and judgment; (2) to influence the decision on response or the selection of the response; (3) to enrich or elaborate the response, and (4) to reorganize the situation.

When the resources of the individual are activated by nonlogical relations to the situation, I call it an associative use of knowledge. By nonlogical relations I mean contiguity, resemblance, frequency, effect, and the familiar laws of association. There are also many variations in the nonlogical relations. For example, resemblance can be iconic, structural, functional, analogical, and metaphorical.

Much of the reaction to situations that require an aesthetic response, for example, utilize previous learnings associatively. The reading of poetry presupposes an imagic store that is spontaneously activated by the poem (Broudy, 1970b). Depth of meaning depends on tapping various layers of this imagic store. In turn, the study of poetry enriches the imagic store in ways that everyday experience may not. If, as is often argued, metaphor is a key operation in cognition, then cognition itself depends on rich stores of imagery (Ortony, 1975).

For our purpose, two points about the associative use of schooling have to be made. First, the associative use of the school input cannot be tested directly by recall, because it is not intended to be recalled on fixed cues; it would lose its usefulness if it were tied to such cues. Second, formal schooling introduces into experience images and meanings honed and fashioned by artists and thinkers, which are highly concentrated and vivid versions of their counterparts in every-day experience. Much of the effect of humanistic studies is at the associative level (Broudy, 1973).

Interpretive use of knowledge refers to categorization, classification, predication, and inference. In contrast to the associative use, the interpretative elicits a response that is logically related to the situation. The categories and concepts of the various disciplines guide our expectations, perceptions, and judgments with respect to both fact and value. But interpretation, although essential to application, does not *by itself* yield any technology which can cause change. And although the interpretation of the situation invariably involves some use of a previous experience, it cannot be reduced to simple replication of that experience.

As with the associative use, the resources for interpretation need not be explicit or conscious at the moment of use. For example, the concept of bacterial infection as learned in biology can operate even if only a skeletal notion of the theory and the facts supporting it can be recalled. Yet, we are told of cultures in which such a concept would not be part of the interpretive schemata. The argument for general education should be that the schooled man thinks, perceives, and judges with everything that he has studied in school, even though he cannot recall these learnings on demand. This would explain why the difference between a schooled and an unschooled man is fairly easy to discern but difficult to explicate. Interpretation is not confined to the use of scientific schemata. Humanistic studies supply value schemata with which to think and feel.

III. GENERAL EDUCATION FOR CONTEXTUAL KNOWING

In addition to the more familiar modes of knowing — knowing *how* and *that* — there is also and perhaps always an implicit knowing *with*. This type of knowing eludes the straightforward storage-retrieval model of the replicative uses of schooling and the hypothetico-deductive mode of problem solving entailed by the applicative use. When these models are used to explain the uses and effects of general education, they render its continuation anomalous, because so little of what has been studied can be retrieved at will or applied to solving situational predicaments.

So if general education is not useless, it must have other uses. Another way of putting it is to say that knowing *with* furnishes a context within which a particular situation is perceived, interpreted, and judged. Contexts can function without being at the center of consciousness, without being recalled verbatim, and without serving as hypothetical deductive premises for action.

What does context contribute to cognition? Context can be regarded as a pattern for construing the import and relevance of its constituents. Granted that propositions have their own lexical meaning, yet without a clue as to context they can become equivocal and ambiguous, if not unintelligible. For example, the locution, "Jack Nicklaus is dead" has its own meaning in the context of heartbeats, brain waves, and obituaries. Yet, uttered in the context of an important golf tournament in which Jack's putt on the 18th hole will determine his chances of winning, the locution has quite a different meaning.

Context is a form of tacit knowing. The context is at the periphery of attention and is known "subsidiarily", while the task of the situation is at the focus. And, as Polanyi noted, while an item can be moved sometimes from periphery to focus and vice versa, the same item cannot be both at the periphery and focus at the same time. Thus, context can be built up out of items that at one time were at the focus of attention and learned explicitly. For example, when we studied theorems of Euclid in school we kept them at the focus of our attention. Many years later they constituted a geometrical context for situations to which they were relevant. When studying geometry we were acquiring a knowledge of a branch of mathematics, and we learned how to prove certain theorems — indeed knowing how to prove them might be regarded as evidence for our claim to knowing them. When listening to talk about putting space capsules into orbit around the earth or the moon we may no longer know certain mathematical truths or how to prove them, but we think *with* these truths as context for our understanding the space talk. There are many contexts for the comprehension of space talk: technological, astrological, literary, and political. Each lends different significance to the space talk, and it is important not to mix the contexts indiscriminately.

Contexts can be cognitive, affective, aesthetic, moral, social, religious. Within each of these types, contexts can be thought of as more or less precise, clear, refined and, "educated", that is, formulated in the categories of an academic discipline. This latter distinction is of the utmost importance for formal schooling, because the social milieu furnishes commonsense contexts for which little or no formal tuition is necessary.

This much about *knowing with*, it seems to me, can be said on the basis of some evidence from Gestalt psychology and from a phenomenological analysis of various modes of mentation (Petrie, 1974). However, given the importance of context for cognition, imagination, judgment, and decision, there is still much that is not known about the epistemology, psychology, and the pedagogy of contextual knowing or knowing with.

One context aides our evaluation of evidence justifying a factual proposition, another context guides us in following the steps of hypothesis formation and verification, and still another context must operate if the steps in a deductive proof are to become valid. It has been shown, for example, that children with perfectly good logic give mistaken explanations of phenomena. Given the conceptions that constitute their interpretive context, their conclusions follow. Genetic epistemology, is the search for the categorial system with which thinking is done at various stages of development. Educators are interested in the conditions that stimulate, elicit, or inhibit the developmental patterns (Witz and Easley, 1976).

Also epistemological in nature (although not so directly related to educational processes) are such questions as: Are there pure givens in scientific thinking? Do scientists choose to study problems on the basis of personal as well as scientific factors (Rudner, 1953)? Is scientific observation theory and value dependent?

Perhaps the most proximate relationship between tacit knowing, contextual knowing, knowing *with*, and the pursuit of knowledge are to be found in the paradigms to which Thomas Kuhn alluded in his work on scientific revolutions (Kuhn, 1962). The paradigms of a prospective professor of physics are not those of a professor of mechanical engineering, while the paradigms of a professor of humanities may have little in common with those of a social worker devoted to humanizing the social order. Types of knowledge and disciplines are distinguished by paradigms of this sort, and they often function tacitly.

From the psychologist one would like to learn more about how contexts are built into and summoned from experience. This order may be too large and unmanageable. Yet, it might be possible to trace — at least in case-study form — the odyssey of a school input through the adult life of the individual. John Livingston Lowes cites an example in which 30 years after reading Oliver Wendell Holmes's *Autocrat at the Breakfast Table* he recalled a passage from it. Holmes had said, "Put an idea in your intelligence and leave it there an hour, a day, a year without ever having occasion to refer to it. When, at last, you return to it, you do not find it as it was when acquired. It had domiciliated itself, so to speak — become at home — entered into relation with your other thoughts, and integrated itself with the whole fabric of your life." But when Lowes recalled this passage, it was in the form of something "germinating and expanding . . . with white and spreading tentacles, like the plant which sprouts beneath a stone" (Lowes, 1927).

This is truly a strange transformation, but perhaps no more so than when barnacles, weeds, and perhaps flowers surround, engulf, and encrust stones thrown into the ocean. What remains, for example, of the poetry we memorized in high school? What has become of the French or Latin we studied, not to mention the history and science courses we passed with flying colors? I have suggested elsewhere that the interpretations a person gives to reading materials might provide clues as to how school studies or the absence of them function in such reading. The same sort of life tasks might also afford an entry into the mysteries of the associative and the interpretive uses of schooling (Broudy, 1972).

It is often argued by educational reformers that if school inputs are to be used associatively or interpretively in life, why teach them in school as disciplines, that is, as formal conceptual structures? Why not make the curriculum a series of problem-solving, or at least problem-discussing experiences? The famous project curriculum that issued from Dewey's influence on W. H. Kilpatrick is only one application of this argument. The principle invoked is: Whenever possible, practice the desired outcomes directly rather than relying on indirect results through transfer. The disciplinarians have usually and indignantly resisted this approach on the grounds that it substitutes watered-down, pseudoknowledge for the real thing; that, at best, it provides a vague familiarity with the phenomena and at worst the illusion of knowledge.

This direct experience approach also finds its plausibility in the orthodox view that a school input, if it functions at all, will be recalled as learned. But what if systematic study is required to supply the ingredients out of which contexts are later constructed and used? And what if these ingredients undergo transformation, transmutation, and indeterminate permutations as experience grows? What if a process of selective forgetting, and not retention, is a necessary condition for context building? These are conjectures, but there is evidence for them in literature, analytic psychology, and ordinary experience. Is the systematic study of such phenomena a proper task for educational psychology?

For school people the thesis being argued here is of paramount importance, if general or liberal education is to be given a rationale not now provided by the replicative and applicative uses of schooling. It seems incredible that for centuries influential members of society have found general or liberal education so personally important even though it could not pass the replicative and applicative tests. If my thesis is plausible, the influential members of society have not used school tests of achievement to measure the importance of general education, but rather the richness of experience and interpretive power that they attributed to it. Perhaps the schools rather than the public needs a new rationale for general education.

IV. SUMMARY AND CONCLUSIONS

Fundamental to the differences among the several kinds of knowledge is the dichotomy between the concrete flow of experiences and the conceptual systems that are abstracted by thought from them. In time these systems acquire a Platonic subsistence of their own that is more and more remote from their origins. The difference between the *abstracta* and the *realia* becomes greater as the logical relations between concepts become sharper. By leaving out many details of experiences, obstacles to logical traffic between concepts are removed. But men have to live within the realm of their experiences whether they are praying, feeding, or doing mathematics; and so the tension between being and knowing is constantly renewed.

Logical purity has its price even within its own enterprise. Bertrand Russell reminded us that by "... examining the basis of our beliefs we can be brought to see the mutual independence of propositions that had been thought to be logically connected ... As logic improves, less and less can be proved ... the result of logical analysis is to increase the number of independent premises that we accept in our analysis of knowledge" (Russell, 1944, p. 684). This is a fairly high price because it makes it more difficult to provide logical continuity between existential propositions.

But logical clarity has its price in other forms of tension. Established academic disciplines move further and further away from the life problems that provided the original impetus to the inquiry that established them. Workers within a discipline are separated into those who develop theory and those who apply theory. The several disciplines tend to grow away from each other as their logical structures become more refined and differentiated, and within the individual the difference between the *abstracta* of thought and the *realia* of life becomes more acute.

This tension provides problems for epistemology, psychology, and education. Epistemology, having successfully discovered and deepened the chasm between the certainty of constructed conceptual systems and the dubiety attending the contingent statements of the empirical and humanistic studies, has spent centuries in trying to bridge it. There is little likelihood that the task will ever be accomplished or abandoned.

For psychology, the dichotomy presents the task of studying man's experience, the logical system which emerges from it, and creating a conceptual system that explains the emergence.

The educator must present a balanced curriculum of selected conceptual systems to pupils who, on the whole, would rather be immersed in the existential flow. On the other hand, they must reorganize the existential flow of their tutees in terms of the conceptual systems studied. It is an arduous juggling act.

I have suggested that this juggling may be understood better, if one notices how conceptual systems are used in relation to the way they are learned. The proposal avoids being a truism if the orthodox view of this relationship is re-examined. I have tried to do this, venturing the hypothesis that restricting the uses of schooling to the replicative and the applicative makes the faith in general education anomalous. To remove the anomaly, it is argued that school inputs can function associatively and interpretively as context suppliers. This view commits one to something akin to the tacit knowing suggested by Polanyi, but also raises questions about what happens to school inputs as experience grows. If contextual knowing restores the unity that abstract learning necessarily ruptures, then the study of its nature, that is, the nature of *knowing with*, deserves the attention of both epistemology and psychology, and may yield more help to the educational enterprise than the study of learning alone has been able to give.

REFERENCES

Berlin, I. *The divorce between the sciences and the humanities.* The Second Tykociner Memorial Lecture, Urbana, Ill. 1974.

Broudy, H. S. Kierkegaard on indirect communication. *Journal of Philosophy*, 1961, 58, 226–233.

Broudy, H. On knowing with. *Proceedings of the 26th Annual Meeting of the Philosophy of Education Society*, 1970. (a)

Broudy, H. Tacit knowing and aesthetic education. In R. A. Smith (Ed.), *Aesthetic concepts and education.* Urbana: University of Illinois Press, 1970. (b)

Broudy, H. The life uses of schooling as a field for research. *The 71st Yearbook of the National Society for the Study of Education.* Part I – Lawrence G. Thomas (Ed.). Chicago: The University of Chicago Press, 1972.

Broudy, H. Research into imagic association and cognitive interpretation. *Research in the Teaching of English*, 1973, 7, 240–259.

Broudy, H. Science, technology, and the diminished mind. *Journal of College Science Teaching*, 1976, 5, 292–296.

Kuhn, T. S. *The structure of scientific revolutions.* Chicago: The University of Chicago Press, 1962.

Lowes, J. L. *The road to Xanadu: A study of the ways of the imagination.* Boston: Houghton Mifflin, 1927. P. 57.

Ortony, A. Why metaphors are necessary and not just nice. *Educational Theory*, 1975, **1**, 45–54.

Petrie, H. Action, perception, and education. *Educational Theory*, 1974, **24**, 33–45.

Polanyi, M. *The tacit dimension.* New York: Doubleday, 1966.

Rudner, R. The scientist qua scientist makes value judgments. *Philosophy of Science,* 1953, **20**, 1–6.

Russell, B . *The problems of philosophy.* New York: Holt, 1912.

Russell, B. *The philosophy of Bertrand Russell.* P. A. Schilpp (Ed.), The Library of Living Philosophers. Evanston, Ill.: Northwestern University, 1944.

Ryle, G. *The concept of mind.* London: Hutchinson's University Library, 1949.

Vico, G. *The autobiography of Giambattista Vico.* Translated by M. H. Fisch and T. G. Bergin. Ithaca, N. Y.: Cornell University Press, 1944.

Vico, G. *On the study methods of our time.* Translated by E. Gianturco. New York: Bobbs-Merrill, 1965.

Witz, K. G., & Easley, J. A., Jr. A new approach to cognition. In L. Van Dem-Daele, J. Pasqual-Leone, & K. Witz (Eds.), *Neo-Piagetian perspectives on cognition and development.* New York: Academic Press, 1976.

COMMENTS ON
CHAPTER 1 BY BROUDY

Hugh G. Petrie

University of Illinois at Urbana-Champaign

Harry Broudy's contribution, drawing on much of his previous work and pointing to the crucial epistemological role of what he calls "knowing with" and the centrality of the concept of *context* in discussions of knowledge, learning, and schooling, is an insightful and rewarding adventure. It is particularly significant in that several other participants in this conference also point to the significance of context or schemata or frames, or scripts or some similar such notion for understanding the acquisition and use of knowledge. Because of this kind of convergence on the concept of *context,* I propose to abandon the more traditional commentator's role of pointing out the difficulties in Professor Broudy's paper, and instead concentrate on this particular hare of *context* he has started, in hopes, if not of running it to earth, at least avoiding some false trails.

What I shall do is the following: First I shall briefly recapitulate the path that Broudy followed in arriving at his emphasis on context. Next I shall note an interesting and pervasive ambiguity in the concept of *context* between context as the existential situation in which a knower is operating and context as the conceptual framework the knower brings to bear on the existential situation. I shall urge that this ambiguity actually points to a central feature of *context* — namely, the necessity for an interaction *between* the actual situation and any categorization in the knower's cognitive repertoire. I then suggest that attempts to account for context solely in terms of a representation, no matter how rich and varied, is to miss the point of an appeal to context and to raise once again at a new level just the problems context was introduced to solve. Finally, I suggest that a cybernetic model of action and perception apparently provides just the right mode of handling the notion of *context.*

CONTEXT

Broudy's main concern is to sketch a possible explanation of the apparent contradiction between our persistent inability to show how the learning of formal abstract material in school affects the quality of our lives on the one hand, and our continued faith that it must, on the other. In brief, Broudy suggests that our faith is justified, and our failure to understand how school learning is related to later life is due to "an indifference to the difference between the criteria for learning and the criteria for use of what is learned." Abstract school learning is not to be thought of as *replicated* in later life tasks nor *applied* to these tasks. Rather it forms the knowledge *with* which we approach these tasks. Broudy appeals here to Polanyi's notion of tacit knowledge as an appropriate means of elaborating on *knowing with:* "Perhaps another and more familiar way of putting it is to say that knowing *with* operates by furnishing a *context* (my emphasis) or a ground against which a particular situation is perceived, interpreted, and judged." This emphasis on context provides a way of understanding how abstract school learning can provide a knowledge that can be used associatively and interpretively by the student. But the associative and interpretive uses of knowledge are neither replications nor direct applications of the knowledge which was originally learned. Thus, the difference between a schooled mind and an unschooled mind is easily apparent but *not* explicable in terms of the kinds of tests which call for the replication or application of the original learning.

However, if we can come to understand the way in which knowing *with* works, we may at long last have a handle on understanding the connection between theory and practice, or in Broudy's terms, between the *abstracta* and the *realia.* This connection is illustrated by Broudy in his discussion of three of the many categorizations of knowledge to be found in the history of thought. The distinction between knowledge as structure and knowledge as process illustrates the abstracta—realia distinction in that the real mental processes of scientists (or students) coming to know result in a product which can be characterized in an abstract way as a conceptual system of interrelated statements. (One needs to add that psychological processes too can be characterized in an abstract conceptual system, but the distinction between the real processes and their abstract characterization remains.) The schooling question then becomes, why teach the abstract system representing the results of the thinking of physicists when our primary goal seems to be to have students think and act like physicists?

The second distinction between scientific and humanistic knowledge illustrates the abstracta—realia distinction in a more indirect way. Broudy claims that "Science is concerned primarily with truth; humanistic studies about authenticity." Scientific truth concerns the correlation, or lack of it, between our representations of reality, and reality. Authenticity is concerned with what people are willing to *do* in the world. The schooling question here becomes the relation between thought and action. In moral education, for example, it is the age-old question of whether morality conceived as a system of thought can have any connection with moral action.

Broudy's third distinction between the validity and utility of knowledge illustrates the abstracta–realia dichotomy in yet another of its guises. To paraphrase, the distinction is between what makes an abstract representation a good representation and what determines what an abstract representation is good for. The schooling question is how does good abstract theory enable one to pursue the real goods of life – and we are right back where we began – by providing a "context or ground against which a particular situation is perceived, interpreted, and judged."

TWO SENSES OF CONTEXT

What is a context? Broudy suggests that it is "an interpretive code for construing import or significance"; "a form of tacit knowing"; and analogous to Kuhnian paradigms. He suggests that "contexts can be cognitive, affective, aesthetic, moral, social, religious . . ." and that they "can be built up out of items that at one time were at the focus of attention and learned explicitly." In the main, Broudy seems to conceive of contexts as conceptual schemes or parts of conceptual schemes which we bring to bear on particular situations. To use Wittgenstein's *seeing as* terminology, an economic context is what is operative when we see the space program as a tremendous expenditure of money (see Petrie, 1971, pp. 155–160); (Wittgenstein, 1958, Part II, Section 9).

On the other hand, context also seems to mean the particular existential situation with which we are concerned. Broudy comes closest to recognizing this sense of context in discussing the locution, "Jack Nicklaus is dead," when he asks us to consider the changes in meaning of the locution when "uttered in the context of an important golf tournament in which Jack's putt on the 18th hole will determine his chances of winning. . . ."

This "existential" sense of context is even more pronounced, I think, in recent psychological literature. For example, Anderson and Ortony (1975, p. 179) have recently argued that "models of memory should invoke understanding, and that understanding is not just parsing; it is processing to a level whose depth depends on the degree of interaction with the *context* (my emphasis) and the existing knowledge base." Anderson and Ortony's rejection of a static organization of the knowledge base in network theories of memory is strikingly parallel to Broudy's claim that "propositions may have their own lexical meaning, yet without a clue as to context, they can become equivocal and ambiguous if not unintelligible."

Anderson and Ortony's evidence relies heavily on an experiment which manipulates simply intrasentence context, but they claim the extension to larger and different contexts is straightforward. Basically their experiment is suggestively explained by their introductory paragraph (p. 167):

> A gedanken experiment: a group of subjects is presented with the sentence *The container held the apples;* another group sees *The container held the cola.* Later each group is given two retrieval cues, *bottle* and *basket.* There are two questions: which cue will best facilitate recall for each group, and why?

Their results are as one would have intuitively predicted — namely that "bottle" best cues the cola sentence and "basket" best cues the apples sentence. Their explanation is basically that the differing intrasentential contexts for the term, "container," cause a different processing of the sentences resulting in a different memorial representation. Thus the two sentences are differentially accessible by the two different cues.

The point I wish to emphasize beyond the general similarities of position between Broudy and Anderson and Ortony is that Broudy seems primarily to treat context as a part of a conceptual scheme, whereas Anderson and Ortony tend to treat it primarily as the particular existential situation. How is one to understand this apparent divergence?

THE INTERACTION OF THE TWO SENSES OF CONTEXT

The basic idea is this: Although there may be only one reality which human beings attempt to know, it does *not* seem to be the case that there is only one way in which one can represent that reality. Thus, one of the central questions of knowledge becomes how one can rationally choose among alternative representations of reality without being able to compare the representations with "reality itself." Our inability to have any direct access to, or knowledge by acquaintance with, the world is by now well accepted as a result of philosophical investigations into the necessity for all experience to be categorized in some way or another to be intelligible (see Feyerabend, 1970; Hanson, 1958; Kuhn, 1970; Polanyi, 1962; Toulmin, 1972).

But if this is so, then human experience will be the causal result of two analytically distinguishable, but factually inseparable features: the concepts and categories we bring to experience — Broudy's sense of context — and the existential features of the particular situation itself — Anderson and Ortony's sense of context. The conceptual framework sense of *context* and the existential particularity sense of *context* are but two sides of the single coin of human experience.

Thus, when Broudy speaks of different kinds of contexts, which can be made subsidiarily appropriate to experience, he is emphasizing the fact that particular portions of reality can be represented in a variety of ways. When he asks about the usefulness of "educated" contexts, contexts formulated in disciplinary categories, he is raising the question of the usefulness of that kind and mode of experiencing. Context in Broudy's sense of one's conceptual and categorial framework structures experience. And since different contexts are possible, different experiences with respect to "the same" piece of reality are also possible. Recall Broudy's example of the geometrical, astronomical, literary, political, and economic contexts which are possible for the apprehension of space talk.

But now an ugly two-headed problem appears. If all of these contexts and more *can* be used to understand space talk, how do we, psychologically, come to apply or use one or another of these contexts, and second, how do we, epistemologically, come to decide which of these contexts is *appropriate* to the situation? Must we somehow have an independent access to the situation which then enables us to run through our stock of contexts checking off features of the situation against features of the contexts to decide which is psychologically and epistemologically appropriate? Do we, at a level once removed, have to *apply* the context to the situation after all? Is Broudy's knowing *with* reducible to the applicative use of knowledge?

It is precisely this idea of *application* to be found in the semantic features theories of language comprehension that Anderson and Ortony argue against. Their evidence seems to show that one can *always* find particular contexts which will alter the straightforward application of framework to event. The concept of "apples" subtly affects what kind of container is appropriate. Nor can we, without a complete reproduction, not mere representation, of the world in our conceptual schemes account for all the gradations in kinds of containers within our representation of "container." Concomitantly, we cannot possibly represent all of the fine-grained differences which *may* prove relevant in any individual case of the application of an economic context. Note, for example, how long it took for economists to recognize opportunity cost as an appropriate part of cost—benefit analyses.

To put the point oversimply, our concepts and contexts cannot contain as a part of their mental representation unique decision rules for their application. In a deep sense, one cannot speak of the "application" of contexts *to* experience; rather contexts must be found already *in* experience. But how does that happen?

Anderson and Ortony recognize this problem at a certain level in that they continually speak of an "interaction" between context (in the existential sense) and the existing knowledge base. This "interaction" kind of talk is a step forward in that it counteracts the tendency to ask how an independently given conceptual framework is "applied" to an independently given particular situation. Still the particular situations are already highly categorized in terms of representations even in Anderson and Ortony's discussion. It is just that in the context, some of these presupposed categories are not problematic. However, *they could be made so.* In *most* situations, the particular kind of container makes no difference in "The container held the cola." Anderson and Ortony create a plausible context in which conceiving of the container as bottle or basket, *does* seem to make a difference. My point is that the process of dreaming up contexts is absolutely indeterminate. Consider, for example, the context in which I am exploring a primitive area and I can only carry my *cola* in the water proof *baskets* made by the indigenous natives.

Anderson and Ortony seem to argue that we need to loosen our knowledge models to allow for the representations of things like baskets, bottles, and containers, interacting with the representation we have of things like apples and cola. The reason seems to be that otherwise we cannot account for the rich variety of knowledge we do have. But the limitation is that it is still just *representations* which are interacting and *qua* representations, the question can always be raised as to the nature and adequacy of the relation between representation and represented. Clearly the relation is not one of identity, nor even of iconic "picturing" in the logical atomist sense.[1] This means that the adequacy of *any* of our knowledge models to reality is always potentially up for grabs. And it also means that we must *somehow* have access to the complete existential situation or else we are just whistling in the dark when we speak of knowledge of the *world*.

CYBERNETICS IN CONTEXT

What I have urged thus far is that the concept of "context" is crucially important for psychologists, epistemologists, and educators in understanding the nature and use of knowledge. This is so because it brings together and focuses on the point at which the abstracta of our conceptual schemes interact with the realia of the world to form our experience. And I have argued that although we have no access to the world independently of our concepts and representations, we must allow, in our accounts of how we come to know, for an influence of the world on our experience. How can this be?

In the very short space remaining, I simply want to assert that cybernetic models give great promise for understanding this interaction (Petrie, 1974; Powers, 1973). The crucial point is that a negative feedback system resists disturbances to its input, rather than controlling its output. In terms of a very gross analogy the heating system of a house does *not* have some complex representation of all of the heat states the house may be in and then *apply* the appropriate heat to each of these states. Rather it simply senses the temperature near the thermostat and if that temperature is different from the set temperature, it drives the furnace until the sensed temperature and controlled temperature are identical. And it will do this, *no matter what* the world of the house really is. It will do its job if the house is well, moderately, or poorly insulated, if the ducts are partially clogged or open, if a window is open or not, if a lamp is near the

---

[1] Compare Wittgenstein (1961), containing a view of the way representations might "picture" reality, with Wittgenstein (1958), in which this view is rejected.

thermostat or not. In short, the actual state of the world within certain ranges is largely irrelevant; the system needs only to be able to represent one feature of that world – temperature near the thermostat – and react to disturbances of that feature no matter how they arise in the world.

I cannot emphasize too much the revolutionary nature of changing from the idea of controlling outputs to that of monitoring inputs. It completely eliminates the nagging problem I had of explaining how one knows when context in the conceptual framework sense is appropriate to context in the particular situation sense. One no longer "applies" concepts to inputs at all. Rather various features of the world are represented by means of our concepts, and, as they are compared with what we want to see, we act on the world; – which action in turn initiates causal chains in the world in all its particularity, which chains may then end up changing our representations.

This emphasis on our active involvement in the world was prefigured in Broudy's dichotomies. We can engage in the *process* of knowledge acquisition only insofar as we do this in terms of the structural *products* of knowledge which enable us to represent the results of our activities in intelligible categories. What we are willing to *do* in the world in the humanistic sense of authenticity determines in part what features of the world it will be worth our while to represent in our scientific and humanistic conceptual schemes. And this is, of course, connected to the validity–utility distinction. Valid, that is, adequate, modes of representing reality are those which enable us to do most of the things we as human beings want to do, and in an evolutionary kind of way, the systems of representation we currently count as valid have stood the test of being able to provide the conceptual contexts in terms of which particular contexts have their effects on us.

I need to point out here that although accounting for an indefinite number of mildly different existential contexts in terms of a cybernetic system affords a great advance in our ability to understand context, it is not the only way. Sometimes what is at issue are contexts which call for *changes* in the cybernetic systems we have been utilizing up to that point. The growth of knowledge can then be understood as comprised primarily of two different processes. On the one hand we assimilate a wide variety of experience to our existing concepts, but occasionally, on the other hand, we need to accommodate our concepts to radically new experiences (Petrie, 1975). This latter process also forms a central theme for several of the conference participants.

In summary, I have agreed with Broudy that the concept of "context" is crucial for an understanding of knowledge acquisition and use. I have also agreed that "context" suggests an indirect, nonapplicative, interpretive approach to the use of knowledge. Expanding on this, I pointed out the curious dichotomy in "context" as conceptual framework and as particular situation. At the same time, I argued that these two senses are really just two different perspectives on the concept of experience. Finally, I suggested that to avoid the problem of how to understand the "applying" of conceptual frameworks to particular situations, the problem for which "context" was first introduced, one might look to the cybernetic model. That model with its view of controlling inputs no matter what the particular situation along with showing how the two senses of context can be joined seemed to offer a great deal of promise.

Educationally, what this seems to imply to me is principally an emphasis on learning how to represent different features of the world rather than on the processing of given representations. It points to the importance of perceptual rather than propositional categories in learning, and to the centrality of human activity in the world. And, I think, in consonance with Broudy's hope, it may, when developed, point to a more adequate way of relating school studies to life outcomes. For if school experiences provide ways of structuring our basic experiences, nay even partially *constitute* those basic experiences, there will indeed be a large "difference between the way knowledge is used in cognizing and responding to a situation and the way school studies are tested at the end of instruction."

REFERENCES

Anderson, R. C. & Ortony, A. On putting apples into bottles: A problem of Polysemy. *Cognitive Psychology,* 1975, 7, 167–180.

Feyerabend, P. Against method: Outline of an anarchistic theory of knowledge. In M. Radner & S. Winokor (Eds.), *Analyses of theories and methods of physics and psychology.* Minnesota Studies in Philosophy of Science, Vol. IV. Minneapolis: University of Minnesota Press, 1970.

Hanson, N. R. *Patterns of discovery.* Cambridge, England: Cambridge University Press, 1958.

Kuhn, T. S. *The structure of scientific revolutions.* Chicago: University of Chicago Press, 1970.

Petrie, H. G. Action, perception, and education. *Educational Theory,* 1974, 24, 33–45.

Petrie, H. G. Evolutionary rationality: Or can learning theory survive in the jungle of conceptual change. Paper presented at a meeting of the Learning Research and Development Center, University of Pittsburgh, September 1975.

Petrie, H. G. Science and metaphysics: A Wittgensteinian interpretation. In E. D. Klemke (Ed.), *Essays on Wittgenstein.* Urbana: University of Illinois Press, 1971.

Polanyi, M. *Personal knowledge* (rev. ed.). Chicago: University of Chicago Press, 1962.

Powers, W. T. *Behavior: The control of perceptions.* Chicago: Aldine, 1973.

Toulmin, S. *Human understanding.* Princeton, N.J.: Princeton University Press, 1972.

Wittgenstein, L. *Philosophical investigations.* New York: Macmillan, 1958.

Wittgenstein, L. *Tractatus logico-philosophicus.* London: Routledge & Kegan Paul, 1961.

OPEN DISCUSSION
ON THE CONTRIBUTIONS
BY BROUDY AND PETRIE

Ortony: I'd like to address a question to Hugh Petrie about the negative feedback model. It seems rather nice in terms of both an individual's output and the perceptions that control the behavior. What I do not understand is how that model applies when one is speaking in terms of the individual's comprehension of an input.

Petrie: I do not have very much to say about this, because it does seem that the advantages of the cybernetic model depend on having an answer to that kind of question. That is, the cybernetic models that I have seen simply assume there is some kind of input function which appropriately translates the actual causal influences on the organism into perceptual categories which can then be further processed in the presupposed comprehension system. So, in a sense, part of the question you are asking is one that I just do not have an answer to, namely, how are these perceptual input functions organized, how do they come to change, how do they in fact pick out various sorts of features of the environment, etc. However, I wanted to concentrate on comparing the perceptual inputs with various kinds of reference signals, allowing for output through an indefinite range of particular contexts.

Wyer: I also have a question about the logic of this negative feedback model. It seems to me that your emphasis is on monitoring of the input to produce a given output. The real question seems to be how you select that output. The output that you want is itself defined in relation to some context. I can envision a second, higher-order servomechanism loop that could help to understand this question. But it seems at some level, you have to get out of the servomechanism and understand how the output is going to be interpreted and evaluated. And I do not see how the servomechanism can really operate at that highest level. Take the temperature example, and say you want to maintain the house at 75° or 70°. Why? Why not 65°?

Petrie: The answer to that question — where do the reference signals come from — clearly is hierarchical feedback loops, and those do have to come to an end somewhere or another. I will just assert (see Powers, 1973, for explication) that utlimately the way in which that has to be accounted for is by some kind of modified drive reduction. There will ultimately be those old discredited drives which will come back in at a basic level. They will serve as the stopper of the feedback systems, providing the basic kinds of organization that you want. Old drive-reduction theories tended to get discredited on grounds that the satisfaction of the drives lead to the cessation of activity of the organism. That does not happen in this system. Indeed, in order to reduce some of these drives, a great deal of activity by the organism is required.

Broudy: Adding to Dr. Wyer's question and to Dr. Petrie's response, I think something has been hit on that may also be a suggestion for the connection between the *abstracta* and the *realia.* Namely, in addition to heating systems and temperature desiderata, there are value schemata, which in time become the parameters of permissible oscillation. In the second footnote to the chapter, I've developed just a little the notion of linguistic parameters. This might be an answer Dr. Petrie might make.

Take the standard Aristotelian virtues: courage, integrity, magnanimity, or even the theological virtues, if you like, that have become operative over a long period of time. They may act as existential parameters that delimit the points of tolerance. For example, we are going through that now with Women's Liberation and the whole chastity problem. The range, I suppose, is between an iota above bestiatlity and an iota below the angels, and it is a wide range. But still, there are limits. Linguistically, however, see what happens. If you say courage is a virtue in this society, this becomes an existential parameter of behavior. But if you find someone in your group who does not understand, or has not had the experience of confronting fear, he would be ruled out of the group as nonhuman, not as a coward. There are all kinds of sanctions against cowardice. What do you do with someone who has no fear; when he recognizes danger, he runs away, and does not feel guilty. In other words, the meaning of the term tends to stabilize the behavior that will be permitted under that name. Thus, while chastity or honesty or courage change their behavioral equivalents from time to time, there are parameters which define the concepts and which at the same time define the existential manifestations that will be permitted. I think, Dr. Petrie, that there, too, you get the same kind of cybernetic control, and the example perhaps will not draw the kind of questions that arise from talking about heating systems rather than human systems.

Sherif: If we accept the notion of "knowing with" which you (Dr. Broudy) talked about, then it seems to me that one could think of schooling as a vast institutionalized definition of what is right, that is set up to provide some kind of common context. It then becomes, presumably, an institution of social control, so that everyone will have a common context. Someone who comes along and says to you, "Bestiality is the best," or "Total abstinence is the only solution for civilization — we're too far gone," is going to fall outside and be treated as deviant. Now, this is a fantastic example, but in fact we live in a society in which there are strikingly different definitions of what should be the context, or the "knowing withs," in which we encounter specific situational contexts and react and interact to them. Do we not then have the problem of the relationship between this vast institutional setup of schooling and the way people actually live their lives? In short, they have other contexts, and in responding to social change they sometimes do develop assertions that are quite contrary to common contexts taught in schools.

Broudy: Let me respond from the point of view of a formal school system that is fairly well organized with special divisions of labor and so forth. Philosophically speaking, there is no criterion of truth that any sophomore in college cannot demolish. As Russell said: the better our logic, the more we show that certain propositions are independent of each other. For example, propositions about matters of fact are independent of matters of value. The better our logic, as he says, the harder it is to prove any connection. In that sense, I am not trying to find a criterion to which any sophomore in college, or any professor, or any right-minded person could not find a counterexample. I am speaking of schools as institutions, in the same sense that you are. What criteria can they use? Not philosophical, certainly. What then? The credentialing system of the culture. Everything I said about guilds you can translate into indenturing systems, legitimating systems, and so forth. Why do they have credibility? Certainly not because they produced the better human beings. You can find numerous examples in Nazi Germany of people who had an excellent education according to any criterion. We accept the authority of the credentialing system in terms of its canons of inquiry, which are public and contain the means for their own correction. That's the *best* we have. The only defense against the charge that academia can make today, is that the means for correction of the evils that are part of a rigidified, institutionalized system lie within that system. If they do not, then they become arbitrary, they become matters of political power. Can we sustain that claim? I think in many areas of truth seeking we can. I am suggesting that as far as schools are concerned, the tradition has within it the very tools for its own criticism. And there has never been a time in any of the disciplines when the proponents have not been confronted by the skeptics.

Sherif: When you say tools, you are speaking of intellectual tools, I presume?

Broudy: No, not only intellectual tools. As I tried to indicate, the arts and the humanistic studies are not purely intellectual. They give us images of feeling, they give us value schemata, but they also give us the criticisms of these schemata. There has never been a time when an intellectual tradition has not been without its critics. Socrates was the critic of the Sophists. That's the weakness and the great strength of the tradition. The divorce of the *abstracta* from the *realia* enables us to play these games, to say "on the other hand." That is their great strength, but it is also their existential weakness. Every so often intellectuals begin playing games with what is not a game. I think the school system has to say that it stands for the best criteria that are available, formal schooling.

Petrie: There is, of course, a sense in which the contexts are similar. But I think the interesting thing about this is that the similar part of it interacts with quite idiosyncratic parts, too. So the very same "knowing with" which is a form of social control is not going to be totally complete and comprehensive because of the fact that you have this local school board with its particular idiosyncracies which will have a modifying effect. On the individual level, you have individuals who are in different existential situations interacting with this common context. In that sense, they provide experiences which will be slightly different for one individual than for another. I think this goes back to what Dr. Broudy said. Since there are still the differences within the similarities, there is the potential for actually criticizing, improving, and changing the context which you continue to impose more or less similarly.

REFERENCE

Powers, W. T. *Behavior: The control of perception.* Chicago: Aldine, 1973.

2

Schooling and the Facilitation of Knowing

John D. Bransford
Kathleen E. Nitsch
Jeffrey J. Franks

Vanderbilt University

... we have heard frequent and justified complaints that many decades of research and study by psychologists interested in human learning and memory have not yielded many significant insights that could be used for the improvement of education and for the betterment of learning in classrooms. If it is true that past research in human learning and memory has been concerned primarily with episodic memory, and if it is true that classroom learning has little to do with students' remembering personally experienced events, then it is not surprising that empirical facts and theoretical ideas originating in verbal learning and human memory laboratories have little bearing on theory and practice of acquisition of knowledge.

E. TULVING

The quotation from Tulving (1972, p. 401) expresses a concern currently held by many psychologists. Despite many decades of research devoted to studying human learning and memory, the gap between basic theory and educational application still remains wide. The present paper explores some of the reasons for this discrepancy. It will be argued that current research and theories concerning episodic or even semantic memory (see Tulving, 1972) are not oriented toward the types of problems faced in most educational settings. This does not mean that current research is irrelevant, but rather that it is not necessarily accompanied by a framework for understanding both its relevance and shortcomings with respect to educational applications. A framework is needed which focuses more directly on relevant educational problems, and which can provide a general perspective for interpreting and evaluating the significance and usefulness of laboratory work.

I. DEFINING THE FOCUS OF THE PRESENT APPROACH

We propose a framework that focuses on the problem of "experts" rather than on subjects in typical learning and memory situations. One could concentrate on expert tennis players, expert readers, expert problem solvers, clinicians, teachers, rememberers, etc. Yet even the study of "already arrived" experts is not sufficient. The basic problem involves the processes of *becoming* an expert and maintaining that expertise; that is, the general problem of *growth.*

Consider what it means to be an expert. The title "expert" does not imply a static, fixed end point. It refers to one's abilities relative to other individuals in a particular domain. In the time scale of history, for example, the decisions of the expert medical diagnostician of the 1300s would probably qualify that person as a rank amateur in the twentieth century. Similarly, today's expert in some area could well be tomorrow's "also ran." Surely the process of *becoming* an expert cannot be defined statically. Even *being* an expert does not imply a static state. It follows that a statement like "Experts have more knowledge than non-experts" is most probably a truism, but it begs the crucial questions. It does not tell us how people become experts nor how they maintain their expertise relative to other individuals. To understand experts one must focus on understanding what they do to gain increasingly greater skill, clarity, and understanding rather than concentrate on the knowledge they have already attained. The problem is to identify the *processes* involved in going about knowing rather than to focus on the *products* of these processes.

As an example, consider once again our hypothetical expert medical diagnostician of the 1300s. It seems reasonable to assume that this person would be a good candidate for excellence if he grew up in today's culture, including present day medical school curriculum. If so, the person's potential for being an expert must be measured in terms of his abilities to know what to do in order to further understand or know something rather than in terms of the particular content of his knowledge. Our basic problem is therefore to understand how to go beyond a current state of knowing. From this perspective, it seems useful to point toward a potential ambiguity in the title of this conference; that is, "Schooling and the Acquisition of Knowledge." It is possible to interpret this as suggesting that education involves the accumulation and storage of "pieces" of knowledge, thus emphasizing the *products* of knowing activities rather than the *processes* of knowing. An alternate title might be "Schooling and the Facilitation of Knowing." This title emphasizes the methods used to facilitate knowing, that is, going beyond one's present state of clarity and understanding. Learning to do this should be an important educational goal.

II. CONTRASTING THE PRESENT ORIENTATION TO OTHERS PREVALENT IN THE FIELD

The present orientation emphasizes the problem of becoming and being experts. It therefore focuses on the problem of learning what to do to go beyond one's present state of knowing. In this section, we contrast this orientation with those emphasizing episodic memory, semantic memory, and "verbal learning" research.

A. Comparison with Theories of Episodic Remembering

Few would deny that education involves something more than merely remembering. Despite this, the relationship between memory and the development of expertise (e.g., learning) is not necessarily clear. For example, it is frequently assumed that learning results in the formation of "traces" or "memories." Research on remembering might therefore be directly relevant to issues about learning, since remembering should be related to the degree to which one has learned. From this perspective, research on learning and remembering seem closely intertwined.

However, consider some contexts where emphases on learning and remembering are widely divergent. Playing tennis represents a case in point. The problem of specifying what it means to learn to play tennis is very different from the typical concerns of the memory theorist. The latter is more likely to request his subjects to "Remember the strokes you made during the last five minutes of the game," or "Remember where the ball bounced during the last three minutes." The problem of becoming a tennis expert seems clearly different from the problem of remembering what one just did (see Bransford, McCarrell, Franks, & Nitsch, in press; Bransford & Franks, 1976, for more detailed discussion of these points). Similarly, one can learn to become better and better at remembering; that is, one can become a "memory expert." However, one does not become a memory expert simply by memorizing a book about memory experts. Instead, one must learn how to use such information to carry out memorizing acts.

B. Comparison with Theories of Semantic Memory

The fact that learning is not necessarily equivalent to remembering is often handled by appealing to "semantic" as opposed to "episodic" memories (see Tulving, 1972). One may *know* something (e.g., an inference) following some experience like reading a passage, yet avoid the trap of falsely believing that he *remembers* explicitly experiencing that particular information (see Kintsch, 1974; Tzeng, 1975). If one assumes that *knowing* depends on semantic memory and *remembering* depends on contact with episodic memory, then theories concerned strictly with episodic memory are clearly inadequate to characterize all the processes involved in education.

However, our present emphasis on learning what to do in order to go beyond one's current level of clarity and understanding also differs from the problems addressed by most theories of semantic memory (e.g., Collins & Quillian, 1969, 1972; Freedman & Loftus, 1971; Loftus & Freedman, 1972; Meyer & Ellis, 1970; Meyer & Schvaneveldt, 1971; Rips, Shoben, & Smith, 1973; Smith, Shoben, & Rips, 1974). These theorists attempt to account for the speed and ease of certain acts of knowing by making assumptions about the preexisting structure of already acquired information. Their emphasis is on describing how one can know *given* certain preexisting structures rather than on discovering the processes by which certain "structures" might be formed (see Bransford & Franks, 1976, for a more detailed discussion of this problem).

As an example of semantic memory models, consider the fact that it is easier to verify that "A canary is yellow" than it is to verify that "A canary has skin." According to many models (e.g., Collins & Quillan, 1969, 1972), this is due to the fact that "yellowness" has been directly stored with canary, whereas "skin" has been stored with animals. One must therefore "search" longer in order to verify that a canary has skin. Similarly, it may be easier to verify that *nurse* and *doctor* are both words than to verify that *nurse* and *butter* are both words (e.g., see Meyer, Schvaneveldt, & Ruddy, 1972). Typical theoretical explanations assert that the former two words are stored more "closely together" in semantic memory, hence, "spreading activation" can more readily occur (e.g., see Meyer, Schvaneveldt, & Ruddy, 1972; Loftus, 1975). Theories of semantic memory therefore attempt to account for knowing solely on the basis of the structure of already acquired information. So-called "process" models of semantic memory are involved with explaining how to use *already stored* information in retrieving facts, making comparisons, etc. However, these notions of "process" are not equivalent to the processes involved in the development of knowing. The latter involve discovering how to *go beyond* what is already known.

A simple example can help clarify the difference between semantic memory models and the present orientation. One could compare the ability of Einstein and a nonphysicist to solve a physics problem. The differences in their problem-solving abilities could be "accounted for" by assuming that Einstein already had knowledge about relativistic physics whereas the novice lacked such knowledge. Such an "account" would be equivalent to the form of most models of semantic memory. But note that the latter models provide no clues to processes by which Einstein *arrived at* his knowledge of relativistic physics. The present orientation is most primarily concerned with this question. Models of semantic memory are at best paraphrases of the objects of our knowing activities (see Bransford &

Franks, 1976, for further discussion). They fail to provide insights into the processes by which people learn what to do to go beyond what they know at a particular time.

C. Comparisons with "Verbal Learning" Research

As a final contrast between the present orientation and others, consider the orientation of a number of "verbal learning" studies purporting to study meaningfulness. A host of studies document the intuitively obvious fact that meaningful material is more easily learned than less meaningful material. For example, Johnson, Doll, Bransford, and Lapinsky (1974) examined the effects of repetition on recall of anomalous sentences versus recall of these same sentences made meaningful by context manipulations. They found that repetition facilitated recall for meaningful sentences much more than recall for the anomalous sentences.

It is both interesting and important to ask *why* meaningfulness increases repetition effectiveness, but again this misses a crucial point. Most theories that attempt to explain why inputs perceived as meaningful are better learned deal with the *products* of previous acts of knowing at state 1, 2, 3, etc. In the above case, the products are divided into two classes: meaningful and anomalous. Explanations for the varying effectiveness of repetition typically attribute differential structural or normative characteristics to these products of previous knowing activities. The critical point such approaches neglect is the question of how one learns to do things to make inputs meaningful in the first place. How does one get from one state to another? With respect to the problem of experts, the question is not so much what they know, but how they became experts and how, as experts, they continue to go beyond their present state of knowing.

III. UNDERSTANDING EXPERTS:
SOME FACTORS INVOLVED

The preceding discussion suggests that many current psychological theories do not directly address problems most crucial to education. A more direct focus on the processes involved in becoming experts would appear to have greater relevance for education. However, studies of experts appear to emphasize a very pervasive but aesthetically unappealing principle; namely that exposure and practice are the major variables. For example, in discussing and extending de Groot's (1965) classic studies of chess experts, Chase and Simon (1973) conclude that practice is the major independent variable underlying skill acquisition. They emphasize the *products* of practice and exposure; for example, the exceedingly large number of distinct chess configurations recognizable by chess experts. Indeed, there is a sense in which practice and exposure *are* major variables.

Despite well-intentioned desires to find magical shortcuts, a certain amount of drudgery is generally necessary for achieving expertise in any domain. However, a naive emphasis on practice and exposure is never sufficient. This ignores the question of *which* exposures or practices are most valuable. Furthermore, it does not help one understand what learners must do in order to make exposures maximally effective.

A. Practice and Exposure: Is That All There Is?

Consider a task in which most of us are probably "experts"; that is, "imaging" our own living rooms. Why are we so adept at this? Is our expertise merely a function of lots and lots of exposure, or something else? On introspective grounds, mere exposure is not sufficient to guarantee expertise at "imaging." For example, one of the present authors has been exposed to a certain situation (e.g., a two-block stretch of Hennipin Avenue in Minneapolis) hundreds of times, yet has only the most vague unarticulated images of it. This problem cannot simply be due to some general "inability to image," since the author can "image" other situations readily. Additional factors must be involved.

A set of studies conducted by Nitsch, McCarrell, Franks, and Bransford was designed to investigate the preconditions for achieving "expertise" at imaging a particular situation given equivalent amounts of exposure. All subjects in the experiments were given a one-minute exposure to a colored picture of a living room. Different groups of subjects were given orienting tasks designed to prompt them to act in different ways. Group I subjects were told that the picture contained from 0 to 3 inked-in Xs. Their task was to scan the picture first horizontally, then vertically, then horizontally, etc., until told to stop. At that time they were to report the number of Xs they had found. Group II subjects were given the same instructions, except they were told that all Xs would be located on the *contours* of objects. They therefore searched contours until told to stop. Group III subjects were told that we were interested in the types of actions that they might perform on the objects in the living room. They expected to report only on actions they generated and not on the visual layout of the room. Group IV subjects were given intentional recall instructions. They were told to study the picture with the intent of recalling the objects and relative locations of the objects that it contained. Following the one minute exposure, all subjects were given a surprise recall test (of course, the test was no surprise for Group IV). All subjects were asked to verbally recall as many objects as they could, and to indicate their relative positions on a recall sheet.

The results were quite dramatic. There were nonoverlapping distributions between Groups I and II versus III and IV. Group I and II recalled and located from 3 to 8 objects. The range for Group III and IV subjects was from 25 to 32. Following free recall, all subjects were presented with questions such as "Was there a window (and where)?", "Was there a wine glass (and where)?", etc. Even when given these cued recall probes, the nonoverlapping distributions of recall scores persisted. Subsequent analysis indicated that the cued recall increment over free recall scores was about three items for subjects in all of the four groups.

The X-scanning results indicate that differences in performance cannot merely be due to the amount of exposure. What is important is exposure in relation to the activities that subjects perform. Given a certain criterion task (in this case a recall test), certain activities are more fruitful than others for performance on that task. The X-scanning studies underscore the importance of some of Cassirer's (1946) arguments. He suggests that it is the purposive nature of our activities that guides the selection of information. What we articulate is not determined so much by the *content* of our experience as it is by the *significance* of certain information for our *acts* and *intents*. Cassirer suggests that only what is important for the activity and scheme of life is selected from the flux and noticed in the midst of this flux. The X-scanning studies illustrate that pure exposure is not sufficient to gain expertise in a particular area. In short, one does not merely learn *from* experience, one learns *to* experience. Purpose affects activity, which, in turn, determines the effects that particular exposures have.

B. Further Factors in Developing Expertise: Flexibility of Activities Performed

The development of expertise involves much more than learning a fixed set of activities that are optimal for acquiring any input. Experts must be flexible, since "optimal" acquisition activites must be defined relative to subsequent activities that one wishes to perform.

As an example of the need for flexibility, consider an area in which we all develop some expertise, that is, the area of remembering. Developmental researchers (e.g., Brown, 1975; Flavell & Wellman, in press) have begun to study children's acquistion of knowledge about how to go about remembering. During early stages of development, children may not even know to explicitly rehearse to-be-remembered items. Gradually they learn many more efficient and elaborate activities to perform. Most college sophomores, for example, exhibit some skills in gearing their acquisition activities to anticipated behaviors. They seem to encode and rehearse differently depending on whether they expect serial versus free recall, recall versus recognition, etc. (e.g., V. Bacharach, personal communication, 1975, Tversky, 1973). Yet even college students are not especially sophisticated in acts of remembering. For example, Wilson and Bransford (in preparation) have designed an *incidental* task that results in much better recall than an *intentional* memory task. When left to their own devices, even college students do not necessarily know what is best to do.

College sophomores often become experts at something else as well; namely at being expert subjects in memory experiments. They learn *not* to interrupt, *not* to ask questions that might disturb the experiment, etc. No self-respecting memory expert would put up with the way psychologists run most memory experiments. Experts would ask questions like "What must I remember?", "How many items?", "How much time will there be?", "What's the nature of the test?", etc. They would know what they needed to know in order to perform optimally — and would settle for nothing less.

In the context of memory experts, it is instructive to look again at the relationship between understanding (or meaning) and remembering. As mentioned above, it is generally assumed that meaningful processing facilitates remembering. For example, "semantic" processing is assumed to be better than "formal" processing (e.g., Jenkins, 1974), greater "depth of processing" is assumed to produce better memory (e.g., Craik & Lockhart, 1972; Craik & Tulving, 1975), etc. Yet the relationship between degree of understanding and remembering is usually talked about in terms of the *items* to be remembered rather than in terms of one's understanding the total task he must perform. In the present discussion, being an expert involves knowing what to do in order to perform optimally. This includes knowing the nature of the initial exposure situation, the nature of later criterion tasks, and the potential relations between the two. It seems reasonable to assume that the better one knows precisely what to ask in order to understand the total task, the better will be his performance. Yet increased understanding of a task can mean that one will choose to process items at a *less* rather than *more* " meaningful" level (in the sense in which the term "meaning" is generally used).

As an example, consider a "levels of processing" experiment conducted by a number of us at Vanderbilt (i.e., Morris, V. Franks, Stein, J. Franks, Bransford, unpublished data). In a within-subjects design, subjects either decided if an acquisition target word rhymed with a preceding word (rhyme acquisition) or if it fit meaningfully into a sentence frame (semantic acquisition). A recognition test indicated that semantic processing produced superior recognition to rhyming processing (hence replicating results from Craik & Tulving, 1975). It is therefore easy to assume that semantic processing results in "better" memory. But better for what?

A second group of subjects received the identical acquisition list but a different type of test. They were presented with a completely novel group of words at recognition and asked to decide which ones rhymed with the acquisition stimuli. Under these conditions, the subjects were better at recognizing rhymes of acquisition words that had initially been processed in a rhyming rather than a semantic mode. The "goodness" of memory resulting from different acquisition activities is therefore relative to the subsequent activities that one wants subjects to perform. A memory expert who realized that his task would be similar to that of Group II (rhyme recognition) would surely choose a "less meaningful" mode (i.e., auditory rather than semantic) for processing the acquisition stimuli. The expert would determine the nature of the total task and gear his acquisition activities to the nature of the test.

As another example of the relationship between understanding and remembering, consider the pictures in Fig. 1a and b. Which one might a memory expert choose to study during acquisition? As is well known in the imagery literature (e.g., Paivio, 1971), coherent scenes (like Fig. 1a) are much better recalled than jumbled scenes. Are coherent ("meaningful") scenes therefore better for all types of memory tasks? A study conducted by McCarrell, Nitsch, and Bransford illustrates that the value of particular acquisition conditions depends on the nature of the test. The subjects saw either Fig. 1a or b for 90 sec with the instruction to study the inputs because they would later be asked to remember what they had seen. Following acquisition, all subjects were presented with information like that depicted in Fig. 2 and asked to decide which member of each pair of elements they had actually seen. Those subjects who had seen the jumbled elements (Fig. 1b) were far superior to subjects who had studied the coherent scene.

An ideal memory expert should be able to choose the optimal acquisition conditions and activities as a function of the particular type of test used to measure retention. In short, the ideal memory expert would be flexible. He must know what to do (including what to ask) in order to best achieve a particular goal.

C. Expertise and Problems of Growth

Issues concerning flexibility by no means exhaust the problem of understanding experts. Experts can be flexible by adapting past knowledge and techniques to current problem situations. There remains the extremely important problem of understanding how experts *go beyond* their current level of competence. How are they able to perform activities which enable them to grow?

Consider the problem of growth in the context of memory experts. Like any expert, a true memory expert is always becoming. His most important skills are knowing what to do to go beyond his level of competence at any particular time. Of course, one could learn a fixed set of memory techniques and operate relatively flexibly and efficiently for some time. But these particular techniques could easily break down as soon as someone changed the nature of the memory game.

The problem of growth is clearly an issue that transcends the domain of memory experts. Indeed, the issue becomes more important as one attempts to be an expert in areas that do not permit as much structuring of situations as frequently occurs in memory demonstrations. That is, a memory expert can remain a performer whose audience must assimilate their tasks and questions to his prearranged "game plan." By contrast, an expert clinician, for example, must

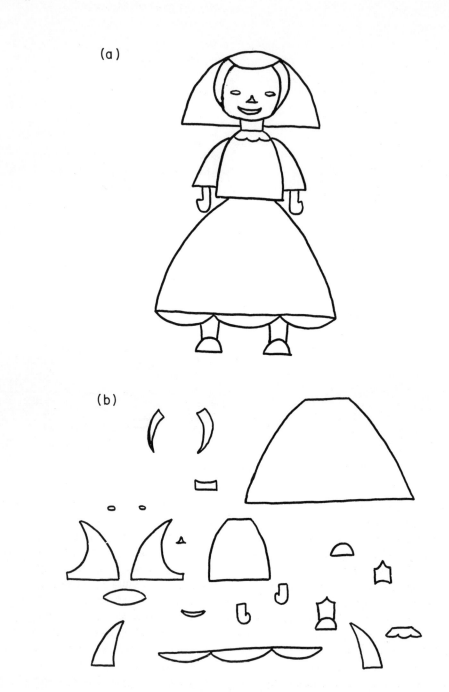

(a)

(b)

FIG. 1 (a) and (b). Two different acquisition conditions.

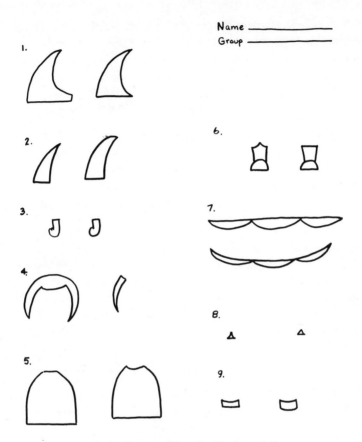

FIG. 2.   Test condition for Fig. 1a and 1b.

be able to accommodate his activities to the particular constellation of problems that his client presents.

While clinical psychologists often disagree about the type of training necessary to develop expert clinicians, most would probably agree that clinical programs should provide training in knowing what to do to clarify, evaluate, and go beyond one's current level of competence. Therapeutic techniques can easily become faddish, yet the needs of clients frequently change. Like the example of the memory expert, a therapist trained only in a set of techniques might fail to accomodate to changes in clients' needs and problems. Therapists must be oriented toward their own growth as well as their clients'. The pervasive importance of learning what to do in order to promote growth is succinctly stated by Toulmin (1972) in his *Human Understanding*: "A man demonstrates his rationality, not by a commitment to fixed ideas, stereotyped procedures, or immutable concepts, but by the manner in which, and the occasions on which, he changes those ideas, procedures, and concepts (P.V.)."

IV. PROBLEMS IN KNOWING
WHAT ONE NEEDS TO FURTHER KNOW

From an educational perspective, understanding the processes by which people are able to go beyond their current state of knowing appears to be the most important (yet difficult) aspect of the problem of understanding experts. Whether a teacher wants to help students learn how to learn on their own or simply needs to decide what to teach next, the same issue prevails.

Consider some activities that people spontaneously engage in when attempting to go beyond their current level of understanding or knowing. As a simple example, assume that someone walks into a room and can only vaguely perceive a particular object. The person must act in order to clarify his perception. In this case, the activity is very simple. One uses his legs to walk closer and clarify what is before his eyes. Similarly, assume that someone can adequately perceive an object, but needs to understand more about it. One might touch it, taste it, smell it, bounce it, etc. Certain activities must be engaged in in order to better understand. At more advanced levels of inquiry, one asks questions in order to further his understanding of some event or object: "What is it?", "Where did it come from?", "What is it used for?", "How do you know that?", etc. Indeed, the process of becoming an expert in some field seems to be more closely related to the ability to ask appropriate questions than to the possession of a prescribed set of facts.

Therefore, there appear to be commonalities among such diverse sets of activities as an infant's exploration of his rattle by placing it in his mouth, an adult's walking across a room to get a better view, a student's questioning of his teacher, a teacher's prompting of students' questions, a teacher's presentation of examples, etc. All are attempts to clarify one's own or another's understanding. But how do students know whether they need further clarification? How does a teacher know whether students understand a message? The problem of developing criteria for determining whether one needs to perform certain activities in order to go beyond a particular level of knowing represents one of the most important and pervasive problems that educators and students face.

Dewey (1933) cites an episode from Charles Darwin's autobiography that illustrates the difficulties in knowing what one needs to know in order to adequately understand something. Darwin notes that, as a youth, he once found a seashell in a particular gravel pit. He mentioned his discovery to the geologist Sidgwich, whose immediate response was something like, "That's impossible." Sidgwich then clarified his statement. He was not questioning Darwin's honesty, but rather questioning the authenticity of the finding. According to Sidgwich, the shell must have been placed there by someone. If it had actually been lodged there for centuries, all extant theories about the geological formation of that particular area would have been in serious doubt. From Darwin's perspective, finding a seashell was finding a seashell. For Sidgwich, the identical event was potentially a much more significant (and different kind of) fact.

The Darwin–Sidgwich example can be used to illustrate the problem of knowing what one needs to know in order to understand something. Assume that Sidgwich believed the shell had *not* merely been placed or dropped there by some recent visitor. If Sidgwich had only one chance to determine details regarding Darwin's discovery, what questions would he ask? Which aspects of the event would make it a significant fact from Sidgwich's point of view? Would it matter precisely *where* the gravel pit was located? Would the exact location of the shell within the gravel pit count? Would it matter whether the seashell was tropical or nontropical? Would its color, shape, composition, etc., count? Would it matter whether Darwin had touched the shell with his hand as opposed to having held it with a cloth, etc.? In the absence of knowledge about Sidgwich's theoretical framework it is difficult to determine the answers to these questions. Knowledge of an appropriate framework sets the stage for knowing what needs to be further known in order to adequately understand something. In the absence of a general framework, it is even difficult to know *whether* further questions need to be asked (Bransford & Franks, 1976).

Now assume that Sidgwich had been a detective rather than a geologist. Assume further that he was investigating a case where someone was murdered in the gravel pit and a prime suspect had a fettish for collecting tropical shells. From a detective's perspective, different "features" of the event would presumably be relevant. For example, the *exact time* of Darwin's discovery would probably be more relevant to a detective than a geologist. Understanding *where* it was found would also differ. For the geologist, "where" would probably refer to a particular rock or soil stratum, and such a stratum might encompass the total perimeter of the pit. For a detective, "where" would refer to a spatial location at a particular point (and might encompass a number of possible horizontally-delineated strata). In addition, whether Darwin had picked up the shell with a cloth or his hands would be significant to the detective. In short, the same "facts" (and their "features") assume different meanings depending on the framework from which one views them (Bransford & Franks, 1976; Kuhn, 1970). Some framework is necessary to guide the search for new information that seems necessary to insure an adequate understanding of a particular event.

The preceding examples illustrate one of the most difficult problems faced by both students and teachers — the *criterion* problem. People frequently have no idea of what they need to do (e.g., ask) in order to insure that they adequately understand particular "facts" or events. Indeed, they frequently do not realize that they need to do anything at all. John Holt (1964) provides numerous examples illustrating the criterion problem within the context of education. He argues that many students do not even realize that a particular subject matter could "make sense." According to Holt (1964), the following illustration is representative of the approach a large number of students adopt:

> One boy, quite a good student, was working on the problem, "If you have 6 jugs, and you want to put $2/3$ of a pint of lemonade into each jug, how much lemonade will you need?" His answer was 18 pints. I [Holt] said, "How much in each jug?" "Two-thirds of a pint." I said, "Is that more or less than a pint?" "Less," I said, "How many jugs are there?" "Six" I said, "But that doesn't make any sense." He shrugged his shoulders and said, "Well, that's the way the system worked out." [p. 181]

Certainly students who have no expectation that what they study will make sense are in a very poor position to develop the ability to decide whether or not they have adequately understood.

In contrast, consider what happens when a student approaches the same subject matter with the realization that it does in fact make sense. Students who know that arithmetic operations with fractions are lawful and reasonable exhibit a markedly different approach to dealing with such problems. Holt relates the following example of how such a student reacted to the erroneously solved math problem, "$1/2 + 1/3 = 3/4$":

> Barbara . . . instantly said, "No! $1/3$ isn't the same as $1/4$." It took me [Holt] a second or two to see what she meant. Since $1/2 + 1/4 = 3/4$, $1/2 + 1/3$ cannot equal $3/4$. [p. 113]

The two preceding examples illustrate the contrast in how students approach the issue of an erroneous problem solution. However, understanding that a particular subject matter "makes sense" can do much more than enable a student to recognize a wrong answer. As we have noted previously, becoming an "expert" entails knowing what to do to go beyond one's present level of understanding. What sort of reasoning does a student use when he or she does not know the answer to a particular problem? The student who does not expect fractions to make sense would simply make a wild guess or leave the following problem unanswered: "$2/4 + 3/5 = ?$" However, Holt relates that one of his students, while unable to give the correct answer, did demonstrate the ability to systematically narrow down the range of possible answers in a clever fashion:

> Betty said, "$2/4 + 3/5$ is 1 or more. You need two more fifths to make 1, and $2/4$ is more than $2/5$, so the answer must be bigger than 1." [p. 114]

Clearly, Betty had a good idea of how to use what she did know to clarify her understanding of this problem. Despite her failure to provide the correct answer, she did appear to understand the problem in a meaningful way.

The preceding examples highlight an extremely important problem. Why do some students know what to do to make problems meaningful while others fail to do so? Subsequent sections consider two aspects of this question: (1) How to characterize the problem of meaning, and (2) How to characterize the processes by which the meaningfulness of inputs can be grasped.

V. DEVELOPING FRAMEWORKS THAT PROVIDE CRITERIA
FOR KNOWING WHAT ONE NEEDS TO KNOW

We have argued that organisms must learn what to do to clarify and go beyond their present level of understanding. For example, they must know how to *make* things meaningful. What does it mean to make things meaningful, and what happens to the organism's system when it performs such clarifying acts?

A. Different Meanings of Meaning

Consider first what it means to make things meaningful. What is the problem of "meaning" here? One use of the term meaning involves contrasts between letter strings such as *gex* versus *paper*. English speakers know the meaning of *paper* but not *gex* (cf. Bransford, McCarrell, & Nitsch, 1976). This use of "meaning" is most closely related to the idea of meanings as products of previous knowing acts, in which such products are assumed to be stored in memory for later retrieval. Thus, this use is related to those theories that look at knowing in terms of stored products or things. However, there is a second use of the term "meaning" that is often much more important than the first in the context of education. This is the problem of understanding the significance of events. To adequately comprehend, one must understand the significance of artifacts (cf. Bransford & McCarrell, 1974), gestures (cf. Bransford, McCarrell, Franks, & Nitsch, in press), utterances (cf. Bransford, McCarrell, & Nitsch, 1976), data (cf. Kuhn, 1970), etc. For example, one can learn to understand the significance of brush strokes given the framework of certain artists, styles, cultures, etc. Or consider the task of understanding the significance of a statement like *Altitude precedes window*. Here one must adopt a framework that focuses on surface features like orthography and realize that the statement refers to an ordering on an alphabetic scale.

Significances arise in the context of particular frameworks for knowing. Increasing awareness of the significance of certain aspects of phenomena follow from increasing expertise with respect to particular domains. For example, Hanson (1970) discusses how theoretical frameworks for aerodynamics allow one to understand the significance of otherwise seemingly incoherent and unrelated aspects of wing shapes. Similarly, Stent (1972) traces various premature scientific discoveries that have occurred in the domain of physical sciences. He argues that such findings were premature because scientists lacked a framework appropriate for helping them understand what the data meant. The previously mentioned Darwin–Sidgwich example in Section IV also illustrates how various frameworks determine the significance of events (including what counts as significant "features"). There appear to be endless potential variations in the significance of any event depending on the framework from which it is viewed.

This emphasis on significances suggests that "meanings" cannot simply be construed as "things" that are stored as particular entities. Instead meaning appears to be better conceptualized as a momentary place or pattern in a changing relation structure or framework. As frameworks change, significances change as well. It is for this reason that problems such as contextually induced flexibility pose such major difficulties for *product* approaches to meaning (e.g., Barclay, Bransford, Franks, McCarrell, & Nitsch, 1974; Anderson & Ortony, 1975; Bransford, McCarrell, & Nitsch, 1976). It would seem more fruitful to focus on the *processes* of creating significances as a function of the changing frameworks from which events are viewed.

An emphasis on significances also cautions against assumptions like "sentences are already meaningful" (see Lesgold, Curtis, DeGood, Golinkoff, McCormick, & Shimron, 1974). Of course, sentences usually are meaningful to a listener at some level, but this does not insure that a listener (e.g., a student) understands the particular significance that a speaker (e.g., a teacher) intends. Indeed, this latter situation illustrates the educational dilemma. The dilemma is that the significance of the "facts" that are taught depend on the existence of a more global, abstract framework. Yet the framework cannot be adequately acquired without exposure to a number of exemplary illustrations or "facts." In short, educators face a version of the chicken—egg problem. The problem is magnified when teachers' frameworks remain tacit and they are unable to communicate them to students. The students are left with a mere array of facts that do not cohere to form meaningful patterns. They then lack a framework to guide them in determining what else they need to know in order to adequately understand.

B. Characterizing the Growth and Changes in Frameworks

We have argued that "meanings" (i.e., significances) are not things but rather are momentary places or relations in changing frameworks of knowing. We have further argued that certain frameworks are necessary in order to know what to do to go beyond one's present state of knowing. We now focus in more detail on what it might mean to develop frameworks that can facilitate subsequent acts of knowing. In short, the focus is on growth.

How might one characterize the changes that accompany growth or learning? Does the organism simply store the products of previous acts of knowing so that these are now available for subsequent retrieval? Does growth simply involve an accumulation of more and more contents (features, facts, ideas, images, principles, schema, etc.) plus greater numbers of interconnections among them? Many models of episodic and semantic memory seem to imply that growth essentially involves an accumulation of more and more content. However, if growth simply involves an accumulation of knowledge, that is, of products, then why don't experts have *more* difficulty than nonexperts? Experts should have more knowledge, so it should take them longer to "sort through" it in order to find what is relevant for a particular task. Yet de Groot's (1965) studies of chess experts show that it is the nonmasters who have to explicitly evaluate all kinds of alternatives, many of which result in dead ends. In contrast, experts are flexibly selective and can readily eliminate nonoptimal hypotheses and thoughts. As Chase and Simon (1973) note: "Masters invariably explore strong moves, whereas weaker players spend considerable time analyzing the consequences of bad moves. The best move, or at least a very good one, just seems to come to the top of the Master's list of plausible moves for analysis" [pp. 216–217].

The present authors assume that growth is not simply an accumulation of "pieces of knowledge." Indeed, the growth of embryos, plants, faces, etc., is anything but a mere accumulation of more "pieces" (e.g., see Piaget, 1971; Shaw & Pittenger, in press; Thompson, 1942). Growth seems to be better viewed as a "remodeling" of a structure as a whole. What might it mean to view psychological growth as a remodeling of one's perspective or framework for knowing rather than the mere accumulation of more and more things that are known?

First, it seems clear that there are many levels of remodeling. In therapy, for example, a client may come to realize that it is irrational to believe himself inadequate. However, this level of remodeling may not be sufficient to allow him to *feel* differently and to *act* in different ways. Similarly, the experience of reading the Castaneda volumes (e.g., 1974) may remodel one's perspective at some level, but not at a level where one can comfortably function in Don Juan's world. One can learn to think *about* his framework, but to think *in terms of* it is a different matter indeed. Yet to become an expert in Don Juan's world, one must think in terms of his framework. One must learn to "see" the world in a different way.

This emphasis on learning to see differently is also stressed in the work on chess experts. As Chase and Simon (1973) note, the research by de Groot (1965, 1966) indicates that ". . . the most important processes underlying chess mastery are immediate visual-perceptual processes rather than the subsequent logical– deductive thinking processes" [p. 215]. De Groot (1966) suggests the following:

> We know that increasing experience and knowledge in a specific field (chess, for instance) has the effect that things (properties, etc.) which, at earlier stages, had to be abstracted, or even inferred are apt to be immediately perceived at later stages. To a rather large extent, *abstraction is replaced by perception*, but we do not know much about how this works, nor where the borderline lies. . . . As an effect of this replacement, a so called "given" problem situation is not really given since *it is seen differently* by an expert than it is perceived by an unexperienced person, but we do not know much about these differences [pp. 33–34].

Indeed, de Groot (1965) notes that expert chess masters have a difficult time respecting nonexperts. The experts are often unable to appreciate how a nonexpert can spend 30 min. figuring out a move that is immediately obvious to them.

How might one begin to conceptualize the remodeling processes that allows organisms to "see" differently? Can an emphasis on remodeling provide a more fruitful orientation toward growth than one which emphasizes the accumulation of more and more facts? In many respects, an emphasis on remodeling is congruent with J. Gibson's (1966) claim that learning involves the education of attention. According to Gibson (1966), learning depends on past experience but not on contact with stored traces or products of past experiences. In short, learning is assumed to involve something different from the accumulation of stored facts that must be retrieved through the "Hoffding step" (i.e., the matching of a new input to a stored memory trace; e.g., see Shaw & Bransford, in press).

We suggest that viewing growth as a remodeling process focuses on the changes that occur as one progresses from thinking *about* things to thinking *in terms of* things. An emphasis on what people think *about* focuses on the products of their knowing activities. An emphasis on what people think *in terms of* focuses on the processes responsible for determining the significance of the objects of knowing (i.e., the products) that people create. Our notion of thinking *in terms of* appears to be similar to Broudy's (Chapter 1, this volume) concept of *knowing with*. From the present perspective, past experience provides an increasingly precise and differentiated framework that sets the stage for perceiving, understanding, and acting. Such a framework permits experts to be optimally selective and efficient because it permits them to rule out or inhibit all kinds of ultimately unfruitful possibilities (e.g., see Bransford & Franks, 1976). Effective learning therefore seems closely akin to perceptual learning where the latter involves a process of differentiation rather than enrichment by storage of subsequent facts (e.g., see Gibson & Gibson, 1955).

Consider how certain acts of clarification help someone think *in terms of* rather than merely *about* a concept. Suppose one seeks clarification by asking for an example. What does this process do? Assume that students are told that "retrieval is the key to remembering." They need a definition of retrieval in order to adequately understand the statement, but they also need more than this in order to "see" what is meant. One thing needed is a number of examples involving retrieval. By hearing various examples, students learn to understand them *in terms of* the concept of retrieval. They do not simply learn by storing and retrieving the examples but instead clarify their concept of what the examples stood for. Gradually they learn to think *in terms of* their increasingly refined knowledge of the concept of retrieval. They gradually eliminate the necessity for recreating the explicit definition of retrieval, for recreating a list of previously heard examples and comparing these to new situations, etc. Gradually, they learn to "see" more directly. Indeed, students can *forget* the examples and still retain the framework acquired from these examples; they gain expertise regarding the global concept of "retrieval." Kuhn (1970), for example, discusses the role of paradigmatic problems and problem solutions that shape scientists' global view of a field.

Of course, increasing accuracy in performance does not necessarily imply that learners are remodeling frameworks or perspectives which will set the stage for subsequent acts of knowing. Learners often *can* simply retain facts and answer on the basis of these. For example, Anderson (1975) compared the performance of subjects who memorized a number of facts as opposed to only one fact about a particular topic. Under these conditions, subjects who had *more* knowledge were *slower* in deciding whether they had actually heard a particular statement during the acquisition task. Related to this, Holt (1964) discusses differences between "answer memorizers" and those who learn to "see the problem." According to Holt (1964), the former student might think: "Let's see, what did I do last time I had a problem like this?' If they remember their recipes and don't mix them up, they may be good at the answer-hunting game, and the answers they bring home may often be right ones" [p. 119] . Holt contrasts these thinking activities to those of other students. The latter derive formulas, principles, etc., from their perception of the problem itself. As discussed above, "memorization" is not what makes one an expert. Experts learn to "see" problems more adequately and hence can more efficiently act (see de Groot, 1965).

C. Additional Factors in Progressing from Thinking *about* to Thinking *in Terms of* Things

From the present perspective, the process of moving from simply thinking *about* to thinking *in terms of* information can result in the elimination of many cumbersome steps previously necessary to insure adequate understanding. Experts who have learned to think in terms of various frameworks can immediately apprehend information that others may have to laboriously compute. De Groot's (1965) studies of chess masters provide one example. Another involves development of competency or expertise in speaking a language. For example, adult speakers of English can readily perceive that the statement *John hit Mary* is semantically equivalent to the statement *Mary was hit by John.* In contrast, young children have great difficulty with this type of task (Olson, 1974). Yet these same children can perform very well *if* they are provided with additional contextual information. Olson (1974) found that informing children about the identity of actors, providing them with a plausible rationale for the interaction, etc., greatly increased performance in the above-mentioned type of task.

A potentially important factor in becoming an expert therefore seems to involve a process of *decontextualization.* Knowing becomes less and less context bound. Experts may no longer need explicit, specific contextual support in order to understand something. They may eliminate the need to perform certain previously necessary activities as well. For example, consider the possibility that explicit pronunciation may be a crucial process during *initial* stages of reading acquisition. The necessity for this explicit "mediating" step seems to eventually drop out later. Of course, it can return under conditions where one confronts especially difficult material and has to resort to explicit pronunciation in order to understand. The automatization that accompanies increasing expertise is therefore *not* assumed to simply involve a process of performing the same activities faster and faster. *What* one must do to understand will change as well (see Kohlers, 1975).

VI. OVERALL SUMMARY AND CONCLUSIONS

Many participants in the present conference have questioned the adequacy of basic psychological theories for providing insights into problems of education. Our contribution has attempted to elucidate some of the reasons for this gap. It was argued that many theories based on current research in experimental psychology are not directly oriented toward problems faced by educators. In particular, research and theories concerning episodic memory, semantic memory, and verbal learning do not necessarily address the crucial problems involved with understanding psychological growth. We have focused on the problems of growth, stressing the problem of learning how to go beyond one's current state of clarity and understanding. Growth could be *represented* by detailing the products of different states of understanding. However, this ignores the crucial problem of which acts of knowing or clarification must be performed in order to get from one state to the next. In the context of education, helping students learn what to do in order to achieve greater clarity and understanding seems much more important than the mere transmission of content. Content can quickly become obsolete. In contrast, the ability to know what one needs to do to clarify and further his present understanding of this content never becomes stale or static. This ability helps one continually grow.

Can a theoretical and empirical emphasis on experts help reduce the gap between education and basic psychological research? At one level, a positive answer to this question might seem doubtful. Since practice and exposure appear to be major variables that influence acquisition, there may be very little one could say except "Go practice." However, this discussion has raised additional questions. For example, it has been demonstrated that equivalent exposures do not necessarily result in equivalent acquisition of information (e.g., the X-scanning study). Students must be helped to make exposures work. In short, an exposure is not an exposure is not an exposure. The effects of exposure depend on the current framework for articulating the significance of inputs. For example, exposure to chess positions would have little positive effect unless an individual had some understanding of the nature of chess. Similarly, students who are exposed to a list of examples will be less able to use this information in a new situation if they initially had no idea of what the examples were supposed to illustrate. As a related illustration, consider the notion of exposure in learning a language. It is extremely doubtful that children could learn a language simply by being exposed to it spoken over a tape recorder in a dark, contextless environment. Without perceptual support from the context of natural world artifacts and actions, children would have no framework for articulating the significance of those utterances, and hence for understanding linguistic meaning and cracking aspects of the syntactic code (e.g., see MacNamara 1972; Nelson, 1974).

We have argued that a basic problem of education is to help students learn what to do to make exposures meaningful. Effective teachers use a variety of intuitively based techniques for helping students perform such acts of knowing: They prompt students to ask and answer particular questions, they relate novel inputs to already acquired information by way of analogy, and they provide both positive and negative examples to help clarify points. Despite the important role of such activities, they remain intuitively based. Ideally, theoretical psychology should provide a framework that helps clarify what is happening when one chooses to prompt certain acts of knowing. Such a framework could help teachers understand the growth process so that they could continually clarify, evaluate, and go beyond their momentary levels of expertise.

Unfortunately, theoretical psychology fails to provide a coherent framework suitable for understanding the growth process. For example, theories of episodic remembering certainly do not perform this function. They may be useful for understanding questions such as "Why are students better able to recall concrete examples than abstract principles?", but they fail to clarify the processes by which students learn what the examples are examples of. Similarly, theories of semantic memory fail to provide insight into the growth process. Rather than focus on the *processes* of acquisition, their major orientation aims toward predicting the speed and ease of knowing *given* that one had already acquired information in a certain form.

As a step toward developing a framework for clarifying the growth process, we have suggested that the development of expertise must involve something more than the mere accumulation of more and more content. Growth appears to involve a remodeling of one's perspective that enables one to "see" differently. Such remodeling involves developing a more global, abstract framework that one acts *in terms of* and that sets the stage for providing concrete particulars with their distinct significance and place (e.g., see Hayek, 1969).

The present orientation suggests the need to contrast conditions of acquisition that appear to promote remodeling as opposed to the mere accumulation of content. The work presented at this conference by Allan Collins (Chapter 10, this volume) represents a case in point. What are the advantages of learning via a student–tutor dialogue versus simply being told factual information? Research is needed to determine whether dialogue trained students can better transfer to other domains.

At Vanderbilt, Mary Lessick Hannigan (1976) has begun some extremely promising work that contrasts the remodeling of a global perspective with the mere accumulation of content. In Hannigan's studies, all subjects are exposed to identical lists of acquisition sentences (e.g., *The man used the hubcap to carry water; The man used the box to reach the branch*, etc.) Her subjects simply rate the comprehensibility of each sentence they hear. The major variable involves the manner in which subjects are induced to process the acquisition sentences. The subjects in Group I simply hear each sentence as a factual statement; those in Group II are told that each sentence represents a hypothetical activity that one might perform in order to survive on a deserted island. The assumption was that the latter type of processing would help students articulate a general perspective regarding problems of surviving on a deserted island that they could begin to think in terms of. These students should therefore have acquired something more than a simple list of facts.

Following acquisition, Hannigan exposed all subjects to a set of test sentences. These sentences were embedded in white noise and subjects were simply asked to repeat each sentence after hearing it. Some of the sentences were old and had occurred during acquisition; some were new but related to the general problem of survival on an island; and some were new but unrelated to a survival theme. Pilot data revealed large and consistent differences between the two groups of subjects. Those in Group II performed much better on both the old sentences as well as the new sentences related to a survival theme.

Although a great deal of additional research is needed, Hannigan's results are very promising. It appears possible to begin studying the effects of various activities at acquisition on subjects' subsequent apprehension of related domains. Of course, the ability to detect information through white noise is not a direct test of expertise, but it does seem to correlate with the degree to which one is able to make inputs meaningful.[1] By articulating a general perspective regarding problems of survival, the subjects in Group II were better able to detect old information as well as new information that could be understood in terms of this framework. The subjects in Group I performed more poorly, despite exposure to equivalent content during the acquisition task. We suspect that acquisition processes permitting the remodeling of frameworks may be responsible for the important priming effects that appear to underlie skilled activities such as oral comprehension, reading, etc. Research is under way to compare procedures that promote remodeling with ones facilitating accumulation of content in a variety of task domains.

ACKNOWLEDGMENTS

This paper was supported in part by grant NEG-00-3-0026 to J. D. Bransford and J. J. Franks. The authors are extremely indebted to Sue Bright for her help in preparing this manuscript.

[1] J. R. Barclay (personal communication) is currently conducting research concerning the effects of context on subjects' abilities to shadow sentences embedded in white noise. The success of his research influenced the decision to use a white noise task as the dependent measure in these studies comparing modes of acquisition that facilitate remodeling with ones facilitating content accumulation.

REFERENCES

Anderson, J. R. Item-specific and relation-specific interference in sentence memory. *Journal of Experimental Psychology: Human Learning and Memory*, 1975, **104**, 249–260.

Anderson, R. C., & Ortony, A. On putting apples into bottles – a problem of polysemy. *Cognitive Psychology*, 1975, *7*, 167–180.

Barclay, J. R., Bransford, J. D., Franks, J. J., McCarrell, N. S., & Nitsch, K. E. Comprehension and semantic flexibility. *Journal of Verbal Learning and Verbal Behavior,* 1974, **13**, 471–481.

Bransford, J. D., & Franks, J. J. Toward a framework for understanding learning. In G. Bower (Ed.), *Psychology of learning and motivation,* Vol. 10. New York: Academic Press, 1976.

Bransford, J. D., & McCarrell, N. S. A sketch of a cognitive approach to comprehension. In W. Weimer & D. Palermo (Eds.), *Cognition and the symbolic processes.* Hillsdale, N.J.: Lawrence Erlbaum Associates, 1974.

Bransford, J. D., McCarrell, N. S., Franks, J. J., & Nitsch, K. E. Toward unexplaining memory. In R. E. Shaw & J. D. Bransford (Eds.), *Perceiving, acting and knowing: Toward an ecological psychology*. Hillsdale, N.J.: Lawrence Erlbaum Associates, in press.

Bransford, J. D., McCarrell, N. S., & Nitsch, K. E. Contexte, compréhension et flexibilité sémantique: quelques implications théoriques et methodologiques. In S. Ehrlich & E. Tulving (Eds.), *La memoire sémantique.* Paris: Bulletin de Psychologie, 1976.

Brown, A. L. The development of memory: Knowing, knowing about knowing, and knowing how to know. In H. W. Reese (Ed.), *Advances in child development and behavior.* Vol. 10. New York: Academic Press, 1975.

Cassirer, E. *Language and myth.* New York: Dover, 1946.

Castaneda, C. *Tales of power.* New York: Simon & Schuster, 1974.

Chase, W. G., & Simon, H. A. The mind's eye in chess. In W. G. Chase (Ed.), *Visual information processing.* New York: Academic Press, 1973. Pp. 215–281.

Collins, A. M., & Quillian, M. R. Retrieval time from semantic memory. *Journal of Verbal Learning and Verbal Behavior,* 1969, 8, 240–247.

Collins, A. M., & Quillian, M. R. How to make a language user. In E. Tulving & W. Donaldson (Eds.), *Organization of memory.* New York: Academic Press, 1972. Pp. 309–351.

Craik, F. I. M., & Lockhart, R. S. Levels of processing: A framework for memory research. *Journal of Verbal Learning and Verbal Behavior,* 1972, **11**, 671–684.

Craik, F. I. M., & Tulving, E. Depth of processing and the retention of words in episodic memory. *Journal of Experimental Psychology: General,* 1975, **104**, 268–294.

de Groot, A. B. Perception and memory versus thought. In B. Kleinmutz (Ed.), *Problem solving: Research, method and theory.* New York: Wiley, 1966.

de Groot, A. B. *Thought and choice in chess.* The Hague: Mouton, 1965.

Dewey, J. *How we think* (rev. ed.). Boston: Heath, 1933.

Flavell, J. H., & Wellman, H. M. Metamemory. In R. V. Kail, Jr. & J. W. Hagen (Eds.), *Perspectives on the development of memory and cognition.* Hillsdale, N.J.: Lawrence Erlbaum Associates, in press.

Freedman, J. L., & Loftus, E. F. Retrieval of words from long-term memory. *Journal of Verbal Learning and Verbal Behavior,* 1971, **10**, 107–115.

Gibson, J. J. *The senses considered as perceptual systems.* Boston: Houghton Mifflin, 1966.

Gibson, J. J., & Gibson, E. J. Perceptual learning: Differentiation or enrichment? *Psychological Review,* 1955, **62**, 32–41.

Hannigan, M. L. The effects of frameworks on sentence perception and memory. Unpublished doctoral dissertation, Vanderbilt University, 1976.

Hanson, N. R. A picture theory of theory meaning. In R. G. Colodny (Ed.), *The nature and function of scientific theories.* Pittsburgh, Penn.: University of Pittsburgh Press, 1970. Pp. 233–274.

Hayek, F. A. The primacy of the abstract. In A. Koestler & J. R. Smythies (Eds.), *Beyond reductionism*, Boston: Beacon Press, 1969.

Holt, J. *How children fail.* New York: Dell, 1964.

Jenkins, J. J. Can we have a theory of meaningful memory? In R. L. Solso (Ed.), *Theories in cognitive psychology: The Loyola symposium.* Hillsdale, N.J.: Lawrence Erlbaum Associates, 1974.

Johnson, M. K., Doll, T. J., Bransford, J. D., & Lapinski, R. Context effects in sentence memory. *Journal of Experimental Psychology*, 1974, **103**, 358–360.

Kintsch, W. *The representation of meaning in memory.* Hillsdale, N.J.: Lawrence Erlbaum Associates, 1974.

Kohlers, P. A. Memorial consequences of automatized encoding. *Journal of Experimental Psychology: Human Learning and Memory*, 1975, **1**, 689–701.

Kuhn, T. S. *The structure of scientific revolutions* (2nd ed.). Chicago, Ill.: University of Chicago Press, 1970.

Lesgold, A. M., Curtis, M. E., DeGood, H., Golinkoff, R. M., McCormick, C., & Shimron, J. The role of mental imagery in text comprehension: Preliminary studies. Pittsburgh, Penn.: University of Pittsburgh, Learning Research and Development Center, 1974.

Loftus, E. F. Spreading activation within semantic categories: Comments on Rosch's "Cognitive representations of semantic categories." *Journal of Experimental Psychology: General*, 1975, **104**, 234–240.

Loftus, E. F., & Freedman, J. L. Effect of category-name frequency on the speed of naming an instance of a category. *Journal of Verbal Learning and Verbal Behavior*, 1972, **11**, 343–347.

MacNamara, J. Cognitive basis of language learning in infants. *Psychological Review*, 1972, **79**, 1–13.

Meyer, D. E., & Ellis, G. B. Parallel processes in word recognition. Paper presented at the meeting of the Psychonomic Society, San Antonio, Texas, November, 1970.

Meyer, D. E., & Schvaneveldt, R. W. Facilitation in recognizing pairs of words: Evidence of a dependence between retrieval operations. *Journal of Experimental Psychology*, 1971, **90**, 227–234.

Meyer, D. E., Schvaneveldt, R. W., & Ruddy, M. G. Activation of lexical memory. Paper presented at the meeting of the Psychonomic Society, St. Louis, Missouri, November, 1972.

Nelson, K. Concept, word, and sentence: Interrelations in acquisition and development. *Psychological Review*, 1974, **81**, 267–285.

Olson, D. R. Towards a theory of instructional means. Invited address presented to the American Educational Research Association, Chicago, Illinois, April, 1974.

Paivio, A. *Imagery and verbal processes.* New York: Holt, Rinehart, & Winston, 1971.

Piaget, J. *Biology and knowledge: An essay on the relations between organic regulations and cognitive processes.* Chicago, Ill.: University of Chicago Press, 1971.

Rips, L. J., Shoben, E. J., & Smith, E. E. Semantic distance and the verification of semantic relations. *Journal of Verbal Learning and Verbal Behavior*, 1973, **12**, 1–20.

Shaw, R. E., & Bransford, J. D. (Eds.), *Perceiving, acting and knowing: Toward an ecological psychology.* Hillsdale, N.J.: Lawrence Erlbaum Associates, in press.

Shaw, R. E., & Pittenger, J. Perceiving the face of change in changing faces: Implications for a theory of object perception. In R. E. Shaw & J. D. Bransford (Eds.), *Perceiving, acting, and knowing: Toward an ecological psychology.* Hillsdale, N.J.: Lawrence Erlbaum Associates, in press.

Smith, E. E., Shoben, E. J., & Rips, L. J. Structure and process in semantic memory: A feature model for semantic decisions. *Psychological Review*, 1974, 81, 214–241.

Stent, G. S. Prematurity and uniqueness in scientific discovery. *Scientific American*, 1972, 227(6), 84–93.

Thompson, D. A. W. *On growth and form* (2nd ed.). Cambridge, England: Cambridge University Press, 1942.

Toulmin, S. *Human understanding. Vol. I: The collective use and evolution of concepts.* Princeton, N.J.: Princeton University Press, 1972.

Tulving, E. Episodic and semantic memory. In E. Tulving & W. Donaldson (Eds.), *Organization of memory.* New York: Academic Press, 1972.

Tversky, B. Encoding processes in recognition and recall. *Cognitive Psychology*, 1973, 5, 275–287.

Tzeng, O. J. L. Sentence memory: Recognition and inferences. *Journal of Experimental Psychology: Human Learning and Memory*, 1975, 1, 720–726.

COMMENTS ON CHAPTER 2
BY BRANSFORD, NITSCHE, AND FRANKS

Michael Scriven

University of California at Berkeley

These comments are primarily aimed toward the preliminary written version of the paper which was sent to me, and must be excused insofar as they are not exactly what I would have picked up if I had seen the paper in final form. For example, the title of the paper I received was " 'Tuning' and the Acquisition of Knowledge," which was abandoned later. But, since the term "tuning" has been quite frequently used in discussing these issues lately, I retain my remarks on it for their general interest, and because they support the authors' decision to drop it!

What does "tuning" mean? Presumably it is intended to have some relation to "comprehension," since that was the original topic in the program, and it is a term that frequently recurs here. But what relation? Does it have enough metaphorical meaning to be useful without explanation or definition? – in my view, clearly not, in the use it gets here. It is hard enough to analyze the concept of comprehension or indeed that of knowledge, without having a new term on one's hands, one that gets applied to the process of teaching or learning, to the state resulting from those processes, and apparently to various other conditions and processes. E. D. Rosen has introduced the term "psychobabble" for the currently popular jargon picked up from encounter groups and the drug/rock culture, language that seems meaningful enough to its users – indeed, terribly meaningful (!) – but it is just about devoid of any testable content and any useful insights. I do not want to put "tuning" into that category without reservations, but I do want to say that it will have to face that fate unless it is considerably clarified.

The chapter opens with a quotation that admirably points up the possibility that most psychological research on "learning" has been irrelevant for education because it has focused on the wrong kind of examples of learning, and, it is hard enough to see what learning nonsense syllables and maze learning by rats has taught us about anything, let alone schooling. Unfortunately, most of the examples therein, quoted from recent or current research, have little more relevance to schools. Learning to recognize words, within or without context, is a negligible part of school learning, and, when it does occur, significantly it occurs with subjects whose cognitive structure content is totally unlike that of the college-age subjects used here. It would not be a bad idea, in my view, if funding agencies would simply refuse to support, and journals refuse to publish, research on learning/schooling/comprehension, etc. that deals with anything except examples of learning that are not only taken from classrooms, but meet two further conditions. First, that they were worth spending time on in the classroom (for example, they should involve nontrivial difficulty levels and mastery should be valuable to some educational or social group other than teachers). Second, the analysis of the examples should be correct. There are *some* examples in this paper taken from serious classrooms situations, thereby meeting the first of these criteria, but some of them have more difficulty in meeting the other criteria, as will be shown in a moment. My main point here is that we have enough evidence from the history of psychology to support total rejection of research psychologists' instincts as to what simplified examples of learning are usefully relevant to the real problems in learning/teaching/training. (The approach of the *Journal of Applied Behavior Research* perhaps comes closest to the one that I advocate.) At the very least, we should avoid spending thousands of pages and hours discussing examples of undemonstrated relevance, except as intellectual puzzles for the research gang.

To illustrate the situation referred to a moment ago, of an example from the classroom which is incorrectly — or shall we say, dubiously — analyzed, let me use the question about whether the first graders' problem of learning to read is that of mapping auditory knowledge of language "onto a visual code." The fact that an undergraduate class agreed with this is taken to show that they had not understood "the context-dependent nature of language." It could equally well be taken to show that the author in question had not understood exactly the same thing. All the reasons produced to show why the students' answer is wrong can be taken perfectly well as reasons for thinking that it is *hard* for first graders to map their auditory knowledge of language into a visual code. These reasons certainly do *not* show that the answer given by the students is wrong. Decontextualizing, a popular term with the authors in talking about their alternative approach, can be seen (how else?) as *part of* the process of changing the mode or coding the linguistic knowledge.

Another major problem in dealing with the chapter is to decide when something novel and significant is being said, as opposed to some old knowledge being redescribed or rediscovered. This is the more difficult because *certain* redescriptions of all facts *do* provide insight, by restructuring our perceptions — as the authors of this paper would be the first to emphasize. But there are a good many examples used here which I find it hard to get under that umbrella. For example, do we really need a review of the literature through the ages to establish that "informal education tends to result in much less transfer from one situation to another," whereas learning an abstract rule makes transfer easier? Doesn't teaching algebraic identities or the rule for solving quadratic equations make this obvious — or any of 50 examples from the history of medicine, if one wants cultural data? (Similar arguments apply to the research quoted to show that the use of relevant examples facilitates learning; but the research on embedded questions *might* be an exception, and would be convinced of that if Rothkopf and Anderson are impressed by it. At first sight it would seem to need both replication and the use of regular texts to make it generalizable.)

The core insight of the chapter, judged by the frequency of repetition, is probably the claim that a repetition is not a repetition is not a repetition, a claim with interesting self-referent properties. Second only to that slogan in its popularity for the authors is the theorem that knowledge is in the form of tools that set the stage for future acts of knowing. The trouble with this idea is that it is circular. On various occasions, the circular use of "acts of knowing" is unpacked, or replaced, following Dewey, with "clarification of experience." Here we run into the opposite problem from that of triviality, namely falsehood. The first example used was the expert tennis player. What clarification of experience results from knowing how to play tennis? No doubt, one can stretch the terms to cover the case, but it is probably more sensible to agree that Dewey was talking about cognitive rather than psychomotor knowledge. In fact, this difference shows why the "tuning" metaphor fails to be useful. It vaguely covers both cases — but careful analysis shows that you need to use different models for different subtypes of learning, and Dewey's model is no good for tennis. And it is worth remembering that intellectual skills may be more like tennis skills than they are like philosophical insights. It is not clear that even the central example — de Groot's example of the chess masters — is a case of clarifying experience. It is, on the face of it, more plausible to say that the chess masters simply have a skill, than to say that they have a better way of thinking about chess positions. I would say the same applies to the skills involved in the application of the calculus, for example, solving differential equations, or integrating complex functions. Moreover, we should not get carried away with an account that ignores simple knowledge, knowing, and learning. "Knowing the date of one's birthday" doesn't seem to involve anything very fancy, certainly nothing that refutes the simple storage model of memory.

There are, to me, interesting omissions from the references cited that I would find it enlightening to have explained: Rothkopf for one, the literature on the picture theory of meaning, Ryle on the knowing-how versus knowing-that distinction, Ausubel, even the Bloom taxonomy, and a good slice of the Gestalt discussion of isomorphism, all seem pretty relevant. The references are very comprehensive, and I mention these others not in the interests of encyclo-paedism, but because I feel acutely aware of the absence of these influences on the work done.

These are pretty critical remarks, but they are offered in the spirit of constructive criticism. It is all too easy for a group of researchers working in a particular field to fall into language and perceptions and — if one will pardon the expression — cliches, that enhance group bonds by becoming symbols of membership, but which lack real scientific importance. Sometimes it is possible for a quasi-outsider to notice these more easily than somebody closer to the current research. Perhaps I have here and there hit on a point worth making. I am sure, however, that in many cases the criticisms are not as serious as they looked to me at first sight. In the discussion, it became clear that the remarks are not so far off base as to produce a merely numbing silence. Reacting to a couple of points that were raised then, I stressed that I am all too well aware that moving towards the study of crucial problems of comprehension in the schooling situation *can* lead to difficulties that are as great as those involved in using rather remote examples. My feeling is only that the balance is — despite the fact that Bransford is perhaps one of the least "guilty" in this respect — still too much in the direction of abstract example. Let me give a hint of what I have in mind as follows: What is it about ex post facto explanations that often leads them to seem plausible, when in fact they do not produce comprehension? What is it about astrological explanations that make them seem plausible, when in fact they do not produce real comprehension? What is the difference between learning to enjoy and recite poetry, and learning to understand what it means? What is the difference between a psychoanalytic description of a patient and — what is in some cases very different — a truly enlightening description of the patient? (Ditto with respect to a "behavior mod" description.) At what point would you be persuaded that a parrot did comprehend the language that it was uttering? (I do not mean, what would be a case where you would certainly be convinced; I mean what would be the minimum performance that would be required to convince you?)

I do not think that talking about "schema" or "schemata," or "frameworks" does very much for us that "tuning" does not, or that "Gestalt" did not.

OPEN DISCUSSION
ON THE CONTRIBUTIONS
BY BRANSFORD, NITSCH,
FRANKS, AND SCRIVEN

Anderson: I want to comment on Dr. Scriven's remarks. There are two aspects that concern me. The first is his charge that psychological research inevitably lacks ecological validity. He argues that in order to be assured of doing something important, psychologists had better sample some real-life tasks. Based on considerable experience with applied educational research, it is my judgment that you can muddle along in a cut-and-dry, technological, highly empirical way with these tasks, every once in a while stumbling upon a minor insight, but getting no fundamental or profound view of the nature of the human condition, the nature of knowing, the nature of perception. We do need bottom-up work which concerns itself with direct practical purposes, with school-like tasks. However, from the shards and pieces of practical knowledge that arise from this, we are never going to get a coherent view of the human condition. So, I think it wrong just to make a blanket dismissal, despite the fact that every one of us here would concur with Tulving's assessment about the past irrelevance of psychology to the educational enterprise.

I think Dr. Scriven really missed the point of Dr. Bransford's paper, which had to do with the recurrent notion of schema. It is a different perspective on what a schema is, namely the framework within which we currently perceive and interpret the world. According to Bransford a schema does not grow by accumulation, and function by retrieval of its pieces, but can, in his phrase, be "remodeled" so that you look at the world differently.

Scriven: I would like to add a note to Dr. Anderson's comment. I want to stress that although a lot of research does not lead to generalizations, it is my feeling the recent work, in the evaluation area, has led more and more to outcomes that can be generalized (for example, in the individualization thesis). You felt I did not come to grips with the main point of the paper, frameworks and schema. I did not really disagree very much with this. That is why I raised the question about the Gestaltists. It is not clear that Dr. Bransford's conceptualization is different from, say, an interactive process of holistic perception.

Bransford: In regard to the Gestaltists, their brain model clearly does not work. That is one problem. The other problem has to do with the problems of education. In all the intuitive techniques that we all know are good, "think of it in this context" or "make examples" and all that, what is it that they do? Why do they work? How do they shape somebody's framework so they think in terms of certain things and not others? What I am worried about right now is not so much how to characterize what the framework is that gets shaped, but rather how to characterize what you need to do to take someone from one state to the next.

Ortony: It seems to me that Dr. Bransford is proposing a mixture of Wittgenstein's "seeing as" and Plato's doctrine of recollection. The doctrine of recollection is particularly puzzling: you have for years been influenced by the work of Hayek and I would like to address a specific question about the primacy of the abstract. It seems to me that that notion has a presupposition built into it which is very difficult to deal with, namely that kids are born with a whole host of given universal concepts which then get applied according to starting frameworks. What is it going to buy? In particular, how are you going to deal with the question of development given this notion?

Bransford: I want to get out of the preformism assumption underlying the primacy of the abstract. I do not think it necessarily implies that. The developmental problem, or the whole problem of a path for growth is very difficult to resolve. The answer, I think, is in terms of starting out with some kind of genetically preattuned types of things that you react to. Then it is going to be a function of what you do, your activities with respect to clarifying those things, the changes from one framework to the next. When I use the term framework, it is very intuitive right now. I do not know how to characterize it, and you could say it is just like Minsky's. He presupposes a frame. He does not tell me how I go from one to the next, and that is the problem. It is those seams between these state by state accounts in all our models that is really the problem that education has to face. It is the nature of your activities in clarifying things that I think counts.

Ortony: Insofar as you propose a kind of model of knowing, it is a model of knowing very much based on the notion of intention or interest or reason or wanting to interpret some kind of input. That still seems to me to have a very severe problem with respect to the very early development of children. It just does not make sense to me to say that a newborn baby is intentional in the sense in which you seem to suggest.

Bransford: Look how little is known about early vocalization, when a child first starts to cry. It is not intended; it is evoked. What you need to do is go in and look at what the kid is doing. You need some really pragmatic ecological approaches, but eventually you get the notion there is a real change in crying. It becomes intentional. I do not know what kinds of things lead to that. I do not have a model of knowing. All I'm trying to say is "this is the nature of the problem." We need to look at what people do.

Gagné: Dr. Bransford, could you say why you gave up the concept of tuning?

Bransford: I was using it in one sense to mean knowledge, and in another sense to mean a kind of process of becoming. I did not want to use the word learning simply because I think learning is usually seen as laying down memories that are retrieved and so forth. I realized what I needed to know is how we know. What do we have to do to go beyond where we are? That seems much more important. It is very easy to get out of that. I keep falling into a static trip and saying, "Let's look at where you are right now and what you can do," instead of how you make transitions.

Petrie: It seems to me that we use a very healthy balance that must always exist between these two kinds of things. For one of these purposes, I think your tuning metaphor is not bad at all. One learns something new, gets a new way of looking at the world which may or may not be important in a particular task. Once that is established, then, in terms of tuning, you are refining. In a certain sense you are not going beyond; you are simply getting better at doing that particular kind of thing.

Bransford: I think you are absolutely right. We have to emphasize both problems. For example, working in terms of a science, you need a paradigm in order to figure out how it is you can go beyond it. I think what we are going to need is an abstract theory of change: changes in behavior, which is the first order of change (where you are really homeostatic), versus changes in a way of behaving, which somehow involves moving beyond.

Olson: You [Dr. Bransford] mentioned the occasions for keeping up new orientations. I think you made it quite clear how the purposes or the goals that you are trying to achieve will specify what sort of information is critical. To a large extent, development consists of simply taking on new purposes. One picks out different aspects of an event to relate them in a different way, to recode or redescribe them. Each time that you carry out one of these new activities, you are equipping yourself with a new way of seeing events.

I'd like to raise another thing that I think you and Dr. Scriven disagreed on. He seemed to imply that you should take actions apart from knowledge, that action is one sort of thing, knowledge another, perceiving still another. It seems to me that you are very interested in, and I think quite successful in, putting those things together. I am saying those things really cannot be reasonably differentiated.

Bransford: If you think about what's involved in the skill of playing football, a big part of it is how your actions affect your perceptions. If you're going to block somebody, you've got to know where he's going to go. The same thing in tennis. Action and perception are intrinsically one, and I think it's the same basic problem whether we are talking about motor skills or "cognitive-conceptual" knowledge. Different things are emphasized, of course.

Scriven: When you get down to it, you are interested in enlightenment, the clarification of experience. Do you really want to say that what happens to the good football player is that his experience is clarified?

Bransford: His experience on the football field? Sure. A good football player knows exactly what to look for.

Scriven: He does not know what to look for. He knows where to get his shoulder in order to prevent the punt.

Bransford: No, no.

Scriven: Well, let us get clear about whether we really are going to use knowledge simply to cover something which the individual can be said to be able to identify as propositional. Is there anything propositional here or not?

Olson: I think that it is worth talking about aspects of knowledge which are propositionalized, and aspects of knowledge which may be tied to regulating ongoing performances. However, I think it is fundamentally wrong to think that knowledge in one case is legitimate knowledge and knowledge in the other case is merely tied to practical actions. In my estimation, they are both knowledge appropriate to carrying out certain kinds of activities. If you are interested in making proofs, for example, then the knowledge has to consist of a set of routines for identifying problems, casting it into an appropriate form to achieve a certain effect. It is just that the goal of making logical arguments is not identical to the goal of blocking in football, but the conceptual apparatus and the recruiting of prior knowledge to carry out that activity is probably quite similar.

Collins: One of the central features of frame approaches, particularly Winograd's, is that you need a very tight integration between procedural knowledge and factual or static knowledge.

3

The Languages of Instruction: The Literate Bias of Schooling

David R. Olson

Ontario Institute for Studies in Education

The structure of our knowledge is so closely entwined with the structure of our language that it may seem foolhardy to try to disentangle them. Yet it is necessary to do so in order to make some assessment of the consequences of using language, especially the language of literate prose, as the predominant means of instruction in the schools. It is clear that knowledge may be acquired through a variety of means: private experience, observation of a model, or explicit instruction. I have labeled these *muddling, modeling,* and *meddling* (Olson, 1976a). Whether for reasons of effectiveness or of economy, educators have settled for learning out of context through means that are primarily symbolic (Bruner, 1966). That is, schooling involves the acquisition of knowledge that possesses at least two distinctive properties: (1) that knowledge is divorced from practical action, and (2) that knowledge is represented in terms of linguistic symbols. What are the consequences of instruction that relies predominantly on written prose?

Naive psychology, according to Fritz Heider (Baldwin, 1967), assumes that the effects of experience can be considered as knowledge, that knowledge is conscious, and that knowledge can be translated into words. Conversely, words can be translated into knowledge; therefore, knowledge can be acquired by being told. Congruent with this is the belief that what differentiates the child from the adult is knowledge and that the primary goal of the school is to impart knowledge through the formal method of pedagogy.

In actuality, much formal schooling, especially at the primary levels, has moved away from instruction through formal, explicit prose, perhaps, in response to virtually all programs of educational reform. Comenius, Dewey, Piaget, and Bruner have all criticized the decontextualized and symbolic nature of the formal school and emphasized that schooling should be more in the context of practical activity and less dependent upon the language of formal verbal instruction.

Even these efforts at reform have not dramatically altered the major bias of the schools; schools remain predominantly literate enterprises. That is, the major aspirations of the schools are concerned with literacy, and the means of instruction are predominantly literate. Schooling is a matter of mediating the relationship between children and printed text. My concern in this chapter is to examine some of the cultural and personal consequences of this reliance upon literate forms as the primary means of instruction in the schools. Some understanding of the consequences of literate forms of instruction may permit some inferences about the means of instruction generally.

What are the consequences of translating all knowledge into such literate forms as logical propositions? Perhaps none. The predominant views of language learning and of the nature of writing lead one to believe that knowledge and its expression are relatively independent. The predominant view about language acquisition is not that language gives a special form to a child's prelinguistic cognitions, a view that was popular until this decade, but rather, that the child's cognitions are very sophistocated prior to the learning of a language and the language is acquired primarily by mapping that language onto an already elaborated conception of the world (Bloom, 1970; Cromer, 1974; Macnamara, 1972). Hence, the structure of knowledge that a child possesses is given its shape prelinguistically by the child's experience in the physical and social environment; his language merely expresses or "represents" what he knows. In instructional contexts, the meanings that the child assigns to a sentence are assumed to be determined by the nonlinguistic knowledge he can bring to bear upon the sentence.

Similarly in regard to writing, the predominant view is that nothing substantial happens to the child's language when that language is written down. It is merely a different medium of expression; the content of that language remains unchanged.

We have then a simple equality statement (what we could call meaning-preserving transformation). Cognitions or knowledge may be transformed into statements without altering that knowledge, and oral statements may be translated into written ones without altering their meaning. This is merely a more complex way of restating the naive theory. Written statements and the representations of direct or practical experience are taken to be more or less equivalent. And that view has to be maintained if we are to accept uncritically the assumption that the study of formal texts is a suitable alternative to actual experience or vice versa. Furthermore, that view is assumed in most models of semantic memory. Norman and Rumelhart (1975) and Anderson and Bower (1973), for example, assume that various forms of experience, regardless of the form of encounter, are stored in memory in a common propositional format, that is, they contribute to a common representation of reality. The origin of the knowledge is irrelevant to the storage and structure of that knowledge.

Ordinarily, this is both a valid and powerful assumption. Knowledge acquired in one context by one particular means, whether muddling, modeling, or meddling is appropriate to other contexts and other activities. But that common structure, I would suggest, is not an automatic consequence of experience. Rather, that generality is the consequence of the application of particular activities, usually in some symbolic form, to the "knowledges" appropriate to more specific activities. Dewey (1916) was making this point when he said, it is a matter of "going over one's past experiences to see what they yield (p. 157)." In other words, it should not be assumed that knowledge is generalized and transferable as an automatic consequence of assigning meaning to an experience.

The alternative is that knowledge is relatively specific to the purposes for which it was acquired; knowledge is the picture of reality constructed to sustain some pattern of action. Different patterns of action therefore result in the construction of different knowledge structure, in different pictures of reality. To apply this to the issue at hand, I would suggest that written, logical statements are not merely representations of knowledge but a particular form of activity that specifies reality in its own biased form. More importantly, schooling has fallen into the habit of both relying upon that form of activity and of taking the picture of reality appropriate to that form of activity as if it were an unbiased picture of reality. What I shall try to show is that literacy in general and schooling in particular are instrumental in the construction of a *particular* form of knowledge that is relevant to a *particular* set of socially valued activities.

Before we examine in some detail what these forms of knowledge are and the actions they are invented to sustain, it may be helpful to illustrate some of the ways that knowledge is tied to a particular set of activities. Illustrations, though not proofs, may be drawn from a whole range of sources. Their most general form comes from literary and artistic criticism in the theory that "nature imitates art" (there was no fog in London until Whistler painted it). That is, the arts provide the means for exploring events in novel ways; various forms of artistic expression, such as painting, demand that the artist discover features of the world that were previously undetected. Gombrich (1960) goes further in arguing that making comes before matching. The artist has to invent solutions to this representational problem. He invents a form of representation and then sees the representation is appropriate to the subject at hand. Gombrich describes human representations as a type of formulary; if there is some information in the environment which cannot be entered in the formulary, it is so much the worse for that information. This point is also made by Cezanne, who pointed out that the artist does not copy the world in his medium, but rather recreates it in terms of the structure of his medium. In general, this line of argument suggests that there is not just one picture of the world which may be called knowledge, and which may then be formulated into a text and taught to children. There are a number of pictures of the world, one appropriate to each of the forms of human activity. When such a picture of reality has been formalized, it becomes a part of the culture and may be taught systematically to children. Language is only one such form of representation and written prose is only one form of language.

Another way of demonstrating that knowledge is *not* a general, coherent, and consistent picture of reality, independent of purposes and independent of the form in which it is represented, comes from the work of Piaget (1972). Piaget's epistemology is premised on the notion that knowledge is not a simple copy of reality but rather that knowledge is the consequence of activity. Each form of activity may therefore be expected to yield a somewhat different form of knowledge. Knowledge is the consequence of human action, and it is biased to serve those human functions. Knowledge is not "objective."

Third, there is some evidence from empirical studies that tends to support this claim. That knowledge is limited by the purposes for which it was acquired is illustrated in the experiments by Duncker (1945) and Maier (1931) and others on "functional fixedness." Using pliers as a gripping tool makes it difficult to perceive them as a pendulum bob; what you know about pliers depends on what you habitually do with them. Maier, Thurber, and Janzen (1968) provided evidence that if information was coded in a form appropriate for recall it was somewhat inappropriate for problem solving. More recent experiments on verbal recall and recognition reported by Bransford, Nitsch and Franks (this volume) and by Frost (see Hunt, this volume) make a similar point. Tversky (1973, 1974) has shown that if a set of pictures is learned for recall, the knowledge is less appropriate for recognition while if it is learned for recognition it is less successfully recalled. Different information from the encoded stimuli was utilized in performing each test; the representation is not independent of the function it is to serve. Some studies by Rothkopf (1972), Frase (1972), and Frederiksen (1972) can be interpreted in a similar way. If students read a text to answer a particular set of questions, they are less able to answer other questions that logically follow from the text. The information people acquire, whether written or pictorial, is selective. It is selected on the basis of its appropriateness to the task at hand.

Finally, some evidence on this point comes from the cross-cultural studies reviewed by Schribner and Cole (1973) and Goodnow (1976). Generally, the findings are that tasks which have been found to be related in our culture are not related in traditional cultures. The simplest cases are on such tasks as reversal learning on which traditional subjects appear to treat each task as if it were a novel problem; transfer does not occur in contexts where we have come to expect it. The more complex case is that described by Gladwin (1970) in *East is a big bird*. The interesting fact is that while the Puluwat possess an incredibly sophisticated navigational system for calculating routes and destinations, that system, by our standards, is not logically consistent; yet, it is a supurb navigational aid. But, if we expect all knowledge systems to be similar, we are surprised to find such logical inconsistency.

All of these lines of consideration cast doubt on the simple view that our knowledge, our picture of reality, is independent of the purposes for which it was acquired. I am suggesting that knowledge is activity and context specific, and that the cognitive problem is to account for how that specific knowledge becomes generalized and suited to new activities performed in new contexts. There must be some correlation between these knowledge structures in that their corresponding forms of action are all performed in the same world. But that would not account for all the relationships and certainly not for the nontransfer effects cited above.

If different forms of activity result in the construction of somewhat different representations of reality, what about the different means of instruction that may be found in schools? I shall introduce this question by suggesting that *different means are means to different goals, not optional routes to the same goal.* Hence, different means of instruction or experience generally are not interchangeable. They result in somewhat different pictures of reality that are appropriate to different goals. Therefore, the assumption that experience and instruction are alternative means to the acquisition of the same knowledge is perhaps false. The adoption of a means of instruction immediately implies the achievement of a certain set of goals at the expense of other goals. For conventional schooling, those goals become the mastery of literate forms of expression and literate modes of thought accompanied by the devaluation of any other forms of expression or any other modes of thought. The nonliterate ones are taken as simply irrational. My claim is therefore quite general. It is that the coding of experience that we call knowledge is not knowledge in general; it is that picture of reality that is constructed to sustain the specialized literate activities of science and philosophy. That which we call language is not language in general, but a specialized form of language appropriate to written text. That which we call rationality and intelligence is not rationality in general, but mental procedures appropriate to the knowledge represented in formal text. Schools are the institutions primarily responsible for the transmission of this particular structure of knowledge and these particular literate forms of competence. They do it not so much for the achievement of a set of educational goals, as an unintended consequence of the reliance upon a particular form of instruction, namely, written prose.

Since the seventeenth century, critics have claimed that schools are bookish, detached from reality, devoid of personal meaning, and useless practically. Yet, schools have not basically changed their character. Why? Perhaps because the type of knowledge that the school develops and the intellectual competencies that it fosters fits quite closely with the literate biases of the culture as a whole. The bias of the school toward a particular form of knowledge and its dependence on a particular form of expression is a description of Western culture as a whole. Hence, an understanding of Western scientific and literate thought would be a description of "schooled" forms of competence.

The main part of this discussion therefore, is concerned with the distinctive properties of human knowledge and intellectual competence that arise from the invention and mastery of a particular cultural artifact, namely, written language. After we have considered the particular qualities that writing has given to knowledge, language, and rationality, it should be clear why schooling is so often detached from "life" and why children, particularly those from less literate homes, have so much difficulty with school instruction.

Let us then turn to an examination of the more fundamental issues, the effects of literacy on knowledge, language, and rationality. We need not consider these independently. Our concern is with the nature of written language and its distinctive functions. As we shall see, the language of ordinary oral conversation serves a somewhat different function than does written text. Further, they generate distinctive pictures of reality or forms of knowledge. It is these differing pictures of reality that we shall be concerned with first.

SCIENTIFIC KNOWLEDGE AND COMMONSENSE KNOWLEDGE

Let us consider, then, the representations of reality associated with oral language and those associated with written text. They are important because they serve to differentiate the conception of reality that is a part of every day practical experience from the picture of reality coded in formal academic disciplines. Furthermore, they differentiate the picture of reality the child brings to school from that which the school attempts to create. The first may be called commonsense, the latter scientific or philosophical knowledge. William James (1907), in his lectures on *Pragmatism* described what he took to be the basic irreducible mode of knowing as commonsense knowledge and contrasted it with the more "educated sisters," scientific and philosophical knowledge. Although scientific knowledge, he admits, puts the control of nature into our hands, it is commonsense that is more universal because it has "turned all of ordinary language into its ally." Unlike his successors, James never attempted to reduce all legitimate knowledge to a single form. While for James and Dewey these "modes" of knowing consisted of the major cultural achievements of mankind, such as science, religion, law and so on, for me, it is the "languages" in which that knowledge is represented, the structure of media and symbols, that give knowledge and the cognitive processes their distinctive properties. While there are presumably a large number of such languages, two of these are most critical: oral language and written statements, or "utterances" and "texts" (Olson, in press b). But our concern here is with the pictures of reality sustained by these forms of language: What is the relation between the two?

Historically, the Western, literate culture has had extremely low regard for commonsense knowledge. For Francis Bacon, it constituted the "idols of the tribe"; for the Enlightenment, common sense was that collection of irrational superstitution to which unreasonable people appealed when they were stuck for a rational argument. It remains the body of beliefs and presuppositions that "go without saying" or that "any fool can see." Science is usually described as the process of discarding commonsense knowledge, of differentiating history from myth, facts from superstition, laws from theories and so on.

The holders of these differing orientations, the intellectual or man of science and the proverbial "man on the street," regard each other with suspicion. The practical man's first question for any new theory is "What is the use (good) of that?" If an idea cannot be shown to have immediate usefulness it is discarded as "so much theory." Men of science regard the simple search for what works as an intellectually barren opportunism.

Three classes of humans have served primarily as representative of this commonsense orientation: the nonliterate members of traditional societies, "Savages"; the uneducated or unspecialized members of our own society, the ignorant; and the inexperienced young, children. The cognitive patterns of all three are described roughly as irrational. They all, for example, perform poorly on IQ tests. While there are wide differences between these groups, some rough characterization of commonsense knowledge can be given and contrasted with that of scientific and theoretical knowledge (Dewey, 1938; Lonergan, 1957; Schutz & Luckmann, 1973).

First, commonsense knowledge is coded for action. It involves a plan for contingent action, not a conception of universal truth. Commonsense expressions appearing to be general truths, are in fact admonitions to action. The proverbial expression "haste makes waste" actually says "slow down."

Second, commonsense knowledge is specialized in the particular and the concrete. Each situation we encounter is to some extent unique and commonsense knowledge is tuned to that uniqueness; it is, therefore, extremely context sensitive.

Third, commonsense generalizations, in order to reflect the variability of events, are often coded in terms of proverbs or aphorisms. While in science an exception disproves the rule, in common sense, an exception proves the rule.

Fourth, commonsense experience results in elements of knowledge that are not in complete agreement with each other. This inconsistency arises because knowledge is acquired in heterogeneous situations and it is retrieved only if it is relevant to a situation. Unlike science, there is no motivation to reorder it into a small set of coherent logical propositions. The navigational system of the Puluwat Islanders, cited earlier, is a case in point. Similarly, when the Greek epics were written down some of their inconsistencies became apparent; history and myth went their separate ways, while for commonsense experience they remained, and still remain, undifferentiated. Hence, proverbs, an important part of the oral language of common sense, are often contradictory (for example, "a stitch in time saves nine" versus "haste makes waste").

Fifth, common sense is value laden, and forced to choose, the man of common sense knows to put "first things first."

Sixth, its intellectual tools are illustration and example rather than definition and deduction. Huizinga (1954) described how, in the Middle Ages:

> ... every event, every case, fictitious or historic, tends to crystallize, to become a parable, an example, a proof, in order to be applied as a standing instance of a general moral truth. In the same way every utterance becomes a dictim, a maxim, a text [p. 227].

Seventh, commonsense is socially conceived and structured rather than logically based. To illustrate, in a commonsense argument the winner of the argument depends not on the number or quality of arguments but on who gets the last word. That is, truth is a matter of authority.

The features of scientific, theoretical knowledge contrast with those of commonsense knowledge. It is coded for reflection, not for action. It seeks universal laws that are free from exceptions and contradictions, and it cuts its ties to values to become "the disinterested search for truth." On the other hand, Lévi-Strauss (1962) and Horton (1970) have pointed out that these differences are not as fundamental as is often supposed. One cannot be simply described as "primitive" or concrete. Both forms of thought involve abstraction, they both involve the representation of complex events in terms of simpler underlying processes, and they both permit prediction and inference. Yet they are obviously very different.

The primary difference between these orientations takes us back to the nature of language. Horton (1970) and more explicitly Gellner (1973) trace differences between traditional and scientific modes of thought to the specialization of one of the uses of language at the expense of others. It is primarily a matter of tooling up the language to better serve the functions of explanation and prediction. To defend this view it is necessary to consider the nature of spoken language and the bias of written prose (Olson, in press b).

UTTERANCES AND TEXTS

The history of the attempt to create autonomous text, statements that in fact say what they mean, is neither well established nor well known. One of the first expressions of this new orientation to text, which occurred contemporaneously with the invention of print and the development of a relatively wide reading public, is represented in the work of Martin Luther.

Prior to the time of Luther, it was generally assumed that meaning could not be stated explicitly. What was written served rather to prompt the recall of information that had already been committed to memory. This was so for two reasons. First, the writing systems tended to be too ambiguous to permit the decoding of novel statements (Havelock, 1973; Goody & Watt, 1963). There was some discrepancy between deep structure or meaning and logical form. Second, the important cultural information, the information worth writing down, had already been shaped by oral statement and memory. Statements that were memorable and elliptical rather than explicit required interpretation by an authority. Luther's claim marked a substantial change in orientation to texts: "The meaning of Scripture depends, not upon the doctrines of the church but on a deeper reading of the text." Luther assumed that the Scriptures said what they meant. The meaning was in the text, not in the interpretation given by the Church. With that assumption, texts were read in a new way: as statements that specified a set of explicit logical meanings, not authority relations between speaker and listener. The ultimate expression of this assumption was in the assertion of the logical positivists which stated that meaning was the set of truth conditions it specified (Ayer, 1936; Carnap, 1947). This orientation had a symmetrical effect upon the writer. Texts were written in a new way, namely, to make the meaning completely explicit, and not open to interpretation. The attempt was to create autonomous text, text in which what was said was a fully conventionalized representation of what was meant.

The latter enterprize was expressed emphatically in the charter of the Royal Society of London formed in 1662. According to its historian Sprat (1667), the Society had "a constant Resolution, to reject all amplifications, digressions, and swellings of style: to return back to the primitive purity, and shortness, when men delivered so many *things,* almost with an equal number of *words*" (p. 113). Locke (1690) too claimed that:

> If we would speak of things as they are, we must allow that all the art and rhetoric, besides order and clearness; all the artificial and figurative applications of words eloquence hath invented, are for nothing else but to insinuate wrong ideas, move the passions, and thereby mislead the judgement; and so indeed are perfect cheats. . . ." (II:ii, p. 146)

Two consequences of this reform in language are of interest here. First, the functions of language were altered. Second, the structures of language were altered in order to serve better the change in functions.

The functions of language have been variously tabulated (Buhler, 1934; Austin, 1962; Searle, 1969). Two are of primary concern here: (1) the function of maintaining social relations between the participants, and (2) the logical relations within and between sentences. These two are roughly Austin's (1962), pp. 144–145) distinction between constative utterances and performative utterances or between locutionary and illocutionary acts. With the first we may make judgments of the truth or falsity of the utterance and with the second we may make judgments as to whether the utterance is in order. If one claims with Henny Penny that "the sky is falling" the utterance may be judged against these two considerations. First, is it *true* that the sky is falling? That is, does the sentence correspond to the state of affairs? This aspect of meaning is the set of truth conditions specified by the sentence. Second, whether or not it is true does one have the right, that is, *is it in order,* for one to declare that the sky is falling? This aspect of meaning depends upon the authority relations assumed by the sentence. The latter depends on one's authority, one's status, and the like.

Any "real" utterance meets both sets of conditions and includes both social and logical components. The first of these sets of considerations, normally is that of the allowances made for the relations that exist between the speaker and listener, considerations that may be called *rhetorical.* The second is the logical or truth value considerations. Speech is always directed to an individual or group of individuals in which the degree of social status and influence are key factors. Hence, the rhetorical function is predominant over the logical function. If you fail to maintain appropriate social relations with the listener, the conversation simply terminates.

My primary hypothesis is that the invention of writing, and particularly the attempt to create autonomous text, resulted in the realignment and specialization of the rhetorical and logical functions. Consequently, the language was specialized to better serve the truth functions at the expense of the social or authority-maintaining functions. More precisely, if the statement was true, that was a sufficient condition for its being "in order." This was the major innovation of the British empiricists in their insistence that all statements correspond to the observations. The authority was passed from ecclesiastical and political authorities to "nature." Statements became the specialized instruments for description and explanation replacing their traditional function of maintaining social and authority relations. And the members of The Royal Society took this specialized tool of science and philosophy to be a "natural, naked way of speaking" (Sprat, 1667).

To better serve this specialized logical function, language has to be brought up to a higher level of conventionalization. Meaning must be formulated into a set of explicit definitions; strict grammatical structure must be shaped up to better indicate logical structure. Expressions in which the logical and grammatical structures are not well correlated are described by Ryle (1968) as "systematically misleading expressions". Furthermore, the logical apparatus for specifying implications and conclusions has to be rigorously conventionalized and followed. Explicit prose is the language of science and philosophy; but it is not "ordinary language". It is the specialized tool of analytic thinking and explicit argument, *and* it is the tool that has been adopted as the predominant form of school instruction.

Much the same conclusion has been drawn by Robin Horton and Ernest Gellner in their analysis of the relation between primitive thinking and modern science. The difference they claim is due to the specialization of language as an instrument of modern science. Horton (1970) says: "People come to see that if ideas and language are to be used as efficient tools of explanation and prediction, they must not be allowed to be tools of anything else" [p. 164]. Gellner (1973) adds: "It is the essence of the savage mind, as of savage institutions, that there is a lower degree of functional specificity. . . . The enchanted [savage] vision works through the systematic conflation of descriptive, evaluative, identificatory, status-conferring, etc. roles of language" (p. 174). And I suggest that the use of writing was the primary factor responsible for the specialization and realignment of functions.

Hence, it seems necessary to conclude that "standard English" is not a general model of the mother tongue but rather the specialized instrument of the description and explanation functions of literate prose. We have let the one function predominate at the expense of the others. Hence, to take explicit written prose as the model of language, knowledge and intelligence has narrowed the conception of all three, downgrading the more general functions of ordinary language and commonsense knowledge.

Four points about schooling follow. First, literate uses of written text provide the only route to certain forms of intellectual achievement. To participate in any highly formalized discipline or in any highly organized bureaucracy may depend upon the development of these highly specialized uses of language. Schooling, in such cases, may provide the instrument for their development.

Second, because it is a tool specialized for the achievement of certain goals, it is not appropriate for all goals. The tailoring of the language of schooling into the language of explicit written texts, makes schooling inappropriate to the achievement of many other goals, especially to sets of practical competencies and furthermore, makes the language of schooling inaccessible to many children.

Third, and most generally, the language of schooling is textually biased, and out of phase with the child's mother tongue. Frequently, teacher's statements, like parental statements, are accepted because of the status and authority of the teacher. Children therefore have difficulty arriving at the convention that the sole grounds for the appropriateness of an assertion is its truth value. Many experimenters have commented informally on the difficulty young children have in seeing a statement as logical or true when it is incongruent with either social, rhetorical, or contextual constraints. In answering questions on such tests as the Binet, young children will repeatedly look at the adult for some suggestion as to the expected answer, rather than look at the test item or display. Similarly, adults whose language has not been specialized often treat logical questions as if they were pragmatic ones (Cole, Gay, Glick, & Sharp, 1971; Luria, 1971).

Finally, the degree of specialization of language appears to differentiate the social classes as Bernstein (1971) has shown. In fact, the Restricted code is one primarily attuned to the social or authority relations while the Elaborated code is one primarily specialized for the descriptive functions of written language. And, as Bernstein has shown, only the latter is the language of the school.

THE LANGUAGE OF SCHOOLING

I have tried to show that explicit prose is a specialization of language serving a very limited number of functions extremely well, particularly those involved in description and explanation. Because it is a specialized form of language, it is not a mother tongue. Here then is our dilemma. The child comes to school the master of a mother tongue, but the dominant means of instruction and communication in the school is the language of formalized written prose. All children have some difficulty moving into that special language, and some children find it largely inaccessible.

The schools, with their tie to literate means of instruction, are committed particularly to the logical uses of language. Yet, the school cannot honor these logical or truth considerations consistently. The teacher is expected to maintain order, to command respect, etc. Hence, teacher statements are a peculiar mélange of violations of both types of language. The language of instruction is frozen into the language of explicit text, yet its truth functions are not consistently honored. Children hearing such statements cannot tell if they are true because they correspond to the facts and observations or because they are uttered by the teacher. I have already remarked how young children will look at the teacher's face for some indication of what is expected from them rather than examine the problem displayed in front of them. While we may be tempted to think that children are not "thinking" or paying attention to the expressed content of instruction, they may in fact simply fail to single out the logical aspects of the statement from its authority-maintaining functions. When they do not make that differentiation, they are in fact using the mother tongue appropriately. They just have not yet mastered the peculiar specialized language of formal schooling.

The distinctive properties of explicit written prose differ in two primary ways from the language of the mother tongue. First, the authority or rhetorical functions are subordinated to the logical functions. Second, the requirement for logical, descriptive autonomous statements requires that the language be more explicit and conventionalized than the mother tongue. For text to serve its functions, meanings and the ways they will be used must be conventionalized so that the reader will retrieve the appropriate meaning. The reader cannot ask the text what it means. In conversations, on the other hand, the meanings may be negotiated and agreed upon by the participants in the course of the conversation (Cole, personal communication, 1975). These differences are substantial enough to put a distinctive bias on the language of schooling. Children's encounters with text or their preparations for those encounters constitute the one absolutely distinguishing feature of schooling. One of the children's first encounters with this special language, which is critical to their further success, is learning to read. The conflict between these "languages" may be seen in the first of the books that the child encounters in school, the reading series.

There is an overwhelming wealth of reading programs developed by publishers to teach children to read. Textbooks, especially the reading series, have improved gradually since Comenius first popularized them in the common schools in the seventeenth century. All of them have evolved to meet a small set of criteria — controlled levels of difficulty, appropriate subject matter, appropriate accompanying activity and the inevitable workbooks. They take this form not because they honor any explicit pedagogic theory or any theory of human cognition but because they are a practical solution to a particular educational problem and perhaps because they match our particular literate cultural bias.

While they all succeed in the same way, they also fail in the same way. They fail to address the particular child in the personal, direct way that speech does. There is no possibility of the text speaking to the child and the child speaking back. There is no negotiating of meanings, expressions, or ways in which those expressions are used. The conventions employed and the meanings specified are lodged unalterably in the text itself. The text makes no allowances for the individual scanning it. The child will have to extract that fixed textual meaning.

The lack of flexibility in "autonomous text" is, as I suggested, what makes this specialized use of language the powerful tool of science and philosophy. It is also what makes schooling difficult for most children and completely inaccessible for others, depending on the predominant uses of language in the home (Bernstein, 1971).

The difficulties children have with such text is frequently but inappropriately attributed to something like an unalterable low IQ. However, these competencies can at least in part, be traced back to the same literacy skill that they are supposed to predict: defining terms, drawing logical implications, etc. (Olson, in press a). Furthermore, since it is also usually assumed that valid knowledge must take the forms represented by texts, there is no alternative but to try to school children in textual knowledge and the formal uses of literate prose. Now, if the preceding argument is valid, it should be clear that the prose text is not *the* structure of language and the knowledge represented by that text is not *the* structure of knowledge, but the form of knowledge appropriate to one specialized technology. To master that form, as I have repeated, it is necessary to master that technology. It is only one specialized technique, however, and that technique is appropriate only to one specialized form of knowledge. Compared to conversational language, dialogue and commonsense knowledge, it is personally a relatively less significant one.

My conclusion is simple. Schools are tied to a specialized language and to a specialized form of knowledge as a consequence of our reliance upon written prose. Literacy is not only a primary goal of schooling, it is deemed necessary for the achievement of other goals. The advantage of that bias of schooling is that virtually every activity becomes an occasion for developing competence with that use of language and that form of knowledge. The disadvantage of that bias is that all forms of knowledge and competence come to be translated into prose text, and the translation of some forms of knowledge and competence into formal text makes that knowledge irrelevant. It also makes that knowledge accessible only to those who already possess a high degree of literacy skills.

Forms of practical activity such as using a rifle, being an officer, or becoming a teacher could be learned informally (Scribner & Cole, 1973). However, they are translated into a set of explicit verbal representations and taught to the learner in formal schooling. While the translation has the advantage of teaching the information to large groups and perhaps leading to new insight into the activity itself, it has the disadvantage of frequently not transferring back to the practical activity. One knows the theory but cannot apply it. Second, the translation of an activity into a verbal list makes the knowledge primarily accessible to those with higher literacy skills. People who, because of their lower verbal skills, have sought out practical activities find that the form of instruction is again biased against them both in terms of the admission requirements and in terms of the demands of the training program. This conjecture would help to explain two well known facts about such training programs: verbal IQ predicts performance in the training program, but performance in the training program does not predict performance on the job (Hoyt, 1965).

Henry Reed's poem *The naming of parts* provides an interesting illustration of how the most practical of activities can be translated into a set of literate skills. The memorizing of a list of names and descriptions replaces the actual manipulation and operation of the rifle. But his description could equally apply to much of schooling. Here is part of Reed's poem:

Today we have naming of parts, Yesterday,
We had daily cleaning. And tomorrow morning
We shall have what to do after firing. But today,
Today we have naming of parts. Japonica
Glistens like coral in all of the neighboring gardens,
    And today we have naming of parts.

This is the lower sling swivel. And this
Is the upper sling swivel, whose use you will see
When you are given your slings. And this is the piling swivel
Which in your case you have not got. The branches
Hold in the gardens their shy, eloquent gestures,
    Which in our case we have not got.

As long as our primary concern is with the development of literacy, it is completely appropriate to translate every kind of intellectual or practical task into a literate one. But if we value a wider range of competence, commonsense knowledge and conversational language should be incorporated so as not to exclude people from access to important but nonliterate forms of competence.

But the more social aspects of literacy skills is not our primary concern. Rather, it is to specify the form of knowledge appropriate to prose text, and then to generalize the relationship between the structure of knowledge and the forms of instruction generally. I have taken the first of these as far as I can at present. I now turn to the problem of means of instruction generally.

MEANS OF INSTRUCTION

The preceding discussion of the biases of formal, written text would seem to lead to the conclusion that there is essentially no optionality in the means of instruction.

Means are not optional routes to the same goal; they are optimal routes to different goals. The knowledge acquired in two ways may be equivalent for some purposes but more often that knowledge may be only superficially related. Indeed, this appears to be the case in the military training and teacher training contexts I mentioned earlier; translating complex practical activities into verbal formulas has the effect of removing the correlation between succeeding in learning the instructional program and success in learning the practical performance. That is, people who learn the lists well are not necessarily the ones who perform the activity well. There is a gap between "theory and practice."

In simpler cases, such as that of learning a picture list, different purposes result in the learning of somewhat different content. To return to the studies by Tversky (1973) and others, subjects who look at a set of pictures to recall them, encode them differently than if they are looking at the same pictures with the expectation that they will have to subsequently recognize them.

There is, of course, considerable overlap between the two types of representations; subjects expecting a recall test can succeed on many of the recognition items and vice versa. As long as those representations are constructed to represent the same situation or event, we may expect that those representations will at least be correlated. That correlation however, does not invalidate the point being made here, namely, that those representations are constructed to serve somewhat different purposes. And making them suitable for one'purpose limits their usefulness for other purposes. Improving the suitability of a cutting instrument for chopping makes it less appropriate for whittling. The same is true for representations of knowledge.

A theory which proposes to assign psychological significance to means of instruction, must, however, go somewhat deeper. In instructional contexts, the goals are often chosen prior to and independently of considerations of means, or so it is claimed. However, the choice of any means requires that the goal be reformulated or translated into the structure of that particular means. The original goal may or may not be lost in the translation. But it will inevitably be altered. The criterion or goal of a certain standard of performance out of school is replaced, as we have seen, by the criterion of performance on a test of verbal recall; moral conduct similarly is replaced by comprehension or recall of moral principles and so on.

But even in cases in which the purpose or goal remains unchanged and only the means of instruction is altered, alterations may occur in what is learned. We have begun a series of experiments in our laboratory that attempt to get at the relation between means of instruction and the knowledge that is acquired. Thus far, these studies have provided some evidence to show that if subjects are taught the same content in two different ways, they are in fact not learning the same content but a somewhat different but related content. These differences may or may not show up, depending upon the nature of the posttests employed. That is, these forms of instruction are equivalent for some purposes such as recall as most of the earlier studies of "means" and "methods" have shown (Travers, 1963; Olson, 1974). However, these means of instruction are simultaneously unequal for other purposes such as transfer. The latter is important not only in that they alter the effects of new experiences, but also in that they constitute the unintended consequences of schooling. These studies are very preliminary and, thus far, seem to reflect rather minor effects in the means of instruction. Hopefully a full understanding of the effects of texts will reveal some of the biases of schooling generally.

Two of these studies involved the use of various forms of mnemonics for the recall of word pairs (Rohwer, 1971). Typically subjects in these experiments are given word pairs under one of four different experimental conditions: (1) subjects in the Control group were asked to learn each word pair in such a way that when given the first word of each pair, they could recall the second; (2) subjects in the Rehearsal group were asked to repeat aloud each pair until the next pair was presented; (3) subjects in the Presented Sentence group were given a sentence relating the nouns in the noun pair; and (4) subjects in the Generated Sentence group were asked to construct their own sentence relating the noun pair. Basically, Rohwer's findings were threefold: first, subjects who are either given sentences or asked to construct sentences linking the nouns do better on recall than do subjects asked to rehearse or simply left to their own devices; second, efforts to teach second graders the strategy of constructing their own sentences were not as successful as simply presenting them with elaborated constructions; and third, the strategy of creating their own sentences without adults making any suggestion is a late development, beyond 14 years of age, if it develops at all.

Consider in more detail the first finding, namely, that the Presented Sentence (PS) and the Generated Sentence (GS) groups were superior to the Rehearsal (R) and Control (C) groups. Now the question is, are the subjects in the three groups learning the same thing? Were those in the Sentence groups simply learning it better than those in the Rehearsal and Control groups? Are different means responsible for learning the same content more effectively? Or are the three groups of subjects learning somewhat different although related content. Do different aspects of this content show up on different types of posttests? Let us suppose that the process of generating and understanding sentences recruits a different set of mental processes than that used by the Rehearsal and Control groups. For example, subjects in the Sentence groups may have been learning to treat word pairs as if they were sentence fragments. If so, subjects in the Sentence-Generated group may have learned, or made some progress in the skill of formulating and understanding sentences relating arbitrary events, subjects in the Sentence-Presented group may not have mastered this procedure as well, while subjects in the Rehearsal and Control may not have learned it at all. Such complex habits are presumably related to a long history of such attempts and it is a little dangerous to look for any change in a brief experimental episode. Nonetheless, in our first experiment, Ruth Pike and I presented to fifth-grade children tasks similar to those described by Rohwer. Like Rohwer, we found that children performed better on a recall task in the Sentence-Presented and Sentence-Generated conditions than in the Rehearsal condition (Figure 1a). But did the subjects learn the same thing, but in varying degrees? When given a new list of noun pairs without instruction, differences in what was learned become apparent. Subjects who had previously been in the Sentence-Generated group performed in a superior fashion to those in the other two groups. Those in the Sentence-Presented group reverted to the simpler strategy of rehearsal, as measured by a posttest interview; consequently their recall fell to the same level as the Rehearsal subjects. These findings are shown in Figure 1b. On the posttest for recall, subjects in all four groups appeared to have learned the same content to differing degrees. On the test of transfer to new lists, however, it became clear that subjects had in fact learned somewhat different things. Those in the Sentence-Generated group now learned the new lists better showing superior recall to the subjects in either of the other groups. We could say that the

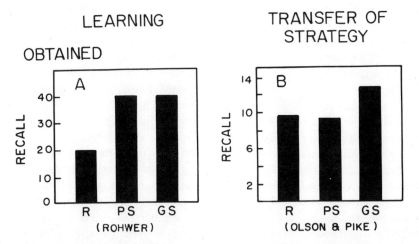

FIG. 1. Recall of word pairs and transfer to new word pairs as a function of means of instruction (Experiment 1).

knowledge children acquired was somewhat different as a consequence of having been taught by a particular means. These differences are the unintended consequence of a particular form of instruction. As Harlow (1959) would say, we fail to see the consequences of experience because we throw away our subjects too quickly.

In a more recent study, Angela Hildyard and I conducted a similar experiment with sixth graders. This study involved a more thorough form of initial learning followed by a longer series of transfer tests designed to assess the effects of that original learning. As in the previous study, subjects were assigned to one of three groups: (1) Those in the Rehearsal group were asked to repeat aloud each pair until the next pair was presented. (2) Subjects in the Sentence-Presented group were given sentences linking the noun pairs. (3) Those in the Sentence-Generated group were asked to generate a sentence linking the noun pair. The first list was treated as a training session in which subjects in each of the groups were trained to use the strategy effectively to reach the criterion of 90% recall. The series of posttests following the learning session involved new noun-pair lists in which subjects were reminded to apply the procedures they had learned the preceding day. On the succeeding day, they were given another new list, this time with the simple instruction to remember as many of the word pairs as possible. One week later, the subjects were recalled and given two more posttests again with new lists, in counterbalanced order. For one of these, they were given word pairs plus appropriate sentences linking them, the second consisted only of a list of word pairs with the instruction to generate a sentence linking the word pair. Two findings are of interest. First, although all groups had 90% recall on the first list, there were large, consistent and significant differences between the groups on all of the posttests with new lists including those delayed one week. These results are shown in Figure 2. Secondly, while both of the sentence groups were better than the Rehearsal group, they were not different from each other. The reason subjects in the Sentence-Presented group did not revert to the Rehearsal strategy after a delay may be due either to the greater training at the outset or to the greater age of the subjects. Again, then, we can conclude that although the "content" given to the groups was superficially similar, subjects in these different treatments had in fact learned different things. As concerns the explicit purpose of the learning, the recall of the original list, differences between means may be negligible or, as in Experiment 1, ordered for efficacy.

The major differences in what was learned show up on the appropriate tests of transfer. Ideally, appropriate transfer tests would have shown that the other means of instruction had resulted in subjects acquiring more or different knowledge than that measured simply by the recall posttest. If for some subjects the word pair was simply a list to be memorized and for others it was a pair of sentence fragments, the question can be raised more seriously as to whether subjects had learned the same thing. I would suggest that any "content" under the application of some new means or method or form becomes a somewhat

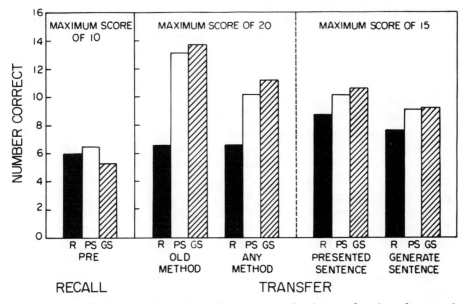

FIG. 2. Recall of word pairs and transfer to new word pairs as a function of means of instruction (Experiment 2).

different content. For some purposes this content is equivalent but for other purposes it is quite different. Again, means are not alternative routes to the same goal, but single routes to different goals.

In a third experiment,[1] Nancy Nickerson and I taught a series of proverbs to a group of subjects, again employing three quite different means. Again, the concern is whether subjects learned the same thing when they were taught the same "content" by different means. Sixty sixth-grade children 10 to 12 years of age were taught a list of 15 proverbs, 5 proverbs each day for three days, under one of three experimental conditions. The training procedures were similar to those mentioned previously. The Rehearsal group subjects were told, "A good way to remember a proverb is to say it over and over to yourself;" Paraphrase-Presented subjects were told, "A good way to remember proverbs is to also learn a sentence that tells you what the proverb means;" Paraphrase-Generated subjects were told, "A good way to remember a proverb is to try to make up a sentence that explains what the proverb means." Subjects recall of the content was scored in two ways: one reflecting the actual phrasing of the proverb; and one reflecting the meanings of the proverbs. Memory was assessed by probed recall, choosing semantically similar proverbs, or structurally similar proverbs. A final series of tests looked for the effects of these means of training on the

[1] We are indebted to Peter Gamlin and Robert Bracewell for the use of their materials and for their advice on this experiment.

comprehension of new proverbs. In one of these posttests, subjects were required to pick out of a set of four, the most appropriate paraphrase of a new set of proverbs. In the second, they were required to generate an appropriate paraphrase to a further set of new proverbs.

Again the results are simple. While subjects in the Rehearsal group produced more verbatim recall than the Paraphrase groups, subjects in the Paraphrase groups recalled the meanings of the proverbs just as well as the Rehearsal groups. Subsequent recall tests failed to differentiate the groups altogether. They had learned the same content. However, on the transfer conditions, given new proverbs, and even given elaborate instructions and practice items on what was required for a "good paraphrase", subjects who had been in the two Paraphrase groups during the training trials outscored the subjects in the Rehearsal groups. These differences are shown in Table 1. Again, it may be concluded that although the means of instruction had some immediate effect on verbatim recall, delayed recall failed to show any differences in what was learned from the instruction sequence. Yet, when appropriate transfer tests were applied one week later, subjects were shown to have learned something quite different and relatively permanent from the different means of instruction. What the subjects had learned was quite similar for some purposes, in this case simple recall; but, what they had learned was quite different for other purposes. We may conclude that different means of instruction resulted in the acquisition of somewhat different knowledge. These differences constitute the unintended consequences of instruction.

In earlier papers on this problem (Bruner & Olson, 1974; & Olson, 1976b) such differences would be described in a somewhat different, and I now think, inferior way. Previously, the effects of different means of instruction would have been explained by saying that the different means had conveyed the same knowledge, but they had recruited different skills. Hence, the difference in transfer would be attributed to differences in skill. Currently, I would prefer to put knowledge and skill back together and argue that each form of activity in which one can be skilled, specified a representation of the world appropriate to that activity. It is this representation that may be called knowledge. Further, there are as many pictures of reality, forms of knowledge as there are types of activities. Finally, these representations may be equivalent for some purposes and different for others.

These differences in means, however, are relatively minor. Of much more significance are those means of instruction that make up the predominant "language of instruction," namely, written prose, to which we return.

KNOWLEDGE AND THE MEANS OF INSTRUCTION

What then are the consequences of the reliance upon predominantly literate or textual means of instruction. The translation of knowledge into essayist prose is

TABLE 1

Recall of Proverbs and Transfer to New Proverbs as a Function of Means of Instruction (Experiment 3)

Group	Training		Probed		Recognition				Choose: Good para.	Generate: Good para.
	Verbatim score	Meaning score	Verbatim score	Meaning score	Correct responses	Verbatim confusions	Meaning confusions	Other confusions		
R.	31.7	33.7	14.6	15.2	13.95	2.3	.35	.15	8.45	8.6
P.P.	29.75	33.45	11.15	12.45	14.5	2.15	.15	.15	10.1	10.0
P.G.	23.2**	32.8	11.1	15.35	13.9	1.65	.45	.30	10.0	11.6*

$*p < .05.$ $**p < .01.$ R = Rehearsal, P.P. = Paraphrase Presented, P.G. = Paraphrase Generated

not simply a "representation" problem. The translation of the knowledge appropriate to one kind of activity or language into that appropriate to a second kind of activity alters that knowledge. We can grasp this point more readily by recalling the point made by Cezanne that the artist does not copy nature but reconstructs nature in terms of the structure of his medium. Each medium, or form of activity, or "language," has its own particular characteristics and to code information in such a language is to give that information a particular bias. In regard to instruction, then, we can ask two questions. First, does the translation preserve the information critical to the achievement of the particular goal? Second, and perhaps more significant, what is the set of goals for which that translation is appropriate?

I have been suggesting that while for some purposes text may be a simple alternative to other forms of experience; it contributes to a representation of reality that is very different from those resulting from alternative means of experience. The picture of reality suited to the requirements of texts is, as I pointed out earlier, the "objective" world. It is a world represented in terms of language specialized for its functions of logic and truth. That specialized use of language and the corresponding knowledge is responsible for many of the cultural achievements of man, science, law, and much of literate literature. But because prose is such a valuable intellectual tool, we have underestimated the bias it puts upon knowledge. It is not the most appropriate tool for the establishment and maintainence of social and authority relations. It is inappropriate to practical actions in immediate social and physical contexts. It loses many of its rhetorical functions, such as those involved in negotiating meanings between hearer and listener. It is certainly not the only, or even the most powerful tool for exploring novel and personal meanings. Above all, it is not a "mother tongue"; it requires a particular book-oriented home environment and years of schooling to master it.

But because of the general cultural bias toward text, schools have been unrestrained in their translation of all knowledge into it. We come to define knowledge as "prose statements known to be true." That is, knowledge comes to be defined as that picture of reality appropriate to the requirements of a particular technology, explicit written text. The means has become the end. The acquisition of knowledge has become nothing other than the construction of a particular view of reality appropriate to the requirements of explicit logical text. That assumption is unsound both epistemologically and pedagogically.

It is unsound epistemologically in that it assumes that the translation can be complete. The meaning of a poem is not given by some prose paraphrase; its meaning is tied inextricably to that particular form of expression. Each form of activity results in a conception of reality appropriate to that particular form of activity whether practical, social or symbolic. No one system of representaiton can exhaust that reality.

It is unsound pedagogically because the exclusive reliance upon text may lead to the undervaluation of practical knowledge and of the mother tongue. Coding of all knowledge in terms of text may make that knowledge inaccessible to people with lesser literacy skills. Further, the translation may lose the distinctive properties of the original form of expression, as when a novel is made into a film or poetry is translated into prose. There are many forms of activity including those in symbolic media, and knowledge is the consequence of the application of any of them.

In conclusion, recall that we began with the idea that knowledge is conscious, that it may be translated into language (without changing that knowledge), and reciprocally, that language may be translated, as a form of instruction, into knowledge. Hence, one can learn by being told. I have denied that this translation is neutral in its effects. Knowledge, I have argued, is constructed in terms of the functions it is to serve. The knowledge appropriate to practical and social actions, as mediated by a mother tongue, may be considered as commonsense knowledge, and is primary both in its acquisition and its personal and interpersonal significance. But it is the particular picture of reality constructed in terms of the requirements of explicit text which has become both a predominant goal of instruction in the schools, as well as the primary means for the achievement of other goals. Yet, the choice of this particular means of instruction affects or biases the knowledge which is acquired. Hence, the choice of a means of instruction, like the choice of a content, must be based upon a consideration of its personal and social consequences, and we are beginning, I believe, to understand what those consequences are.

ACKNOWLEDGMENTS

The research project on which this paper is based was supported by Grant No. S74-0999 from the Canada Council. I am also grateful to Nancy Nickerson for her assistance in the preparation of this manuscript.

REFERENCES

Anderson, J., & Bower, G. *Human associative memory.* Washington, D.C.: Winston, 1973.

Austin, J. L. *How to do things with words.* London and New York: Oxford University Press, 1962.

Ayer, A. J. *Language, truth and logic.* London: Gollancz, 1936.

Baldwin, A. L. *Theories of child development.* New York: Wiley, 1967.

Bernstein, B. *Class, codes and control, Vol. 1.* London: Routledge & Kegan Paul, 1971.

Bloom, L. *Language development: Form and function in emerging grammars.* Cambridge, Mass.: M.I.T. Press, 1970.

Bruner, J. S. On cognitive growth. In J. S. Bruner et al. (eds.), *Studies in cognitive growth.* New York, Wiley, 1966.

Bruner, J. S., & Olson, D. Learning through experience and learning through media. In D.

Olson (Ed.), *Media and symbols: The forms of expression, communication and education.* 73rd Yearbook of the NSSE. Chicago: University of Chicago Press, 1974.

Buhler, K. *Sprachtheorie.* Jena: Verlag, 1934.

Carnap, R. *Meaning and necessity.* Chicago: University of Chicago Press, 1947.

Cole, M., Gay, J., Glick, J., & Sharp, D. *The cultural context of learning and thinking.* New York: Basic Books, 1971.

Cromer, R. The development of language and cognition: The cognition hypothesis. In B. Foss (Ed.), *New perspectives in child development.* London: Penguin Education Series, 1974.

Dewey, J. *Democracy and education.* New York: Macmillan, 1916.

Dewey, J. *Logic: The theory of enquiry.* Toronto: Holt, Rinehart, & Winston, 1938.

Duncker, J. On problem solving. *Psychological Monographs,* 1945, **58**, 270.

Frase, L. T. Maintenance and control in the acquisition of knowledge from written materials. In R. Freedle & J. B. Carroll (Eds.), *Language comprehension and the acquisition of knowledge.* Washington, D.C.: Winston, 1972.

Frederiksen, C. H. Effects of task-induced cognitive operations on comprehension and memory processes. In R. Freedle & J. B. Carroll (Eds.), *Language comprehension and the acquisition of knowledge.* Washington, D.C.: Winston, 1972.

Gellner, E. The savage and modern mind. In R. Horton & R. Finnegan (Eds.), *Modes of thought.* London: Faber & Faber, 1973.

Gladwin, T. *East is a big bird: Navigation and logic on Puluwat atoll.* Cambridge, Mass.: Harvard University Press, 1970.

Gombrich, E. H. *Art and illusion: A study in the psychology of pictorial representation.* Bollingen Series XXXV. New York: Pantheon Books, 1960.

Goodnow, J. The nature of intelligent behavior; Questions raised by cross-cultural studies. In L. Resnick (Ed.), *The Nature of intelligence.* Hillsdale, N.J.: Lawrence Erlbaum Associates, 1976.

Goody, J., & Watt, I. The consequences of literacy. *Comparative Studies in Society and History,* 1963, **5**, 304–345. Republished in J. Goody (Ed.), *Literacy in traditional societies.* Cambridge, England: Cambridge University Press, 1968.

Harlow, H. F. Learning set and error factor theory. In S. Koch (Ed.), *Psychology: A study of science.* New York: McGraw-Hill, 1959.

Havelock, E. *Prologue to Greek literacy. Lectures in memory of Louise Taft Semple, second series, 1966–1971.* Cincinatti, Ohio; University of Cincinatti, Press, 1973.

Huizinga, J. *The waning of the middle ages.* New York: Doubleday, 1954.

Horton, R. African traditional thought and western science. In B. R. Wilson (Ed.), *Rationality.* Oxford: Blackwell, 1970.

Hoyt, D. P. The relationship between college grades and adult achievement: A review of the literature. *American College Testing Program Research Reports,* 1965, **7**, 1–58.

James, W. *Pragmatism.* New York: Longman's, 1907.

Lévi-Strauss, C. *The savage mind.* London: Weidenfeld & Nicolson, 1966. (First French edition, 1962.)

Locke, J. *An essay concerning human understanding,* London: Ward, Locke & Bowden, 1690.

Lonergan, B. J. F. *Insight: A study of human understanding.* New York: Philosophical Library, 1957.

Luria, A. R. Towards the problem of the historical nature of psychological processes. *International Journal of Psychology,* 1971, **6**, 259–272.

Macnamara, J. The cognitive basis of language learning in infants. *Psychological Review,* 1972, **79**, 1–13.

Maier, N. R. F. Reasoning and learning. *Psychological Review,* 1931, **38**, 332–346.

Maier, N. R. F., Thurber, J. A., & Janzen, J. C. Studies in creativity: The selection process in recall and in problem solving situation. *Psychological Reports,* 1968, **23**, 1003–1022.

Norman, D. & Rumelhart, D. *Explorations in cognition.* San Francisco: Freeman, 1975.

Olson, D. Culture, technology and intellect. In L. Resnick (Ed.), *The nature of intelligence.* Hillsdale, N.J.: Lawrence Erlbaum Associates, 1976 (in press, a.)

Olson, D. From utterance to text; The bias of language in speech and writing. In H. Fisher & R. Diez-Gurrero (Eds.), *Language and logic in personality and society.* New York: Academic Press, (in press, b.)

Olson, D. Notes on a theory of instruction. In D. Klahr (Ed.), *Cognition and instruction.* Hillsdale, N.J.: Lawrence Erlbaum Associates. 1976.   (a)

Olson, D. Towards a theory of instructional means. *Educational psychologist,* 1976, **12**, 14–35.   (b)

Olson, D. (Ed.) *Media and symbols: The forms of expression, communication and education.* 73rd Yearbook of the NSSE. Chicago: University of Chicago Press, 1974.

Piaget, J. *Principles of genetic epistemology* (translated by Wolfe Mays). London: Routledge & Kegan Paul, 1972.

Rohwer, W. D. Prime time for education: Early childhood or adolescence? *Harvard Educational Review,* 1971, **41**, 316–341.

Rothkopf, E. Structural text features and the control of processes in learning from written material. In R. Freedle & J. B. Carroll (Eds.), *Language comprehension and the acquisition of knowledge.* Washington, D.C.: Winston, 1972.

Ryle, G. Systematically misleading expressions. In A. G. N. Flew, (Ed.), *Logic and language.* Oxford: Blackwell, 1968.

Schutz, A., & Luckmann, T. The structure of the life world (translated by R. Zaner & H. Engelhardt). Evanston, Ill.: Northwestern University Press, 1973.

Scribner, S. & Cole, M. Cognitive consequences of formal and informal education. *Science,* 1973, **182**, 553–559.

Searle, J. R. *Speech acts: An essay in the philosophy of language.* Cambridge, England: Cambridge University Press, 1969.

Sprat, T. *History of the Royal Society of London for the improving of natural knowledge.* (1667), J. I. Cope and H. W. Jones (Eds.), St. Louis: Washington University Press, 1958.

Travers, R. M. W. *Essentials of learning: An overview for students of education.* New York: Macmillan, 1963.

Tversky, B. Encoding processes in recognition and recall. *Cognitive psychology,* 1973, **5**, 275–287.

Tversky, B. Eye fixations in prediction of recognition and recall. *Memory and cognition,* 1974, **2**, 275–278.

COMMENTS ON
CHAPTER 3 BY OLSON

Ernst Z. Rothkopf,

Bell Laboratories

Olson in his provocative contribution states clearly his concern that excessive reliance on written instruction biases the student's perceptions and thoughts in an undesirable manner. Olson's views on the literate bias of schooling is good news for serious students of instruction. The reason is that the paper is a clear signal that the lessons of 25 years of instructional research are beginning to penetrate the rose thickets of academic psychology. The moment may not be far off when a noble but earthy kiss will awaken the slumbering beauty of traditional learning theory. Judging from Olson's paper, the name of the charger that will carry the prince through the thorny barrier may be *task analysis*. Sleeping beauty will never be the same again and she may even live happily ever after.

Task analysis is important to the position taken by Olson, because it provides means for understanding why *apparently* equivalent instructional means produce different results and why *apparently* sufficient instructional messages fail their purpose. Olson points out that verbal knowledge cannot always be translated into appropriate acts, as illustrated in the ambiguous cliché about the gap between theory and practice. The experiments reported by Olson provide convincing evidence that very gross descriptions of learned performance are misleading because this performance has important process substructures. It is not sufficient to speak about recall of learned information but necessary to specify conditions of testing, for example, recognition, cued or free recall. More important, it is desirable to specify the cognitive substrate which supports performance: the learned underlying concepts, their relationships to each other, and their relationships to performance.

These kinds of complexities have been slighted, if not ignored, by academic learning theorists in their search for rigorous, quantitative, theoretical models. Olson provides a valuable service in drawing attention to them even though he does so indirectly. In fairness, it needs to be said that applied learning theorists have long recognized the importance of task structure in instruction and in the design of other supports of performance. The work of Gagné (1965) on the analysis of the hierarchical structure of skills is an example of this applied work.

Techniques have evolved during the last two decades, following the pioneering work of Robert Miller (1962, 1963), on the analysis of tasks. These methods are not completely objective and have substantial shortcomings. But the value of task analysis has been demonstrated in many instances, most notably in instructional design. It is unfortunate that task analysis has until very recently been almost completely ignored by learning researchers. Olson's paper does not make explicit reference to this work but the research which he describes, as well as his general remarks about the results from overly bookish education, points strongly to the need for analyzing the cognitive substrates of performance.

Olson makes substantial assumptions about the prevalence of reading assignments in primary and secondary schools. Little reliable quantitative information is available about assignments, their frequency, monitoring, and compliance. I question whether schools are really as completely in the thrall of text as Olson asserts. Curriculum content is probably closely tied to available text. That seems a benevolent relationship, because it ties the school into the general weave of our culture. But I seriously wonder how extensively the achievement of substantive instructional goals depends on reading by the student. It is easy to overestimate the importance of text on the basis of homework assignments, outside reading projects, and the like. But this is only nominal instructional content. If compliance with assignments were considered in the estimates of the influence of text, Olson might have moderated his assessment of the importance of text in schooling. It is easy to underestimate the role of the book as an amulet and a sign in the intellectual twilight zone. The acquisition of books and holding them near are often vicarious acts for the acquisition of knowledge. Assigning readings is probably often a substitute for teaching.

Olson raises an interesting issue about the apparent discrepancies between our logical standards, presumably fostered by the literate bias of our teaching, and "logically inconsistent" inventions such as the sophisticated navigational system of the Puluwat. He says, "if we expect all knowledge systems to be similar we are surprised to find such logical inconsistency" (page 69). I suspect that the bias that would be involved in any surprise is not the bias produced by printed educational means, but the bias of a sector of our intellectual establishment. Useful action guided by means which are not logically integrated or which are very incomplete have a long and honorable history in our culture. We use technological products effectively without much understanding. Our assumptions about how things work are often not only incomplete or logically inconsistent, but wrong. And yet people cook, tune their color television sets, and start their cars on cold days. Nomographs and other performance aids are used to make decisions and guide complicated acts without their users knowing the principles or relationships on which the nomograph was based. It is clear that effective practical action is and has never been thought to depend exclusively on rational analysis. The bias for logical consistency is probably not harbored by the doer who reads heavily, but rather by the academic intellectuals who write too much. As a matter of fact, the argument is attractive that logical consistency is not a general characteristic of language nor even a peculiar characteristic of written language. Instead, it seems plausible that the logical style or tone represents aesthetic values, the *production values,* of academic writers.

Olson portrays, with disturbing power, the narrowing and distorting effects of excessive reliance on print in learning concepts. The picture that he creates is that of the book constricting and biasing the world of the student. This jaundiced view would be appropriate if bad texts were the only books used in schools. But that is hardly the case. The student is brought into contact with the literature of his language; the experiences and thoughts of other human beings. These would not be as conveniently accessible if books were not available. There are books of adventure and exploration that provide substantive knowledge while they fascinate and entertain. There are biographies that portray other individual choices and fates and that can serve as models for questioning young minds. There are the creations of the artistic imagination that allow the reader glimpses of the human condition. Olson need not worry about Luther forcing us to accept text as immutable truth. Books are not only sources for literal facts or deducations, they also provide inductive bases for knowledge, opinions, and attitudes. The creative literature of the English language includes not only the fictional voices of wise men and oracles, but also of liars, knaves, and pontificating fools. If reading can teach caution and skepticism, we better douse the fearsome bonfires that Olson has tried to kindle.

REFERENCES

Gagné, R. M. *The conditions of learning,* New York: Holt, Rinehart, & Winston, 1965.

Miller, R. B. Analysis and specifications of behavior for training. In Robert Glaser (Ed.), *Training research and education,* University of Pittsburgh Press: Pittsburgh, 1962.

Miller, R. B. Task description and analysis. In R. M. Gagné (Ed.) *Psychological principles in system development,* New York: Holt, Rinehart, & Winston, 1963.

OPEN DISCUSSION
ON THE CONTRIBUTIONS
BY OLSON AND ROTHKOPF

Broudy: This dichotomy between the uses of language to express common sense and language that is to have autonomous meaning, objectivity, and logical coherence leaves the place of the humanities unsettled. *Literas,* as you know, was connected in Cicero's mind with *humanitas.* Humanitas was also supposed to contain truth of a kind. It seems to me either you are going to get rid of humanitas and call it nontext, or, if text, allow that it has a very large difference in characteristics from the kind of language used to express propositions of fact with truth conditions. This is why humanistic truth, it seems to me, is a problem for us. The interpretive schemata for receiving that language is not the same as it is for the reception of scientific statements.

Olson: I agree that written language, once it is created, is put to all sorts of functions. You cannot identify language with the service of any one of them. I have simply taken one function, as applied in one kind of context, and tried to indicate the properties of that system. I really do not have a good explanation of what happens, for example, to written conversation. Conversations are presumably commonsense representations, and yet they may be, in fact, written. So, they will take some of the characteristics of both of those kinds of systems. There is certainly no clean break between these forms. You can have someone speak only in formal propositions, and you can have someone who writes and reports only dialogues.

Broudy: As far as schooling is concerned, what do we do with this intermediate group, the humanities. Should we throw it out because it is not commonsense? It is commonsense refined by sensibility, which then translates into a set of symbols which are no longer accessible to commonsense. You now have to be literate. But you cannot construe the humanities in the same way that you construe scientific discourse. What do we do with them in the curriculum?

What happens to your distinction between commonsense and text language, since the humanities are textual, but not the language of action?

Olson: I would see these in terms of a branching tree with literacy being the most critical partition.

Rothkopf: Let me add that the distinction between the commonsense and the "literate" is even found in oral speech in societies that are preliterate. For example, among some Plains Indians public speech was restricted to some individuals. People with speech defects or accents were not allowed to speak in public councils because the Indians were concerned with passing down language in pure form from one generation to the next.

Olson: I take that to be quite an important point that I have implied, but possibly never specified. Any use of language, whether it is written or oral can be specialized to serve different kinds of functions. It is not that we create logic through learning to read and write, it is that learning to read and write permits you to specialize in one set of considerations while holding the others constant.

Broudy: What you seem to be talking about is formalization in the sense of stylization. You can stylize any communication, and the minute you introduce form to it, you have already moved away from the ordinary, natural, spontaneous, ad hoc use of language.

Petrie: I wonder if it would be helpful to look at the distinction between the languages of the humanities, science, and commonsense this way. If you start with social functions, social relations, and rhetorical functions, as main uses, it may turn out that in the development of mankind a couple of these functions become tremendously important. Let me oversimplify just to pick out the two that we have been talking about. Regarding the truthseeking function, no matter what our social relationships are, periodically they bump up against the world. However much we might like the world to be such and such a way, it just is not. So it is very socially useful to find out how the world is in certain kinds of ways. In another sense, it may be that the social relations are such that they bump up against, for example, the moral dimension, how the world ought to be. The constant "bumping up against" in general areas of social language uses may well have led to the idea that those functions have got to be institutionalized. Take the scientific example now. We can institutionalize the truth seeking function and we now say you have the "right" automatically to say something if it is true. That takes the "right" out of the social relationships and puts it into this very institutionalized scientific use of language. Something analogous could be developed for the moral and the aesthetic realms as well.

Olson: I would think that moral and realistic considerations are built into all of these representations. For example, the world has to be honored in a commonsense orientation. It is honored in a very subtle way. It is not that there is ignorance there, but that truths are not tailored according to a certain recipe, namely, written prose. I wonder if it is just that the world is a problem and that leads you to specialize. I think you specialize because you have access to a new means of analysis which have certain advantages; for example, allowing generalizations about the truth value of statements across time and space. Once you try to push your knowledge into that recipe, it specializes massively. But I would not say that it is a better fit to reality. It is just a fit of reality according to a new type of recipe.

Petrie: One could, with the kind of view I offered earlier, help resolve the continuity problem that Dr. Broudy pointed to. It is not quite as neatly divided as you suggest. It might help us to understand in what sense these specialized institutions which develop truth seeking, beauty seeking, goodness seeking, and specialized uses of language with those kinds of purposes (I like your functional emphasis) really could be refined common sense, still serving the function of guiding action, but in a better way.

Rumelhart: I would like to raise two points. In the first place, informativeness is a requirement not only on spoken material (as Grice would argue), but also on written material. Contrary to Dr. Olson's claim, being true is not a sufficient justification for written material any more than it is for spoken speech. You would not want a paper full of tautologies, for example.

Second, it seems to me somewhat dangerous, from the point of view of the psychologist, to want to divorce the two types of language as much as Dr. Olson advocates. In particular, in the context of such issues as concept learning or comprehension, it seems wrong to suppose that these processes go on in fundamentally different ways in the two different kinds of situations. Take as an example the presumed context-free nature of text. I cannot imagine a text that is truly context free. Even in the most rigorously written scientific paper, you can rarely pull a sentence out of context and try to make sense of it. It has to be in the context of the paper. Moreover, even the whole paper probably would not make much sense, if it were not in the context of some theory or discipline. To suppose that Luther was correct in saying that the meaning was in the text and nowhere else seems to be wrong. Rather, it would seem that our understanding of text is really an extrapolation of our ordinary ways of dealing with what Dr. Olson calls commonsense.

Olson: I agree that texts that require no private interpretation are quite scarce. But it seems to me that you can still differentiate two ways of analyzing a statement. One way is in terms of whether you are going to assimilate it into what you know, in which case it is a matter of interpretation. This is the same point Dr. Spiro made earlier about Dr. Meyer's paper. Did you hear anything that is of interest or use to you? The other way to read text is to accommodate, as Piaget would say. What is the text, in fact, saying? Try to suspend private interpretation and honor only the conventionalized meaning. Even if text never becomes completely autonomous, those are still immensely different procedures to apply to the analysis of a sentence than the ordinary conversational ones.

Spiro: I think Dr. Olson might not really want to argue that the logical function is, in a sense, inherent in the characteristics of text per se. It is very possible that students initially come into school trying to do what they always try to do, namely, to use processes geared to old functions. These would certainly be of the commonsense kind. What they run up against is the uses which the schools require. These are geared mainly to the kinds of texts which reward this sort of sterile, logical, literate approach. So, it is not so much the text per se as what they know they have to do with the text. I would not be surprised if the child's initial approach to text is more like the commonsensical than the textual. From some perspectives, that may not be disadvantageous. In short, what you do with information will depend on its function, and what use it will have to be put to.

Olson: That is right.

4

The Representation of Knowledge in Memory[1]

David E. Rumelhart

University of California at San Diego

Andrew Ortony

University of Illinois at Urbana-Champaign

INTRODUCTION

While originating from the senses, knowledge is not a blind record of sensory inputs. Normal people are not tape recorders, or video recorders; rather, they seem to process and reprocess information, imposing on it and producing from it knowledge which has structure. The human memory system is a vast repository of such knowledge. Some of this knowledge seems to be in the form of specific memories of particular events which we have experienced; some of it seems to be in the form of more general abstractions no longer tied to any particular time, place, or source. It is one of the tasks of a theory of the representation of knowledge to provide a characterization of the way in which knowledge is structured so that progress may be made toward answering other important questions: how is memory organized so as to usually permit relevant information to be accessed when required? how is old knowledge employed in the acquisition of new? how does our current knowledge state modulate our actions? No theory we know of provides a completely satisfactory answer to questions such as these. Nevertheless, substantial strides toward answering them have been made during the past five or ten years. It is, we believe, a tribute to these strides that a paper on the representation of knowledge can be found in a volume such as this.

---

[1] The paper originally presented at the Conference by Rumelhart and discussed by Ortony has been replaced by this joint effort. Hence the absence of formal and open discussion.

The progress to which we refer can be regarded as the focal point of a new emerging discipline called Cognitive Science. The research of an increasing number of people working in artificial intelligence, cognitive psychology, and linguistics on problems concerned with the representation of meaning and the structural and processing aspects of knowledge, reveals a substantial convergence of opinion on the essential components of systems for representing knowledge. Recent papers by Bobrow and Norman (1975), Minsky (1975), Norman, Rumelhart, and LNR (1975), Rumelhart (1975), Schank and Abelson (1975), and Winograd (1975) all attest to this convergence. While differing from one another, sometimes in important ways, there is nevertheless agreement on the broad outline stated or implied by these authors. In this paper we will sketch this broad outline and develop some of the arguments in favor of the general approach. Although many aspects of the ideas we will develop differ from those of earlier approaches, it is not our purpose to critically review any of them, nor to attempt any explicit comparison between our approach and that of others. Rather, we have drawn upon what we consider the best aspects of each of these other developments and constructed what seems to us the most reasonable composite view. To the degree that technical detail is required we have formulated our ideas in the context of the Active Structural Networks of Norman, Rumelhart, and LNR (1975) and as a synthesis of the work of Rumelhart and Levin (1975), and of Rumelhart (1975).

While we will not be comparing our account of knowledge representation, which we will express in terms of "schemata" (singular — "schema"), with the accounts of others, it is appropriate that we indicate the concepts with which proponents of similar views are associated. The theory proposed by Minsky (1975) is based on what he called "frames." Winograd (1975), Charniak (1975), and other workers in Artifical Intelligence have largely followed Minsky's usage. Bobrow and Norman (1975) and Norman (1975) have used the term *schema* much as it is used in this paper. Norman, Rumelhart, and LNR (1975) have used the term *definition* where we will use schema. Schank and Abelson (1975) and Schank *et al.* (1975) use the term *script* to refer to one class of schemata and the term *plan* to refer to a class of somewhat more abstract schemata. Rumelhart (1975) also uses the term schema to refer to a set of abstract schemata similar to Schank and Abelson's *plans*.

SCHEMATA

A central theme in work of the kind referenced above is the postulation of interacting knowledge structures, which, as indicated already, we shall call "schemata." The term finds its way into modern psychology from the writings of Bartlett (1932) and it is to him that most workers acknowledge their debt. It is interesting to note, however, that in his *Critique of Pure Reason*, Kant (1787) utilizes a notion of schemata that in many ways appears to be more similar to ours than is even Bartlett's.[2]

Schemata are data structures for representing the generic concepts stored in memory. They exist for generalized concepts underlying objects, situations, events, sequences of events, actions, and sequences of actions. Schemata are not atomic. A schema contains, as part of its specification, the network of interrelations that is believed to generally hold among the constituents of the concept in question. Schemata, in some sense, represent stereotypes of these concepts. Although it oversimplifies the matter somewhat, it may be useful to think of a schema as analogous to a play with the internal structure of the schema corresponding to the script of the play. A schema is related to a particular instance of the concept that it represents in much the same way that a play is related to a particular enactment of that play.

There are, we believe, at least four essential characteristics of schemata, which combine to make them powerful for representing knowledge in memory. These are: (1) schemata have variables; (2) schemata can embed one within the other; (3) schemata represent generic concepts which, taken all together, vary in their levels of abstraction; and (4) schemata represent knowledge, rather than definitions. In the remainder of this section we discuss these four features in turn, illustrating by example aspects of each. The section on variables is long because in it so many notions are introduced for the first time.

Variables in Schemata

Just as a play has roles that may be filled by different actors on different performances so schemata have variables that may become associated with, or bound by, different aspects of our environment on different occasions. In the context of linguistics these variables have been called "cases" by those who advocate case grammars following Fillmore (1968). We might, for example, have

---

[2] Kant says:

[This] representation of a universal procedure of imagination in providing an image
No image could ever be adequate to the concept of a triangle in general. It would never attain that universality of the concept which renders it valid of all triangles . . . The schema of the triangle . . . is a rule of synthesis of the imagination . . . The concept 'dog' signifies a rule according to which my imagination can delineate the figure of a four-footed animal in a general manner, without limitation to any single determinate figure such as experience, or any possible image that I can represent *in concreto,* actually presents.

He goes on: . . . the *image* is a product of the empirical faculty of reproductive imagination; the *schema* of sensible concepts, such as of figures in space, is a product and, as it were, a monogram, of pure *a priori* imagination, through which, and in accordance with which, images themselves first become possible. These images can be connected with the concept only by means of the schema to which they belong.

a schema for GIVE that would have three variables: a giver, a gift, and a recipient. On different occasions the variables in the GIVE schema will take on different values. These values are determined by aspects of the environment, that is, by contextual and situational factors, as well as the to-be-comprehended stimulus. Thus, the environment provides referents for the mental conceptualizations which become associated with the variables in the schema. But, while the variables may be bound by different aspects of the environment on different occasions, still the relationships internal to the GIVE schema will remain constant. In particular, the giver will somehow cause the recipient to get the gift, and in normal cases this is true regardless of the identity of the giver or recipient, or the nature of the gift. We say "in the normal case" advisedly, for in certain cases that will be discussed later, exceptions can be found to these generalizations.

Figure 1 illustrates the Active Structural Network representation for the GIVE schema discussed above. (For a detailed discussion of active structural networks see Norman, Rumelhart, & LNR, 1975). The uncircled upper case term represents the name of the schema. The pointer labeled "iswhen" points to the internal structure of the schema. The variables X, Y, and Z are pointed to by arrows labeled "giver," "recipient," and "gift," respectively. The encircled terms represent subschemata. The arrows pointing from the subschemata show how the variables of the schema relate to those of the subschemata. Thus, the "giver" of the GIVE schema is the "agent" of the CAUSE subschema. Note also that the GET subschema plays the role of the "caused event" for the CAUSE subschema. As we shall see, actual schemata are rather more complex. The representation given here is solely for purposes of illustration.

Just as certain characteristics of the actors are specified by the playwrite (e.g., sex, age, appearance), so too a schema contains, as part of its specification,

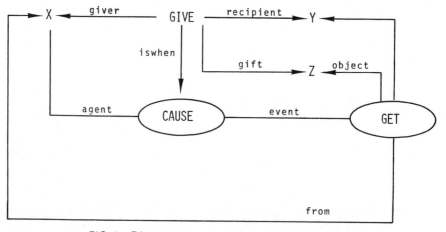

FIG. 1. Diagrammatic representation of a GIVE schema.

information about the *types* of objects that may be bound to the various variables of the schema. Thus, in our GIVE example above, we might, for example, have specifications within the schema to the effect that the "giver" must be capable of willful action (animate?). Such constraints on the values that variables can take serve two important functions: (1) they tell what sorts of objects might realistically be bound to each variable; and (2) when there is insufficient information they can allow good guesses to be made about at least some of the variables.

The following example is intended to clarify the process whereby variable binding occurs. Suppose we have a schema for the concept of someone breaking something. We can imagine at least three variables associated with the schema: the breaker, the object, and the method whereby the object is broken. We might expect the breaker to be an agentive force, the object to be rigid or brittle, and the method to be some action of which the breaker is capable and which is believed to be sufficient to break the object in question. Figure 2 illustrates how such a schema might be represented as an active structural network.

Consider, now, the following sentences:

(1) John broke the window.
(2) The ball broke the window.
(3) John broke the bubble.

In each case, using our analogy of a play, we can say that the sentence describes an enactment of the BREAK play. Nevertheless, we get quite different images of

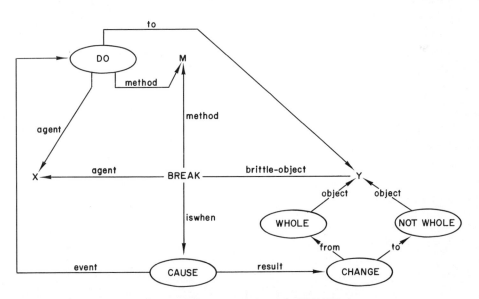

FIG. 2. Diagrammatic representaiton of a BREAK schema.

the relationships between the subjects and objects of these sentences. That is, in spite of the surface similarities among the sentences, the roles are assigned so as to produce quite different enactments of the play.

Compare first sentences (1) and (2). Suppose, perhaps, because the word "break" appears in the sentence, that we have been led to consider our BREAK schema as a possible account for these sentences. We must now somehow associate the other concepts referred to in the sentences with the variables of the schema. The variable constraints can help us do that. In both cases "the window" will probably be taken as the "object" and associated with variable Y (in the figure). The window clearly meets the criterion of being a rigid object. In sentence (1), John will also easily be determined to fit as the "breaker," X, since John is presumably the name of a person and since people are stereotypical agentive forces. However, in sentence (2) "the ball" is not easily bound to variable X because it is not easily considered an agentive force. Thus, we must make a guess about the identity of variable X. We know that X can be bound to an unspecified person or "someone." But what about "the ball." There is another variable in the break schema that can be used to account for "the ball," namely, the method. Thus, we have "someone caused the window to become broken by using the ball." But what action did this "someone" perform? We are given no direct information and must again make a plausible guess. We know from the variable constraints that whatever it was, it must have been sufficient to cause a window to break. We could leave it at that, or we could look back to the ball schema, or we could search our memories for other cases of objects like balls breaking objects like windows and see what sorts of activities were involved. Were we to carry out this extra step of inference, we probably would determine that the ball (perhaps a baseball) was somehow propelled through the window. In this way, although the particular method was nowhere stated, the variable constraints within the schema have enabled a probable value to be assigned to one of the variables. This assignment of inferred values to variables we refer to as the assignment of *default values* (Minsky, 1975). Note, however, that these default values need not be fixed independently of the values of the other variables. Instead, they are filled contingently, the value being assigned to a particular variable (such as the method in our example) depending on the value of other variables (such as the object in our example).

Now contrast sentence (1) with sentence (3). Binding the X and Y variables (the breaker and object, respectively) causes no problems. In both cases John is the breaker. In one case the object is "the window" and in the other it is "the bubble." However, we probably get quite different images of the method involved in these two cases. This difference presumably results from the knowledge we have about what sorts of activities are sufficient to break an object of the strength of a window as opposed to what sorts of activities are sufficient to break something of the rigidity of a bubble. This information could have already been abstracted and directly associated with the BREAK schema or it could be discovered by consulting our memories for various instances of things like windows and bubbles having been broken.

To summarize, schemata have variables with which are associated variable constraints. These serve two functions. First, they help in the assignment of values to variables by specifying the sorts of things that can fill the various roles in the schema. Second, when such an assignment cannot be made merely on the basis of the current input or from memory, the constraints can help to generate default assignments. Once an assignment of variables has been made, either from the environment, from memory, or by default, the schema is said to have been *instantiated.* It will transpire in our discussion of comprehension. that the instantiation of schemata is only the first step in comprehension. From there the process of activating subschemata or dominating schemata may continue, thereby perhaps modifying the original assignments of variables. This process of activating related schemata is akin to Craik and Lockhart's (1972) notion of depth of processing.

Before leaving our discussion of variables and variable constraints, it should be mentioned that variable constraints are seldom absolute. It is rarely the case that a variable *cannot ever* accept a value of a certain sort. Rather it is useful to think of variable constraints as as representing *distributions* of possible values. A particular variable can take on any of a range of possible values, but some values are more typical than others. Empirical evidence for the view that distributional information has to be represented can be found in Walker (1975) who found that judgments about values of attributes of physical objects were quickest when these values were rated as being either extreme or typical. The primacy of prototypical values is argued for by, for example, Rosch (1973). Thus, "give" tends to require the giver to be a person, but of course governments and other institutions can give in much the same sense as a person; such values, however, are less typical. If we have a choice, the variable constraint will prefer values closer to the "average" of the distribution, but will *accept* deviant values if no other interpretation can be made.

In fact, the set of variable constraints for a given schema should be considered to form a multivariate distribution with correlations among the several variables. Thus, as our example with BREAK illustrates, when filling an unfilled variable we prefer values close to the "average" for that variable *conditional on* the values of the already filled variables. Halff, Ortony, and Anderson (in press) describe data showing just this kind of context-sensitivity with adjective—noun pairs. The extent to which a particular schema fits a particular state will roughly depend on how probable that particular configuration of variables is for that particular schema. One might regard some of the experimental findings in language comprehension as mild support for this last claim (Anderson & Ortony, 1975; Barclay, Bransford, Franks, McCarrell, & Nitsch, 1974; Johnson, Bransford, & Solomon, 1973).

Schemata Embed

In much the same way as the entries for lexical items in a dictionary consist of other lexical items, so the structure of a schema is given in terms of relationships among other schemata. As we shall see, in some cases schemata can even be embedded within themselves, that is, some schemata are recursive structures. In this section, we shall restrict our discussion to simpler schemata such as those illustrated in Fig. 1 and 2 where the terms in circles are the names of embedded schemata, that we call the *subschemata*. These are represented within the schemata in which they appear, the *dominating schemata,* by names or labels, not by their entire structures. Clearly, representing the structures themselves would have the absurd consequence that every schema in memory would contain the knowledge to be found in at least most, if not all, of the other schemata in memory. This explosive multiplication of knowledge representations is arrested by incorporating only uniquely identifying references to the subschemata, for such names do not themselves incorporate other names.

Consider the FACE schema illustrated in Fig. 3a which is based on the model described by Palmer (1975). It contains within it references to schemata for eyes, ears, mouth, and so on. The substance of the FACE schema is the specification of such normal constituent parts, the subschemata, and the specification of the relationships that normally hold between them. Notice that the schema for EYE in Fig. 3b has as its subschemata those for pupil, iris, eyelid, etc., none of which appear in the FACE schema.

The overall organization which results is hierarchical, not just in the sense of a hierarchy of concepts related by class inclusion (as in Collins & Quillian, 1969), but in a more general way. This organization seems to lead to an infinite regress, in which each schema is characterized in terms of lower level constituents, or subschemata. Presumably, the dependence that schemata have on lower level subschemata must ultimately stop, that is to say, some schemata must be atomic in the sense that they are not characterized by reference to any other constituent schemata. These atomic schemata correspond to what Norman, Rumelhart, and LNR (1975) call *primitives.* Many of them probably represent basic sensory-motor procedures, while others may represent unanalyzable conceptual components of human knowledge such as that of "causal connection" which, as Hume pointed out two hundred years ago, cannot be extracted from experience alone. Thus, our entire knowledge system would appear to ultimately rest upon a set of atomic schemata.

The property of embedding which schemata have provides a number of important advantages. Foremost among these is that a situation or object can be comprehended in terms of its major constituents without necessary reference to the internal structure of the constituents themselves. Yet, at the same time, a "deeper" understanding can be achieved if reference is made to the internal structure of these constituents. Thus, for example, a face can be thought of as a certain configuration of eyes, nose, mouth, etc., rather than an enormously

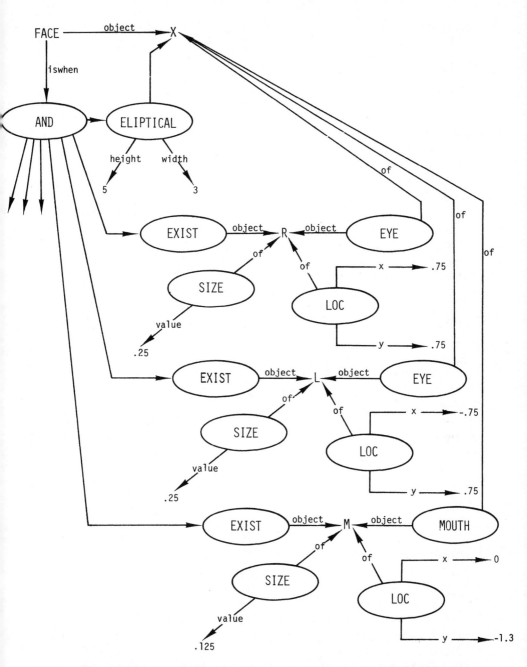

FIG. 3. Diagrammatic representation of (a) part of a FACE schema, and (b) part of an EYE schema. The indicated values should not be taken to represent distances in terms of some standard metric. Rather, they represent numerical approximations of knowledge concerning relative sizes and distances.

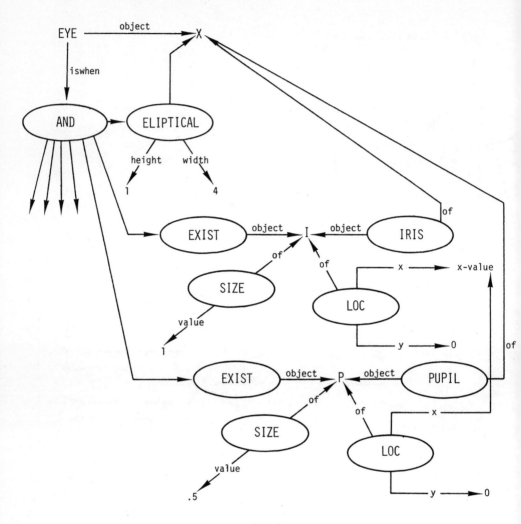

FIG 3B

complex configuration of those elementary perceptual attributes upon which the perception of a face must be presumed to ultimately depend. Similarly, the structure of a schema allows us to distinguish between the relationships that exist between the subschemata and those that exist between the constituents within any one of those subschemata. Thus, suppose that an event is observed in which two people are sitting next to one another talking. Because the PERSON schema is utilized, the feet of one person are seen as being more closely tied to the head of that person than to the feet of the second person. The event would be perceived in this way, even though their feet might in fact be physically closer than either person's feet were to that person's head. Put another way, we can say that our knowledge about people guides us in perceiving people as people and inhibits us from mindlessly grouping objects together on the basis of similarity or proximity. Objects *are* grouped together, but only on the basis of the schemata which are being employed in their interpretation.

A second advantage of embedding, related to the first, is that of representational economy of variables. In the last section we discussed a GIVE schema. A subschema which appears in it will be for one of the several senses of "cause." The particular sense of "cause" in question can be roughly translated as being "do and (thereby) cause." There will be a schema for this sense of "cause" that will include, but not be identical with, the atomic schema for "cause." The DO schema is much closer to some primitive action schema than is the GIVE schema or the BREAK schema in which we have it referenced directly. Consequently, one way or another, it will be accessible from almost all schemata which represent higher level action verbs (where "higher level" means "more remote from primitives"). Thus, sometimes, as in the GIVE schema, DO will be accessible from the schema for the appropriate sense of "cause" and other times, as in the BREAK schema, it may itself be a subschema. In any event, associated with some low level schema such as DO will be various subsidiary variables, those appropriate to answering such questions as When? Where? Why? and How? Thus, instead of requiring variables for such aspects of actions as time, place, reason, and manner to be associated with every single high level schema representing a kind of action, the binding of these variables can often take place in the DO schema. It may or may not be an interesting observation that when we are told that John broke a window, we tend to ask "When (where, why, or how) did he *do* it?" at least as readily as we ask such questions about his *breaking* it. Perhaps our ordinary language sometimes reflects the role that these underlying structures play. However, one should not exaggerate the significance of such observations.

Schemata and Levels of Abstraction

The third major characteristic of schemata emerged clearly at the end of the last section. There are schemata at all levels of abstraction. This characteristic deserves special mention because it is this aspect which most completely sets apart our position from earlier attempts to represent semantic memory. In general, previous works (see Anderson & Bower, 1973; Kintsch, 1972; Quillian, 1968; Rumelhart, Lindsay, & Norman, 1972; Schank, 1972) have concentrated on representing the internal structure of, at most, lexical items. Not until very recently have attempts been made to represent conceptualizations at more abstract levels such as action sequences or plots of stories. The work that has been done in this area is very much in its infancy (see Charniak, 1972; Rumelhart, 1975; Schank & Abelson, 1975). The need for theories of knowledge representation sufficiently powerful to be able to handle higher level conceptualizations becomes more obvious when one considers how essential they seem to be to account for our ability to organize, summarize, and retrieve information about connected sequences of events. Particularly, if one includes the reading of connected discourse in this context, as of course one must, it would seem that such activities constitute the vast bulk of the information processing that people do, both in and out of formal educational settings. It is indeed rare that comprehension is required completely out of context, and on those occasions when it is, we seem to have an uncanny ability to construct a context within which, or perhaps, by means of which, to interpret the input.

Thus, we envision the human memory system as containing countless packets of information, each packet referring to other packets which normally form its constituents. Such packets represent knowledge at all levels of abstraction ranging from basic perceptual elements, such as the configuration of lines which form a square, to abstract conceptual levels which allow us to give cogent summaries of sequences of events occurring over substantial periods of time. We see no great discontinuity between perception and comprehension. Perception is comprehension of sensory input. Nor do we see any great discontinuity between plans and actions. Perhaps actions can be viewed merely as plans instantiated with motor values, which may themselves be either action schemata, like swimming, or primitive actions such as those required to swim. Indeed, in performance, the use of action schemata without reference to the internal structures of their constituents may be regarded as being those "automatic" performances which, Polanyi (1958, 1966) reminds us, become marred if the performer tries to attend to the constituent actions.

Schemata Represent Knowledge

In the discussion so far, reference has frequently been made to the fact that schemata represent the constituents and interrelations that are "normally" to be found. In the section discussing the embedding of schemata we noted, for example, that the FACE schema gave a specification of the "normal constituent parts" and of the relationships that "normally hold between them." We also suggested in the section on variables that the variable constraints are best regarded as distributions rather than inviolable limits. This notion seems to accord well with some recent psychological research as well as the linguistic analyses of Labov (1973) and Lakoff (1972).

If the three characteristics of schemata that we have so far discussed were the only ones; schemata would be much closer to dictionary entries than we would like to imply. To be sure, the fact that schemata can be at all levels of abstraction does exclude many of them from being candidates for dictionary entries. However, there are at least two additional reasons why it should be emphasized that schemata are not the same kinds of things as dictionary entries. First, schemata represent knowledge that is encyclopaedic rather than definitional in character, and even when "essential" characteristics are represented, they are represented in most cases as characteristics which normally or typically pertain. Second, while dictionaries attempt to provide records of "the meanings of words," schemata represent knowledge associated with concepts. Consequently, they are not linguistic entities, but abstract symbolic representations of knowledge which we express and describe in language, and which may be used for understanding language, but which are nevertheless not themselves linguistic.

The characteristic of flexible variable constraints is a very important feature of schemata and it provides a way of seeing one of the differences between definitions and knowledge. We do not fail to understand the story about Odysseus and the Cyclops when we discover that the Cyclops is a one-eyed giant, nor do we deny that the Cyclops has a face, for a face is still a face, even if it has only one eye. Just how many, and to what extent, normal characteristics can be distorted before the schema in question no longer will provide an adequate account is largely an empirical question. But that such distortions and deviations from the typical occur is indisputable, and in representing what is normally true, rather than what is necessarily true, schemata have the capacity to tolerate such deviations, rather than to fail because of logical contradictions between variable constraints and attempted assigned values. Knowledge has to be structured in such a way as to allow that dead animals are nevertheless animals, and that one-eyed faces can still be faces. It is precisely for reasons like these that semantic feature theories, in so far as they require defining features for concepts, seem to us inadequate (see Rips, Shoben, & Smith, 1973). Schemata attempt to represent knowledge in the kind of flexible way which reflects human tolerance for vagueness, imprecision, and quasi-inconsistencies.

THE FUNCTIONS OF SCHEMATA

The characterization of schemata offered so far has portrayed them as the basic building blocks of the human information-processing system. In this section, we propose to elaborate on some of the ways in which schemata fulfill this role. We discuss their primary role of comprehension, for which we take them to be the central mechanism. In addition, we discuss their function in creating records of experience, and memories, as vehicles for inferential reasoning, and of representing and organizing action structures.

Comprehension

Schemata are the key units of the comprehension process. Within the general framework presented here, comprehension can be considered to consist of selecting schemata and variable bindings that will "account for" the material to be comprehended, and then verifying that those schemata do indeed account for it. We say that a schema "accounts for" a situation whenever that situation can be interpreted as an instance of the concept the schema represents. Thus, the bulk of the processing in a schema-based system is directed toward finding those schemata which best account for the totality of the incoming information. On having found a set of schemata which appears to give a sufficient account of the information, the person is said to have "comprehended" the situation. In this view, when a person uses a schema to comprehend some of the aspects of the situation, the schema constitutes a kind of theory about those aspects. Thus, in general, the process of comprehension can be regarded rather like the process a scientist goes through in testing a theory; evidence is sought which either tends to confirm it, or which leads to its rejection. Upon finding a theory which, to our satisfaction, accounts for the observations we have made, we feel that we understand the phenomenon in question.

One of the most important aspects of theories that is shared by schemata is the role of prediction. We need not have performed every experiment to be able to predict with some confidence the outcome of many proposed experiments. Thus, for example, astronomers, confident in their theories, were able to predict the existence and location of Pluto before they were able to observe it. Similarly, a schema allows us to predict aspects of the input which have not been (and perhaps never will be) observed. For instance, once having determined satisfactorily that a certain object is an electric lamp, one tends to assume that it has an on/off switch even though it has not been observed. Similarly, on being told that someone went to a movie, it is normally assumed that the person, or a companion, went to the ticket window and bought a ticket prior to watching the movie. We make these assumptions because the schemata we employ in comprehending the scenes in question, or linguistic descriptions of them, predict that those aspects very probably exist by providing variables for them. It is often possible, in effect, to run the experiment by looking for the switch or inquiring about the purchasing of the movie ticket. In fact, we rarely do this, because first we have enough confidence in the schemata correctly predicting the outcomes of such "experiments," and second, the aspects of a situation which are left to be assumed in this way are usually not very important. Certain environments, such as courts of law, are interesting because very often neither of these reasons pertain.

As a means of introducing a more detailed discussion we now deal with one of the objections that could be raised against theories of the kind we are proposing. If comprehension is achieved by utilizing a schema or set of schemata to account for the input, how is the absurd conclusion that there exists a schema for every conceivable input to be avoided? The first response to this objection is to accept, as we do and must, that there are not specific schemata available for every situation we might encounter. Yet, it is equally true that we could not *understand* every situation we might encounter; indeed, in reality we do not even understand all those situations we *do* encounter. Of course, we do usually manage to achieve at least partial comprehension; that is to say, while we may not be able to find a single schema which fully accounts for some particular situation, we may well be able to find schemata to account for particular aspects of it. The problem, then, is only that we cannot find a single schema which satisfactorily accounts for the entire situation.

This first response, however, appears to leave the objection standing, for we do not deny that we often can understand situations for which the postulation of a specific schema for understanding it would be gratuitous. Thus, a second response is required, and this is that novel situations can generally be handled by using not only specific schemata, but also high level abstract schemata, as we will try to illustrate with the following example:

(4a)   Mary heard the ice cream man coming.
(4b)   She remembered her pocket money.
(4c)   She rushed into the house.

Sentences (4a)–(4c) together constitute a kind of story snippet for which most of us can rather easily get a good interpretation. Presumably, this interpretation is along the lines that Mary heard the ice-cream man coming and wanted to buy some ice cream. Buying ice cream costs money, so she had to think of a quick source of funds. She remembered some pocket money she had not yet spent which, presumably, was in the house. So, Mary hurried into the house trying to get the money by the time the ice-cream man arrived.

An interpretation of Sentences (4a)–(4c) of the kind we have given is an ordinary language interpretation, but how is it achieved using schemata? Clearly, we do not have a detailed schema like the GIVE schema or FACE schema to account for cases of "hearing ice-cream men." However, we probably do have a rather abstract "problem solving" schema which, in conjunction with a number of less abstract schemata, will account for the inputs.[3] Suppose our problem-solving schema has roughly the following structure:

Problem-solving schema (Person P, Event E, Goal G)

1. E causes P to want G.
2. P tries to get G until P gets G or until P gives up.

That is, a problem solving episode is one in which something (E) happens to someone (P) which initiates in him a desire for something (G). The person then continues to make attempts to get the goal until he finally attains it or he gives up. Suppose, further, that the TRY schema has the following internal structure:

Try (Person P, Goal G)

1. P decides on an action A which could lead to G.
2. While any condition A' for A is not satisfied, P tries to get A'.
3. P does A.

[3] A detailed discussion of these problem solving schemata is presented in Rumelhart (1975) and in Rumelhart (1977a).

Thus, the TRY schema consists of three parts: deciding on an appropriate plan of action (A), fulfilling any preconditions (A') on that plan of action, and finally carrying out the plan itself.

Let us now consider how these schemata might help in the comprehension of the sentences. On encountering the first sentence, (4a), the comprehension system activates a number of schemata based on the surface clues in the sentence. (In the general case, schemata may also be activated by contextual clues, but more of that later.) In this particular case, therefore, "Mary" and something like "the coming of the ice-cream man" will be bound to variables in the HEAR schema. Similarly, a schema for ICE-CREAM MAN will be activated, which, in turn will activate its subschemata which together constitute our knowledge about ice-cream men. These will include the SELL schema with "ice-cream man" already bound to the *vendor* variable and "ice cream" bound to a variable representing "goods." However, the variables for *buyer* and *money* have yet to be bound. Meanwhile, since one of the things we know about ice-cream men is that they sell ice cream, the ICE-CREAM schema is activated, thereby making available our knowledge about ice cream. Part of this knowledge is the fact that many people like ice cream. This gives rise to the expectation of finding such a person, and the assignment of any such candidate to the *liker* variable in the now activated LIKE schema. At this point some of the unbound variables in the LIKE and SELL schemata can be identified with one another, since one ordinarily likes what one buys, the still unbound *buyer* of the SELL schema is a good candidate for the first variable of the LIKE schema, the *liker*. Similarly, "ice cream," which binds the *goods* variable in the SELL schema, is a good candidate for the second variable of the LIKE schema, the liked *object*. Thus far, the only candidate for the buyer is Mary and, "Mary" being the name of a person, the requirements for the *buyer* in the SELL schema are apparently satisfied and a tentative assignment of "Mary" to the *buyer* variable is made. At this point we have activated at least the schemata for ICE-CREAM MAN, SELL, ICE CREAM, and LIKE. Now once the LIKE schema is available, the WANT schema is activated, since we often want what we like. Thus, we are able to interpret (4a) by concluding that since ice-cream men sell ice cream to buyers, and since buyers usually like what they buy and want what they like, and since Mary is a good candidate for a buyer, Mary probably wants ice cream.

Before proceeding with the analysis, a couple of observations should be made. Even though we have taken a page or so to account for the comprehension of one simple sentence, our account is still not as detailed as we would like. We have doubtless still made some questionable assumptions and taken some dubious turns. Nevertheless, we hope that the general mechanism whereby schemata function to produce comprehension has been adequately described. It should at least be clear that the process is a complex one. The immediate result is a kind of inference, but it neither is, nor is intended to be, a deductively valid one. Rather, it relies very heavily on stereotypical, default values for variables, that is why we say things like "one ordinarily likes what one buys." Information of this kind will be incorporated into the SELL schema (and also into its "mirror image," the BUY schema), but its incorporation will be as a default assignment determined from the variable-constraining distributional information alluded to earlier. Such assignments are only made in the absence of conflicting information. They combine to give rise to probable interpretations which would render certain sequel sentences, at least, unexpected. Thus, were Sentence (4a) to be followed by Sentence (5)

(5) She drew her revolver and shot him.

we suspect that, in the absence of any contextual cues, a certain degree of reinterpretation would be required to modify some of the variable findings made in Sentence (4a) as a result of the sequel, Sentence (5).

Returning now to our example, we have concluded that Mary probably has a desire for ice cream. It is at this point that we invoke our abstract problem-solving schema, because desires are often parts of problem-solving episodes. Consequently, among others, the problem-solving schema outlined above will be activated. This schema requires an event which causes the desire to come to the fore. In this case, the event of becoming aware of the ice-cream man's arrival is a sufficient cause. Thus, the event variable E of the problem solving schema would become bound by the event of Mary hearing the ice-cream man, the P variable by "Mary" and the G variable by "ice cream." The second line of the problem-solving schema tells us that P tried to get G. We can therefore expect to find evidence for Mary trying to get the ice cream. Probably even before this processing is completed we have taken in the next sentence, (4b), about Mary's pocket money, and we now have a good reason for trying to interpret this as at least related to an attempt by Mary to get the ice cream. In order to do this, we need to make use of our TRY schema which reveals that the first step is deciding on a plan of action which could lead to the accomplishment of the goal. Now we already have an appropriate schema available, namely, that of Mary as the buyer of the ice cream from the ice-cream man (the instantiated SELL schema). This choice is supported by the evidence provided by Sentence (4b), for the buyer needs money; Mary remembers her pocket money, so she has probably decided to buy the ice cream. We now expect to find input either about Mary buying some ice cream, or about her trying to satisfy some precondition for so doing. Thus, when in Sentence (4c) we see Mary going into the house we may conclude that she was intending to get her pocket money from the house. Upon making these associations and upon finding no more input, we conclude our processing with the interpretation outlined above. That is, we have comprehended the story snippet by settling upon a configuration of schemata and their variable bindings which appear to account for all aspects of it, even though we had no single schema for dealing with the particular event described.

The abstract schemata that were used to illustrate the comprehension of Sentences (4a)–(4c) are really very general. They can be used to cover very many instances of trying and problem solving. Consider the following somewhat more complex example from Schank and Abelson (1975):

(6a) John knew his wife's operation would be expensive.
(6b) There was always Uncle Harry. . . .
(6c) John reached for the suburban telephone book.

Again, these sentences can easily be interpreted using the same two abstract schemata. John's awareness that his wife's operation would be expensive binds the *event* variable in the abstract problem-solving schema. John is thereby caused to want something, namely money, and he therefore tries to get it. He decides to borrow it from Uncle Harry. A condition on borrowing is asking, and asking requires contacting. One way to contact is by phone. A phone book is used as a part of telephoning. Thus, John is trying to phone Uncle Harry to ask for the money.

If comprehension does indeed proceed in the way we have suggested, one might suppose that it would be possible to produce a computer simulation of the process. In fact we know of cases in which the details of the operation of such a system have been adequately specified to determine whether or not comprehension can be so achieved. Schank *et al.* (1975) have developed a computer system called SAM which can apply schemata at an intermediate level of abstraction and one of us (DER) has developed a computer system called STORYWORLD which is able to apply very simple versions of the problem-solving schema just mentioned. Still, no one has yet developed a processing system of sufficient sophistication nor a knowledge base so rich that we can say with certainty that these proposed mechanisms will work at the level we are suggesting.

Schemata and Memories

A complete discussion of the representation of knowledge cannot restrict itself to *generic* knowledge alone. It must deal not only with what has traditionally been called *semantic* memory but also with what Tulving (1972) called *episodic* memory. The content of episodic memory, episodic knowledge (see Ortony, 1975a) is more specific, being those memories for particular events which we have directly or indirectly experienced. By contrast, generic knowledge is the knowledge that we have of concepts, abstracted from such memories. In this section we discuss the relationship between episodic knowledge, memories, and schema theory.

In a sense, our memories are natural side effects of the comprehension process. In comprehension various aspects of the input are associated with a configuration of schemata, and these instantiated schemata constitute our *interpretation* of the input. What gets stored in memory is, in effect, a copy or partial copy of these instantiated schemata, that is, what gets stored is not the input itself but the interpretation that was given to that input as a result of the comprehension process. In fact, these memory traces are probably not complete copies of the originally instantiated schemata, but a more or less complete set of fragments of them. Perhaps such partial information storage results from some incompleteness in the original copying process due to time pressures or some inherent difficulties in the process. Perhaps various aspects of the memory trace decay, or become inaccessible over time. In any event, after some time only fragments of the copies of the originally instantiated schemata remain and we must use these fragments to try to reconstruct the original interpretation and thereby "remember" the input situation. This reconstruction is not, however, unguided, but utilizes schemata to assist in interpreting the fragments, just as comprehension utilizes schemata to assist in interpreting the sensory inputs. There is thus a kind of continuum between understanding and remembering, where in the former we have the imposition of an interpretation primarily on incoming "sensory fragments," and in the latter, we have the imposition of an interpretation primarily on "memorial fragments." In both cases schemata are employed. It should be emphasized that although remembering can be thought of as perceiving with memory as the modality, the episodic memories on which it is usually based are not merely fragments of the initial sensory input, but a fragmentary representation of our interpretation of that input.

Notice that this view of memory yields two sources of "importation" and "distortion" in our recollections. On the one hand, the initial comprehension process involves a "filling out" of the original sensory skeleton — this filling out invariably allows some latitude on the part of the understander. On the other hand, our reconstruction of the original interpretation may very well lead to the imposition of yet a slightly different interpretation. It seems to us that the experiment reported by Spiro (1975) provides support for both of these sorts of processes.

Having already suggested a close relationship between remembering and understanding, we will now introduce another very important connection between them. In our discussion of comprehension, it may have seemed that the entire process required only the generic knowledge captured by schemata. But this cannot be right, for the interpretation of the outside world very often makes demands not only on generic knowledge but also on specific memories. For example, when we hear a sentence, although some of it is *new* and does not require reference to old memories (although it does, of course, require existing schemata if it is to be understood), some of it is presupposed to be *given* and may well require reference to stored memories (see Clark, 1973, for a discussion of the *given-new* distinction in linguistic inputs). Thus, when binding variables, certain variables are bound to aspects of the current situation, other variables are bound to aspects of our memories of a related situation. It is presumably through such bindings that new information becomes interrelated with old in our memories, thus providing a way for memories about particular events to become directly related to one another.

Finally, the fact that our memories are representations of interpreted inputs rather than of inputs themselves has some important consequences for retrieval. Since the particular schemata which will be activated at the time of comprehension depend not only on the input but also on the context, different contexts may give rise to different patterns of schemata available for comprehension even though the input be the same. A second presentation of the input (or part of it) will tend to be helpful as a retrieval cue to the extent that it can be interpreted in the same way as the original. Consequently, changes in the contextual conditions prevailing at retrieval time, compared with those at the time of presentation, may result in a failure to recognize the second presentation as being the same item as the original. For the same reason, fragments of the original presented as retrieval cues may also be relatively ineffective. In this way schema theory accounts for the *encoding specificity* results of Tulving and Thomson (1973) and others.

Making Inferences with Schemata

We have discussed the use of schemata for comprehension, storage, and retrieval of input information. In addition to these, schemata serve an important function as powerful devices for making inferences.

Perhaps the most obvious way schemata serve to make inferences is as predictors of as yet unobserved input. Upon finding a schema which gives a good account for an input situation, we can infer likely aspects of the situation which we have not observed. Thus, if someone tells us that he went to a restaurant for dinner, we can *infer* that he was probably given a menu, gave his order to the waitress, and paid for the meal after eating. We can make such inferences because the RESTAURANT schema has things like *dining* (see Schank & Abelson, 1975, for the specification of a RESTAURANT DINING schema) as subschemata. The activation of such subschemata and their constituents serves as a vehicle for such inferences. Related to this is another inferential process that we have already discussed, namely, inferring the existence of a whole from the observation of a part. Thus, for example, if we see an eye, we can often infer the existence of a face. This inference is involved in the natural course of comprehending an input, and comes about by the activation of dominating schemata by their subschemata. A third kind of inference already discussed involves filling unspecified variables. The variable constraints along with our knowledge of particular cases allow us to make rather good guesses about unspecified variables by assigning typical default values. Thus, in our *break* example, we make a guess about the sort of action that was involved in breaking the bubble without actually having been told.

In addition to these sorts of inferences which naturally occur during comprehension, schemata are useful for what Collins, Warnock, Aiello, and Miller

(1975) call *functional reasoning*. Consider Sentence (7b), which answers the question (7a) cited by Collins *et al.* as an example of functional reasoning:

(7a) Is the Chaco the cattle country? I know the cattle country is down there.

(7b) I think it's more sheep country. It's like western Texas, so in some sense I guess it's cattle country.

To account for Sentence (7b) we can postulate a schema for "producing farm goods" (a not unreasonable assumption for students of geography). There are presumably many climatic variables such as temperature, rainfall, and vegetation which determine what agricultural products can be produced. The answer to Question (7a) can be generated if one assumes that first the climatic variables of the schema are fixed by being bound by their values for Chaco. A search can then be initiated for a related schema or memory in which the variables in question have the same or comparable values. If such a search successfully reveals a candidate, one can check to see if "cattle" is a value of its *agricultural products* variable. In the case of Sentence (7b) the person answering presumably determined that since Western Texas matched on values of climatic variables and that cattle were raised there, indeed they might well raise cattle in the Chaco. Collins and his colleagues give a number of similar examples which illustrate the same reasoning process. It appears, then, that a typical reasoning strategy is to fill certain variables of a schema and then search for cases which match those variables and assume that the unspecified variable has the same value as the instance we found. This is exactly the same process that we discussed for filling unspecified variables by consulting episodic memory. Apparently, this process can be applied as a general reasoning strategy.

Functional reasoning is a kind of analogical inference. Schemata seem to play an important part in explicit analogical reasoning. Consider the following analogy problem:

(8) Neil Armstrong is to the moon as Christopher Columbus was to what?

A schema-based system would have to first find an instantiated schema, or memory in which there were at least two variables, one bound by "Neil Armstrong," the other bound by "the moon." It would then substitute "Christopher Columbus" for "Neil Armstrong," replace "the moon" by a free variable, x, and search memory for another instantiated schema which matched on all (or most) other variables (not values). At that point, it would permit as a response the value of the variable, x. In case this procedure failed to find a match, a new schema relating "Neil Armstrong" to "the moon" can be found and the process repeated. Presumably, we would eventually find that Neil Armstrong led an exploratory expedition to the moon and that Christopher Columbus led an exploratory expedition to America. Thus, we could produce the answer "America."

In addition to the particular inferential procedures such as those just described, there are also much more abstract *reasoning schemata* which will allow conclusions to be drawn from premises. In many cases, such schemata will be general statements of the kinds of rules frequently found in logic textbooks. Like other schemata, they may contain variables which get bound when the schemata are utilized; and like still other schemata, they can vary in their level of abstractness. Thus, while there is probably a general-purpose TRANSITIVITY schema with complicated variable constraints, there may also be more specific ones in which the *relation* variable is fixed. Thus, for example, if the *relation* variable in the transitivity schema is fixed for "physical cause" we would get the special-purpose CAUSAL TRANSITIVITY schema below:

Causal Transitivity (event E_1, event E_2, event E_3).

1. If E_1 causes E_2 and E_2 causes E_3, then certainly E_1 causes E_3.

The use of such a schema would be identical to that of schemata in general. It would be activated at appropriate times (see the section on processing principles for a more detailed discussion of activation of schemata) and once activated, available candidates for binding the variables would be sought. Thus, the reasoning strategies which people normally employ can readily be incorporated into a schematic representation of knowledge such as the one we propose. These principles may not only include, but may also transcend, the "laws of thought" which are described in textbooks. Finally, at a more general level, it is interesting to note that one can regard the entire comprehension process in schema theory as itself being a case of analogical reasoning. When we determine that a situation fits a certain schema we are in a sense determining that the current situation is analogous to those situations from which the schema was originally derived. Moreover, when we make inferences about unobserved aspects of the situations we are, in effect, assuming their existence *by analogy* from the situations from which the schemata were derived.

Schemata and the Structure of Actions

At the end of the section on the characteristics of schemata we indicated that schemata can also constitute the underlying knowledge used to perform actions. We turn now to a more detailed examination of this idea.[4]

---

[4] The application of schemata to actions is not new. Bartlett (1932) suggested that we have motor schemata for such activities as playing tennis. Much more recently, Schmidt (1975) has proposed a schema theory of motor skill learning which further develops Bartlett's notions. Many of the particular ideas discussed in this section derive from those

Most people know how to toss an object from one hand to another. The problem that concerns us is how to represent that knowledge. How do we characterize a TRANSFER schema that organizes and coordinates the set of actions involved? The schema below could serve this purpose. Like all other schemata, it has variables and subschemata:

TRANSFER (object O, from hand H_i, to hand H_f, at time T).

1. TOSS O from H_i to location (H_f) at T.
2. CATCH O with H_f at $T + \delta T$.

H_i is taken to be the initial hand which holds the object (O) at the outset (time T) and H_f is the hand which finally holds the object as a result of the transfer. In this case, then, TRANSFER is assumed to have four variables and two embedded subschemata — TOSS and CATCH. TOSS and CATCH themselves are of course complex schemtata with variables, and they are, in turn, represented by a configuration of subschemata. Thus, for example, CATCH may have roughly the following internal structure:

CATCH (object O, with hand H).

1. POSITION H at INTERCEPTION-POINT (of O with H).
2. When O contacts H, GRASP O with H.

The invocation of the CATCH schema will result in the activation of something we might call the TRAJECTORY schema. (by way of the interception-point schema). The TRAJECTORY schema will enable the values of some of its variables to be fed back to the CATCH schema. This, in turn, would allow the POSITION SCHEMA to move the hand closer to the interception point. Ultimately, the fine tuning which takes place is probably best regarded as being under the control of a negative-feedback system with the perceived disparity between the hand position and the object's position being successively reduced (Petrie, 1974; Powers, 1973).

Of course, the TRANSFER schema can itself serve as a constituent of more abstract action schemata. Consider, for example, the case in which we have an object in each hand and want to EXCHANGE the objects by tossing each to the other hand:

EXCHANGE (object O_1, with object O_2, from hand H_i, to hand H_f, at time T).

1. TRANSFER O_1 from H_i to H_f at T.
2. TRANSFER O_2 from H_f to H_i at APEX (O_1).

---

discussed by D. A. Norman, Ross Bott, and other members of the LNR Research Group at the University of California, San Diego, during a number of research meetings in the fall of 1975.

The APEX schema enables the determination of a region within which the object is at its highest point. Clearly, some kind of distribution of positions will have to be represented, although the coordination of transfers does not depend upon an object being exactly at the highest point. The initiation of step 2 in the EXCHANGE schema could thus vary within limits. An interesting feature of the APEX schema is its subtle blend of cognitive and motor aspects; it involves understanding or interpreting perceptual inputs and perceptual tracking. We doubt that any sharp separation of action schemata from those we have discussed already as means for interpreting inputs can usefully be made.

Directly or indirectly, the action schemata we have just described all find their place as subschemata within a yet more complex schema, namely, juggling by the cascade method. Assuming that of the three objects, two (O_1 and O_2) start off in the right hand (H_r) while the third (O_3) starts in the left (H_L) we have a JUGGLE schema as follows:

JUGGLE (object O_1, object O_2, object O_3, at time T).

1. EXCHANGE O_1 with O_3 from H_r to H_L at T.
2. JUGGLE O_2, O_3, O_1 at APEX (O_3).

Juggling is thus represented recursively as invoking first an EXCHANGE of two objects and then, as EXCHANGE is being completed, reinvoking the JUGGLE schema, which in turn initiates a new EXCHANGE, and so on.

With these examples we have tried to show that knowledge underlying the performance of actions can be represented in the same way as knowledge underlying comprehension. For clarity of exposition, we can distinguish between these two kinds of knowledge as being based on action schemata and comprehension schemata. At the same time it should be emphasized that these schemata are almost always highly interdependent. The coordination of many actions requires an interpretation of perceptual cues which are often selected because activated comprehension schemata are purposefully "looking for" variables relevant to the action in question. The interdependence of action and comprehension schemata in the other direction was discussed when we dealt with the TRY schema which has an action schema as a constituent.

Schemata appear to handle the representation of actions and action sequences rather naturally because the basic characteristics of schemata map conveniently onto some of the crucial characteristics of actions. In the first place, the existence of *variables* in action schemata permit the flexibility required for the performance of actions. Thus, when we shoot a basketball, we are probably doing so from a position on the floor from which we have never before shot. Nevertheless, we make some estimate of the distance and angle (both variables in a schema for shooting basketballs) and thus determine how forcefully and in what direction the shooting should be initiated. Secondly, the *embedding* of action schemata within one another also captures some important intuitions about actions, in particular, the fact that they have constituent structures. Thus, although juggling is a single action, it does have complex subactions as constituents. Papert (personal communication) reports that people learn to juggle faster if the subactions corresponding to our TRANSFER and EXCHANGE schemata are mastered first. This suggests that these subschemata are *real* constituents of juggling in spite of the apparent unity of the actions for skilled jugglers. Finally, the existence of action schemata at *all levels of abstraction* in principle allows us to account for the relations between *plans* (very abstract action schemata) and the execution of those plans, even down to the smallest finger twitches.

SCHEMA ACQUISITION AND MODIFICATION

For the most part, our discussion to this point has taken schemata as givens, cognitive tools that exist from the start. We have postulated no mechanisms whereby new schemata can grow and old ones evolve. Indeed, this is a central problem for schema theories and very little work has been done on it. Nevertheless, the nature of schemata suggests a number of plausible mechanisms whereby new schemata can be produced. In this section we will concentrate on two such mechanisms, specialization and generalization, both of which can be regarded as kinds of learning.

Schema Specialization

Schema specialization occurs when one or more variables in a schema are fixed to form a less abstract schema. The BREAK schema discussed earlier and illustrated in Fig. 2 will serve as an example. It would be quite possible, for instance, to fix the *object* variable, *Y*, to "bubble." Since, as was mentioned in the discussion on variables, the variable constraints interact, fixing the *object* variable to "bubble" would have repercussions for the constraints associated with other variables, such as the *method* variable. Thus, the original BREAK schema could be specialized to produce a new BREAK BUBBLE schema, or a BREAK WINDOW schema, and so on. Similarly, the abstract problem-solving schema that was used in the interpretation of the sentences about Mary and the ice cream, Sentences (4a)–(4c), could be specialized to produce a BUY ICE CREAM FROM AN ICE-CREAM MAN schema. Notice that there are no constraints on the complexity of our ordinary language descriptions of schemata. The concepts which schemata represent are not restricted to concepts for which there are simple lexical items in the language.

The fact that schema specialization can occur tells us nothing about the circumstances under which it does occur. Presumably the criteria for schema specialization are frequency and utility. If a schema is frequently used with the same values assigned to some of its variables then the generation of a more specialized schema with those values fixed may occur. At the same time, some schemata may be so general that their utilization involves a great deal of work and leaves a great deal of uncertainty as to the probability of default assignments fitting. Since schema specialization constrains the default assignments and reduces the amount of work to be done, its use may be more effective. Thus, in the ice-cream example, a good deal of processing was required to determine that the problem-solving schema should be invoked and exactly how the variables within the subschemata should be bound together. Were we to construct a more specific schema much of this processing could be bypassed.

Consider another more extreme example of the usefulness of this specialization process. Suppose we have a schema for a *thing* or physical object. Suppose that among its variables were, its name, and a list of its properties. If it turned out that a significant number of those properties correlated highly with the "name" of the concept it may well be useful to build a specialized schema for that subset of *things* which went by that particular name. It might well be that the prior existence of a number of such abstract schemata coupled with the machinery for specializing these schemata might be enough to account for all of our schemata. A final example of the potential role of schema specialization in learning comes from the learning of motor skills and the operation of action schemata. Consider what happens when we learn, say, how to throw a dart at a bullseye. At first we invoke a rather general THROW schema and attempt to determine the proper variable values for throwing particular kinds of darts particular distances. The THROW schema is very general, but there are many variables to set and our ability to set these properly may not be great. However, once we have thrown a particular dart several times we become increasingly better at determining the proper angle, amount of force, etc., for throwing it. It would thus make sense that we might well build these values into a THROW DART schema which could later be called upon when we again want to throw darts. The tremendous savings on relearning motor skills would appear to support such a view.

A final point should be made about specialization and that concerns the question of the storage/processing tradeoff. One of the virtues of relatively general schemata is that they are able to assist in the comprehension of a diverse array of inputs. Specific schemata, on the other hand, provide a faster, more detailed interpretation of a smaller range of inputs. If we allow the generation of too many specialized schemata, the differences between them may not be sufficient to enable the correct ones to be isolated. Consequently the processing saved in comprehension may be taken up in selection, and little would be gained. In general, the more structures there are in memory, the greater are the storage demands and processing time for selection. For this reason, the production of specialized schemata has to be limited to cases where a reasonable payoff can be expected.

Schema Generalization

Schema generalization is, of course, exactly the converse of specialization. That is, some fixed portion of an old schema is replaced with a variable to construct a new and more abstract schema. This mode of learning would be especially useful when we have a case in which no schema fits a particular situation exactly, but one schema gives a very close fit to the situation except for one aspect. If we repeatedly encounter such a situation we might very well construct a new schema similar to the old one, but in which the troublesome constant has been replaced by a variable. The variable constraints for this new schema would presumably be determined by the distribution of values we actually observed which forced us to create this new variable.

Again the BREAK schema from Fig. 2 will be useful for illustration. One might decide that an object's being rigid or brittle only represents a subset of particular cases and that the object should have more general characteristics. Suppose that the object were constrained so that it either possessed a natural structure, or that it was normally used to perform some function. Now the required action would be different. It would have to be some action which was capable of destroying the natural structure, or fouling up the normal performance of the object's function. If this were the case, one could view the BREAK schema in Fig. 2 as a particular case of a more general BREAK schema. The virtue of the more abstract schema would be that it could handle other cases of breaking as in Sentences (7) and (8):

(7) John broke the sewing machine.
(8) John broke his promise.

In these cases our original BREAK schema would be inadequate, more so perhaps for Sentence (8) than for Sentence (7). In the case of Sentence (7), we clearly have some notion of destroying the normal function involved in our understanding of it, for a broken sewing machine normally is a machine that no longer functions properly, rather than a physically mutilated, twisted, unrecognizable lump of metal. In the case of Sentence (8), a promise can be viewed as serving a social function of providing a certain kind of commitment or guarantee. The original examples (1), (2), and (3) can also be handled by the more general schema. In the case of Sentences (1) and (2), both concerned with the breaking of a window, the normal function of the window can be regarded as having been fouled, indeed, one might well maintain that the difference between a broken window and a cracked one lies in just this fact. In the case of Sentence (3), the natural, generally convex structure of the bubble, is destroyed. All that would be required for the more general schema to be applied would be knowledge of the natural structure or normal functions in the schemata representing the objects in question.

If the more general BREAK schema we have just sketched can be used to account for a greater range of "breakings" than the more specific one of Fig. 2, the question again arises as to whether and why we need both. Again, the answer is that it depends on whether or not the more specialized BREAK schema is sufficiently useful sufficiently often for it to be stored as a separate schema. The particular distinctions within schemata that an individual has, will depend on their utility for that individual. It would be entirely reasonable to expect a football player to have a special schema for the concept of "breaking a tackle," separated from his general purpose BREAK schema. Such a specialized schema would incorporate a great deal of more specific knowledge and would presumably be used rather frequently.

The GIVE schema shown in Fig. 1 can also be used to illustrate the point. Whereas the most common sense of the word "give" concerns causing something to change possession, when someone "gives you trouble" there does not seem to be any object changing possession at all. Yet, one does end up "having the gift" when someone gives it to you. It would thus appear that the sense of "give" in "giving trouble" is a kind of generalization from a more specific, and probably prior, GIVE schema. Thus, generalized schemata may also constitute a means for interpreting what Gentner (1975) calls "metaphorical extensions."

The importance of generalization of schemata for learning is obvious. Schemata need to be generalized to the extent that they permit the interpretation of the inputs to the system. Thus, a great deal of learning may be dealt with by supposing that when a radically new input is encountered, a schema without variables is constructed. Then, when comparable inputs are encountered, which are sufficiently close to the original schema, a new one is created in which the differences become variables and the consistencies get built into the structure. In the other direction, more general schemata may be acquired as a result of learning, for example, general principles, and such schemata may become more specialized as the range of their application becomes more apparent.

In addition to these two modes of schema formation, there appears to be one other related learning mechanism natural for schema theories. This is related to, but not identical to, the generalization mechanism. Suppose we encounter a situation in which we cannot find a schema which will account for the entire configuration of subschemata we have discovered. In this case, we can store our partial interpretation of the situation, a number of unrelated aspects. If, subsequently, we encounter very similar configurations of schemata for which we again can find no overall schema, we might well build a new schema whose internal structure matches the similar aspects of the configurations and whose variables match the variable portion of these situations. In this way, we can find repeatedly co-occuring configurations of schemata and thereby gain a specification of a new, more abstract schema.

Before leaving our discussion of schema change, it should be noted that it seems reasonable to suppose that not only can new schemata be grown (by the mechanisms outlined above) but old schemata can evolve or be "tuned." Within schema theory as we have developed it here, there are three ways in which this can come about. First, we can get more precise information on the nature of the "distributions" underlying the variable constraints. Everytime we determine that a particular schema gives a good account of a situation we can use the value of its variables to modify the variable constraints and the correlations among the various variable values. Second, we can drop out apparently irrelevant aspects of a schema. If a certain variable is rarely filled from the input situation, it is probably not a very important aspect of the schema and perhaps could be dropped from the specification of the schema. A similar argument would apply for presumed, "fixed properties" of a schema. If such properties simply are rarely or never observed, they cannot be very important aspects of the schema. Finally, old schemata can be tuned by adding new variables or fixed properties that appear to be relevant. If a given schema always differs from the situations for which it is intended to account by a small constant difference, that constant element should be added to the specification of the schema.

A real case in point is that of a five-year-old boy we know who currently believes that a sauna "is a wooden room where a lot of men sit around." Presumably, in the not too distant future, this child, with or without being influenced by the Women's Movement, will relax the constraint on sauna users to include women, and, hopefully will introduce variables for purpose, and for temperature, with a default value like "hot"!

Our discussion of learning has been necessarily vague. Nevertheless, it does appear that there are a number of mechanisms which can operate naturally within schema theory allowing for the natural growth and evolution of a schema system which can carry out the tasks required of it.

PROCESSING PRINCIPLES

It used to be fashionable for a rather sharp distinction to be made between cognitive structures and cognitive processes. More recently, however, emphasis on this distinction has waned for two related reasons. In the first place, models have been developed in which knowledge has been represented procedurally (see Hewitt, 1975; Winograd, 1972)). Second, models have been developed which represent many cognitive processes as structures identical in their characteristics to those used to represent more static knowledge. Our own suggestions for general problem-solving and inference schemata are good examples of this latter development. Yet, it is still the case that some more global processing principles are required in order to account for the availability of the right concepts at the right time. A theory of knowledge representation ought not to ignore this issue. Throughout the course of this paper we have repeatedly used such terms as "activation" and "invocation" which have cropped up at key points in our discussions of almost all aspects of the theory. It is therefore now necessary for us to take a somewhat closer look at them.

The entire memory system contains an enormous number of schemata and memories. At any one time only a few of them are required and no procedure of random search could possibly lead to their efficient discovery. The search for likely candidate schemata must, therefore, be somehow guided, and it must be sensitive to the context, for the "correct" choices often depend on the context in which the processing is occurring. The same input is differentially interpreted by an observer depending on the conditions under which he observes it, what he has just observed, and what he expects to observe. In addition, although expectations are obviously important, unexpected events can be interpreted without going through all possible interpretations first. Thus, what seems to be required is a process which allows for the convergence of information so that information derived directly from the input can be combined with expectations to lead (more or less directly) to plausible candidate schemata.

We believe that schemata have characteristics which readily enable these requirements to be satisfied. The convergence is achieved by the combination of *bottom up* and *top down* processing. Bottom up processing occurs when aspects of the input directly suggest or activate schemata which correspond to them and when these schemata themselves activate or suggest dominating schemata of which they are constituents. In our example of Mary and the ice-cream man, Sentence (4a)–(4c), the occurrence of a word like "hear" (or a cognate) in the input would directly activate the HEAR schema. The HEAR schema may itself activate a dominating schema like one for "becoming aware" and this being an event would suggest the problem-solving schema. In general, we want to say that schemata activated by their own constituents are activated from the bottom up, so that bottom up processing is the activation of dominating schemata. Top down processing, on the other hand, arises from schemata activating their constituent subschemata. In our ice-cream example, the activation of the SELL schema by the ICE-CREAM MAN schema is a case in point, as is the activation of the TRY schema by the general problem-solving schema. These processes are called "top down" because they lead from conceptual expectations towards the data in the input where the satisfaction of these expectations might be found. In fact, such processes need not go all the way back to the input since they can meet with the bottom up processing. Bobrow and Norman (1975) call this latter type of processing *conceptually driven,* since it is ultimately concepts which generate a search for particular constituents which they suggest. They contrast this with *data driven* processing in which it is ultimately the input data which generates suggestions for particular concepts.

It may be helpful to think of these processing issues in terms of a computer-programming metaphor, for one can think of a schema as being a kind of *procedure.* Procedures have *subroutines* and one can think of the activation of a schema as being like the invocation of a procedure. The variables of a schema are thus analogous to the variables of a procedure while the subschemata are analogous to the subroutines which may be invoked from within it. The activation of subschemata within a schema is like the calling-up or invocation of the subroutines within a procedure. This is the paradigm case of conceptually-driven processing. However, unlike ordinary procedure calls, in which the flow of control is only from procedure to subroutine, the flow of control in a schema system operates both ways. It is as though a given procedure not only could invoke its own subroutines (conceptually driven processing), but also could invoke those procedures in which it was itself a subroutine (data driven processing). Finally, one must imagine these procedures as operating simultaneously.

If the combination of data driven and conceptually driven processing exhausted the processing mechanism, we would have a serious problem on our hands. For, were this to be the case, there would appear to be no way of preventing every schema in memory from becoming activated as soon as one was activated. The solution to this problem lies in the notion of "accounting for the input" which was discussed in the section on comprehension. In the normal course of processing, some schemata will find more evidence for themselves than will others, and in general, these will be schemata which are suggested from a number of different sources. It is upon these that processing will focus. "Finding good evidence" happens in a number of ways. First, a schema needs to find good bindings for its variables. Thus, if the GIVE schema is invoked there should be candidates for the giver, the recipient, and the gift. Second, a schema should find some evidence for its subschemata, so that for the GIVE schema there should be some evidence to suggest that a recipient did indeed GET the gift and perhaps that it did not happen by chance. Third, it should be possible to find a dominating schema which to some extent offers a good fit. Those schemata which fail to find such evidence cease processing and are deactivated so that the dominating schemata in which they occur can use the failure-to-fit information toward the assessment for their own goodness of fit. The details of the evaluation mechanism are beyond the scope of this paper, but a detailed mathematical formulation of it can be found in Rumelhart (1977b).

We mentioned earlier that contextual and situational factors influence the way in which inputs are interpreted. Since schemata are structures which provide interpretations for inputs in all modalities, the simplest way to understand the mechanism whereby such factors affect comprehension is to regard the input as including those factors. For example, consider hearing an utterance of (9) in the rather different situations of a bar and a children's birthday party.

(9) I would like something to drink.

In a bar one is continually seeing and hearing things connected with bars and one thus anticipates that many bar-related schemata will be activated, unless, that is, one is totally oblivious to one's surroundings. When (9) is encountered in such a situation and it activates a DRINK schema, drinks which can be found within the BAR schema are going to be suggested from more sources than they would at a children's party where they might well not be currently active at all. So, in the context of a bar one would expect to find beer and liquor suggested more strongly and one would expect to find more evidence for them than one might for lemonade and milk which would presumably be more prevalent at the party. Thus, the utterance of Sentence (9) will give rise to different expectations in different situations. More local context effects, such as the influence of what immediately went before, are handled in exactly the same way. To summarize, information (including both the "stimulus" and the context) enters the system and directly suggests certain plausible candidate schemata to account for it. At the same time as this data driven processing is going on, such postulated schemata activate their dominating schemata, which in turn look for other as yet unsuspected aspects of the situation. This conceptually driven processing allows internal contextual constraints to be effective.[5] A schema is said to provide a good account of (aspects of) the input situation when it can find good evidence for itself.

CONCLUSIONS

We claim that the schema theory provides both the concepts and the vocabulary for theorizing about the organization of knowledge. Indeed, the prevalence of schema-related notions in this volume attests to this fact. At the same time, it cannot be denied that the terms we utilize need to be constrained so as to prevent them from being absorbed into all manner of incompatible accounts, and to this end, we have tried to characterize the concepts to which they correspond in greater detail. A schema theory cannot be expected to completely describe the makeup and machinery of the mind, but as part of it we think it is promising.

The notion of schemata as varying in their abstractness relates rather directly to the findings of Meyer as reported not only in this volume but also in Meyer (1975) and Meyer and McConkie (1973). Meyer's research indicates that an independent objective characterization of the logical structure of a prose passage enables quite specific predictions to be made about the relative memorability of different ideas occurring within it. In particular, higher level ideas, ones which are more dominant in the logical structure, are better remembered than particular details, and, they are better remembered if their order of appearance in the passage is congruent with their priority in the structure. As Meyer herself points

---

[5] It should be noted that variable binding comes about as a result of either or both types of processing. A schema may be actively looking for an (aspect of the) input to bind to one of its variables (conceptually driven) and/or such an input may demand some variable to which it can itself be bound (data driven).

out, these findings tend to support Ausubel's (1963) claims about the importance of having a higher-order structure to which to attach the details. This can be translated very readily into schema theory. In fact, Rumelhart (1975) describes in some detail the structure one might anticipate certain kinds of STORY schemata to have, in particular, children's stories with "morals." Since a STORY schema can be regarded as a partially ordered set of rewrite rules, and since these rules (the STORY grammar) embody the (presumed) logical structure of a class of stories, it would follow with minimal assumptions that less processing would be required to fit a story to a schema when the story corresponded more closely to the schema structure than when it did not and, if understanding is considered to be finding such a fit, one can conclude that it is easier to understand a story whose structure closely matches that of the STORY schema. Arguing from better understanding to better "memory for gist" is not difficult. It can be done on both empirical and theoretical grounds. A story is just a special case of a prose passage and there is no reason to believe that Meyer's findings could not be replicated in the domain of children's stories.

Expressed in terms of schema we could thus come to two conclusions. First, if the binding of variables within a schema is normally assumed to proceed most smoothly from the top down, then providing information in a structured form most closely resembling the structure of the schema which will be required for its interpretation maximizes the likelihood that the interpretation will be appropriate and minimizes the processing required. In such a case, each successive piece of information, as it is assimilated, provides additional support that the interpretation will be appropriate and minimizes the processing required. In such a case, each successive piece of information, as it is assimilated, provides additional support that the interpretation so far achieved is indeed appropriate or "satisfactory." Second, and by parallel argument, one might expect to "unpack" some used schema in recall, and this unpacking will be most efficient if it is done from the top down. In this case, the major structural aspects would appear before the details, which are themselves less predictable as they become more specific.

The implications that schema theories, or indeed any other theories of knowledge organization, have for education must still be regarded as only potential. Awaiting more detailed models, we can nevertheless point to a few general considerations. It is certainly the case that one of the purposes of instruction is to provide the kind of knowledge that will prove useful to a person in processing new information and dealing with novel situations. This goal can be regarded as equivalent to that of producing knowledge structures in which new information can be processed and understood. The provision, therefore, of new knowledge structures which do not have this characteristic is as pointless as is the provision of new information for which no interpretive structure can be found. The purpose of a schema is that of a cognitive template against which new inputs can be matched and in terms of which they can be comprehended. Thus, the role of examples in instruction can be regarded as providing individual cases in which a schema can have its variables bound; well-chosen examples will fully exploit such a schema by showing the nature and bounds of values that its variables can take. The generation of new knowledge structures and demonstrations of the way in which they can be used can thus be regarded as one of the principle goals of instruction. Ortony (1975b) has argued that metaphor is a powerful instructional device. In the current context, one might regard metaphors as aids to selecting an old schema, which with relatively little modification, can be used to produce a new one. One might thus use a "flowing water" schema as the basis for the generation of an "electric current" schema. The former might incorporate knowledge concerning unidirectionality of flow, branching, capacity of the conduit, and so on, all of which would have their analogs in an "electric flow" schema. Good instruction would clarify the metaphor of electricity in wires as water in pipes by specifying which variables stay and which go. What makes it a metaphor, after all, is that some of the new information will not fit into the old schema.

The generation, modification and instantiation of schemata seems to us to characterize both informal learning and formal schooling. There are many ways in which they can occur, ranging from discovery through play, to insight through instruction. In all cases, existing knowledge is utilized in and required for the acquisition of new knowledge. We leave the implications of this for the new born child for the consideration of biologists and philosophers.

ACKNOWLEDGMENTS

The work reported herein was supported in part by Grant NS 07454 from the National Institutes of Health, by Grant NIE-G-74-0007 from the National Institute of Education, and a grant to the second author from the Sloan Foundation.

REFERENCES

Anderson, J. R., & Bower, G. *Human associative memory*. Washington, D.C.: Winston, 1973.

Anderson, R. C., & Ortony, A. On putting apples into bottles – A problem of polysemy. *Cognitive Psychology*, 1975, 7, 167–180.

Ausubel, D. P. *The psychology of meaningful verbal learning: An introduction to school learning*. New York: Grune & Stratton, 1963.

Barclay, J. R., Bransford, J. D., Franks, J. J., McCarrell, N. S., & Nitsch, K. Comprehension and semantic flexibility. *Journal of Verbal Learning and Verbal Behavior*, 1974, 13, 471–481.

Bartlett, F. C. *Remembering*. Cambridge, England: Cambridge University Press, 1932.

Bobrow, D. G., & Norman, D. A. Some principles of memory schemata. In D. G. Bobrow & A. M. Collins (Eds.), *Representation and understanding: Studies in cognitive science*. New York: Academic Press, 1975.

Charniak, E. *Toward a model of children's story comprehension.* Unpublished doctoral dissertation, Massachusetts Institute of Technology, 1972. (Also, MIT Artificial Intelligence Laboratory Tech. Rep. AI-TR, 266, 1972.)

Charniak, E. Organization and inference in a frame-like system of common sense knowledge. In proceedings of *Theoretical issues in natural language processing: An interdisciplinary workshop.* Cambridge, Mass.: Bolt, Beranek, & Newman, Inc., 1975. Pp. 42–51.

Clark, H. H. *Comprehension and the given-new contract.* Paper presented to a conference on "The role of grammar in interdisciplinary linguistic research," University of Bielefeld, Bielefeld, Germany, December 1973.

Collins, A. M., & Quillian, M. R. Retrieval time from semantic memory. *Journal of Verbal Learning and Verbal Behavior,* 1969, 8, 240–247.

Collins, A. M., Warnock, E. H., Aiello, N., & Miller, M. L. Reasoning from incomplete knowledge. In D. G. Bobrow & A. M. Collins (Eds.), *Representation and understanding: Studies in cognitive science.* New York: Academic Press, 1975.

Craik, F. I. M., & Lockhart, R. S. Levels of processing: A framework for memory research. *Journal of Verbal Learning and Verbal Behavior,* 1972, 11, 671–684.

Fillmore, C. The case for case. In E. Bach & R. I. Harms (Eds.), *Universals in linguistic theory.* New York: Holt, Rinehart, & Winston, 1968.

Gentner, D. Evidence for the psychological reality of semantic components: The verbs of possession. In D. A. Norman, D. E. Rumelhart, & the LNR Research Group, *Explorations in cognition.* San Francisco: Freeman, 1975.

Halff, H. M., Ortony, A., & Anderson, R. C. A context-sensitive representation of word meanings. *Memory and Cognition,* in press.

Hewitt, C. Stereotypes as an ACTOR approach towards solving the problem of procedural attachment in FRAME theories. In proceedings of *Theoretical issues in natural language processing: An interdisciplinary workshop.* Cambridge, Mass.: Bolt, Beranek, & Newman, Inc., 1975.

Johnson, M. K., Bransford, J. D., & Solomon, S. K. Memory for tacit implications of sentences. *Journal of Experimental Psychology,* 1973, 98, 203–205.

Kant, E. *Critique of pure reason* (1st ed. 1781, 2nd ed. 1787, translated by N. Kemp Smith). London: Macmillan, 1963.

Kintsch, W. Notes on the structure of semantic memory. In E. Tulving & W. Donaldson (Eds.), *Organization of memory.* New York: Academic Press, 1972.

Labov, W. The boundaries of words and their meanings. In C. J. Bailey & R. Shuy (Eds.), *New ways of analyzing variation in English.* Washington, D.C.: Georgetown University Press, 1973.

Lakoff, G. Hedges: A study in meaning criteria and the logic of fuzzy concepts. *Papers from the Eighth Regional Meeting, Chicago Linguistics Society.* Chicago: University of Chicago Linguistics Department, 1972.

Meyer, B. J. F. *The organization of prose and its effects on memory.* Amsterdam: North-Holland Publ., 1975.

Meyer, B. J. F., & McConkie, G. W. What is recalled after hearing a passage? *Journal of Educational Psychology,* 1973, 65, 109–117.

Minsky, M. A framework for representing knowledge. In P. H. Winston (Ed.), *The psychology of computer vision.* New York: McGraw-Hill, 1975.

Norman, D. A. *Resources and schemas replace stages of processing.* Paper presented at the Sixteenth Annual Meeting, The Psychonomic Society, Denver, Colorado, November 1975.

Norman, D. A., Rumelhart, D. E., & the LNR Research Group. *Explorations in cognition.* San Francisco: Freeman, 1975.

Ortony, A. How episodic is semantic memory? In proceedings of *Theoretical issues in natural language processing: An interdisciplinary workshop.* Cambridge, Mass.: Bolt Beranek & Newman, Inc., 1975. (a)

Ortony, A. Why metaphors are necessary and not just nice. *Educational Theory,* 1975, **25**, 45–53. (b)

Palmer, S. E. Visual perception and world knowledge: Notes on a model of sensory-cognitive interaction. In D. A. Norman, D. E. Rumelhart, & the LNR Research Group, *Explorations in cognition.* San Francisco: Freeman, 1975.

Petrie, H. G. Action, perception and education. *Educational Theory,* 1974, **24**, 33–45.

Polanyi, M. *Personal knowledge.* Chicago: University of Chicago Press, 1958.

Polanyi, M. *The tacit dimension.* New York: Doubleday, 1966.

Powers, W. T. *Behavior: The control of perception.* Chicago: Aldine, 1973.

Quillian, M. R. Semantic memory. In M. Minsky (Ed.), *Semantic information processing.* Cambridge, Mass.: M.I.T. Press, 1968.

Rips, L. J., Shoben, E. J., & Smith, E. E. Semantic distance and the verification of semantic relations. *Journal of Verbal Learning and Verbal Behavior,* 1973, **12**, 1–20.

Rosch, E. H. On the internal structure of perceptual and semantic categories. In T. E. Moore (Ed.), *Cognitive development and the acquisition of language.* New York: Academic Press, 1973.

Rumelhart, D. E. Notes on a schema for stories. In D. G. Bobrow & A. M. Collins (Eds.), *Representation and understanding: Studies in cognitive science.* New York: Academic Press, 1975.

Rumelhart, D. E. Understanding and summarizing brief stories. In D. LaBerge & S. J. Samuels (Eds.), *Basic processes in reading: Perception and comprehension.* Hillsdale, N.J.: Lawrence Erlbaum Associates, 1977. (a)

Rumelhart, D. E. Toward an interactive model of reading. In S. Dornic (Ed.), *Attention and performance, VI.* Hillsdale, N.J.: Lawrence Erlbaum Associates, 1977. (b)

Rumelhart, D. E., & Levin, J. A. A language comprehension system. In D. A. Norman, D. E. Rumelhart, & the LNR Research Group, *Explorations in cognition.* San Francisco: Freeman, 1975.

Rumelhart, D. E., Lindsay, P. H., & Norman, D. A. A process model for long-term memory. In E. Tulving & W. Donaldson (Eds.), *Organization of memory.* New York: Academic Press, 1972.

Schank, R. C. Conceptual dependency: A theory of natural language understanding. *Cognitive Psychology,* 1972, **3**, 552–631.

Schank, R. C., & the Yale A. I. Project. *SAM – A story understander* (Res. Rep. 43). New Haven, Connecticut: Yale University, Department of Computer Science, August 1975.

Schank, R. C., & Abelson, R. P. Scripts, plans and knowledge. In *Advance Papers of the Fourth International Joint Conference on Artificial Intelligence.* Tbilisi, Georgia, USSR, 1975. Pp. 151–157.

Schmidt, R. A. A schema theory of discrete motor skill learning. *Psychological Review,* 1975, **82**, 225–260.

Spiro, R. J. *Inferential reconstruction in memory for connected discourse* (Tech. Rep. No. 2). Urbana, Ill.: Laboratory for Cognitive Studies in Education, University of Illinois, 1975.

Tulving, E. Episodic and semantic memory. In E. Tulving & W. Donaldson (Eds.), *Organization of memory.* New York: Academic Press, 1972.

Tulving, E., & Thomson, D. M. Encoding specificity and retrieval processes in episodic memory. *Psychological Review,* 1973, **80**, 352–373.

Walker, J. H. Real-world variability, reasonableness judgments, and memory representations for concepts. *Journal of Verbal Learning and Verbal Behavior,* 1975, **14**, 241–252.

Winograd, T. *Understanding natural language.* Edinburgh: Edinburgh University Press, 1972.

Winograd, T. Frame representations and the declarative-procedural controversy. In D. G. Bobrow & A. M. Collins (Eds.), *Representation and understanding: Studies in cognitive science.* New York: Academic Press, 1975.

5

Remembering Information from Text: The "State of Schema" Approach

Rand J. Spiro

University of Illinois at Urbana-Champaign

The initial concern in this contribution is with the issue of accuracy in recall of connected discourse. It is very important to note that the accuracy referred to is not verbatim or even gist reproduction, but the absence of gross semantic distortions and importations of ideas possibly not even consistent with or inferrable from the original text's semantic representation. The question of accuracy in discourse recall has played a central role historically in distinguishing between competing theoretical orientations for explaining the nature of memorial functioning. Bartlett (1932), based on his finding of pervasive gross inaccuracy in recall of stories, concluded that discourse recall is a constructive process. Cognitive structures (schemata) are cumulative, holistic, assimilative blends of information. Recall is more than mere passive reproduction of stored memories since the memories no longer exist in their original form. Particular to-be-remembered information must be isolated from other assimilated information in relevant schemata by some vague inferential process of "turning round upon one's schemata."

Following Bartlett's lead, other researchers have made accuracy in discourse recall the crucible for theory verification. Typical of this approach is the work of Gomulicki (1956), who failed to replicate Bartlett's finding of pervasive inaccuracy. Reproductions resembled summaries or abstracts of the stories (in fact, subjects were unable to distinguish between generated abstracts and recall protocols). The accuracy in recall led Gomulicki to reject the active reconstruction theory in favor of an "abstractive-trace retrieval" theory. The to-be-remembered information has a particular identity immune from assimilative effects of other knowledge and subsequently encountered relevant information.[1]

---

[1] A considerable body of research is accumulating on the topic of "construction", deriving from the seminal paper by Bransford, Barclay, and Franks (1972). Examples include research by Barclay (1973), Frederiksen (1975b), and Honeck (1973). These experiments

Recall is a matter of passive retrieval of stored traces, with selectivity of omissions a function of structural importance in the abstract.

The abstractive-trace retrieval theory apparently receives support from the common finding of freezing effects (Kay, 1955) in discourse: in repeated reproductions (even with reinstatement of the original) the initial reproduction acts as a fixed model with little deviation other than omissions (e.g., Bartlett, 1932; Howe, 1970; Spencer, 1973). Further apparent support obviously is provided from the many studies that have replicated Gomulicki's finding of pervasive accuracy in recall, for example, Johnson (1970), Meyer (1974), Meyer and McConkie (1973), and Spencer (1973).

The lack of any studies replicating the kind of inaccuracy Bartlett found has led theorists to reject the reconstruction hypothesis. For example, after examining the available evidence, Bartlett's student Zangwill (1972) concluded that the emphasis in memory research and theory must be on reproduction rather than reconstruction, and that Bartlett's theory, "in my view never very plausible, is best forgotten" (p. 127). Zangwill's conclusion is implicitly accepted by those who attempt to account for discourse recall solely in terms of structural relations internal to the discourse, for example, Johnson's (1970) structural importance and the hierarchy depth concept of Meyer and McConkie (1973). The latter two approaches are typical of the modus operandi in contemporary research on memory for connected discourse (e.g., Crothers, 1972; Kintsch, 1974). The factors that perpetuate these approaches will be discussed later.

There is, however, an ubiquitous fallacy underlying the relation between data and theory in all of the research discussed above. The fallacy is the assumption that recall accuracy has anything at all to do with distinguishing between active reconstructive theory and passive abstractive-trace retrieval theory. The fallacy results from a basic misunderstanding shared by all researchers in the area, including Bartlett, and attributable to the vague and nonoperational quality of initial statements of the reconstruction hypothesis, of what is and is not entailed by what in this paper will be referred to as *reconstructive theory*.

Reconstructive theory must allow for accurate recall, examples of which are certainly plentiful in everyday life. The conditions under which recall should be inaccurate are specifiable on an a priori basis in reconstructive theory. One can then reexamine the experimental literature to determine whether conditions for inaccuracy were present or not in a given study. Accuracy per se is irrelevant. Evidence against reconstructive theory would be provided only by accuracy in conditions where the theory would predict inaccuracy. It will be argued that

---

demonstrate that inferential elaboration is a necessary part of *language comprehension*, that "meaning" is constructed (as compared to an "interpretive" approach to semantics). Gomulicki allowed for that possibility. This research does not, however, have any implications for the reconstruction hypothesis in *recall*.

none of the studies supportive of abstractive-trace retrieval theory meet the requirements for a critical test of Reconstructive Theory.

Given the assumption of assimilative schemata with chronologically recent additions exercising some form of schema dominance (see Bartlett, 1932, for the arguments in support of this assumption), conditions for inaccurate recall become evident. First, the likelihood of inaccuracy increases with the degree of interaction with pre-existing cognitive structures. The more one relates discourse to prior knowledge, the greater the assimilation into those structures with the resultant loss of particular identity of the discourse. The boundaries between the to-be-remembered information and the prior knowledge become increasingly fuzzy over time (see the discussion of the nature of the assimilative process in the second part of this paper). It is certainly true that a discourse can be treated as irrelevant to preexisting knowledge structures and intentionally kept distinct from them (for example, if the discourse is perceived to be fictional and with no future usefulness). If such is the case, reconstruction is straightforward since falliable inferential processes for disentangling the information in the discourse from other information it may have been assimilated with would not be required. Essentially, the information to be recalled would comprise a self-contained schema.

Second, and more important, schemata to which the information in the discourse has been related must be modified by subsequently encountered information, leading to the loss of dominance resulting from chronological recency for the information in the discourse. When this occurs, it is possible that current schematic states at recall will differ from the preassimilation states at the time of comprehension. If such is the case, the past schematic states must be inferred from the current states; remembering will then be a reconstruction based on what is stored rather than reproduction of what is stored. Depending on the nature of the change in the schematic states, the personal rules of inferential reconstruction will lead to either accurate recall or inaccurate recall (as, for example, when the two schematic states are psychologically contradictory). The inaccuracy resulting from faulty inferences based on schematic states at recall will be referred to as reconstructive errors.

If the first condition (cognitive interaction) is present but the second one (subsequent schema modification) is not, reconstructive theory would predict an increase in inferential elaboration at comprehension with no evidence in recall of localized reconstructive errors (the distinction between construction and reconstruction again; see Footnote 1). Frederiksen's (1975a,b) data may be interpreted as support for this contention.[2] It must be repeated once again, however,

[2] In Frederiksen (1975a,b), more inferences were made in a problem-solving condition than in a memory condition. The frequency of inferences did not decrease with repeated reinstatements of the original, suggesting that the inferences are made at comprehension rather than being fabrications at recall to fill gaps. Since there is no systematic subsequent schema modification, these results are consistent with Reconstructive Theory.

that the level of recall accuracy is not a necessary indicator of the existence of reconstructive processing in remembering. Accuracy can be the result of either the differentiation of information in the discourse from cognitive structures or the absence of schema modification, rather than being *general* support for abstractive-trace retrieval theory. Inaccuracy can be the result of active elaborative processing at comprehension or merely bad guessing, with low confidence, to fill gaps in memory, rather than being the high confidence product of a natural and common process of inferential reconstruction which would generate accurate recall in exactly the same way that inaccurate recall was generated.

It is contended here that none of the studies of memory for connected discourse meet the two criteria for a critical test of Reconstructive Theory. Arguments have been advanced elsewhere (Spiro, 1975) in support of the claim that certain characteristics of laboratory experiments conspire to minimize the likelihood of reconstructive error. The demand characteristics of the experimental situation, the nature of the experimental materials, and the isolated context in which discourses are presented all increase the likelihood that the discourses will be maximally differentiated from pre-existing cognitive structures.[3] The primary norm of self-presentation (Kiesler, Collins, & Miller, 1969) is to remember as much as possible. Any awareness by subjects that interaction with cognitive structures could lead to confusion at recall will make such interaction less likely. Furthermore, subjects tend to believe experimenters want "pure" effects, unconfounded by one's idiosyncratic knowledge (Spiro, 1975).

In general, the subject can be expected to assume that the information in the discourse is of no future usefulness. The discourses are typically and clearly fictional. Even if they are perceived as true, their truth and any other considerations regarding the topical content vis-à-vis prior knowledge are irrelevant to the purposes of the experiment. The usefulness of the discourses begins and ends with the experiment. One of the main reasons in everyday life for relating new information to old is negated: selectively processing information in order to update one's knowledge (that is, keeping the knowledge "current") of issues which are personally interesting or important. It would be foolish to update one's knowledge with the useless, isolated, and probably false information usually found in experimental prose. Furthermore, the normal basis for determining importance (for example, personal interests) are inoperative in the

---

[3] Obviously, some interaction with cognitive structures must go on. It is certainly not intended here that knowledge of the language should be separated from knowledge of the world. Such separation is clearly impossible (e.g., Lakoff, 1971). What is contended is that the use of prior knowledge in memory experiments will be lazy, that is, just sufficient for construction of a minimum plausible and consistent semantic representation. Bartlett's (1932) results are interpretable in this context. Since his stories were very bizarre and contained many logical gaps, greater "effort after meaning" was required for formation of even a minimum plausible semantic representation than is the case with less bizarre and more consistent text. Hence, the greater incidence of importations.

experimental situation. All of the information is important for a high recall score. The selectivity effects that are usually found are functions of the internal structural relations of the text. The "important" elements are the ones that tie together the most information, for example, ideas that are superordinate in a hierarchical text parsing (Meyer, 1974; Meyer & McConkie, 1973). If subjects are keeping a discourse isolated from prior knowledge, it is not surprising that the greatest directing force would be exerted by endogenous factors rather than by one's pre-existing knowledge structure.

If one considers the primary sources of extratextual extension, their absence in conventional discourse memory experiments is striking. There is no prior linguistic context, the context of the situation is the experiment itself (which is obviously not related to the topical content of the discourse), ego-involving attitudes are not relevant given the topics usually used (Spiro & Sherif, 1975), and knowledge about the communicator which might effect inferences about intentions and communicative function are also orthogonal to the topical content of the prose. All of these factors tend to enrich a given prose passage, to give it a particular and idiosyncratic "significance" or "aboutness" (Bransford & McCarrell, 1975) or meaning (if one considers psychological meaning to be what something "means" to an individual, that is, the interactive product of the semantic relations in discourse *and* the contextually determined extratextual relatedness). Extratextual extensions of meaning are without basis, unwarranted, and usually impossible in conventional discourse memory experiments (with the exception of those extensions necessary to form a *minimum* plausible semantic representation of discourse which is bizarre, has gaps, etc.; see Footnote 3).

The factors that minimize the extent of relating to preexisting cognitive structures also reduce the likelihood of subsequent modification of relevant schemata, the essential condition for reconstructive errors to occur. Even if one were to inadvertently encounter information related to the topical content of the less esoteric discourses, they would not be related to, or used to update, the isolated representation of the material for the same reasons mentioned above for the *initial* differentiation from other knowledge structures. In any case, it is certainly true that none of the studies which can be taken as support for the abstractive-trace retrieval theory have systematically provided subsequent schema-modifying information which would be predicted to result in reconstructive errors in remembering the original. In other words, none of the aforementioned studies have provided an experimental or manipulative test which would critically distinguish between predictions of abstractive-trace retrieval theory and the reconstructive approach based on altered schematic states outlined in this paper.

The only known research which provides an appropriate test of reconstructive theory with verbal materials is an experiment by this writer (Spiro, 1975).

The subjects read one of two stories dealing with an engaged couple. One aspect of both stories deals with Bob's ardent desire not to have children and his reticence and delay in informing his fiancée, Margie. In one story, he finally tells her and finds that she feels the same about having children as he does, and they are both relieved. The "having children" aspect of this story is grossly representable using a structural balance model (Heider, 1958), and is balanced (see Figure 1a). The other story is exactly the same except for the last few sentences, in which Margie is horrified by what Bob tells her since having children is very important to her. This story ends as a bitter discussion begins (imbalanced story; see Figure 1b).

Some subjects were told they were participating in a memory experiment (Memory condition), the other subjects thought the experiment concerned reactions to situations involving interpersonal relations, and that the story was true and the experimenter knew Bob and Margie personally (Cognitive Interaction condition). Approximately 8 min were spent on administrative tasks (for example, subjects filling out consent forms) following the reading of the story. The experimenter, apparently to kill time while collecting the forms and for no apparent purpose, then casually mentioned either that Bob and Margie did eventually get married and are still happily together, or they never did get married and have not seen each other since the engagement was broken, or nothing was mentioned to the subjects at that time. The Memory subjects were additionally informed that the story was true at this time. The "married" ancillary information can be considered consistent with general expectations likely to have been formed after reading the balanced story, but would be more

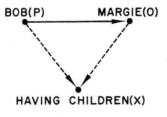
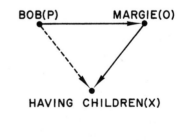

FIG. 1 Structural balance representations of an aspect of the balanced and imbalanced stories.

likely to contradict expectations engendered by the imbalanced story. On the other hand, the "unmarried" ancillary information is consistent for subjects who read the imbalanced story and contradictory for the balanced story.

Subjects returned either two days, three weeks, or six weeks later and were told to recall the story as best they could. The Cognitive Interaction groups were clearly informed that the purpose of the experiment solely involved memory and that they should include in their reproduction only ideas explicitly present in the story they had read on bright yellow paper. They were told *not* to include any personal reactions they may have had or inferences they may have made.

Reconstructive theory predicts that, for subjects in the Cognitive Interaction condition, schemata concerning knowledge of how interpersonal relations usually work will be activated and the information in the story will be related to those schemata. Memory of the story then will be inferentially reconstructed in a predictable way based on three integrated factors, that is, factors having fuzzy or no boundaries or particular identities: accessible elements of the presented story, the ancillary information, and the activated schematic knowledge regarding interpersonal relations.

When either no ancillary information or consistent ancillary information is received by subjects, the reconstructive model would predict basic accuracy in recall. If anything, consistent ancillary information may bolster existent schemata leading to slight errors in the direction of heightening the degree of balance in balanced stories and the degree of imbalance in imbalanced stories.

However, when subjects are presented with contradictory ancillary information (that is, "married" after imbalanced stories or "unmarried" after balanced stories), recall will be problematic. The subject will have to base his recall on schemata which have been modified in a significant way, an overall evaluation of Bob and Margie as having a favorable relationship changed to a state in which the relationship is unfavorable (or vice versa). If reconstruction requires inference about an earlier schematic state *based on* current schematic states, and the current schematic state is inconsistent with the earlier one, then recall should tend to be erroneous in the direction of producing *reconciliation* of the conflicting elements. Thus, errors in recall (for contradictory ancillary information subjects) should lessen the degree of balance (should be imbalancing) for those who read the balanced story, and the errors should lessen the degree of imbalance (should be balancing) for those who read the imbalanced story. For example, the extent of Bob and Margie's disagreement in the imbalanced story might be remembered as less severe than it actually was or even nonexistent.[4]

These predicted errors in recall can be specified a priori. A finite list of balancing and imbalancing error types has been generated (Table 1) using the

---

[4] The point of view offered here is unrelated to the common finding that "meaningfulness" or "depth of processing" facilitates recall. The present arguments relate to the characteristics of recall rather than the level of recall.

three elements and their interrelations in the balance triads of Figure 1. Again, errors of the balancing kind are predicted for the "contradictory" subjects who read the imbalanced story. The errors consist of changes or distortions of interelement relations, adding relations not specified in the original story, or importations of information which explicitly supersedes the presented balance triad. Table 1 also gives examples of the different kinds of errors.

These predicted errors in recall should not be confused with conscious fabrica-

TABLE 1

Predicted Reconstructive Errors: Bob (*P*), Margie (*O*), Having Children (*X*)

Error types	Imbalancing errors (−)	Balancing errors (+)
$P–X, O–X$	Divergence in original valence (e.g., "Bob wanted to have children and Margie didn't," for the balanced story) or in valence at a later time (e.g., "Bob later changed his mind and fought with Margie about having children," for the balanced story)	Convergence in valence with respect to original or subsequent attitude (e.g., "Margie agreed" [or "later changed her mind and agreed"] with Bob about not having children," for the imbalanced story) or intentions (e.g., "Margie decided she would try to have children soon," for the balanced story)
	Change in the feasibility of X toward divergence (e.g., "for some reason they became aware that it was impossible for them to have children, and this fact made them very unhappy")	Change in the feasibility of X toward convergence (e.g., "the problem was resolved when they found out that Margie couldn't have children anyway")
		Divergence in the relative importance of the relations to X (e.g., "they disagreed, but Bob felt very strongly about the issue and for Margie it was not so important") or a lessening in the importance of X for both of them (e.g., "it was not a very important matter to either of them and was therefore easily resolvable")
$P–O$ relative to $P–X, O–X$		Increase in weight (e.g., "their feelings for each other were much more important than how they felt about any issue")

continued

TABLE 1 (continued)

Error types	Imbalancing errors (−)	Balancing errors (+)
P–O	Change in the negative direction, either in the degree of affect (e.g., "Bob began to realize he didn't like Margie as much as he thought he did") or the degree of unity (e.g., "Bob and Margie began to see less and less of each other")	Change in the positive direction (e.g., "Bob's love for Margie grew continually at a rapid rate")
Other situations	Importation of an imbalanced situation, specific or general e.g., "they had many other serious areas of disagreement")	Importation of a balanced situation, specific or general (e.g., "they had the same attitude on almost everything")
Overriding principle	E.g., "the prospect of marriage is not considered as ideal as it once was"	E.g., "everybody argues and it doesn't mean anything"

tion to fill gaps in memory. Rather, the errors are seen as the outcome of a fallible process which is the essential mode of operation in memory. If the errors are conscious fabrications, subjects should be able to detect them, as they did in an experiment by Gauld and Stephenson (1967). In that experiment, the errors probably were just guesses. The conditions of that experiment were such that reconstructive theory would not predict any normal reconstruction-based errors. If, however, the errors in the present experiment are not conscious fabrications, then it should be hard for subjects to detect them as errors. Since the predicted errors are produced by the same process of inferential reconstruction, in the same specific reconstructive act, and based on the same underlying schemata as the correct aspects of recall, the predicted reconstructive errors should be undifferentiable from the correct aspects of recall. The prediction, then, is that subjects' expressed confidence in predicted errors should not be less than their confidence in correct aspects of recall (considering only subjects in "Cognitive interaction—contradictory ancillary information" conditions). Actually, the reconstructive errors have a firmer basis in the underlying schemata (being constructed by the subjects' own rules for organizing the world) than does most of the information in the original passage (which is arbitrarily provided to the subject, rather than being initially generated by the subject). If this is the case, confidence in predicted reconstructive error could increase relative to confidence in correct aspects as the retention interval increases and assimilation proceeds, with the former eventually becoming greater than the latter.

It is hypothesized that schematic assimilation increases with time. Therefore, all of the predicted effects regarding reconstructive errors in recall should increase as delay prior to recall increases. Furthermore, such an interaction would argue against the alternate hypothesis that the reconstructive errors are the retrieved outcomes of inferential processing at comprehension. The fact that the predicted reconstructive errors are not legitimate inferences based on the text alone (and do not occur in the ancillary information conditions other than contradictory) also militates against the latter hypothesis.[5]

It should be noted that the reconstructive approach makes no predictions regarding the quantity of errors that will occur in recall. A single reconstructive error can reconcile the information from the story with contradictory ancillary information. Therefore, number of recall errors was not used as a criterion variable in the main data analysis.

On the other hand, when subjects read the stories in the context of a conventional memory experiment, the arguments of Reconstructive Theory lead to the expectation that representation of the stories will be maximally differentiated from preexisting schemata (thereby lessening the activation and participation of prior knowledge regarding interpersonal relations) and protected from assimilation with the ancillary information. The prediction, therefore, is that recall under memory conditions will be basically accurate. In particular, the reconstructive errors predicted for the Cognitive Interaction-Contradictory condition should not occur in the Memory-Contradictory condition.

All of the predictions of reconstructive theory were conclusively demonstrated at high levels of statistical significance. For details of the scoring procedures, see Spiro (1975). To illustrate the results obtained, Table 2 presents the data for mean constructive error scores (ranging from +1 to +5 for predicted balancing errors and from −1 to −5 for predicted imbalancing errors; higher absolute values indicate grosser inaccuracies; each subject receives one score). In Table 3 the data is viewed as a function of the absolute value of the reconstructive error scores (in case the results in Table 2 are attributable to a greater likelihood of balancing and imbalancing errors cancelling each other out). The confidence that aspects of recall protocols were *explicitly* expressed in the original story (with inferences to be assigned low ratings) are reported in Table 4 (a nine-point scale is used) for correct aspects and predicted reconstructive errors with absolute

---

[5] Reconstructive Theory does not contend that reconstructive errors can not have their genesis at the time of ancillary information presentation (Figure 2 explicitly allows for this possibility). However, it seems likely that the form and force of the errors change over time as assimilation proceeds. When the ancillary information is presented, there is no basis for the errors to be any more than speculations, "It may be that X" (if X first appears at that time at all). Only later can the errors change, as they do, to the assertion of "X." Furthermore, the distinction between reconstruction of what was said (or thought) and where it was said should be kept in mind. In the case of the latter, it is unlikely the question would ever occur to a subject until the time of recall. In any case, the main issue is whether the initial representation of text maintains a particular identity immune from the assimilative effects of subsequently encountered information and thoughts.

TABLE 2

Mean Constructive Error Scores as a Function of Type of Instructions, Delay, Type of Story, and Type of Ancillary Information[a]

Instruction	Story	Delay								
		2 days			3 weeks			6 weeks		
		Ancillary information								
		None	Consistent	Contradictory	None	Consistent	Contradictory	None	Consistent	Contradictory
Cognitive interaction	Balanced	.1	-.2	-1.4	.0	.9	-3.1	.3	.7	-3.2
	Imbalanced	.2	-.4	1.0	.5	-.3	3.5	.6	.2	2.9
Memory	Balanced	.3	.6	-.2	.2	.2	.6	.0	.9	-.3
	Imbalanced	.1	.4	-.2	.6	.1	-.4	.4	.2	.1

[2] Scores vary from
[a]Scores vary from −5 to +5.

TABLE 3

Means for the Absolute Values of Constructive Error Scores as a Function of Type of Instructions, Delay, Type of Story, and Type of Ancillary Information[a]

Instruction	Story	2 days			3 weeks			6 weeks		
		None	Consistent	Contradictory	None	Consistent	Contradictory	None	Consistent	Contradictory
Cognitive interaction	Balanced	.5	.4	1.4	.8	1.3	3.1	1.1	1.3	3.6
	Imbalanced	.6	.8	1.4	1.5	.7	3.5	1.6	1.4	2.9
Memory	Balanced	.3	.8	.4	.4	1.0	.8	.8	1.1	.5
	Imbalanced	.3	.4	.4	1.4	.7	1.0	.4	.8	1.1

(Column groups "2 days", "3 weeks", "6 weeks" fall under the spanning header "Delay"; the None/Consistent/Contradictory sub-columns fall under "Ancillary information".)

[a]Scores vary from 0 to 5.

TABLE 4

Average Rated Confidence in Correct Aspects of Recall Relative to Rated Confidence in Constructive Errors with Scores of Absolute Value Greater Than Three[a]

	Delay					
	Type of recall					
	2 days		3 weeks		6 weeks	
Condition	Correct	Constructive error	Correct	Constructive error	Correct	Constructive error
Cognitive interaction: contradictory	8.08 (4)	7.58	6.80 (13)	7.39	6.57 (12)	7.42
Cognitive interaction: "none" or consistent	– (0)	–	7.18 (4)	6.63	6.42 (6)	6.17
All delay intervals						
Memory: contradictory	7.50 (3)	4.67				
Memory: "none" or consistent	7.93 (4)	3.00				
Memory: all ancillary conditions	7.74 (7)	3.71				

[a] Numbers in parentheses indicate the number of subjects on which the means are based.

values greater than three. The stringent criterion means a conservative test of the reconstruction hypothesis in relation to the conscious fabrication alternative; since the latter would predict grosser errors, it should be most detectable. condition include the following:

"Balancing" errors by subjects reading the imbalanced story:

___ they separated but realized after discussing the matter that their love mattered more.

___ they underwent counseling to correct the major discrepancy.

___ they discussed it and decided they could agree on a compromise: adoption.

___ she was only a little upset at the disagreement.

"Imbalancing" errors made by subjects reading the balanced story:

___ they had had a severe disagreement about having children at some time prior to their agreeing.

___ there was a hassle with one or the other's parents.

___ they *disagreed* about having children.

___ they at no time discussed their attitudes about having children with each other out of fear of rejection and this led them to separate.

These errors are gross distortions of the actual story. They occur only when reconstructive theory predicts they should occur.

ISSUES IN THE INVESTIGATION OF PROCESSES IN RECONSTRUCTIVE MEMORY

Once the pervasive role of inferential reconstruction in memorial functioning is accepted, certain issues not previously of primary concern become prominent. What is stored? Reconstructive processes must operate on some data base. Specification of details of discourse likely to be stored must be interfaced with stored rules for inferential reconstruction. What is the nature of schemata and what principles govern the assimilative process? How is information that is not directly stored generated at recall, and how does prior knowledge exert its directing force? These are questions that this writer believes will become the focus of a large proportion of memory research in the coming years.

The State of Schema Approach

In the following discussion, a framework for investigating these issues is proposed: the State of Schema (SOS) approach. First, the SOS approach is applied for illustrative purposes to the specific case of the previously discussed experiment. The illustration will serve as a context for the development of answers (sometimes quite speculative owing to the highly underdeveloped state of the art) to the questions proposed above. Finally, some suggestions will be offered regarding the general value of the model presented. The order of exposition is somewhat unusual, proceeding from an ad hoc illustrative case, which is highly developed, to a bare outline of more general approaches. This is justified by the perceived face plausibility of the special case and, more important, by the certainty that the issues generated would have to apply to any model of reconstructive processing.

Figure 2 contains an account of the paths to several possible recall outcomes, as well as the functional determinants of path "activation" for subjects in the Cognitive Interaction-Imbalanced-Contradictory condition. It is assumed that an unspecified period of time has elapsed since initial comprehension of the story. An explanation of Figure 2 is in order before discussing the implicated issues.

The building block of the model is the "State of Schema." The SOS is a representation of a subset of the information hypothesized to be stored in a schema (or a set of related schemata). The information can be, among other things, specific details from a story, general impressions or summary statements (for example, expectations regarding state of balance of outcomes), general types of events that have occurred in prototypal situations, and rules for inferential reconstruction. It should be noted that the form of molecular representation (propositional, graphtheoretic, etc.) is irrelevant at this time. In what follows, at first only paths leading to reconstructive errors will be described.

Figure 2 examines SOS(S) (the state of the schema for the imbalanced story) after the story has been comprehended and some time has passed. SOS(S) is by now assimilated ($\Rightarrow$) into the schema relevant to events (rather than rules) regarding interpersonal relations in general $[\text{SOS}(\text{IR}_G - E)]$, giving SOS(S) at time 1 $[\text{SOS}(S_1)]$:

$$\text{SOS(S)} \Rightarrow \text{SOS}(\text{IR}_G - E) = \left\{ \text{SOS(S)}/[\text{SOS}(\text{IR}_G - E]\right\} = \text{SOS}(S_1).$$

The information that might be stored in $\text{SOS}(S_1)$ includes the following:

(1) negative outcome
(2) important issue: having children (weighted)
    (a) disagreement (weighted)
    (b) Bob does not want children
(3) other facts and details from the story (for example, the fact that Bob and Margie are engaged).

The issue "having children" in the context "engaged" is assigned a weight by referring to the "rules" component of $\text{SOS}(\text{IR}_G)$, that is, $\text{SOS}(\text{IR}_G - R)$, probably in combination with an actuarial consultation of $\text{SOS}(\text{IR}_G - E)$ (to

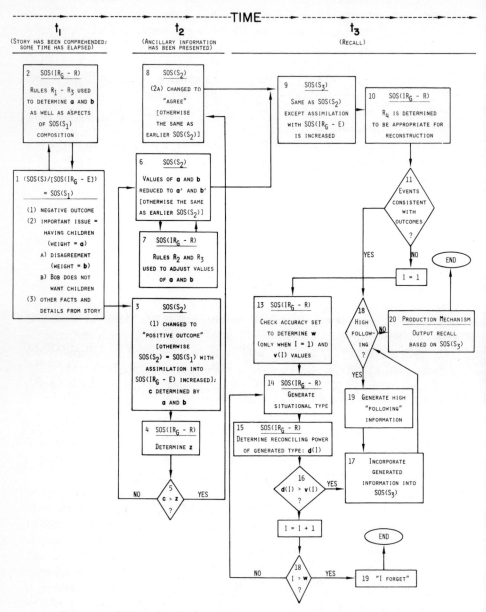

FIG. 2 An SOS model of inferential reconstruction (see text for explanation).

determine what most engaged couples have said and done vis-à-vis the issue). The rules might include:

R_1 : In the context "to be married," assign the weight a (for most people, some high value) if there is disagreement on the issue "having children."

R_2 : Outcome values (negative for this example) are more important than states regarding issues.

R_3 Reduce a by some constant (to a') if the state to the issue is negative (that is, disagreement) and the outcome is positive (that is, the disagreement is less important if things work out all right; since the outcome is negative in this story, the "importance of the disagreement" weight stays a).

Rule 3 is a consequence of Rule 2. The importance weight assigned to the disagreement about having children will subsequently help determine what kind of error is likely to occur in recall. Individual differences are probably quite large in the determination of a (as they probably are in assigning weights and criterion values throughout the model).

The *extent* of disagreement, (2a) in $SOS(S_1)$, is also assigned a weight (b) based primarily on the story, but likely also affected by the importance weight (a). Disagreement that is considered less important is probably also perceived as being of lesser degree (that is, the disagreers are not as far apart).

In (2b) of $SOS(S_1)$, the valence of only one relation of the disagreement (Bob___"having children") is assumed to be stored, since the valence of the Margie___"having children" relation is derivable on the basis of (2a) and (2b). Whether derivable information is stored, and which elements are left to be derived are also subject to individual differences, probably.

Assume now that the contradictory ancillary information ("they did get married") has been received and some time has passed. At Time 2, $SOS(S)$ will now contain the information in No. 3, $SOS(S_2)$. The outcome, (1) in $SOS(S_1)$, is changed to positive.

The "importance of the disagreement" weight (a), and the "extent of disagreement" weight (b) are combined to form a composite value, $c [c = f(a, b)]$, with greater disagreement yielding higher values of c. $SOS(IR_G - R)$ is then referred to for determination of a criterion value z, which is the value of c necessary to conclude that the disagreement must have been dissolved for the outcome "got married" to have occurred (in the absence of other information). Low values of z will be generated when individuals think agreement about having children is essential to agreement about "getting married," and high values of z will be generated when it is considered nonessential. If $c > z$ (with an adjustment for the greater ease of changing if c is low), it is inferred that they must no longer disagree, and 2a is changed in $SOS(S_2)$ from "disagree" to "agree." If $c < z$, (2a) in $SOS(S_2)$ remains "disagreed," but the weights of "importance of the disagreement" and "extent of the disagreement" (a and b, respectively) are reduced (to

a' and b') according to Rules R_2 and R_3 from SOS($IR_G - R$), since the outcome is now positive.

More time passes, and recall is attempted at Time 3. SOS(S_3) is the same as SOS(S_2), except assimilation with SOS(($IR_G - E$), is increased. That is, the boundaries between SOS(S_2) and SOS($IR_G - E$), the latter being in interactive relation with SOS($IR_G - R$), are less clearly defined. Reconstruction of events involving interpersonal relations relies first on the following rule from SOS($IR_G - R$):

> R_4: Events must be consistent with outcomes (though not necessarily vice versa), particularly when outcome information is more chronologically recent (as it is here), unless there are reasons for the inconsistency.

The outcome information of (1) in SOS(S_3) is then compared with detail information, (2) and (3), of SOS(S_3). If (2a) had been changed to "agree" ($c > z$ at t_2), consistency will be found. Recall will then be a straightforward output based on SOS(S_3). A likely reconstructive error is that Margie originally did *not* want children [if (2b) is only "Bob didn't want children," with the Margie ___"having children" relation left to be derived]. Another likely constructive error is that Bob or Margie had a change of mind about the issue (if *both* of the relations with "having children" remain in stored from in (2b), that is, they were not automatically changed when 2a was changed, the subject might think something like "they used to disagree and now I know they agree, so someone had a change of mind").

If inconsistency is found [that is, if (2a) is still "disagree"], inferential reconstruction proceeds as follows. Previously encountered types of situations involving engaged or married couples are generated from SOS($IR_G - E$) in a general (unlabeled as to participants) form. Generation is determined by similarities to the details remaining in (2) and (3) of SOS(S_3) and by some index of commonness of occurrence (a function of the number of labeled instances of the general type). Each generated type of situation is analyzed for its reconciling power for the (R_4-based) inconsistency of SOS(S_3). The reconciling power is then assigned a value (d), based on calculations in SOS($IR_G - R$). The value of d is then compared to a criterion value (v). The latter value is a constant plus a variable which a function of the experiment's accuracy set (Brockway, Chmielewski, & Cofer, 1974). When a premium is placed on accuracy, v will be larger (better reconciliation is required). If $d > v$, the reconciliation is clear (that is, easily derivable). Any time the reconciliation is so easily derivable from (and totally consistent with) stored information, the rememberer simply assumes that another case of not attending to easily derivable information has occurred. The rememberer will then insert the reconciling generated information in recall. An example of how this might work is by generating a common situation where many couples had areas of disagreement with approximately the same importance and extent weights as the (now lowered) a' and b' of SOS(S$_3$). For these couples, their areas of agreement outweighed the area of disagreement and allowed a happy married life. The reconstructive recall error that would result might be something like "they disagreed, but their positions were not too far apart and the issue was not that important to them anyway, so other areas (of agreement) were more important and had a greater effect on their plans and life together."

If for the first generated general situation $d < v$, another situation is generated and the new value of d is compared to a slightly increased value of v (due to the situation's less typical nature and fewer elements in common with stored details of the story). This process continues until a $d > v$ situation is found or until w generations are made. The value of w also depends on the accuracy set of the experiment. If the importance of accuracy is stressed, w will be a small value. After w unsuccessful generations, the rememberer will probably indicate that he or she has "forgotten." The type of process outlined above is assumed to be a common one, and therefore not a conscious indication to the subject of likely error.

Note that it is assumed in all cases that information strongly implied by the contents of the SOS at recall is incorporated into the SOS (Boxes 17, 18, and 19 Figure 2). The consequences of this process for research which builds language comprehension theories based on text reproductions (e.g., Frederiksen, 1975b) is discussed later.

What about recall without reconstructive errors? This will tend to occur under the following conditions (among others): (1) SOS(S) $\Rightarrow$ SOS(IR$_G$) (lack of assimilation and, therefore, lack of a base for subsequent generation at recall); (2) not on relating contradictory outcome information to SOS(S$_1$) or not having contradictory information to relate (leaving nothing to reconcile at t_3); (3) under "memory" instructions (where both of the former two reasons are operative); (4) under cognitive interaction instructions with "none" or consistent ancillary information (since the second reason is operative).

Integrity of To-Be-Remembered Information

A basic tenet of Reconstructive Theory is that the degree of interaction with pre-existing cognitive structures is a continuous variable. The degree can range from near total differentiation to total subordination of new information to many old structures. Some of the consequences of cognitive interaction have already been intimated, for example, greater likelihood that subsequently encountered information will alter states of schemata to which the to-be-remembered information has been related to. Also, a basis for generation of reconciling information in recall is provided (Figure 2, Boxes 13–17). Such information could, of course, be generated even without assimilation into a general schema, but the reconciling power (d) of any generated information would be lessened. Reasons for this, as well as other concomitants of the degree of cognitive interaction will be addressed in the following discussion of functional incidentals. Before proceeding, however, a brief discussion of the determination of related-to schemata and a distinction between two types of cognitive interaction is helpful.

Interaction with prior knowledge may occur solely to facilitate an internally consistent semantic representation of discourse, or it may occur because the discourse content is subordinate in function to exogenous factors. In the former case, the discourse will be referred to as having high integrity, and in the latter case, low integrity. The function of comprehension in the former case is solely to understand the discourse as an independent entity. In the latter case, the function of comprehension is to update knowledge.

In high-integrity discourse, inferential elaboration is auxiliary. Rather than relating new information to old for purposes of keeping knowledge current, the SOS for the discourse only is important. In this case it is likely that the necessary-for-comprehension old information is explicitly incorporated into the SOS for the new information. This is probably accomplished in a manner parallel to and with the same or similar mechanisms as the recall process illustrated in Boxes 14–17, with Box 19 replaced by "I don't understand this discourse" (see Figure 2). The time course of high-integrity discourse is characterized by the low likelihood of schema alteration by new information, and assimilative loss of idiosyncratically incidental and autobiographical aspects only due to second level (between noninterrelated schemata) functional incidental processes (which operate relatively slowly and with great inertia; this process will be described below). The result is a high level of accuracy for this type of discourse. Furthermore, any information that must be generated at recall (Boxes 14–17, Figure 2) will have lower ds if based in noninterrelated schemata, leading to a higher proportion of "I forgets" in situations that would otherwise produce reconstructive errors. It should be pointed out that for bodies of knowledge not previously encountered, cognitive interaction potential is minimal. Recall of such material may imply apparently high-integrity processing. Such "schemata in development" differ from high integrity schemata in the likelihood of and susceptibility to subsequent modification. It is expected, therefore, that similarities in the nature of recall would decrease with increasing delay intervals.

It is probably much more common outside of the lab to encounter low-integrity schemata. Accordingly, in the sections that follow discussions apply to SOSs that are subordinate to more general SOSs. High-integrity SOSs will usually be seen to operate as special cases of the more general low-integrity approach. Which preexisting SOSs are related to is always, to some extent, a function of the content of the discourse. Contextual factors that determine the extent and nature of SOS subordination include the following: prior linguistic context (if earlier discourse resulted in low integrity SOSs, the preexisting superordinate schemata will also be operative in the processing of subsequent discourse); the context of the situation (for example, "I am here because of issue X"); speaker–hearer (writer–reader) relationships (for example, SOSs involving shared presuppositions relevant to the communicative function are likely to be activated); interests and attitudes (for example, when one is ego involved with an issue, the interrelated cognitions and affective correlates that comprise the attitude exert a determining force on recall of attitude-relevant statements even in sterile laboratory conditions; Spiro & Sherif, 1975); task demands [for example, in the experiment discussed earlier, the instructions in the cognitive interaction condition lower the integrity of SOS(S) and induce interaction with SOS(IR$_G$)]; linguistic cues (for example, an author explicitly informing the reader that some point under discussion will be illuminated if considered from a specified, broader perspective); and kind of discourse (for example, Greek myths may not be relatable to any of an individual's preexisting SOSs, which can be considered "functional knowledge").

Subsequent sections illuminate differences between high- and low-integrity SOSs. One point can be made now, however, in regard to sentence memory research like that of Anderson and Bower (1973). It is clear that SOSs for sentences in an acquisition list are of the highest possible integrity. Upon hearing the sentence "The hippie touched the debutante in the park" in a memory experiment, one does not consider, for example, the sociological implications of class differences among young Americans, nor revise prior beliefs on that issue. One is certainly not concerned with the truth value the utterance carries. The sentence stands totally by itself. When it appears in a recognition test, what one "knows" about the behavior of hippies and debutantes in parks is irrelevant. If you have seen the sentence in the acquisition list, you respond "old" even if you have specifically stored knowledge that the specific event has never occurred, and if the sentence was not in the list, you respond "new" even if you saw a hippie touch a debutante in the park on the way to the lab. Clearly, such experiments deal with memory for the most sterile, isolated, and useless of episodes. They can hardly be considered representative of memorial processing in general since they make the peculiar demand on a subject to *disregard* what that subject knows.

Selectivity

What do I mean when I say errors are generated by the same process as accurate recall? One of the most basic characteristics of communication is the high frequency of occurrence of redundant information. The information is redundant either in the sense that it repeats old information, or is strongly implied by prior knowledge. When discourse leads to low-integrity representation, the main function of language comprehension is to update one's knowledge. This suggests a preliminary, partial answer to the following question: What is stored, given that reconstruction must be based upon some stored information? Some details from discourse are specifically stored. These are likely to be details that carry new, knowledge-updating information. Information that is important but redundant will merely strengthen the old representations, rather than leading to a new representation.

It seems obvious, however, that one does not consciously "store" new information. More likely, the new information receives more attention during initial processing. However, even important new information may be redundant. Information can be implied by or "follow" from earlier parts of the text containing new information. "Following" can refer to logical induction and deduction or to more psychological implication, for example, probabilistic connectedness. In any case, the covert response is likely to be something like "Of course, go on," with accordingly less processing and likelihood of salient specific storage. This is particularly true when information-processing capacity is overloaded. If people know they do not pay as much attention to or are not as impressed by important but psychologically redundant information at comprehension, awareness that a reproduction does not include some high "following" information will lead to the assumption that it was not "stored" because of the selective comprehension processes. The information is then likely to be incorporated with high confidence into the reproduction (see Boxes 17, 18, and 19, Figure 2).

There are two important consequences, among others, of this kind of assumption by rememberers. First, under certain conditions it can lead to error in recall. For example, what may "follow" at the time of initial processing may not follow later. New information or qualifications on old information may reduce the extent to which B follows from A (leading to omissions of B) or may increase the extent that C follows from A (leading to erroneous memory). Further, the extent of implication may be overestimated at comprehension when there is confounding with chronological recency. Of course, it is also possible, and certainly more common, that the rememberer's selectivity assumption can lead to generation of high "following" information actually present in the discourse. It is in this sense that the same processes are said to underly accurate recall and reconstructive errors. Second, it calls into question conclusions about *language comprehension* based on text reproduction (Frederiksen, 1975b). Clearly, if the assumptions above are correct, many of the inferences found by Frederiksen could have been generated at the time of reproduction, rather than being an integral part of the language comprehension process. Some method of identifying the locus of inferential processes is required.

At times, the amount of important new information which does not highly "follow" may exceed information processing capacity. In this case, "artificial implication" may be employed. Algorithms, mnemonic aids, and other devices which allow some information to be derivable are consciously stored. For example, "left-to-be-derived" markers of some kind can be tagged on to stored information suggesting paths for elaboration at recall. It seems likely that these markers are relatively unstable members of SOSs over time, possibly because they are extraneous and not directly related to the topical content of SOSs they are a part of. If left-to-be-derived markers of a given age are no longer *generally* available, this may lead to the rememberer assuming they were at one time, leading to a reduction in the "followingness" criterion (Box 13) and greater error in recall with increases in the delay interval. Accurate recall without reconstructive error may then occur when relevant left-to-be-derived markers are still generally accessible, and, therefore, absence of such a marker is not assumed by default to indicate that one did exist. Furthermore, error can result from new information (within the same discourse or subsequently encountered) altering the algorithms for left-to-be-derived elements, leading to incorrect generations at recall.

Finally, effects of selectivity on less important information which receives less attention and does not follow from more important information is discussed in the context of "functional incidentals" below.

The Nature and Consequences of the Assimilative Process: Functional Incidentalness

Schematic states are assumed to be continually in transition. It is postulated that the primary factor governing the restructuring and blending processes of assimilation is functionality. For reasons of cognitive economy and efficiency, aspects of information which are less useful will be less stable over time in memory. The dynamic SOS organization is assumed to be driven by "functional statements," of which individuals need not be consciously aware. Theoretically, any piece of information or rule in SOSs could be assigned a value dependent on the function statements of the SOSs of which it is a part. That value can be called the "functional incidentalness" (FI) level, where high FI can be paraphrased as "information of only incidental importance considered in the context of operative functions."

Some functions are generally operative, others are specific to particular SOSs. For example, information bearing on the truth value of propositions is usually low FI. Therefore, if the source of a message is associated, due to past experience, with a low credibility level, the source information will be low FI (and likely to remain in the SOS over time). If "The head of the CIA said X" is encountered, the source aspect is likely to be low FI. However, source information not associated with past low credibility will be high FI. Thus, if all newspapers are believed to be equally and highly reliable, and there is no a priori reason to doubt X, the source in "The Washington Post reporter said X" will be high FI and eventually lost as function-based assimilation over time occurs. Another example of general functions are those relating to communicative function. Hence, the very strong memory for illocutionary act force of propositions: "I don't remember specifically what X told Y, but I do remember that X was asking Y for something."

Other functions are SOS specific. For example, in SOS(IR$_G$), outcomes are considered important and any information bearing on outcomes would be low FI. For other kinds of situations, for example, those in which outcomes have less importance or are taken for granted, outcome-relevant information may be high FI. As the extent of interaction with cognitive structures (level of integrity) increases, discourse specific functions decrease in importance. Thus, for passages in memory experiments, the functions would all be internally determined (for example, by level of thematic relatedness) and task oriented (toward a high recall score). However, when assimilation into larger SOSs occurs, more general functional common denominators are operative, leading to a much broader range of high-FI information in the discourse, as well as increasing the probability of low-FI intrusions of information (Boxes 13–18, Figure 2).

Regarding the temporal aspect of assimilation in the experiment discussed, it can then be partially attributed to a change in the locus of functional determination over time. Functions tend to differ if one takes a between-SOS rather than within-SOS perspective. Again for reasons of cognitive economy, reduction in the number of distinct SOSs is assumed to go on over time. Since $SOS(IR_G)$ is already the result of such processes of consolidation, one would expect the functions of SOS to be dominant and the consolidation to be more heavily in the $SOS(S)$ to $SOS(IR_G)$ direction. As this goes on over time, FI determination shifts from $SOS(S)$ functions to $SOS(IR_G)$ functions. The latter are basically irrelevant to story maintenance per se, leading to the loss of the story's particular identity. A primary consequence is a decrease in v (Box 13, Figure 2) with increases in the delay interval.

The functional orientation can be seen as a distinct alternative to Tulving's (1972) episodic–semantic distinction, insofar as episodic memory can be paraphrased as "I remember" and is characterized primarily by its autobiographical reference, and semantic memory can be paraphrased as "I know" without autobiographical reference. For example, take one's knowledge about the Civil War. For a time, some of that knowledge might be "episodic," for example, "My seventh grade teacher taught me X about the Civil War on occasion Y." Later, the autobiographical details might be lost with the following result in "semantic" memory: "I know X about the Civil War," where X is incorporated in a body of Civil War knowledge with individual elements not distinguished as to the autobiographical characteristics of the situations in which they were independently acquired. The functional approach would indicate, however, that autobiographical reference is a meaningless basis for distinguishing between types of memory or knowledge. Essentially, autobiographical information would be part of one's semantic memory ("I know") if it is low FI. For example, if the situation in which X was acquired is relevant to the truth value of X, that autobiographical information would endure as a stable qualification on X in memory. Again, where and from whom you learned about the Battle of Gettysburg may not be generally important, but "who" might be if a senile 100-year-old veteran told you, and the fact that you heard it in the South might be functional "where" information, whereas East–West differences would not be functional "where" information. Because of the more general functions which dominate between-SOS assimilation, it is frequently the case that autobiographical information becomes high FI, and thus does not become a stable part of one's general knowledge. However, this correlational fact is not an explanatory concept. What accounts for the phenomenon is the degree of interaction with preexisting knowledge (increasing and accelerating between SOS assimilation) and the schema-structuring force of function. Thus the episodic–semantic distinction may be more profitably viewed in terms of a continuum of cognitive interaction and by specification of SOS functions.

Context Effects and Individual Differences

SOS representations are affected by contextual factors in various ways, and many are not represented in the model (for example, the contextual determination of particularized word meanings as a function of linguistic context, Anderson & Ortony, 1975). Several kinds of context effects are illustrated in the SOS model. In box 1 of Figure 2, the weights assigned to (2) and (2a) are determined under the contextual influence of rules R_1, R_2, and R_3 of $SOS(IR_G - R)$, that is, external to $SOS(S_1)$. These weights, besides having an effect on initial comprehension, have wider ranging effects on the subsequent time course of $SOS(S)$. In particular, the decision at Box 5 is affected, thereby determining the nature of schema change at Time 2 and recall at Time 3.

Note also that the cognitive event represented in Box 6 illustrates a different kind of context effect, that is, the *reinterpretation* of old information in the context of new information (context effects are usually viewed from the reverse perspective). This is, essentially, a form of learning, and one that has usually been neglected.

Finally, the effects of the context of one's attitudes are illustrated by the determination of z, the consequences of that value on SOS changes, and the subsequent possible directions reconstruction may take.

Implicit throughout the SOS model is the powerful determining force of idiosyncratic factors. The qualitative changes in schematic states resulting from individual differences on the issue of having children and its role in marriage plans is an example. It is expected that the reconstructive approach, with its decreased emphasis on the internal structural relations of discourse, will lead to an increasing emphasis in discourse memory research on individual differences in prior knowledge, personal inference rules, attitudes, etc.

SOS Construction

The preceding discussion has been loosely illustrated by the model presented in Figure 2. It was intended that the model would reflect some of the essential characteristics of reconstructive recall: interaction of stored elements and rules for inferential reconstruction; idiosyncratic influence of prior knowledge on reconstructive errors (or their absence); dynamic schema change reflecting assimilative processes and the effects of new information on the representation of old; and a generation-test process for reconciling contradictory schematic states. It is clear that the specific SOS model presented in Figure 2 is not generally applicable. Rather, it is likely that specific SOS models would have to be generated for specific situational types. If this is so, the utility of the SOS model approach can be reasonably called into question.

However, the intended function of the SOS approach is *not* to model the reconstructive processes involved in given situations. What is expected to remain constant across situations is *not* the specific models, but the characteristics incorporated into the models. The model of Figure 2 is intended to be a prototype for construction of SOS models for other situations which would differ in form from Figure 2, but not in the kinds of processes incorporated. Then, by comparing different SOS models, inferences become possible about (*a*) the general processes involved in all specific reconstructive models, and (*b*) the processes by which specific SOS models are created. Knowledge about (*b*) is important because it is almost certain that people must construct specific SOS models for given situations in much the same way as it has been suggested that cognitive psychologists must. To assume anything other than fresh construction of models is to ignore the strongest data available about human cognitive processing: the virtually unlimited flexibility, capacity for nuance, and creativity with which novel but appropriate behavior occurs as a function of an infinite number of contexts. It is probably apparent that Reconstructive Theory views memory as a close cousin of (if not the same thing as) thinking, and no single model could capture the complexity of those processes.

A final word about the generation of specific SOS models is in order. The method of investigation should parallel the method that would be employed to investigate how people think about an area in general. For example, the rules in Figure 2, rather than being generated intuitively, could have been derived from research on social cognition and the social psychology of interpersonal relations.

EDUCATIONAL PRIORITIES

It has for some time been this writer's impression that students approach text in the same way as subjects in a memory experiment. They appear to compartmentalize new information, differentiating it from prior knowledge as much as possible. One has the feeling that students, in part becuase of the nature of the tests they anticipate, insufficiently integrate related knowledge acquired in school (both between grades and within the same grade, and certainly between subjects), and furthermore, treat most school material as unrelated to everything outside of school. The problem may involve the distinction made earlier between comprehension to understand text per se and comprehension to update one's knowledge: should discourse have high or low integrity?

Emphasis can be placed on the characteristics of text that promote highest recall levels. An example is Meyer's suggestion (this volume) that an author should place those ideas most wanted to be remembered near the top of the text's content structure. However, such a suggestion, based on internal structural relations in text, presupposes the desirability of high integrity processing (with concomitant emphasis on high levels of accurate recall as a goal). Such processing certainly may be desirable at times. However, it also seems likely to detract from knowledge integration.

An emphasis on knowledge updating rather than compartmentalization (relating text to preexisting cognitive structures rather than interrelating within text), with a corresponding deemphasis of tests which merely assess replicative ability (Broudy, chapter 1, this volume), could lead to improved generative abilities, since increased assimilation would make reliance on more rote-like retrieval processes an inefficient strategy; and improved "contextual knowing", the ability to provide a rich, particularized interpretation of information as a function of the context in which it is used. These assertions have intuitive plausibility, but obviously require empirical confirmation.

It should be kept in mind, however, that such a shift in emphasis may have as a correlate an increase in certain kinds of inaccuracy in knowledge reproduction. The data presented earlier show that when people think about and personally relate to what they read, which surely is desirable, there is an increase in "error." For example, the ensuing loss of text's particular identity is likely to lead to errors in reconstruction relating to the source of information (misattribution of who said it and where it was said). However, this inaccuracy may be a necessary step toward more integrated cognitive structures. If so, providing it does not persist, it should not be punished. The question becomes one of priorities. The conditions when each of the two comprehension functions is most desirable must be identified, and instructional materials and tests must then be tuned to the desired function.

ACKNOWLEDGMENTS

This research was supported in part by grants from the National Institute of Child Health and Human Development (PHS Training Grant HD-00151), the National Institute of Education (Grant No. HEW NIE-G-74-0007), and the University of Illinois Research Board. Parts of this paper are based on a doctoral dissertation at the Pennsylvania State University. The author wishes to express his gratitude especially to Charles N. Cofer, as well as to David S. Palermo, William F. Brewer, Carolyn W. Sherif, James E. Martin, Richard C. Anderson, James M. Royer, and Paul A. Games for helpful comments. Thanks for secretarial service are due Bonnie Anderson and Charity Armstrong. Phyllis Spiro is thanked for much other support.

REFERENCES

Anderson, J. R., & Bower, G. H. *Human associative memory*. New York: Wiley, 1973.

Anderson, R. C., & Ortony, A. On putting apples into bottles, A problem of polysemy. *Cognitive Psychology*, 1975, 7, 167–180.

Barclay, R. J. The role of comprehension in remembering sentences. *Cognitive Psychology*, 1973, 4, 229–254.

Bartlett, F. C. *Remembering*. Cambridge, England: Cambridge University Press, 1932.

Bransford, J. D., Barclay, J. R., & Franks, J. J. Sentence memory: A constructive versus interpretive approach. *Cognitive Psychology*, 1972, 3, 193–209.

Bransford, J. D., & McCarrell, N. S. A sketch of a cognitive approach to comprehension. In W. B. Weimer & D. S. Palermo (Eds.), *Cognition and the symbolic processes*. Hillsdale, N.J.: Lawrence Erlbaum Associates, 1975.

Brockway, J., Chmielewski, D., & Cofer, C. N. Remembering prose: Productivity and accuracy constraints in recognition memory. *Journal of Verbal Learning and Verbal Behavior*, 1974, 13, 194–208.

Crothers, E. J. Memory structure and the recall of discourse. In R. Freedle & J. B. Carroll (Eds.), *Language comprehension and the acquisition of knowledge*. Washington, D.C.: Winston, 1972.

Frederiksen, C. H. Acquisition of semantic information from discourse: Effects of repeated exposures. *Journal of Verbal Learning and Verbal Behavior*, 1975, 14, 158–169.   (a)

Frederiksen, C. H. Effects of context-induced processing operations on semantic information acquired from discourse. *Cognitive Psychology*, 1975, 7, 139–166.   (b)

Gauld, A., & Stephenson, G. M. Some experiments relating to Bartlett's theory of remembering. *British Journal of Psychology*, 1967, 58, 39–49.

Gomulicki, B. R. Recall as an abstractive process. *Acta Psychologia*, 1956, 12, 77–94.

Heider, F. *The psychology of interpersonal relations*. New York: Wiley, 1958.

Honeck, R. P. Interpretive versus structural effects on semantic memory. *Journal of Verbal Learning and Verbal Behavior*, 1973, 12, 448–455.

Howe, M. I. A. Repeated presentation and recall of meaningful prose. *Journal of Educational Psychology*, 1970, 61, 214–219.

Johnson, R. E. Recall of prose as a function of the structural importance of the linguistic units. *Journal of Verbal Learning and Verbal Behavior*, 1970, 9, 12–20.

Kay, H. Learning and retaining verbal material. *British Journal of Psychology*, 1955, 46, 81–100.

Kiesler, A. K., Collins, B. E., & Miller, N. *Attitude change: A critical analysis of theoretical approaches*. New York: Wiley, 1969.

Kintsch, W. *The representation of meaning in memory*. New York: Wiley, 1974.

Lakoff, G. Presupposition and relative well-formedness. In D. D. Steinberg & L. A. Jakobovits (Eds.), *Semantics: An interdisciplinary reader in philosophy, linguistics and psychology*. Cambridge, England: Cambridge University Press, 1971.

Meyer, B. J. F. The organization of prose and its effects on recall. Research Report No. 1, Reading and Learning Series, Department of Education, Cornell University, 1974.

Meyer, B. J. F., & McConkie, G. W. What is recalled after learning a passage? *Journal of Educational Psychology*, 1973, 65, 109–117.

Spencer, N. J. Changes in representation and memory of prose. Unpublished doctoral dissertation, The Pennsylvania State University, University Park, Pennsylvania, 1973.

Spiro, R. J. Inferential reconstruction in memory for connected discourse. (Tech. Rep. No. 2). Urbana, Ill.: University of Illinois, Laboratory for Cognitive Studies in Education, October 1975.

Spiro, R. J., & Sherif, C. W. Consistency and relativity in selective recall with differing ego-involvement. *British Journal of Social and Cinical Psychology,* 1975, **14**, 351–361.

Tulving, E. Episodic and semantic memory. In E. Tulving & W. Donaldson (Eds.), *Organization of memory.* New York: Academic Press, 1972.

Zangwill, O. L. Remembering revisited. *Quarterly Journal of Experimental Psychology,* 1972, **24**, 123–138.

REMEMBERING: CONSTRUCTIVE OR RECONSTRUCTIVE? COMMENTS ON CHAPTER 5 BY SPIRO

James M. Royer

University of Massachusetts, Amherst

Professor Spiro has presented a most interesting contribution, which revitalizes our interest in a theory which one critic has dismissed as "never very plausible and best forgotten" (Zangwill, 1972, p. 127). Before commenting on Spiro's chapter, it is important to point out that there are two sets of data which have been interpreted as being supportive of a reconstructive theory of memory: the data that Bartlett (1932) reported, and the results of Spiro's research that he has reported to us today.

Barlett's research has been criticized primarily on two grounds. The first is that the considerable inaccuracy in recall over extended time periods that he reported has not been replicated in most subsequent studies (e.g., Gomulicki, 1956; Frederiksen, 1975). These studies have suggested gross inaccuracy in recall is such a transitory phenomenon it can hardly serve as an empirical base for a theory of memory. The second criticism derives from studies (e.g., Gauld & Stephenson, 1967), which have suggested that the inaccuracies which Bartlett reported could have been "guesses" made by his subjects to fill in gaps in memory. Since reconstructive theory considers inaccuracy in recall to be a natural product of the remembering process, the argument that errors in recall are primarily a function of guessing threatens the integrity of the theory.

Given the uncertainty involved in interpreting Bartlett's results, the experiment that Spiro has reported assumes considerable importance, and I direct the majority of my comments to the results from his experiment. First, I would like to review three theoretical positions on the nature of the remembering process, and describe how the data that Spiro has presented relates to each of the positions.

Three conceptually distinct theories have emerged from the efforts of psychologists to account for the remembering process. The first, and certainly the oldest I will describe, is one that Neisser (1966) has labeled the "reappearance hypothesis." The central idea in this position is that remembering involves reviving a memory trace which essentially is a stored copy of a sensory experience. The contents of this trace can be completely described by the sensory event perceived by the learner. Remembering, then, involves locating this trace in memory and bringing its contents to consciousness.

The second theory, commonly referred to as constructive theory (see Anderson & Ortony, 1975; Bransford, Barclay, & Franks, 1972), again involves the idea that remembering involves finding and bringing to consciousness stored records of past events. However, constructive theory differs from reappearance theory in that the contents of the memory trace are not definable in terms of the sensory event that created the trace. Rather, the contents of the memory trace are jointly determined by the sensory experience, the current knowledge structure of the learner, and pertinent features of the environmental context in which the event is perceived. This means that two learners experiencing the same sensory event will be very likely to have different contents in the memory representation arising from that event, and hence, somewhat different memories of the experience. In contrast, reappearance theory would assert that memory of identical sensory experiences should be essentially the same except for omissions of content.

Reconstructive theory is the third theory and it differs markedly from the previous two. In this theory, the essential notion is that remembering frequently does not involve finding and bringing to consciousness the representation of a past event. Instead, remembering involves inferring or reconstructing events of the past on the basis of the current state of the memory "schema." The argument is, that sensory events are integrated into a memory schema, or "organized pattern" to use Bartlett's phrase, and during the integration process the "particular identity" of the experienced events is lost. When recall of past events is necessary, the appropriate schema is located, and the past state of the schema is inferred on the basis of its current state. Bartlett referred to this process as the "schema turning around upon itself." Spiro has presented us with a more carefully worked out explanation of this process, but his central theme is the same as Bartlett's. Remembering does not solely involve the retrieval of stored records of past events. Rather, it frequently involves the reconstruction of past events at the time of recall.

I would now like to examine the data from the experiment Spiro has described and consider how that data relate to each of the theoretical positions I have discussed. I believe that we can discount reappearance theory as providing a plausible account of the data from Spiro's experiment. I cannot imagine how reappearance theory would explain the pattern of inaccurate recall we see in the results, or for the fact that the occurrence of specific kinds of errors increased with the passage of time.

Constructive theory seems to me to be much more difficult to dismiss in terms of providing a plausible account for the data, and I comment more on this later. For the moment, however, let me review those aspects of the data that Spiro cites as being contrary to predictions derived from constructive theory. First, and probably foremost, we have the fact that the occurrence of predicted errors increased with time for those groups who were predicted to make specific errors. In the groups for whom specific errors were not predicted, there was no increase in these errors over time. As Spiro has noted, if we accept the position that constructive theory predicts that any errors (other than omissions) that occur should have their origin in the comprehension process, then we have no basis for accounting for the fact that substantive errors increase in frequency with the passage of time. Second, Spiro has argued that constructive theory does not provide us with the basis for predicting the specific kinds of errors he was interested in. That is, the errors predicted by reconstructive theory are not legitimate inferences from the text materials the subjects read. And, finally, we have the confidence ratings showing that after two days, subjects in the reconstructive-error conditions have more confidence that correctly recalled material was explicitly expressed in the passages than incorrectly recalled. However, at longer recall intervals the subjects had more confidence in errors than they did in correctly recalled material. This pattern of results can be contrasted to that for the remaining groups in the experiment where correctly recalled material consistently received higher confidence ratings than did incorrectly recalled material. As was the case with the accuracy data, it would seem that constructive theory would not predict the kind of interaction I have described between treatment conditions and delay interval. The reason being that confidence in an error formed at the time of comprehension should remain fairly stable over time relative to the confidence expressed for correctly recalled material.

The evidence that I have cited contributed to Spiro's rejection of a constructionist interpretation of his data, and lent support to the reconstruction interpretation. He has argued that the reconstruction interpretation provides a good fit to all aspects of the data, whereas interpretations based on reappearance theory, constructive theory, and a "guessing to fill in the gaps" hypothesis all leave important features of the data unaccounted for.

Having reviewed some of Spiro's data, I must confess that I am unconvinced that reconstructive theory provides the only satisfactory account of his experiment. Rather, I believe that constructive theory can provide an interpretation that is equally as plausible. One assumption in addition to those considered previously must be added to constructive theory to provide an account of Spiro's results. The assumption is that construction of memory traces can occur after the point of comprehension.

I would like to place myself in the position of one of the subjects who received the cognitive interaction contradictory treatment in Spiro's experiment. I have been told that the experiment is concerned with "changes in the way people react to stories involving interpersonal relations when there is a delay prior to giving the reaction." Further, I am told to think about and to react to the story, and that during the second session I will be asked to answer various kinds of questions concerning my reactions. I then read a story that includes a general description of two people who meet, fall in love, and become engaged. Near the end of the story I read a section of the passage which indicates that the issue of having children was a potential point of conflict between the couple. I then read, if I am in the balanced condition, that this issue was resolved in that both parties did not want children, or if I am in the imbalanced condition I read that the couple disagreed on this important issue and that a bitter argument followed. After reading the passage, and before I leave, the experimenter casually mentions that the couple got married in the imbalanced condition, or they broke their engagement in the balanced condition.

As time passes following the experiment, I remember the instructions I received and I think about and react to the story I read. It would seem that a logical focal point for my thought would be on the potential or actual issue of conflict (depending on the experimental condition), and on the fact that the outcome of the relationship conflicted with the information presented in the story. In thinking about the situation, I generate possible events that could have happened between the time point described at the end of the story and the point at which the couple either got married or broke their engagement. These generated or constructed events are then stored as memory traces. I could elaborate on this procedure further, but I suspect that the general drift of this argument is clear. I would now like to return to the important aspects of Spiro's results and describe how my assumption of the storage of generated memory traces might account for the results.

First, let us take the fact that the occurrence of what Spiro has called reconstructive errors increases over time. The alternative hypothesis I have suggested could account for this data in two ways. After only two days the subject could have given little thought to the experiment, and therefore would be less likely to have formed a generated memory trace after this short interval than after a long interval. The second possibility is that the subject has, in fact, generated and stored the "error" memory trace, but after a short interval he has some likelihood of being able to identify the trace as having been generated rather than actually presented in the story. As time passes, the subject could lose the capability of distinguishing between those traces formed as a function of reading the story and those which were generated, and therefore becomes increasingly likely to recall the generated error.

Spiro has also noted that the fact that the reconstructive errors made by his subjects were not logical inferences from the text alone suggests that constructive process could not be the source of the errors. This would be true if memory construction were restricted to the comprehension phase of the experiment.

However, as I have indicated, memory traces could be formed after the time of comprehension and thus would be based on both the textual material and the ancillary information presented to the subject after he has read the text. I believe that the State of Schema (SOS) model that Spiro presented provides a highly plausible account of how such a trace might be formed. The difference between my account and Spiro's is I have suggested that the errors were constructed prior to the request for recall, whereas he has argued that they were reconstructed during recall.

Finally, I would like to consider the confidence data and suggest how the constructive interpretation I have proposed could account for the fact that the reconstructive error groups had more confidence that erroneously recalled material had appeared in the text than correctly recalled material. The data indicated that after two days the cognitive interaction contradictory groups expressed greater confidence in correctly recalled material than in recalled errors. However, after three and six weeks they expressed greater confidence in recalled errors than they did for correctly recalled material. In contrast, subjects in the remaining conditions consistently expressed greater confidence in correctly recalled material at each of the retention intervals.

The interpretation I have suggested could account for this pattern of results if one grants the assumption that subjects will express more confidence in a recently constructed memory trace than they will in a memory trace formed earlier. In my account, since constructed error traces are formed after the subjects have read and comprehended the text, the constructed errors have a recency advantage over the memory traces formed when the subjects actually read the textual material. If we assume that subjects retain some capability for distinguishing between constructed and comprehended (text) material for some time after the experiment, we can explain the fact that after two days correctly recall material is more confidently recalled than erroneously recalled material. But as time passes, the subjects lose the capability of distinguishing between comprehended and constructed information, and the recency advantage of the constructed information influences the confidence ratings. Support for the assumption that recently stored information will be recalled with greater confidence than remotely stored information can be found in Spiro's data on the confidence ratings for correctly recalled material at each of the three delay intervals. There was a steadily declining confidence in correctly recalled material as the delay interval in the experiment increased.

Early in his contribution, Spiro suggested that the viability of reconstructive theory was not likely to be determined by laboratory experiments which demonstrated that recall from textual materials was basically accurate in character. Rather, he argued that "evidence against reconstructive theory would be provided only by accuracy in conditions where the theory would predict inaccuracy."

I agree with this assertion in theory, but I also believe that the current state of formulation of both constructive theory and reconstructive theory makes it unlikely that experiments involving the use of accuracy data will be able to distinguish between the two theories.

I believe that if evidence concerning the viability of the two theories is forthcoming it will not center upon whether recall is accurate or inaccurate. Rather, I believe it will come from experiments examining the differences in processing assumptions contained in the two theories. It seems to me that the critical difference between constructive and reconstructive theory involves assumptions about what processes are activated at the time of recall. Constructive theory suggests that a constructed memory trace is located and brought to consciousness at the time of recall. Reconstructive theory asserts that the past event is formulated at the time of recall. I would think that a process involving searching for the appropriate memory schema and then reconstructing the past state of that schema should involve more processing activity than locating a previously stored memory trace. If so, then it may be possible to design a reaction time experiment which would provide evidence reflecting upon these different processing assumptions.

Having argued that I do not believe reconstructive theory offers the only plausible explanation of the results of Spiro's experiment, I would like to suggest that constructive theory and reconstructive theory are not incompatible. In fact, they may be highly complimentary. Reconstructive theory does not assert that remembering always involves the reconstruction of past events. Indeed, Spiro has identified for us many instances where recall involves the retrieval of stored records of past events. If he were to grant the possibility that memory traces could be constructed after the point of comprehension, we could probably agree that the results of his experiment are not contrary to either constructive or reconstructive theory. If this is the case, what does reconstructive theory add to the way we conceptualize human cognitive functioning?

I believe that Spiro's attempts at providing a detailed model of the reconstructive process represents an important attempt to capture thinking rather than just memory in our psychological models. It is clear that theories of cognitive functioning which do not account for thinking are incomplete. I look forward to further development of Spiro's theory, which I believe has considerable promise as a comprehensive model of cognitive functioning.

REFERENCES

Anderson, R. C., & Ortony, A. On putting apples into bottles — a problem of polysemy. *Cognitive Psychology*, 1975, 7, 167–180.
Bartlett, F. C. *Remembering*. Cambridge, England: Cambridge University Press, 1932.

Bransford, J. D., Barclay, J. R., & Franks, J. J. Sentence memory: A constructive versus interpretive approach. *Cognitive Psychology*, 1972, **3**, 193–209.

Frederiksen, C. H. Effects of context induced processing operations on semantic information acquired from discourse. *Cognitive Psychology*, 1975, 7, 1399–166.

Gauld, A., & Stephenson, G. M. Some experiments relating to Bartlett's theory of remembering. *British Journal of Psychology*, 1967, **58**, 39–49.

Gomulicki, B. R. Recall as an abstractive process. *Acta Psychologica*, 1956, **12**, 77–94.

Neisser, V. *Cognitive psychology*. New York: Appleton-Century-Crofts, 1966.

Zangwill, O. L. Remembering revisited. *Quarterly Journal of Experimental Psychology*, 1972, **24**, 123–138.

OPEN DISCUSSION ON THE
CONTRIBUTIONS BY SPIRO AND ROYER

Spiro: I believe Dr. Royer's positions concerning the processes that may be operative and their temporal locus of operation are largely compatible with my own. For example, the SOS model presented in Figure 2 of Chapter 5 allows for reconstructive errors originating at various points during the delay interval. (However, my contention in the paper that over time the form and force of the reconciling errors made immediately after exposure to the ancillary information would probably change from speculations to assertions should be noted here as a qualification.)

Where we differ is in regard to theoretical delineation. Dr. Royer's second suggestion to account for my results, viz., that the ability to distinguish generated from presented information decreases with time (from nearly perfect differentiability to nearly perfect inability to differentiate), is one of the most basic tenets (the assimilative quality of schemata) of my version of reconstructive theory. It can be distinguished from an alternate theory that would have recall based on retrieval of traces of interpreted (or constructed) experience. In that approach, inferential elaborations would be as much a part of discourse's representation as constructed understandings which bear a direct relation to what was "in the presented discourse." In any case, I agree with Dr. Royer that my data and theory are incompatible with alternate theories of the constructive kind that would keep the reconciling inferential elaborations permanently distinct from nongenerated information (that is, specific story information does not have a sovereign integrity).

I should also add that I find it unlikely that much thought was devoted by subjects to the experimental materials in the interval after two days and before recall at three or six weeks.

Hunt: I still wonder whether there is any need to make a distinction between the constructive and reconstructive approaches. For example, in Elizabeth

Loftus' work with recall of accidents, which is very similar to your research, it has proven just about impossible to discriminate between the two theories.

Spiro: It depends on the version of reconstructive theory one refers to. My data are inconsistent with the two versions which I discussed in my immediately preceding comment. Furthermore, the interaction with delay is at least very suggestive. Another new point in support of the distinction involves the difference between remembering information and remembering where information comes from. A reconstructive error can have its initial appearance at various stages in the delay interval, but the erroneous attribution of that information to the specific discourse probably occurs at recall. There would be no reason for a subject to decide prior to that time what was in the story as opposed to what was a reaction to the story.

With regard to Loftus, her research on memory for visually presented information is certainly in the same family as my research on memory for connected discourse. However, there are differences. For example, since the ancillary information was verbal in Loftus' research, the bias in recall may be interpretable as evidence of dominance (or greater efficiency) of the verbal code much like that found by Carmichael, Hogan, and Walter (1932), among others.

Royer: I think one way of disentangling construction and reconstruction is by the reaction time experiment that I mentioned. It should be the case, if reconstructive theory is correct, that generation of errors should be much slower than retrieval of correct, stored material from the passage.

Spiro: The main problem with such an approach is that the predictions of reconstructive theory with respect to reaction time are ambiguous. A case could be made that the predicted reconstructive errors, since their origin is more firmly grounded in stable pre-existing knowledge structure, would be recalled as rapidly (or even more rapidly) than the discourse information which is imposed upon the rememberer. Reconstructive theory also contends that a substantial proportion of *correct recall* is generated. Therefore, any results of reaction time experiments would not differentially bear upon the two theories.

Ortony: Changing the subject, if inaccuracy only occurs in the Memory condition and students are in any kind of learning situation, of what use is your inaccuracy criterion (even if it only refers to an intermediate and enabling stage of development)? Would you present the material to them in some kind of disguised fashion?

Spiro: Certainly not. I would try to induce an orienting set analogous to the Cognitive Interaction condition in the experiment. Unfortunately, since most school situations have an orienting set more like the Memory condition (a set to store information in some isolated manner to facilitate subsequent regurgitation when tested), my suggestion carries an implicit prescription for educational reform.

REFERENCES

Carmichael, L., Hogan, H. P., & Walter, A. A. An experimental study of the effect of language in the reproduction of visually perceived forms. *Journal of Experimental Psychology*, 1932, **10**, 214–229.

6

The Structure of Prose: Effects on Learning and Memory and Implications for Educational Practice

Bonnie J. F. Meyer[1]

Western Connecticut State College
  and
Educational Testing Service

Most of the knowledge a person acquires comes from reading or listening to prose. Thus, an important goal in education has long been to help people develop the ability to acquire information from their reading and listening. Programs to implement this goal have been severely handicapped by the lack of an adequate theory of learning from prose. There are very few data of the type needed for such a theory. Few studies have asked what people learn from their reading or listening and how this information is acquired.

Research in education dealing with learning from prose (Carroll, 1971) has tended not to examine the influence of aspects of prose itself on which aspects of it are remembered. Instead, the effects of aids such as special instructions (Flanagan, 1939; Welborn & English, 1937), interspersed questions (Rothkopf & Bisbicos, 1967), training programs (Deverell, 1959), or other variables external to the text itself have been examined to ascertain their usefulness in increasing recall from a passage.

In contrast to educators' frequent use of prose in studies, in the past psychologists generally have tended to avoid research with natural prose. This avoidance was not due to a lack of interest, but resulted from a view that learning processes could better be studied with less complex and more easily controlled stimuli, such as lists of nonsense syllables or words, or pairs of these items. Thus, verbal

---

[1] Present address: Department of Educational Psychology, Arizona State University, Tempe, Arizona 85281.

learning research rarely involved the use of prose. Ironically, some of the learning principles consistently found with lists of words were not found with prose (Kirscher, 1971). Not only is prose more complex and more complicated, but it contains an organizational structure designed to deliver a message; this primary attribute of prose materials is not found in lists of words or nonsense syllables.

The lack of techniques necessary to specify the information in prose was the major cause for educators and psychologists to ignore the influence of aspects of prose itself on what is remembered from it. Recent developments in linguistics (Fillmore, 1968; Grimes, 1975; Halliday, 1967; van Dijk, 1972) have provided needed discourse grammars which make this research possible.

My research with prose began by attempting to determine why some ideas from a passage are recalled by almost everyone, whereas other ideas are recalled by very few people. I identified three aspects of a passage and examined their relationships to which ideas were well and poorly remembered from the passage. These aspects were the structure or organization of the content of a passage, the serial position of the ideas in a passage, and the relative importance raters assigned to all the ideas in a passage. The results of this investigation (Meyer, 1971) clearly showed the structure of prose to be the most powerful variable in predicting the recall of content from a passage. In fact, most of the relationship between both the serial position of the content and its recall and rated importance of content and its recall could be accounted for by the relationship of these variables to the structure of the passage. Thus, the structure of prose was clearly seen as an important variable in determining which ideas from a passage a group of people will remember.

In this chapter I focus on this important variable, the structure of prose. The chapter is divided into two main sections. First I present a summary of my research investigating the effects of the structure of prose on what is remembered from it. Second, the implications of this research for educational practice is discussed. Before discussing this research and its implications a general understanding is necessary of the nature and form of this structure of prose.

THE CONTENT STRUCTURE

The prose analysis technique that I use to identify the structure of a passage is based on Fillmore's (1968) case grammar and Grimes' (1975) semantic grammar of propositions. This procedure for prose analysis yields hierarchically arranged tree structures. Nodes in these tree structures contain content words from the passage, and the lines among the nodes show spatially how the content is organized. In addition, labels are found in the tree structures that explicitly state and classify the relationships among the content. This hierarchically arranged display of the content of the passage is called the content structure since it shows the structure or organization of the content in the passage.

The content structure of a passage shows how some ideas in the passage are subordinate to other ideas. Some ideas from a passage are located at the top levels of the content structure, others are found at middle levels, and still other ideas are found at the bottom levels of the structure. Most of the ideas located at the top levels of the content structure have many levels of ideas beneath them and related to them in a direct downward path in the structure. These top level ideas dominate their subordinate ideas. The lower-level ideas describe or give more information about the ideas above them in the structure. The content structure is similar in this respect to the traditional outline; superordinate ideas are located toward the left or top of the outline or content structure, while the subordinate ideas are found toward the right or bottom. The content structure differs in three important ways from the traditional outline. First, the content structure diagrams all the ideas in a passage. Second, the content structure contains labels that specify the relationships among the ideas in a passage. Third, the content structure is built by using explicit rules of the semantic grammar of propositions.

Using this prose analysis technique a passage is viewed as being a complex proposition that can be decomposed into subpropositions bearing certain relations to one another. Propositions are composed of a predicate and its arguments. There are assumed to be two types of predicates, with that term being used in the logician's sense: lexical predicates and rhetorical predicates. Lexical predicates are centered in a lexical item, typically verbs and their adjuncts, and take arguments that are ideas from the content of the text. The lexical predicates are related to the arguments by case or role relationships. Rhetorical predicates are not centered in lexical items, but still take arguments. These arguments can be single ideas from the content of the text, but are more often lexical propositions or other rhetorical propositions. The rhetorical predicates frequently appear at higher levels in the structure of a passage, representing intersentential relationships. They consist of a finite number of labels which classify and describe the relationships, particularly intersentential and inter-paragraph relations, found in prose.

The book *The Organization of Prose and Its Effects on Memory* (Meyer, 1975) gives a complete description of this technique with step-by-step procedures for analyzing a passage, examples, and comparisons of this approach to procedures proposed by other psychologists. This technique has been shown to be reliable when used by investigators trained in the technique. Independent analyses of two prose analysts showed a 95% agreement in the content structures of a passage; differences did not occur in the level of the information in the structure, but in particular role relations or rhetorical predicates identified to label the relationships between ideas in the passage.

This system also provides an extremely reliable method for scoring free recall protocols produced after exposure to a passage. Content units and relationship units, role and rhetorical relations, are scored. The content structure is printed on grid paper. The tree structure is northwest rooted rather than north rooted with indentations to the right representing a node lower in the tree. A second piece of grid paper is lined up with the content structure; one column on the paper is used for the recall protocol of each subject. If a content unit from the content structure is found in the recall protocol, that unit is scored by placing a number in that subject's column in the row that corresponds to the content unit in the content structure. This number indicates that the unit was recalled and also indicates the order in which the subject recalled the idea in his protocol. Thirteen recall protocols from 500-word passages were independently scored by two scorers, who agreed 99% of the time on whether items from the content structure should be counted as present or absent in the recall. Therefore, the use of the content structure in scoring recall protocols is both useful and reliable.

RESEARCH EXAMINING THE EFFECTS OF THE STRUCTURE OF PROSE ON RECALL

Height of Information in the Content Structure

Clear and consistent findings dealing with the height of information in the content structure have emerged from several studies with subjects of different age groups and for different recall tasks. The height of information in the content structure influences its recall. Ideas located high in the structure are better remembered after reading or listening to a passage than ideas low in the structure. Three studies investigating the effects of the height of information in the content structure will be discussed.

Study 1. Three groups of 23 Cornell University undergraduates listened to two 500-word articles extracted from *Scientific American* magazine (Meyer, 1971; Meyer & McConkie, 1973). One group heard each passage once before recalling it in a free recall task, the second group heard each passage twice before recalling, and the third group heard each passage three times. The passages were analyzed into tree structures subjectively, but were similar in structure to my latter analyses based on developments in linguistics. Structures of the passages made by three independent judges were in 91.5% agreement; the idea units were identified for the judges, but they had to arrange them into a hierarchical structure representing the logical relationships in the passage.

The ideas were divided into three groups high, medium and low based on their level in the structure of the passage. Then recall was examined for these ideas high, medium, and low in the passage's structure. For both passages under all three presentation conditions units high in the structure were recalled more frequently than those lower in the structure ($p < .001$), but no consistent difference was found between units middle and low in the structure.

Recall of units at high, medium, and low levels in the structure increased about equally with additional presentations. That is, the influence of the height of information in the content structure appears to have its effect when a person is first exposed to the passage. If idea units high in the structure of a passage can be accepted as being the main ideas of the passage, then this finding relates to the controversy of whether students learn main ideas first, then add details, or whether they first acquire details and only later obtain the main ideas. The first position is advocated by Ausubel (1963); the reader is said first to acquire the main, more abstract ideas of the passage, then to use these to form a structure into which the details are incorporated. Glock (1967), on the other hand, suggests that students should seek first to acquire details and then to learn the main ideas as they are seen to be based upon these details. The results from this study support Ausubel's view in finding that on the first exposure the main ideas tended to be acquired better than ideas lower in the structure. However, it is not true that on further presentations the details were then learned more quickly. After the first trial, position in the structure had little or no effect on the rate of increase of recall frequency. These data also indicate that the learning advocated by Glock, details first and then main ideas, is not the order normally used by college students.

This study also gave evidence for some form of clustering. Subjects tended to recall from a passage groups of units that were related to one another in the hierarchical structure. The overall recall for the passages in this study was about 23%. However, if a particular unit was recalled, then nearly 70% of the time the unit directly above it in the structure was also recalled.

This study indicated that information high in the structure was recalled better than information low in the structure. However, the content of information at high and low positions in the content structure was not controlled. Thus, the results could have been due to different types of information which may tend to be located in high and low positions in the structure. For example, the information high in the content structure might have been more concrete or conducive to imagery. These traits of the content, which investigators (Anderson, 1974; Montague & Carter, 1973; Paivio, 1969; Yuille & Paivio, 1969) have found to facilitate recall, could have been responsible for the differential in recall of information high and low in the content structure. Also, the differential could have resulted from more frequently used terms located high, rather than low, in the content structure, or from more inclusive concepts located high in the content structure and narrower concepts found low in the structure.

In addition, the structure was arrived at subjectively. In the next study to be described the content high and low in the content structure is controlled. Also, the passages for this study were analyzed more objectively using the semantic grammar of propositions.

Study 2.   In order to control for the nature of the content of the passage high and low in the content structure, six passages were carefully produced (Meyer, 1975). Two were written on each of three topics: Nuclear Breeder Reactors, Schizophrenia, and Parakeets. On each of these topics a paragraph was written which was included in both passages on that topic. This was called the *target paragraph.* One of the passages on each topic, the high passage, was written in such a way that, when analyzed, the information in the target paragraph stood at the top of the content structure. The other passage, the low passage, was so written that in its content structure the information in the target paragraph stood at the lowest levels. Both passages on the same topic were the same length, and had the same number of words occurring prior to and following the Target Paragraph. Thus, physical position in the passage was constant.

Two groups of 21 Cornell University undergraduates each participated in the experiment. Subjects in each group read and recalled three passages. Group 1 read the Breeder Reactor High, Schizophrenia Low, and Parakeet High passages. Group 2 read the Breeder Reactor Low, Schizophrenia High, and Parakeet Low passages. The order of presentation was counterbalanced within groups.

The experiment was conducted in two sessions. In the first, subjects read each passage and produced a written free recall of it immediately after reading. In the second session, one week later, subjects were again asked for a free recall of each passage. Then they were given lists of the content words found in the Target Paragraphs of each passage and asked to produce a third free recall of each passage, using these words to aid them. This was called the Cued Recall task.

The recall protocols were scored by assigning them one point for each content unit or relationship from the original content structure, which was included in the recall. They were scored for substantive content, rather than for exact wording.

Recall scores for the Target Paragraphs are presented in Table 1. Delayed recalls of the Parakeet passages have not been scored. As can be seen, in every case recall was significantly higher when the paragraph was high in the content structure, rather than low. This result was marked and consistent. This was not due to differences in passage difficulty, since total recall scores for the entire passages did not differ; 34% of the units were recalled from both Nuclear Breeder Reactor passages, and for the Schizophrenia passages 25% were recalled from the High version and 28% from the Low.

Differences in Target Paragraph recall scores between immediate and delayed testing, and between delayed free and delayed cued testing were computed. An analysis of variance of these data indicated significantly more loss over time for Target Paragraphs were low than when high in the structure, $F(1, 80) = 5.814, p < .005$, with no significant effect for passage topic and no interaction. Differ-

TABLE 1

Mean Recall for Target Paragraphs in High and Low Content Structure Positions for
Immediate and Delayed Free Recall and Delayed Cued Recall Conditions

Target paragraph topic	Recall condition	Content structure position		Degrees of freedom	t	Probability
		High	Low			
Breeder Reactor (46 units in target)	Immediate free recall	18.05	13.43	40	1.931	.05
	Delayed free recall	14.81	4.48	40	5.186	.0005
	Delayed cued recall	25.57	19.67	40	1.945	.05
Schizophrenia (46 units in target)	Immediate free recall	19.71	13.90	40	2.319	.025
	Delayed free recall	14.14	7.09	40	2.823	.005
	Delayed cued recall	26.00	19.57	40	2.527	.01
Parakeets (88 units in target)	Immediate free recall	44.24	34.57	40	2.75	.005

ence between delayed free and cued recall did not vary with passage topic or content structure position. Thus, presence of the cues produced approximately equal increments of recall, over delayed free recall scores, in all conditions.

It appears, then, that information high in the content structure of a passage is more likely to be recalled immediately after reading, and is subject to less forgetting over time.

One explanation for the recall superiority of high information might be that, since information high in the passage sets the theme of the passage, it is repeated more frequently in the passage. To check this explanation, the High and Low versions of the Nuclear Breeder Reactor passage were searched for instances of four types of repetition of content units from the Target Paragraph: verbatim repetition, substantive repetition, detailed restatement, and implicit reference. It was found that 12 of the 46 idea units in the Target Paragraph were repeated at least once in the text of the High version of the passage, while eight were repeated in the Low version. Of these, nine were repeated more frequently in the

High version, and five were repeated more frequently in the Low version. Thus, there was somewhat more repetition in the High version. However, amount of repetition did not seem to be related to likelihood of recall. Of the nine units repeated more frequently in the High version of the passage, eight were recalled better from that version. Of the five units repeated more frequently in the Low version, four were better recalled in the High version. These data were taken from immediate recalls and the delayed recall showed an even greater tendency for better recall of units from the High version, regardless of repetition frequency. Thus, while there was slightly more repetition of Target Paragraph information in the High version of the passage, this could not account for the superior recall from that version.

The three findings of this study were: (1) information is more likely to be recalled from a passage if it is high in the content structure than if it is low; (2) information is more likely to be retained over time from a passage if it is high in the content structure than if it is low; and (3) providing cues for recall one week after the original reading increases the recall of information high and low in the content structure of the passage about equally.

First of all, these findings point out the importance of the content structure of a passage as a determiner of the learning and retention of information from the passage.

Second, these findings bear on various theoretical positions regarding learning from prose. The recall superiority of high information immediately after learning could be accounted for from either a selectivity in learning or a retrieval position. That is, it may be that the content structure guides the reader's attentional processes, causing him to be more likely to select for storage that information high in the passage structure. On the other hand, it may be that high and low information are equally stored, but that the laws of retrieval are such that high information is more likely to be recalled under free recall conditions. The present study does not allow the testing of these two alternatives.

In order to discriminate between these two alternative explanations some data are being collected. Thus far, data have been collected from eighteen teachers attending a night class at Western Connecticut State College. Half of these subjects read the Breeder Reactor High and Parakeet High passages, while the other half read the Breeder Reactor Low and Parakeet Low passages. The subjects produced a written free recall immediately after reading which was immediately followed by a cued recall task. The results show these subjects to recall a third to a half fewer ideas than the subjects in the earlier experiment, but the same pattern of superior recall of the target paragraph high in the content structure is evident. The cues appear to assist recall for both high and low structural positions for both passages to about the same extent. Even with the assistance of cues, information high in the content structure is better recalled immediately after reading the passage. Thus, the data thus far collected support the first alternative that more information high in the structure is actually stored in memory.

The greater loss of low information over time could be due either to a differential rate of loss from memory, or to structural changes which cause lower information to be less accessible to retrieval for free recall, though the information is still present in memory and is accessible in other ways. The subsumption theory of Ausubel (1965) takes the first position, suggesting that peripheral information (that which is lower in the content structure) is subsumed by the more central information (that higher in the structure) over time, thus losing its independent identity and becoming less available for recall. The cued recall data provide some help in discriminating among these theoretical positions. If the recall loss were due simply to structural changes which make the information less accessible to free recall, though still present in memory, it would appear reasonable that it would be recalled under cued conditions. A reasonable prediction might then be that information low in the structure, which has been most subject to loss of accessibility to free recall, would be aided most by the presence of cues. Although the data pattern was in this direction, the differences were not significant. Thus, low information appears to be more rapidly lost from memory or subsumed over time, and not to simply become inaccessible to free recall.

Study 3. Three homogeneously grouped sixth-grade classes in a public school in Connecticut listened to a tape of a 641-word passage about parakeets. This passage, entitled Parakeets: Ideal Pets, was written for the study with college students and a copy of the passage appears in that work (Meyer, 1975). The content, interest level, and difficulty level for listening was gauged to be appropriate for this age group by the students' teachers. The 28 students in the highest ability class of the three classes had a mean IQ of 111 on the Lorge—Thorndike Intelligence Test and the average student in this class was reading a year and a half above grade level as measured by the Reading Subtest of the Iowa Test of Basic Skills. In contrast, the 28 students in the middle ability class had a mean IQ of 100, and the average student read three months below grade level, while the mean IQ for the 21 students in the low ability class was 86 and the students' mean reading level was a year below grade level. After listening to the passage the students were given thirty questions which they were to read silently as their teacher read them aloud. After reading each question the teacher waited for the students to write down an answer.

The parakeet passage has 17 levels in its content structure. Fifteen of the questions administered to the subjects asked for answers from the top eight levels in the content structure, while fifteen other questions tapped information found in Levels 10 through 17 of the structure. The questions from levels one through eight in the structure correspond to questions educators have called questions asking for main ideas, and those questions from Levels 10 through 17 correspond to questions asking for details. The number of correct answers dealing with information located high in the structure was then compared to the number of correct answers from information low in the structure for the three classes of students.

The results of a two-factor analysis of variance with repeated measures can be found in Table 2. The main effects of ability groups and height of information in the content structure were statistically significant and there was no significant interaction. Figure 1 summarizes the data graphically. Thus, all ability groups remembered more information high in the content structure of the parakeet passage than low in the structure. Higher-ability students simply remember significantly ($p < .001$) more ideas from high and low in the content structure than middle- and low-ability students, and middle-ability students remember significantly ($p < .025$) more ideas from high and low in the structure than low-ability students. The parallel findings for the three ability groups on high- and low-level questions displayed in Fig. 1 are very similar to the findings in Study 1 in which groups differed on the number of times they listened to a passage. For all of the groups of sixth-grade children high-structure information is better remembered immediately after hearing the passage, but higher-ability students appear to have a greater capacity to process and remember both more main ideas and details as if they were getting added presentations of the material.

This study was initiated for several reasons. First, it appears important to investigate the possibility of formulating a theory for writing test questions using

TABLE 2

Analysis of Variance of Number of High and Low Content Structure Questions Correct for High, Medium, and Low Sixth Grade Ability Groups

Source of variation	Sum of squares	Degrees of freedom	Mean square	F	Probability
Between subjects		77			
Ability groups	73.69	2	36.85	6.77	.005
Subjects within groups	408.02	75	5.44		
Within subjects		78			
Questions position in content structure	2281.83	1	2281.83	496.05	.001
Ability groups × position interaction	1.94	2	.97	.22	N.S.
Position × subjects within groups	345.25	75	4.60		

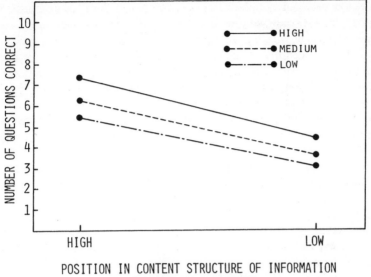

FIG. 1 Number of questions tapping high- and low-level information in the content structure answered correctly by high-, medium-, and low-ability sixth graders.

the content structure of a passage. For example, a certain number of questions for a test of general comprehension of a passage would come from top branches of the content structure, others would test whether the reader understands the relationships between top level content, while still other questions would test for lower level content. This study has shown that questions can be easily written from the content structure. The structure certainly provides a concrete criteria for discriminating between questions asking main ideas and details. For each question the exact levels in the structure involving information in the question and required in the answer could be specified as well as which exact idea units from the structure were involved in the question. Thus, it appears quite feasible to develop a theory of question writing using the content structure.

Second, it seems valuable to ascertain whether the findings related to the height of information in the content structure hold true for age levels other than college students. This study shows that the findings certainly hold true for sixth graders listening to prose. Developmental studies are necessary to look at when and how this differentiation in recall of high- and low-level information occurs both in listening and reading.

Third, it is important to examine data for a possible interaction between ability level of children and their recall of high- and low-level information. This investigation was conducted to see if low-ability students remember more fragmented details and not the main ideas. This was not found with listening, but it may be the case with some children with certain learning or reading disabilities. Although working with only two learning disabled children last year in the public schools, I found that after reading and recalling a narrative they did remember the top-level information, the major sequences in the narrative, and forgot the specific details. More research in this area is needed.

In conclusion, these three studies present consistent results using different modes of presentation of prose, different age and ability levels of subjects, and different recall tasks. Information high in the content structure is remembered and retained much better than low level information. Kintsch and Keenan (1973) using a slightly different prose analysis technique with passages of 20 to 70 words also supported this finding.

Passages with the Same Structure, but Different Content

A study (Meyer, 1975) with Cornell University undergraduates was designed to examine the degree of correspondence in recall frequency patterns from passages differing in the content of units of their content structure, but having the same structural form and the same specific relationships. In order to examine the influence of the pattern of specific relationships in the content structure on recall, the Breeder Reactor High and the Schizophrenia High passages, mentioned previously, were designed to have the same structure and role and rhetorical relationships, but different content.

The recall frequency data from these passages were examined to see the degree to which the same structure results in the recall of the same items regardless of content. A Pearson product-moment correlation coefficient was computed between the recall frequency data for the Breeder Reactor High passage and that for the Schizophrenia High passage. The number of subjects ($n = 21$) recalling a unit in the content structure was tallied for each of the 193 units in the structure. The number of subjects who recalled each idea unit in the Breeder Reactor High passage was tallied. In addition, the number of subjects who recalled each idea unit in the Schizophrenia High passage was also tallied. Then a correlation was run between these recall frequency scores for corresponding units in the two passages. The Pearson product-moment correlation coefficient for the Breeder Reactor High and Schizophrenia High in an immediate free recall condition was .55 ($p < .001$) and .56 ($p < .001$) in a delayed free recall condition.

In examining the .55 degree of relation between the two passages with the same structure of relations, but different content, it is not apparent how much of this relationship is due to the general effect of height in the content structure versus how much is due to the specific similarity of the function of the idea units as guaranteed by the same relationships in the content structures of both passages.

In order to examine this situation, any correspondence due solely to the same specific relationships in the two passages was eliminated. This was accomplished by identifying the height in the content structure of each unit in the Breeder Reactor High passage, and the number of people recalling the unit. Then, the recall frequency of each unit of the content structure was replaced by the recall frequency of another unit with the same height in the structure through random selection. This procedure was followed for every idea unit in the content structure so that the height in the content structure of each unit was preserved while the specific functional relationships characterizing each unit were destroyed. A correlation was computed between these mixed recall frequency scores for the Breeder Reactor High passage and the original recall frequency scores of the Schizophrenia High passage. This provided a measure of the degree of relationship between the two passages due solely to height in the content structure.

The Pearson product-moment correlation coefficient for this relationship was .22 ($p < .001$) when compared with the .55 ($p < .001$) correlation with the presence of both factors of height in the structure and the same pattern of specific relations. Therefore, it appears that most of the relationship between the recall patterns from passages with identical structures results from the similarity of their pattern of specific relationships in the structure and not just to height in the structure. Thus, both the factors of height in the structure and the pattern of specific types of relationships are needed to account for the correspondence in the patterns of recall from passages with identical structures of specific relations and different content.

Through analyzing numerous passages and examining recall data, I came to believe that the pattern of specific relationships at the top levels of the content structure has a dramatic effect on which ideas and relationships will be remembered by almost everyone in a group, which units by some, and which units by few people in a group. That is, although top-level information is in general much better remembered than low-level information, not all top-level information is equally well remembered. The differences in recall of this top-level information appear to be dictated by the relationship of each top-level content unit to the rest of the top-level information in terms of its specific role or rhetorical relations and its location in the configuration of the top level branches. In contrast, the pattern of specific relations low in the content structure appears to have very little effect on which detail is remembered. At the lower levels of the content structure, the particular content of idea units appears to determine whether or not they are recalled rather than the specific function the information takes in the passage in relation to other information. Past research (Meyer, 1971) indicated that even at very low levels in the structure numbers and familiar proper names were recalled unusually well. Data from this study were available to test this hypothesis concerning the differential effect of the pattern of relationships high and low in the structure.

The data used to investigate the validity of this hypothesis were the recall scores for each idea unit in the Breeder Reactor and Schizophrenia target paragraphs high and low in the content structure. The Breeder Reactor and Schizophrenia target paragraphs have the same structure of specific relations and different content. The correlation between the recall frequency scores for the idea units in the Breeder reactor and Schizophrenia target paragraphs when the paragraphs were high in the structure would indicate the influence of the pattern of specific relationships at the top levels of the content structure on which units are recalled. On the other hand, correlations between the recall frequency scores of the idea units when these same paragraphs were low in the structure would indicate the influence of the pattern of specific relationships at the low levels of the content structure on which units are recalled. Thus, if the pattern of specific relations high in the structure greatly influences recall, while this pattern of relations only minimally influences recall low in the structure, where peculiarities of content play the most important role in recall, then a correlation between recall frequency patterns from the paragraphs high in the structure should be high, while the correlations for the same paragraphs low in the structure should be low.

The Pearson product-moment correlation coefficient between the Breeder Reactor and Schizophrenia target paragraphs high in the structure for the immediate free recall condition was .83 and it was .67 in the delayed free recall condition one week later. In contrast, the correlation between these target paragraphs low in the structure for the immediate free recall condition was .09 and −.11 for the delayed free recall condition. Thus, although the content of the ideas for the two paragraphs was different, the same pattern of specific relationships in the paragraphs appeared to have produced similar recall patterns from the two paragraphs when they were high in the structure. On the other hand, correlations between these same paragraphs when they occurred low in the content structures are approximately zero. Thus, these data support the hypothesis concerning the differential influence of the pattern of specific relations in the content structure on recall, depending on height in the content structure.

This study showed that passages with identical structures of specific relations, but different content, produce similar patterns of recall. This structural dimension of prose appears to be a useful dimension on which to classify types of passages. Since the structure of relationships at the top levels of a passage's content structure is more powerful in predicting recall than the structure at the bottom levels of a passage's structure, it may be necessary only to classify passages into various types on the basis of their top-level structures. Classifying passages on this structure variable along with content variables and traditional readability measures would help to insure equivalency of passages often needed in experiments and constructing equivalent forms of reading tests. Future research is necessary to determine whether the pattern of the structure alone at the top levels of the content structure influences what information is recalled, or whether the particular types of role relations and rhetorical predicates that determine recall, or a combination of the two influence what information is recalled. Scoring recall protocols from numerous passages, it has become evident to me that one particular relationship, manner rhetorical predicates, and its corresponding content is consistently recalled by few if any people regardless of the unit's position in the content structure. Manner relations explain how an event was performed, for example, carefully or slowly. I suspect that the later option is true — the pattern of the structure in combination with particular relations influences recall.

Manipulations of the Extreme Top Level Structure

The studies previously discussed suggest that the reader or listener pays particularly close attention to the top level information in the content structure. A study was designed to see if certain top level organizational patterns facilitate memory of the entire passage more than other patterns.

In my first study with prose (Meyer, 1971) using two *Scientific American* magazine articles, I found that one passage was recalled nearly twice as well as the other. The content of the two passages did not appear to differ in difficulty although the fast breeder reactors discussed in the better remembered passage may have been slightly more difficult than the content in the poorer recalled passage dealing with the therapeutic community, a method of treating the mentally ill. It appeared to me that the organization of the breeder reactor passage was tighter and superior; at the top level of this passage's content structure was a response rhetorical predicate which relates a problem or problems to a solution. The problems in this passage were the need to improve the quality of the environment, the need to produce enough electricity, and the need to conserve the nation's finite supplies of coal, oil, and gas. The solution to these problems was the fast breeder reactor, the content that the authors were primarily interested in discussing in their article.

In contrast to the response rhetorical predicate used to organize the content in the passage on breeder reactors, an attribution rhetorical predicate organized the therapeutic community passage. An attribution rhetorical predicate describes qualities of a proposition. The attribution rhetorical predicate related the therapeutic community to a number of descriptions of qualities of the community. The top level organization appeared loose; the author could have used a different top level structure although he would have to add different corresponding content. A response rhetorical predicate could have been the top level predicate; that is, the author could have stated some problems of treating the mentally ill and then presented the therapeutic community as the solution to these problems and then in depth described this therapy. Another possibility would be to use a covariance rhetorical predicate as the primary organizational focus of the passage. The covariance rhetorical predicate relates an antecedent to a consequent.

For example, the author could have described the research and work of a number of individuals as the antecedent, and the consequent would be the treatment method resulting from their work, the therapeutic community which could then be described.

In summary, authors often have a choice in how they will organize the presentation of their material and what content they will include. An author may not consider what organizational structure will be most effective. A study (Meyer & Freedle, 1976) only partially analyzed was instituted to compare the effects of four discourse types or top level structures on the amount of information remembered from prose.

The four discourse types were expository text and were classified according to their top level rhetorical predicates. The rhetorical predicates were *response*: problem and solution, *covariance:* antecedent and consequent, *attribution,* and *adversative*, which relates what did happen to what did not happen. Four passages of 141 words were written about loss of body water. Of the 141 words in each passage 109 were the same for the four passages and 32 were different. The content, structure, and relationships were exactly the same for 58 of the 69 units in the content structures of the passages. Six other units were the same in structure and type of relationships, but not in content. The remaining different units were the top-level rhetorical predicates, which differentiated the discourse types of the passages.

Four groups of 11 Western Connecticut State College graduate students each listened to one discourse type dealing with the loss of body water. Immediately after listening to a passage, the subjects wrote all that they could recall about it. One week later another free-recall task was administered. In addition, the subjects were asked to state the primary message of the passage and to answer questions about the passage to determine what information was stored in memory, but not retrievable without cues. At present, only the immediate and delayed free-recall protocols from the covariance and atribution passages have been scored. A cursory reading of the protocols written after listening to the adversative and response passages indicates that they are more similar to the protocols from the covariance passage than those from the attribution passage.

The effects of the two discourse types, attribution and covariance, were examined on the recall of the 58 identical units in both passages. The results of a two-factor analysis of variance with repeated measures can be seen in Table 3. More information was remembered from the passage with the covariance top-level structure than was remembered when that same information was organized with an attribution rhetorical predicate. This superiority in recall of the 58 units in the covariance passage over the identical 58 units in the attribution passage can be seen graphically in Fig. 2.

Thus, preliminary analysis of the data from this study indicates that certain top level structures facilitate the acquisition of information in a passage more than other top-level structures. These findings have important implications for a

TABLE 3

Analysis of Variance of Covariance and Attribution Passage Recall Scores from
Immediate and Delayed Free Recall Conditions

Source of variation	Sum of squares	Degrees of freedom	Mean square	F	Probability
Between subjects	2505.66	21			
Discourse type	918.21	1	918.21	11.57	.005
Subjects within groups	1587.45	20	79.37		
Within subjects	813.5	22			
Recall task	518.21	1	518.21	36.6	.001
Discourse type × recall task interaction	12.01	1	12.01	.85	N.S.
Recall task × subjects within groups	283.28	20	14.16		

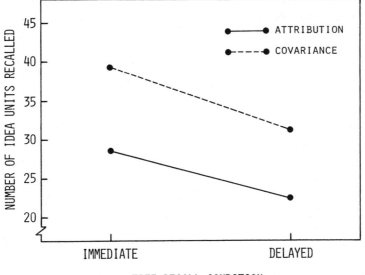

FIG. 2 Number of idea units recalled from covariance passage and attribution passage
under immediate and delayed free-recall conditions.

theory of how people process information from prose as well as practical implications for writers.

In the next section of this paper I deal with the implications for educational practice of these research projects, which have examined the effects of the structure of prose on what information is acquired from prose.

IMPLICATIONS FOR EDUCATIONAL PRACTICE
OF THE STRUCTURE OF PROSE
AND ITS EFFECTS ON MEMORY

There is a great need in education for a comprehensive theory of learning from prose on which to base programs designed to increase students' learning from their reading and listening. Such a theory requires an extensive data base from which to generalize principles of learning from prose. The structure of prose is a valuable tool for use in experiments designed to increase this data base. The findings of the studies presented in this paper will have to be accounted for in such a theory as well as data collected on other aspects of reading and listening.

One reasonable explanation of the data from the studies discussed in this paper involves steps taken by the reader or listener directly related to the structure of a passage. The data suggest that the reader needs to have an organization of ideas presented to him. When exposed to a passage, his strategy usually will be to use the ready-made organizational structure of the passage. The research indicates that some types of these top level structures are better than others for remembering the ideas of a passage. The reader attends closely to this top level structure of the passage, remembering the primary relationships in the top levels of the structure (not such relations as manners) and those top-level relationships tying together large segments of prose. He rehearses and subsequently stores in long-term memory these top level concepts and interrelationships located high in the content structure of a passage. Peripherally related information to this top-level structure, found low in the content structure, is rehearsed less in short-term memory, and what information is processed for long-term storage tends to be particular clusters of content that in some way catch the reader's attention, such as numbers and familiar proper names. In memory the information more centrally related to the top-level structure of a passage is retained longer, whereas the peripherally related clusters of information tend to be forgotten more quickly.

These studies have shown that college students from their reading and listening, and sixth graders through listening, better remember top-level information in the structure (main ideas), than low-level information (details). Developmental research is needed to show when people begin to process the main ideas and filter out peripheral information in listening and in reading. Use of the techniques employed in the studies presented in this contribution to identify the structure of prose will be extremely useful in developmental research. A student and I have recently used this prose analysis technique to prepare narratives for recall experiments with nursery school children and have found the technique useful.

There is potential for creating a valuable diagnostic tool for teachers, reading specialists, and school psychologists from developmental research and research establishing norms for age levels on recall of high- and low-structure information from passages listened to and read. Such a diagnostic tool using the structure of a passage could enable educators to see where a child having difficulties in learning deviates from the norm in what he learns from his reading or listening. A simplification of the structure of prose itself may be a valuable pedagogical tool in helping a child visually comprehend the relationships among ideas in prose and the superordinate and subordinate relationships among these ideas in terms of the organization of a particular passage.

The structure of prose can also be a valuable tool for studying individual differences in learning from prose not only in terms of whether or not an individual deviates from the norm. If a child does deviate substantially from others in what he remembers from a passage, his recall protocol can itself be analyzed as to its structure. Then this structure can be compared for similarities to and differences from the structure of the original passage.

In my studies with college students most of their recall protocols are organized in manners similar to the original passages, but a few deviate markedly. These rare protocols are either organized in a unique manner by the subject, often with distortion of the information from the original passage to match the structure they have provided, or they lack any overall organization and relate only fragmented details. In the first type it appears that the subject did not pick up the passage's top level structure or primary message. In order to provide an organization to tie together the ideas that he remembers from the passage, he seems to produce his own structure and adds details not found in the text and distorted details from the text to support the structure he has devised. Concerning the later type of protocol, I once (Meyer, 1972) compared subjects who recalled the top level structure of a passage to those who recalled primarily isolated clusters of low level information on their performance on the Rorschach Test. For the small group studied there was a tendency for the subjects who recalled the low level information without an overall structure tying the ideas together to have a preponderance of rare detail responses on the Rorschach Test.

In conclusion, research using the structure of prose to study individual differences in learning has much potential. The structure of prose and its effects on learning also have significant implications for writers of test questions, standardized reading and listening tests, textbooks, lectures, and school assignments.

The structure of prose can be readily used as the basis for a theory of writing test questions. Anderson (1972), in his analysis of 130 articles in which one or more experimenter-made reading achievement tests were employed, found that two-thirds of the investigators did not even attempt to give any description of the information tapped by their questions, nor did they give a rationale for asking some questions rather than others. Thus, a difficult problem has existed in selecting questions to evaluate reading comprehension from a passage and specifying the kinds of information that a reader must remember to answer a particular question.

Using principles of transformational grammar both Bormuth (1970) and Anderson (1972) have specified systematic procedures for writing test questions. Although these procedures explicitly state how a question was derived, they provide no guide in deciding which information in the prose about which to write questions, nor much assistance in classifying types of information from a passage necessary to answer certain kinds of information.

Use of the structure of a passage can solve these problems and give test questions greater construct validity. The exact level and idea units in the content structure of a passage can be specified for questions written using this structure as a model. If an examiner wants to test for main ideas and details, the questions can be differentiated and selected by their position high or low in the structure of the passage. The percentage of questions coming from different levels in the content structure could be manipulated according to the type of test desired by the examiner. For example, a test of general comprehension would include primarily questions from the top levels of the content structure with only a few middle and low level ideas. Using the structure of prose to select information for test items, and transformational grammar to write the questions, should improve the validity and reliability of tests.

The structure of prose can be used to describe passages used in reading and listening tests. The research discussed in this contribution shows that the structure itself influences what is remembered from it. Certain top-level structures appear to facilitate recall of a passage more than others and the pattern of specific relationships high in the content structure influences the recall of content and relations at this level of the structure regardless of the particular content of the ideas. Equivalent forms of reading or listening tests are often required in the evaluation of educational programs. The passages with different content on these equivalent tests should have the same structure and specific relationships, particularly at the higher levels of their content structures. In addition, the passages should be made equivalent on aspects of content, such as imagery, as well as readability measures. Also, the test questions on the equivalent forms of the test should come from the same positions in the identical structures of the passage. These procedures would provide evaluators with greater assurance that alternate forms of tests are, in fact, equivalent.

Finally, the results of these studies, examining the effects of the structure of prose on what is remembered from it, have notable implications for writers of textbooks, lectures, and classroom assignments. First, the information that a writer wants his readers to remember should be placed high in the content structure of the prose. Second, a tightly organized top level structure embodying causal or comparative relationships appears to facilitate the recall of the information from prose over a loosely organized top level structure that lists a collection of attributes. Thus, the writer should select a top level structure for his content that will best facilitate its recall. The structure of prose may also be a useful teaching tool in writing classes. It may be beneficial for the teacher and students to diagram the top level structures of a student's theme and examine this structure for its inclusion of the ideas felt to be most important by the theme's writer and for the strength of the top level relationship.

In summary, the structure of prose has been shown to be a powerful variable in determining recall of prose. More specifically, information high in the structure is better remembered and retained than low-level information. Also, the pattern of specific relations in the structure influences the recall of the information in prose. In addition, certain top level structures facilitate recall more than others. These findings have important educational implications in terms of providing data for a theory of learning from prose, information about individual differences in learning, a potential diagnostic tool for educators to identify areas of learning problems, and a model for writers of test questions, texts, and other prose materials. Use of the structure of prose in future research will continue to provide new insights into the processes involved in learning and retaining information from prose.

REFERENCES

Anderson, R. C. How to construct achievement tests to assess comprehension. *Review of Educational Research*, 1972, **42**, 145–170.

Anderson, R. C. Concretization and sentence learning. *Journal of Educational Psychology*, 1974, **66**, 179–183.

Ausubel, D. P. *The psychology of meaningful verbal learning: An introduction to school learning.* New York: Grune & Stratton, 1963.

Ausubel, D. P. Cognitive structure and facilitation of meaningful verbal learning. In R. C. Anderson & D. P. Ausubel (Eds.), *Readings in the psychology of cognition.* New York: Holt, Rinehart, & Winston, 1965.

Bormuth, J. R. *On the theory of achievement test terms.* Chicago, Illinois: University of Chicago Press, 1970.

Carroll, J. B. Learning from verbal discourse in educational media: Review of the literature. Final Report Project 7-1069. Princeton, New Jersey: Educational Testing Service, 1971.

Deverell, A. F. Are reading improvement courses at the university level justified? *Invitational conferences on education.* Canadian Educational Association, 1959. Pp. 19–27.

Fillmore, C. J. The case for case. In E. Bach & R. Harms (Eds.), *Universals in linguistic theory.* New York: Holt, Rinehart, & Winston, 1968.

Flanagan, J. C. A study of the effect of comprehension of varying speeds of reading. In *American educational research on the foundations of American education.* Official report, 1939. Pp. 47–50.

Glock, M. D. *The improvement of college reading.* Boston: Houghton Mifflin, 1967.

Grimes, J. E. *The thread of discourse.* The Hague, Holland: Mouton, 1975.

Halliday, M. A. K. Notes on transitivity and theme in English. *Journal of Linguistics*, 1967, 3, 37–81.

Kintsch, W., & Keenan, J. M. Reading rate as a function of the number of propositions in the base structure of sentences. *Cognitive Psychology*, 1973, 5, 257–274.

Kirscher, M. C. The effects of presentation order and repetition on the free recall of prose. Unpublished master's thesis, Cornell University, 1971.

Meyer, B. J. F. Idea units recalled from prose in relation to their position in the logical structure, importance, stability and order in the passage. Unpublished master's thesis, Cornell University, 1971.

Meyer, B. J. F. Usefulness of the Rorscach test in explaining individual differences on a reading recall task. Unpublished manuscript, 1972.

Meyer, B. J. F. *The organization of prose and its effects on memory.* Amsterdam: North-Holland Publ., 1975.

Meyer, B. J. F., & Freedle, R. The effects of different discourse types on recall. Paper in process, Educational Testing Service, 1976.

Meyer, B. J. F., & McConkie, G. W. What is recalled after hearing a passage? *Journal of Educational Psychology,* 1973, 65, 109–117.

Montague, W. E., & Carter, J. F. Vividness of imagery in recalling connected discourse. *Journal of Educational Psychology*, 1973, 64, 72–75.

Paivio, A. Mental imagery in associative learning and memory. *Psychological Review*, 1969, 76, 241–263.

Rothkopf, E. Z., & Bisbicos, E. Selective facilitative effects of interspersed questions on learning from written material. *Journal of Educational Psychology,* 1967, 58, 56–61.

van Dijk, T. A. *Some aspects of text grammars.* The Hague: Mouton, 1972.

Welborn, E. L., & English, H. B. Logical learning and retention: a general review of experiments with meaningful verbal materials. *Psychology Bulletin,* 1937, 43, i–20.

Yuille, J. C., & Paivio, A. Abstractness and the recall of connected discourse. *Journal of Educational Psychology*, 1969, 82, 467–471.

COMMENTS ON
CHAPTER 6 BY MEYER

John F. Carter

Navy Personnel Research and Development Center

There is probably no proposition concerning learning from discourse that is more intuitively plausible than that the organization or structure of materials that we read or hear should affect our learning. Not only do our intuitions suggest this, but there is even a very substantial research base dealing with the effects of organization on learning word lists which provides a rich source of theoretical and empirical principles in support of this notion. Time does not permit, nor would it be desirable for current purposes to review this basic literature. But, in general, the findings are consistent with the view that learning will be facilitated to the extent that the learner is able to adopt, or construct, an organizational scheme during learning which can act as a specific retrieval plan (Tulving & Donaldson, 1972). While this proposition is straightforward, and the implications for learning from textual materials rather direct, my attempt to make good on these implications has convinced me that it is, indeed, exceedingly difficult to generalize up the "phylolinguistic" scale. That is to say, in the several years that I have conducted research on factors affecting prose learning and have tried to generalize from word list studies in the organization in free recall tradition, I have found that the obvious and straightforward generalizations did not always survive in the crucible of textual learning situations. In fact, if one reviews the history of research on organization or organizational-orienting variables on learning from prose, or educational materials in particular, one seldom finds facilitating effects. Consequently, it was particularly refreshing to read Meyer's description of her research on the effects of discourse structure on learning. This appears to represent a needed exception to the general trend and one which could have important implications for educational practice.

Before going further, however, let me provide an overview of my remarks today. First, in order to provide a context for my comments, I would like to review some of the general literature in this area and relate it to Meyer's work. Then will follow a critique of certain aspects of this research thrust and an attempt to evaluate the proposed implications of this line of inquiry for educational practice.

As Meyer correctly states, there are several different approaches to the study of organizational effects in prose learning. Although these are probably not mutually exclusive, they are sufficiently distinct to be given separate consideration in the context of our discussion today. The first involves studies which attempt to directly influence the nature of the learner's processing of the organizational structure of a passage. Included here are studies going back at least 50 years in which subjects were asked to engage in various activities, such as summarizing, outlining, or underlining text, which it was apparently thought would aid the student to identify and process critical elements in the textual materials. The second involves the manipulation of adjunct materials for the purpose of providing a conceptual framework for material to be studied later. This is what Ausubel (1960) termed an "advance organizer." Third, there are the attempts to manipulate the implicit organization of a prose passage to better understand how learners discover and use structure to facilitate recall. Meyer's work, of course, falls into this last category, as does much of my own.

If there is a unifying theme in these different approaches it would seem to be the hypothesis that somehow knowledge of the superordinate ideas in a prose passage will facilitate acquisition and recall of subordinate ideas. The problem for the prose researcher is to demonstrate that this hypothesis is correct; and for the educational designer, to use this principle, assuming it is correct, to produce more learnable materials.

Now, let us look more closely at the research in each of these areas. In doing so, I will take a somewhat historical perspective since many of the most relevant studies from the point of view of educational practice are fairly old.

Perhaps the first study which attempted to influence the subject's processing of organizational structure, or attention to main ideas, was conducted by Germane (1921). Germane compared the effects of reading and rereading a passage, with reading and summarizing the passage for a 30-minute period with sixth- through eighth-grade school children. Although the study was not well done from a modern perspective, the consistent result was for the rereading group to be superior in performance on what he called "reason" and "memory" questions.

About 20 years later Arnold (1942), using college students as subjects in a study spanning 15 weeks, found rereading to be superior to a variety of subjective organizational techniques such as outlining, underlining, and précis writing. Similar results for several measures of educational performance were reported by Matthews (1938).

More recently, Carter (1972) asked high school students to "subjectively organize" scrambled and logically presented textual materials. This treatment was also not facilitative over free reading on a free recall task.

On the positive side, Beauchamp (1923) and Newlun (1930) reported summarizing and outlining to be superior to reading. However, these studies differed from most of the others in that they were conducted in a natural classroom over a period of several months with school children. (The study by Arnold, 1942, which found negative results, was also conducted under naturalistic conditions.)

On the whole, then, these studies seem to contradict the general hypothesis that procedures aimed at causing subjects to process aspects of the higher level conceptual structure of a passage should facilitate educational performance.

However, if we apply the results from Meyer's research to this problem we may find a way to explain these data. The central finding reported in Meyer's paper is that content high in the conceptual structure of a prose passage is better recalled than content low in the conceptual structure. Furthermore, her data indicate that this effect is independent of the specific content of the material in question. In other words, it appears that learners may spontaneously engage in the very behaviors which the investigators in the above studies sought to influence. If this is the case, then small wonder that simple instructional sets or interventions of short duration were unable to produce significant effects.

The fact that two studies, conducted in a natural classroom over an extended period of time and with children, did produce facilitative effects, suggests that it may be possible to enhance processing of complex prose materials with learners who may not have acquired the sophisticated information search strategies typically possessed by adults. But the clear implication is that these strategies, once acquired, are difficult to influence with traditional experimental interventions.

This brings me to the next general area of organization in prose research, studies of the effects of what Ausubel (1960) termed the "advance organizer." To quote Ausubel (1960), "cognitive structure is hierarchically organized in terms of highly inclusive concepts under which are subsumed less inclusive subconcepts and informational data" (p. 267). This is a conception which is not too different from more recent formulations regarding the structure of semantic memory (e.g., Collins & Quillian, 1972). The implication of this view for Ausubel was that prior exposure to higher level concepts should enable subjects to better store and maintain subordinate information in memory. Without elaborating further on his theory of meaningful learning and memory, let it simply be said that the evidence regarding the advance organizer hypothesis is mixed. Some studies have concluded in favor of advance organizers (e.g., Ausubel, 1960; Grotelueschen & Sjogren, 1968), and some have concluded against (e.g., Allen, 1970; Schulz, 1966). Furthermore, the supporting studies have often been flawed by a failure to control for the direct instructive effects of the advance organizer itself vis-à-vis the performance measure. It may be, therefore, that we merely see the effects of review rather than cognitive elaboration in these studies.

Be that as it may, the interesting point within the context of the current discussion is that, as Meyer points out, her findings are in general agreement with Ausubel's theory. Certainly Ausubel would predict that any examination of subjects' learning should reveal a strong trend favoring greater retention of superordinate ideas. In addition, we could reasonably expect that some manipulation of this upper level structure along the lines suggested by Ausubel would produce beneficial effects on learning. It is surprising, therefore, to find that the efficacy of advance organizers has not been better supported in the literature. Furthermore, the kinds of "advance organizers" which have been reported to facilitate learning in several studies were not of the general, superordinate sort at all, but served instead to make subsequent materials more concrete (e.g., Royer & Cable, 1975). One problem in separating higher level elements of a passage to serve as advance organizers is that it ignores the role of context in defining the conceptual level of the elements, something which Meyer's work indicates is extremely important.

I now come to the third area of organization in prose research – studies which manipulation the inherent structure of the passage itself. As indicated previously, this is where I think Meyer's research belongs, as well as some of my own. Studies in this category include those in which the experimenter added headings or underlined main points in the text, gave subjects an outline, manipulated name versus attribute organization, presented scrambled versus correctly organized versions of the text, or, as in the case of Meyer's research, varied the position of information in the conceptual structure of the passage.

Early investigations of this sort include a study by Robinson and Hall (1941) who found no significant effects for adding headings to prose passages with college students, and a large factorial study by Christensen and Stordahl (1955) who varied the presence of headings, summaries, outlines, and underlining for a passage read by Air Force recruits, with essentially negative results.

More recently, Lee (1965) found differences favoring an elaborated text that included advance organizers, headings, and summaries over unelaborated and scrambled versions. However, the methodology employed by Lee makes it unclear whether these effects were due to the organizational variables involved, or to simple repetition of test-relevant information.

Bruning (1970), using college students as subjects, found that the presence of a topic sentence facilitated factual cued recall, but surprisingly, it did not matter whether the passage with topic sentences was presented in scrambled or logical order. Carter (1972) also studied the effects of scrambled text with similar results.

A problem with studies of this sort is that they have typically used only a single exposure to the materials as the experimental treatment. Hypothesizing that organizational effects require time to develop, Carter and Carrier (in press) varied the number of exposures to scrambled and logical versions of a prose passage for college students and found that logical organization was better only after multiple exposures to the materials. Meyer's findings suggest that this is not because subjects do not process structure during initial reading, but, rather, that information search strategies for main ideas and higher level elements are sufficiently strong for sophisticated learners that little is added to what they can discover for themselves without the benefit of text elaboration techniques, even when the text is presented in less than an optimal fashion. Clustering analyses also support this conclusion in that even with a scrambled text subjects appear to discover to a great extent the inherent conceptual structure of the passage (Carter & Carrier, in press).

Research with passages in which either name or attribute organizations were equally appropriate have, in contrast to the above generalization, found decrements in recall associated with scrambled presentations (e.g., Frase, 1969). However, these passages have typically been quite short in comparison to materials used in the studies mentioned above. Whether subjects get to a point in reading a passage at which organizational manipulations influence their processing strategies would appear, therefore, to be a function of the length and complexity of the materials. The shorter and less complex the materials, the sooner learners will free themselves from a general search for high level conceptual elements and look for specific schemes to aid recall.

This model, if one can even call it that, would seem to account for the many contradictory findings evident throughout this literature. Second, it points to the need for studies using materials and experimental methodologies that more closely simulate the kind of information processing requirements placed on learners who are confronted with the large amounts of textual material, and contingencies on learning, which are associated with the normal classroom. Until this is done I think it will be difficult to extract generalizations which will be useful to educational practioners.

This would seem to lead me to the point of making comments on the implications of Meyer's work and the other research cited above for the process of schooling, the announced purpose for this conference. Meyer has outlined a number of uses for her procedures and results for educational practice. These focus in three areas: diagnosis of individual and developmental differences in textual learning, test construction, and the writing of instructional materials. I have specific comments in each of these areas, but first let me make a general comment which applies not only to Meyer's work but other research in the area, as well, including my own.

Most of this research has focused on free recall as the primary variable of interest. Although free recall may be a useful measure of learning when one is interested in determining the knowledge structure possessed by subjects, or their retrieval strategies, it has limited educational relevance since most educational measurements rely on some form of cued testing to assess learning. Even essay testing, the closest parallel to free recall, typically requires more than simple factual recall. The problem is that educational practice usually involves learning *from* text, while psychologists have tended to study learning *of* text. I think most educators would not place factual learning at the apex of educational goals. This, of course, is not to minimize the importance of studies aimed at understanding memory for prose, but to emphasize that we cannot expect them to have profound implications for education until we begin to study a wider range of educational performances. At least with respect to organizational variables, this has not happened to a sufficient degree.

Now, some comments regarding the specific implications of Meyer's research. She argues that knowledge about the typical pattern of recall is useful as a diagnostic tool. I agree that this would seem to be a reasonable use of her data and procedures. However, there are many reasons why a subject's recall protocol may be discrepant from the norm. For instance, it may only mean that a useful subjective scheme has been applied, or that a degree of creativity has been exhibited. It seems, therefore, that there is a need to assure that discrepant recall patterns imply dysfunctional verbal processing and retrieval strategies, rather than a tolerable, or even desirable, level of individual uniqueness.

I would also agree that structure of prose research has implications for test construction. Combined with the work of Bormuth (1970) and Anderson (1972), as Meyer points out, there appears to be emerging a powerful basis for developing questioning techniques. The major difficulty would seem to be in getting classroom teachers or instructional materials publishers to employ such procedures systematically. I have not seen the specific steps necessary to produce a prose analysis according to Meyer's scheme, but unless it is rather simple and straightforward I question whether teachers would routinely use such methods for test construction. Of course, teacher's manuals might provide item pools which have been developed along these lines, but my experience suggests that test items derived from these sources have seldom been developed using already existing psychometric procedures. Of course this is a problem in implementation, not conception. But I think we often worry too little about such matters.

My final comments deal with the question of using findings from organization in prose research to benefit instructional development. Here I will be more critical, and I fear, pessimistic. As the above review of literature indicated, those variables which are most easily manipulated by developers of instructional materials have generally failed to show facilitative effects in experimental studies. Nevertheless, developers continue to provide outlines, headings, advance organizers, and the like, in the belief that they benefit the student. Are they wrong to labor so diligently to do so? I think not. And the reason I think not is that the purposes served by such appendages are not primarily for the enhancement of recall, but to aid in such educationally common behaviors as reviewing, searching for and retrieving specific information, and separating topics into a convenient size for study assignments. Thus, whether organizational paraphernalia are facilitative of recall or not is largely unimportant, as long as they serve these other useful purposes in the world of everyday education.

I am also not terribly hopeful that knowing that learners tend to recall higher level structure will greatly affect the practice of instructional development. Meyer states, "information that a writer wants his readers to remember should be placed high in the content structure of the prose [p.198]." There are two difficulties with this proposition from a practical point of view. First of all, the level and position of an idea in instructional materials is more determined by the structure of the underlying knowledge domain, and the instructional intent, than by the decision of the developer. If instructional materials are properly developed, one begins with statements of objectives which, in turn, determine the nature of the instructional content and the behaviors required of students. Within this context, the level of an idea in the instructional product is a function of its logical relationship to those objectives, rather than a decision which can be made arbitrarily by the designer.

Moreover, I seriously doubt whether deliberately adding or substracting detail or abstract elements in instructional materials for the sole purpose of elevating or reducing the level of certain ideas in the materials is the proper use of this knowledge. I suspect that the finding that people tend to favor higher level elements in recall is a descriptive fact regarding natural prose of the same sort as the finding that materials with short, active sentences and familiar words have lower readability scores. But as with readability measures, which capitalize on correlative but not necessarily causative factors, it may not be a *prescriptive fact*. That is, it may not imply a rule that can be used for producing new materials. Obviously, research should be done to test this possibility, but if it is to have genuine relevance to the activities of persons engaged in the day-to-day problem of constructing meaningful and effective instructional events, it should be done with materials which have been realistically developed using conventional procedures, and which are clearly tied to instructional intents.

Finally, and in order to end on a more positive note, let me say that Meyer's findings regarding the influence of discourse types on memory for prose content may provide a more manipulable aspect of instructional materials design than is the conceptual level of particular information. It may be that curriculum writers, for instance, could learn to describe ideas in the relational forms which she found to be facilitative, provided, of course, that it does not do violence to instructional intent. Research is needed to see how well this works in educational settings.

In summary, it seems that Meyer has made a useful contribution to our understanding of an aspect of prose learning. Moreover, the potential for this line of inquiry to contribute in a pragmatic way to the improvement of educational practice is relatively high. However, before the statements of educational implications become more than lip service for the purpose of establishing relevance, there must be a significant attempt to test these implications on the front lines, and in the trenches of what we have termed here "schooling."

REFERENCES

Allen, D. Some effects of advance organizers and level of question on the learning and retention of written social studies material. *Journal of Educational Psychology*, 1970, 61, 333–339.

Anderson, R. C. How to construct achievement tests to assess comprehension. *Review of Educational Research*, 1972, **42**, 145–170.

Arnold, H. F. The comparative effectiveness of certain study techniques in the field of history. *Journal of Educational Psychology*, 1942, **33**, 449–457.

Ausubel, D. P. The use of advance organizers in the learning and retention of meaningful verbal material. *Journal of Educational Psychology*, 1960, **51**, 267–272.

Beauchamp, W. L. A preliminary experimental study of techniques in the mastery of subject-matter in elementary physical science. "Studies in Secondary Education I." *Supplementary Educational Monographs*, 1923, **24**, 47–87.

Bormuth, J. *On the theory of achievement test items.* Chicago: Chicago University Press, 1970.

Bruning, R. Short-term retention of specific factual information in prose contexts of varying organization and relevance. *Journal of Educational Psychology*, 1970, **61**, 186–192.

Carter, J. The role of organization in the recall of facts from prose. Unpublished doctoral dissertation, University of Illinois, 1972.

Carter, J., & Carrier, C. Prose organization and recall. *Contemporary Educational Psychology*, in press.

Christensen, C. M., & Stordahl, K. E. The effect of organizational aids on comprehension and retention. *Journal of Educational Psychology*, 1955, **46**, 65–74.

Collins, A., & Quillian, M. How to make a language user. In E. Tulving & W. Donaldson (Eds.), *Organization of memory.* New York: Academic Press, 1972.

Frase, L. T. Paragraph organization of written materials: The influence of conceptual clustering upon the level and organization of recall. *Journal of Educational Psychology*, 1969, **60**, 394–401.

Germane, C. E. Outlining and summarizing compared with rereading as methods of studying. *N.S.S.E. 20th Yearbook*, Part 2: *Silent reading*. 1921. Pp. 101–113.

Grotelueschen, A., & Sjogren, D. Effects of differentially structured introductory materials and learning tasks on learning and transfer. *American Educational Research Journal*, 1968, **5**, 191–202.

Lee, W. Supra-paragraph prose structure: Its specification, perception, and effects on learning. *Psychological Reports*, 1965, **17**, 135–144.

Matthews, C. O. Comparisons of methods of study for immediate and delayed recall. *Journal of Educational Psychology*, 1938, **29**, 101–106.

Newlun, E. O. Teaching children to summarize in fifth grade history. In *Contributions to education*, No. 404. New York: Teachers College, Columbia University, 1930.

Robinson, F. P., & Hall, P. Studies of higher-level reading abilities. *Journal of Educational Psychology*, 1941, **32**, 241–252.

Royer, J., & Cable, G. Facilitated learning in connected discourse, *Journal of Educational Psychology*, 1975, **67**, 116–123.

Schulz, R. W. The role of cognitive organizers in the facilitation of concept learning in elementary school science. Unpublished doctoral dissertation, Purdue University, 1966.

Tulving, E., & Donaldson, W. *Organization of memory.* New York: Academic Press, 1972.

OPEN DISCUSSION
ON THE CONTRIBUTIONS
BY MEYER AND CARTER

Spiro: It seems to me that there are two distinct strategies, among others, that are available in the comprehension of connected discourse. In one strategy, you try to maintain the integrity of a particular passage as much as possible. I think this strategy is very common, for example, in memory experiments, in which the material is typically not of any general usefulness, and the goal is to try to remember as much as possible. When this strategy is operative, it makes a lot of sense that intrapassage structural relations will be a very potent factor in determining the likelihood of recall for the various elements of the discourse. However, there is another strategy which is probably more typical, and, for educators, one which would possibly be considered more ideal — that the function of comprehension can be to update one's knowledge. There is a great deal of redundancy in what one reads and hears; a lot of information that one encounters is old and uninteresting information. A lot of it is new. I think, in this second strategy, you focus on the latter information, and use it to update old knowledge. When this strategy is employed, I think it is very possible that the intrapassage structural relations will be subordinated to the pattern of relations which exist in the preexisting knowledge structure which is being updated. In that case, there is no reason to suspect consonant patterns of superordinateness.

Other factors, for example, attitudes and interests (which may have more "superordinate" standing in prior knowledge) may direct one's attention to elements which may be of low depth in any text-based structural hierarchy. Individuals may then idiosyncratically construct subjective text structures around the low depth elements.

Meyer: I think what you said is true: in the experiment, the person's strategy is to remember all he can from a passage. However, a good deal of reading strategy, I think, outside of the experimental situation involves finding out the author's message. If you are trying to find the primary message of the author, you probably will get the same results as I found. But if you are trying to zero in on the details that are relevant for you, if you have some strategy in which you do not care exactly what the author's primary message is, but just want to increase your knowledge base and pick out of the text information that you do not already have, then I think you would be recalling different information.

Spiro: Even if you are looking for the author's message, once you have related that message to your prior knowledge, the fact that it was that particular author's message may not be very important, and the superordinate nodes which allowed the identification of that message may be very quickly assimilated. Then the functional aspects of the discourse, possibly low in the text-based hierarchy, will still be salient in long-term recall even when you do have to utilize the superordinate nodes initially.

Furthermore, it is certainly true that one's perceptions of a communicator's message are filtered through extratextual knowledge about the communicator. This accounts for phenomen such as "he or she did not say what he or she really meant," reading between the lines, anticipation of the message a person will try to communicate, etc. Therefore, even the initial comprehension of text to discern the "pure" message of the author may not predominantly utilize the proposed intrapassage structural relations.

Another problem relates to generality. All discourse is not as susceptible to hierarchical organization as those used in your experiments.

Finally, there is one other point I would like to make, more in response to Dr. Carter, but also in response to Dr. Meyer. It relates to the tolerableness of uniqueness in recall. Clearly, when somebody has misunderstood a passage and therefore does not evidence any superordinate organizational strategy, that is not desirable. However, there are other kinds of uniqueness which result from the integration of to-be-remembered information with one's idiosyncratic personal knowledge. This may be desirable given the need for the kind of nonreplicative uses of knowledge that Dr. Broudy, for example, mentioned earlier.

Wyer: I am struck by the lack of interactions between Dr. Meyer's hierarchy variables and the other variables manipulated, for example, number of repetitions, or immediate versus delayed recall. If I understand the implications of this, it suggests that cognitive organization per se plays no role in your experiments. The type of information that is high in the hierarchy plays no role in facilitating recall of any other information in the passage because, if that were the case, you would get some facilitation of the low hierarchy information, as a function of number of trials or immediate versus delayed recall. So the lack of those interactions suggests to me that there is very little cognitive organization really going on in the recall process in these data. Actually, it simply says that some information is more salient than others.

Meyer: I do not think you necessarily can reach a conclusion at this time. I think more research is needed into looking at the clustering of recall and perhaps giving cues of higher level information and seeing what information those cues can help you retrieve.

Resnick: I would like to raise some questions about the educational uses of your research. Your paper was largely free of any hypotheses about processing, about what people did as opposed to what the text was like that would produce the effects you were getting. There were a few hints at process notions but really very few, and I think that may place a severe limit on the application to testing. Most current tests of reading comprehension, for example, or of knowledge of any particular subject matter area, are designed as predictive and sorting measures, and the psychometric methods used are extremely good for the purposes for which the tests are intended. I am sure there are potential refinements, but fundamentally those tests do their job quite well. That is, you get high reliability across time as well as good split halves. You can sort people very well, and if that is the aim of the tests, then we do not need to put a whole lot more effort into them (although some psychometricians would disagree). So, the aim of new tests would be precisely what you suggested: diagnosis. However, for diagnostic tests to be at all worthwhile, you have to have a plan for what you would do depending on the different results for different people in your diagnosis. What I am wondering about is how, without a theory of what people are doing as they read your texts, you can have even the beginnings of a theory of differential instructional treatments for people who come out differently on the diagnostic test.

Meyer: Interesting question.

Resnick: I don't mean that as a personal challenge, but maybe it is a challenge for all of us to think about. Perhaps I am pushing too hard on whether or not a process theory is needed.

Anderson: There is another point in addition to the diagnostic one. We aim to validate our instructional treatments against some criterion. The criterion is very shaky when you do not know what you are testing. Without a clear and well-justified criterion, you are counting number correct on a completely arbitrary scale.

Rothkopf: I wish Dr. Meyers could say something more about the procedure that you used in placing the identical paragraph in the high and low position in your passages.

Meyer: The surrounding content to that paragraph in the two passages is different. The target paragraph is the same. Although it is in the same physical position in both high and low versions, when you diagram the structure, it appears at the very top in one and the very bottom in the other. In the passage on parakeets, the target paragraph was about where parakeets originated from, the first color mutations, and details about how the colors that are available on the market today originated. It was at the low level of the content structure of the passage entitled, "Parakeets are Ideal Pets," which talked about why parakeets are ideal pets for people with limited time, space, and money, and informed them that the cost of the bird depends on the color. The other passage dealt with the appearance of parakeets.

Rothkopf: It strikes me that there is a variable that you might consider which would provide either a parallel explanation to your data, or perhaps an alternative one. We are dominated in some sense by the fact that there exists a technological invention called a computer out in the world and everybody looks at the world now in terms of logical trees. This splendid generalization has captured all of our imaginations. There is another, older, and fairly well-tested theory around that says that a critical fact in recall is connectedness among terms. It does not really matter what the sequence and order of this connectedness is, but that the number of paths into a particular node determines the likelihood of recall.

For example, Esther Coke and I have done some work on the recall of long lists where the interitem associative structure — the number of paths — to a particular word, was found to be a good predictor of the recall of a word. Now I wonder whether what you call the top of the hierarchy also happens to be the best connected sets of nodes in your content, and whether that might not be a useful alternative to consider.

Meyer: Because an idea is higher in the structure, that information usually has more nodes beneath it.

Rothkopf: It may be possible, for example, to construct passages such that connectedness is varied without growing a logical tree.

Meyer: Right. Looking at repetition, I tried to determine whether the results were due to just repeating the same thing over and over. That hypothesis was disconfirmed. I will have to look at the phenomena from the perspective you suggest.

Olson: I would like to comment on the point raised by Rand Spiro a little while ago. It concerned the fact that when you have people examine text to try to find out what the structure of the text is, in that case you are doing a fairly unique or peculiar type of thing with language that is quite different from what you are doing if you are using language in ordinary conversations, or if you are telling me something that you think I might be interested in ahead of time, and so on. As Dr. Spiro put it, it is a question of whether you think that the meaning resides in you as the listener and it is up to you to try to find something in the text which is of interest or significance or utility to you. This is opposed to the case where you assume that the meaning is in the text, and it is up to you to come to grips with the text. In your experiments, of course, it is the latter. I think in almost all school enterprises it is the latter; the text is there, the information is there, and it is up to the reader to try to come to grips with it in some way. But that, I think, is a very special enterprise. The much more common one is where you come already equipped with a very elaborate set of expectancies, a host of prior cues, and a set of values as to what is worth looking for, whether it is worth continuing reading, and so on. That would normally bias very strongly what you would recall and what you would relate to other information you had at the moment.

Meyer: The first approach I elected is the simplest. What is exactly in the text, and what the readers recall from that. Then it gets more complex when you consider a particular reader's strategy.

Olson: I certainly don't blame you for doing that as an experimenter. I wonder if it is really simpler for children, though, who, for example, are in the process of learning to negotiate with text in this way. I think it is an extremely difficult enterprise. I think the most difficult thing for people to master in the course of schooling is that ability to sort of suspend, or at least hold in abeyance, all of their expectations and interests while they really try to see what the author is getting at. In other words, it is complicated for psychologists to study that, but the thing that is complicated for psychologists is really the most dominant or most natural or easiest procedure for children to bring to bear.

Spiro: When you [Dr. Meyer] say your approach is simpler, that suggests a difference in degree between what you find rather than in the less controllable but possibly less artificial case. Actually, what you might find is a qualitative or a categorical difference in the processes involved, in the elements of text likely to be recalled, and in the extent to which hierarchical relations within a text might matter at all. If so, the simplicity becomes more serious in its consequences, in that generalizability is severely hampered.

Meyer: Well, that's probably the next step then.

Berliner: Just a comment on watching some primary grade students learning to read, or rather learning to prepare for tests of reading comprehension. They are taught in direct and partly indirect means to take a paragraph, find the topic sentence, subsume under that other kinds of things, and they are directly instructed to work the way your subjects have. It leads to the question of whether there are other cultures, other forms of education, where that would hold. I have the feeling that in our system, from about second grade to about fifth, children are given direct instruction to do what your subjects did, and I think your data are perhaps just a straight outgrowth of the effect of schooling.

Meyer: It would be interesting to see at what age children begin to recall more higher level information or main ideas than details from prose in their reading and in their listening.

Petrie: Just one example of that commonsensical kind of thing seems to be the very distinction in our language between prose and poetry. You are not taught to comprehend poetry; poetry is not the kind of thing that one comprehends at all in the same sort of way as you do prose. In that sense, it may be the case that the structure in the material is not totally independent of the social and prior instructional kinds of experiences. Not only do you have the difficulties that have been alluded to by other commentators here of individuals having their own purposes, desires, and individual methods of comprehending and processing, but it may well be that the culture has objectified in the material a certain way of organizing it that is not in any way immutably fixed. It may be very socially dependent.

Rothkopf: What do you [Dr. Meyer] think is the logical text unit for analysis in the kind of research that you are talking about? It seems to me that there must be some upper limit probably around a thousand words. That limit is of some importance. If you pick a unit that is too large for your analysis, then the resulting structural tree becomes unmanageable after a little while. Do you have any region that you think you'd want to practice in?

Meyer: In terms of words?

Rothkopf: Okay. How would the nodes and linkages grow with number of words? Have you ever looked at that?

Meyer: Well, it also depends on how much detail you want to consider in the analysis. If you break down the passage as far as possible to referential indices rather than leaving some nodes as propositions, it will take you days to analyze even passages of about 640 words. Also, it would be very time consuming to score recall protocols for all of these referential indices. Thus, shorter passages are certainly easier to deal with when analyzing a passage to this degree of detail. For many experiments and most educational situations I would recommend only analyzing a passage to the specificity of node desired, this may be propositions or complex propositions. Analyzing a passage to this level of specificity shortens analysis and scoring time.

7
Cognitive Development and the Acquisition of Concepts

Katherine Nelson

Yale University

The title of this contribution implies a concern with the process of acquiring knowledge (rather than the representation of knowledge or the structure of knowledge). Moreover, I have been asked to discuss "development," which inherently implies a process of change from one state to another. Yet, most of what we know about knowledge at any stage of development has to do with its content and structure rather than how it is acquired, and most of what we know about changes with development has to do with descriptions of content and structure at different stages rather than with how those changes come about.

Regretably, I cannot remedy that situation, and I obviously cannot deal with all of cognitive development in the time and space allotted even if that were possible. I propose instead to present a way of looking at developing conceptual systems, and the process by which they are developed, and try to extract from this view some principles that will enable us to decide what changes and what does not change with age and with exposure to schooling. I hope by doing so to extract what we need to explain in a theory that would deal with the process of acquiring knowledge. The ensuing discussion focuses considerable attention on the *pre*school child primarily to emphasize what the continuities in development are, and to show how the more complex knowledge of the school child and adult is derived from the base established in early childhood.

The most basic question to be addressed here is: What develops? The first consideration will therefore be given to some developmental principles that have been widely proposed as dimensions along which conceptual systems change over time. From there I proceed to a discussion of the acquisition of concepts and the relevance of that process to observed developmental changes. I conclude with a revised view of possible developmental principles.

THE MECHANISMS OF DEVELOPMENT

It is widely recognized that while we know a great deal about the characteristics of stages of development, we know very little about transitions between stages. Piaget, of course, has been the most important contemporary influence on thinking about development and the acquisition of knowledge, and he has demonstrated persuasively that the thought of young children is different in many ways from that of older children and adults. Perhaps even more important, he has taught us to think in terms of developing *structures* of thought and to consider the way in which children's structures influence what they *can* know as well as what they will choose to know from the presentations of the environment. Piaget (e.g., 1952, 1971) has presented a model of development as a continuous active process of adaptation or equilibration involving the dual opposing mechanisms of cognitive assimilation and accommodation. It is not my purpose to expound on Piagetian theory here, however, because, like many others, I have found this to be an attractive metaphor which has guided my thinking about developmental problems, but which has failed to provide a detailed specification that could be tested in any given case of transition. It must be conceded that the most complete theory of development yet proposed is still a theory of stage progression and not yet a theory of transformations.

This is not to belittle Piaget's contribution. There is no alternative theory that does better in this respect. Neither learning nor maturation as theories of development are ádequate to the complexities of the problems. Attempts to specify development in information processing models are also still at the level of stage description. Recently dialectics has been proposed as a general developmental theory (Riegel & Rosenwald, 1975), and it may yet prove to be more adequate than any previous model. Still, we are as far from understanding in any detail how developmental change takes place as we were 10 or 15 years ago (see Kessen, 1962). There are, however, a set of recurrent themes which have been used to characterize developmental change in conceptual systems and it is worth examining these for their potential utility.

Concrete to Abstract Bases of Knowledge

Although this progression has been proposed very widely, the concrete to abstract dimension was probably most completely developed by Goldstein and Scheerer (1941), who considered it to be a fundamental dimension of conceptual development. From one viewpoint this is only obvious. Children must begin with the facts of the world as they encounter them, and these will be concrete, physical, sensory facts. Of course, from a rationalist's viewpoint, the child must begin with certain abstract categories or structures into which the concrete facts can be fitted. And from a constructivist or structuralist viewpoint, cognitive organization must go beyond the immediate perceptual given and is by definition an abstraction. The proper question then is seen as one of what (abstract) knowledge is about, whether more or less concrete, rather than the nature of knowledge itself. That is, the child who operates with a concept of "dogness" such that she can recognize novel instances of dog and predict the behavior of dogs, must be said to have abstract knowledge applied to the concrete topic of dogs.

This issue is related to and often confused with the issue of specific (or particular) and general knowledge, as Braine (1962) pointed out. General knowledge of dogs is abstract only in the sense that it refers to a category rather than to a specific dog, but it nonetheless includes all members of a group of concrete objects. *Animal* is more general than *dog*, but not more abstract. *Species*, however, is an abstract term referring to a class of classes, and is therefore more abstract than *dog*, which is the name of a concrete class. From this viewpoint, Braine showed that young children do not have trouble operating on a general concrete level, but they do not usually operate on an abstract level.

Ordinarily, however, when the concrete—abstract issue is posed, it is posed in terms of generality (that is, the general class of animals in contrast to the less general class of dog) or in terms of the abstract basis for concept formation, often perceptual versus functional bases for forming equivalence classes (see below). A central question here is whether very young children operate with hierarchical systems expressible in taxonomies of the dog—cat: animal type. Let us defer that question to a later point in the discussion, however, and consider first the issue of perceptual and functional bases for forming equivalence classes, and then the specific to general as principles of development.

Perceptual versus Functional Bases of Knowledge

What things are used for has appeared to many people to be on the face of it a more abstract notion, requiring more "going beyond the information given" in Bruner's (1957) term, than what things look like. Thus, the notion that younger children will form concepts based on perceptual attributes whereas older children will form concepts based on their functions appears plausible. In fact, in a test of this hypothesis Bruner and Olver (1963) presented data on the basis of the formation of equivalence classes (asking "Why do these things go together?") that tended to support this notion, although their results were more complicated than a straightforward progression from perceptible to functional formulation might suggest.

However, in a recent test of this hypothesis with six-year-olds and college students, Miller (1973) found no evidence for greater reliance on perceptual features (which he called "concrete") than functional (termed "abstract") by either the children or the adults. Miller's task consisted of eight subtests in each of which the subject was presented with four objects and asked to remove the "one that does not belong." In every case, a subgroup of three objects based on a perceptual attribute such as shape could be formed and another subgroup based on function could be formed. For example, the first group consisted of banana, ball, orange, and plum, which could either form a group of round things, or a group of edible things (or the category fruit). Both child and adult groups tended to form equivalence classes based on abstract or functional dimensions rather than on concrete or perceptual ones. Miller also found that in most cases the children were able to shift readily from one basis of classification to another (contradicting another of Goldstein and Scheerer's claims in regard to the rigidity of immature concepts).

This was hardly a definitive experiment. It does illustrate, however, that both task requirements and the composition of categories and objects presented to the child are important in determining the kind of behavior that the child will exhibit, and in particular whether perceptual or functional bases will be relied on. On the whole, it also seems clear that as a dimension of development the perceptual to functional dimension is misspecified. Concepts referring to objects include both dimensions; which is relied on in any particular situation is less a matter of developmental stage than of utility in a given context. I return to this question and to the problem of what is properly considered functional later.

Specific to General

The progression from specific instance to general class is usually realized in the proposition that the child begins with the most specific case and moves up a hierarchy to more general cases. For example, he or she begins by naming Fido and only later comes to recognize the general category of dogs and then of animals. This formulation reflects one of two very general opposing theories of development, that is, generalization theory. The alternative, differentiation theory, has also recently had its proponents from the linguistic side (Clark, 1973). From this view concepts begin as very global unspecified structures which become more specific, better defined, and more differentiated with development.

Many years ago Brown (1958) asked, "How shall a thing be called?" by a child beginning to talk, and concluded that children would learn the name of a thing according to its level of greatest utility in the society in which they are growing up. This was later redefined (Brown, 1965) to that level that maximally discriminates among similar things in the everyday environment. This principle was set forth in place of either a specific to general naming tendency or a general to specific progression. Anglin (1975) has recently subjected this principle to experimental test and confirms that young children tend to use terms at an intermediate level of generality. That is, they apply the name "dog" rather than "collie" or "animal" to a pictorial instance of dog. At an even earlier point, it has been found that children just beginning to say words begin to use names for specific familiar things, but readily generalize an originally specific term to all similar things (Nelson, 1973; Rescorla, 1976). That is, they seem to operate from the outset with the notion that words apply to general classes of things and *not* to specific objects. Sometimes their categories are more broadly defined than the adults' (some children, but certainly not all, do call horses "doggie" at first), but sometimes they are more narrowly defined, as when a child calls a doll "baby" but does not apply the term to other infants.

The specific to general dimension of conceptual development has recently been proposed on a more advanced level by Saltz (1971; Saltz *et al.*, 1972). They have presented evidence that five-year-old children define general categories such as food more narrowly than eight-year-old children do; that is, younger children are willing to assert that fewer "peripheral" members belong to the category. Saltz and colleagues believe that the child learns which attributes are definitional and which are optional, thus broadening the boundaries of concepts as the child develops. However, even with such categories as food, furniture, and clothing, it does not appear that there is a single progression of this kind. When asked to give members of categories of this type, younger children produce fewer members than do older children, but proportionately as many come from the periphery of the concept as those of older children (Nelson, 1974b). For some general categories (for example, clothing) younger children name fewer "noncore" members, while for others (for example, furniture) they name more than older children do. Thus, neither the specific to general nor the general to specific hypothesis seems adequate to describe the development of early concepts or later hierarchical categories.

Complex to Class

Bruner and Olver (1963), Inhelder and Piaget (1964), and Vygotsky (1962) all presented similar evidence based primarily on grouping experiments ("Put things together that go together") to show that younger children form loose complexes without stable definitional bases rather than true classes which can be defined in terms of logical relations. Piaget (1962) in particular has presented an extensive discussion of the "preconcept" of the preoperational child which emphasizes its organization around a prototype case rather than in terms of critical attributes. However, recent research in concept formation in both adults and children (Bransford & Franks, 1971; Posner & Keele, 1968; Rosch, 1973, 1976) has demonstrated that forming a schema based on a prototype is a general cognitive process that is widely characteristic of natural concept formation at all ages and is not limited to young children. Thus, while there is undoubtedly a restriction on the young child's ability to deal with logical classes as compared with adults, this does not seem to be an appropriate dimension along which to differentiate natural concepts that appear to have similar prototypical structures at all ages.

It would seem then that none of these standard principles, separately or together, is appropriate to the description of conceptual development. Let us therefore consider the process of concept formation and the development of the conceptual system in more detail to determine what dimensions of development *are* relevant.

ACQUISITION OF CONCEPTS

In the remainder of this contribution I consider the acquisition of knowledge in terms of forming concepts which are defined by and embedded in a context or system, initially an *event structure*, later also a *categorical* or semantic *structure*. I also consider the process of acquiring knowledge and the formation of structures into which it fits as interrelated problems, beginning with "natural" conceptual systems as revealed in those of preschool children and contrast these with "context-free" systems found among older children and educated people in general. The effects of schooling on this development and its implications for education are considered in a final section.

The utility of long-term memory is usually viewed as a store of past experience to which we refer incoming information for identification and categorization. I would like to emphasize further that the everyday function of cognitive structures is that of a predictive mechanism, an adaptive function basic to all our activities. The increasing role of prediction in the life of the young child is crucial to understanding development. From this viewpoint, it is important to recognize the extraordinary degree to which the world for the young child is composed of novel objects and events. The essential task of cognitive organization for the first several years of life is to form concepts about these objects and events, and the larger contexts within which they occur, in order to be able to make accurate predictions about more and more recurrent experiences. The more complete the prediction at any given time, the less effort that must be spent in processing new information and the more new information that may be taken in from the present context for future use. The implications of this functional view will, I hope, become clear as the discussion proceeds. At this point, some definitions necessary to that discussion must be developed.

Concepts

Psychologists have always used the term concept as though its meaning were transparent, but their uses of it have not always been in accord with its use in, say, philosophy or linguistics. I intend to use it in what I conceive to be basically its traditional psychological sense, that is, as organized information that is not dependent upon the immediate perceptual array and is at least potentially nameable. Concepts can exist at varying levels of generality and abstraction and may vary from elemental to extremely complex. The term concept here does not imply any necessary logical organization as is implied in the term class, and thus concepts can be said to compose the elements of cognition at all levels of development. This is in contrast to Vygotsky's (1962) and Piaget's (1952) use of the term concept, which both reserve for those structures which meet the conditions of logical classes. This use is also in contrast to another use of the term in Piaget's theory, for example, in the "concept of the permanent object," "the concept of number," "the concept of conservation." In my view these are not properly termed concepts, because they are not potentially (within a limited time space) nameable by those who are said to possess them. Although the mathematician may have a concept of number and Piaget may have a concept of the permanent object, the child has only a system of operations which reveal knowledge of some properties of these concepts. The conceptualization process by definition confers unity on the information that it organizes, and hence nameability (Nelson, in press a). Without this sense of unity, the concept does not yet exist.

If the concept is not necessarily a class, neither is it necessarily a category, although it may be. Categorization implies grouping of diverse instances of objects or events. This appears to be a very basic cognitive disposition (Deese, 1967; Flavell, 1970; Nelson, 1973a; Ricciuti, 1965), and it is undoubtedly important to the young child's exploration and organization of the world. However, the equation of the two has unfortunate implications in terms of process as well as composition; concepts cannot be restricted to groups of more than one instance, nor should they be made dependent on a comparison process. A single instance (for example, the moon) may lead to a concept, and a concept may be formed on the basis of a single experience. For the same reason, the formation of equivalence classes (e.g., Bruner & Olver, 1963; Olver & Hornsby, 1966) should be conceived of as a special case of concept relations. The claim here is that the concept as such does not depend on relations *between* instances and concepts, such as shared attributes. However, concepts do necessarily exist within a conceptual framework and this framework may take different forms. Those to be considered here are the elementary *event structure*, the *script*, and the *category*.

Event Structures

Recent developments in cognitive psychology and linguistics, including those reflected in this volume, have emphasized propositional and dynamic relations in semantic memory. In a related way, working with the problem of first word acquisition, I have tried to show (Nelson, 1974a) how both initial word meaning and possible sentences can be derived from an object concept defined in terms of an *event structure* which contains all of the relations and functions of the object in the experiences of the individual. The event structure initially contains

TABLE 1

Examples of Specific and General Event Structures for
the Concept *Ball*

	Specific:		General:
BALL →	Mother throws Baby catches Rolls − bounces Playroom	BALL →	(Actor) throws (Actor) catches Rolls − bounces Home, outdoors

particular and idiosyncratic information regarding possible actors, actions, locations, results of actions, and so on. With further experience with a given object or similar objects, the event structure of a given concept becomes more general and less specific (see Table 1).

This type of event structure seems quite obviously to be necessarily a product of what has sometimes been called episodic memory.[1] It derives from particular experiences, and on the basis of these it enables the child (or adult) to predict what she can do with something or what others can do, or what the thing itself will do when next encountered.

Scripts

Episodic memory also provides a temporal and spatial framework within which such event-based concepts may fit. Following Schank and Abelson, 1975, I will call these larger event structures or frameworks *scripts*. A script is an event sequence that describes the interaction of a number of different concepts — people, places, and things — organized around a goal, for example, *eating*, at home or in a restaurant, or buying food in a store. Knowledge of scripts for recurrent events enables the child (or adult) to predict what, when, and who in familiar situations.

Categories

Most discussions of conceptual development have been concerned with the development of categorical knowledge — knowledge that groups concepts into hierarchical taxonomies defining superordinate, subordinate, and coordinate relations. Categories are general and context-free structures defining logical, not physical, relations. They cannot therefore be derived directly from episodic

[1] Episodic memory has been used in different ways by different people. Tulving (1972) seems to have attributed a particularistic evanescent momentary quality to it as opposed to the holistic, long-lasting and structural quality of semantic memory. The use here is more in accord with Posner and Warren's (1972) notion of the tape-recorder memory or Schank's (1975) notion of episodic memory, which is not limited in duration.

memory, but the relation between the two is of central interest to concept development.

I believe that the contrast between scripts and categories is equivalent to the contrast between episodic and semantic memory (see Posner & Warren, 1972; Schank, 1974). In particular, the two systems or conceptual frameworks rely on different types of relations between concepts although both describe possible organizations in memory. On the one hand, the episodic script is based on experiential relations in space and time which may be expressed in propositions or stories about concrete real world events. Categories, on the other hand, are based on logical relations between concepts: similarities and differences in attribute structures, for example. Categories require manipulation (analysis, comparison) of information about concepts. Both categories and scripts may provide frameworks for the same concepts; there is no implication that the concepts embedded in either context are different in either content or structure. For example, bears may be part of a zoo script or they might be part of an animal taxonomic category.

One more point needs to be stressed here. The kind of concepts and conceptual systems discussed here exist in the individual. It is misleading to suggest that concepts exist somewhere "out there" to be taught or learned. Concepts may of course be shared among individuals, a group, or community. They may be talked about, written about, read about. However, I would like to avoid talking about the attainment of concepts. It is quite certain that, however great the convergence among a community on definitions of concepts and concept prototypes (e.g., Rosch, 1976), there is variation from individual to individual in the content and structure of the vast majority of concepts, scripts, and categories.

The Basic Process

The most parsimonious assumption that we can make about development is that the basic *process* of acquiring knowledge remains the same regardless of developmental stage. Certainly this is the usual assumption that has been made by psychologists, for example, those in the learning tradition. Does it fit the facts? If this assumption is to hold, it must encompass a process or processes that are simple enough to apply to the very immature child as well as to the older child and the sophisticated adult. It is the beauty of association theory that it provides such a process. Unfortunately, another requirement is that the process must account for the acquisition of not only simple associations, but also very highly complex structures, and association theory has failed to do this. In fact, no process whose complexity is independent of both the knowledge to be acquired and the structure of what is already known can account for the facts.

It is for this reason among others that the dual process of assimilation and accommodation proposed by Piaget has so much appeal. What can be assimilated to given structures and what will be accommodated to by these structures is a joint product of the complexity of the cognitive structure and the complexity and novelty of the real world event. Yet, the basic process of adaptation remains the same throughout development. Unfortunately, as noted above, this idea seems to resist concretizing. It is very difficult, indeed impossible, to make independent predictions in any given case as to what will be assimilated or accommodated (or ignored) because of the difficulty of assessing cognitive structure in a detailed enough way.

At the risk of sounding either grandiose or simplistic, let me propose concept formation as a basic process that can adapt to the structure of present knowledge, and can also handle very simple and very complex knowledge. An important part of this proposal concerns the relational structures, scripts or categories, into which concepts are entered. We need to think in terms of both the basic units of thought, that is, the concept, and the frameworks within which such units operate in order to understand how they are generated.

Our old notions about how a concept is formed suggest that after a certain number of experiences with an object (or event), sufficient associations between the concept name and the attributes of the concept instances have been built up to produce an appropriate and correct concept. Twenty years or so ago the suggestion was made (Bruner, Goodnow, & Austin, 1956) that the persons forming such concepts might be engaged in hypothesis-testing behavior; that is, they might be taking an active, rather than a passive role in the formation of the concept. Still, this process would only take place if the person knew there was a concept to be identified, and if instances of the concept were somehow identifiable as such. The description leaves the person very much at the mercy of environmental presentations and identifications. How can novel concepts be formed, that is, novel to either the individual or the world at large? What would the individual do with a novel object or event?

These questions are crucial developmentally because of the immense importance that novel events and objects must play in the mental life of the young child. At birth, all objects, people, and events that the child experiences are novel. The first year of life is largely devoted to resolving these experiences into familiar, recognizable forms and predictable events. Piaget (1954) has described some of the strategies and the stages that the child goes through in establishing this basic knowledge, and recent experimental evidence (e.g., Cohen & Salapatek, 1975) has shown in detail how the child builds up perceptual memories during this period. Research has not yet resolved the extent of built-in categories (for example, space, color, phonetic features) that aid the child in this task, but whatever these may be they are unlikely to be sufficient to simplify the child's conceptual work significantly.

The immense, unboundable store of our adult knowledge of the world and its relationships begins inevitably with the infant's knowledge about who cares for it, the dwelling and its rooms where life begins, the crib, the toys, the feeding apparatus to which the infant is exposed. Such things form the input for the child's first concepts, and by one year children exhibit impressive knowledge of parents, familiar toys and objects, familiar places and established routines. They exhibit this knowledge not by naming, but by action. When given a new example of a familiar concept, for example, shoe or ball or cup, children at this age will try to put it on their feet, throw it, or bring it to their mouths, respectively and appropriately. They behave differentially (often but not always with reserve and some anxiety) toward strangers in contrast to familiar caretakers or friends. They are familiar with home and its spaces, and can find familiar things in their accustomed or temporary places. They predict event sequences such as going to bed with unshakable conviction. In contrast, in an unfamiliar place and situation, with unfamiliar people, such as a psychological laboratory, the child is likely to show anxiety in the presence of strangers, to spend a lot of time looking around the room, and, if allowed to, exploring the far corners and unfamiliar objects.

What is important here is that the child has both concepts and miniature scripts within which to set these concepts at this early point. These scripts are both spatial and temporal. Before children have learned to talk they have organized concepts on the basis of their own experience which will be named when they get into the naming game with their parents. The scripts themselves are not likely to be named, however. They are rather the ground within which the figures (that is, concepts) fit. Concepts are potentially nameable, but prior to being given the names, children have neither labels to signify a concept nor a method to identify it, whether a given instance is an example of an existing concept or not. They are on their own and must make sense of the world in the best way possible. How can this be done? One way is to lie and let the world go by, accumulate patterns and extract the invariant features from these patterns in order to build up a store of familiar images. In fact, we know from recent infant research that this is not a bad description of at least some aspects of perceptual learning during this period.

Another way to make sense, especially when the infant has gained motor control to the extent that she can both manipulate things and move in space, is to explore those aspects of the world that are *novel* and *interesting*. Bear in mind that the overall tendency of this system is to gain predictive control; to organize knowledge about the environment to the extent that the world to be dealt with is for the most part predictable. As long as most of what the infant has to deal with is novel and unpredictable, the task of living will take enormous cognitive effort. Much of the time will need to be spent in extracting information from the ongoing scene. To the extent that the infant has already established event structures (concepts and scripts) into which she can set the ongoing sequence, and to the extent that objects and people fit into those structures, she can be free of the necessity of constant monitoring of events to figure out what it is all about. The previously established structures provide expectations for the present experience; for example, it is feeding time, or going out for a walk time, or bedtime. Some of the young child's attachments to routines and anxieties in the face of change can be understood within this framework. When the script is seriously violated, the child can no longer predict what is going to happen, and therefore does not know what reaction his own actions will bring. She is thrown back into the chaos from which she was so recently freed. It will take a great deal of experience with old scripts, slightly variant scripts and new but not too different experiences to enable the child to take disruptions in stride.

What has been said thus far is that event structures, both elemental concepts and the sequences or scripts within which they fit, are important organizing structures for the young child. Concepts are defined in relation to larger event sequences in space and time. The selection principle for concept formation, what is novel and interesting, must therefore depend not only on the characteristics of the object or event in itself, but also upon the characteristics of the episodic *structure* within which it occurs. We know very little about event structure memory and how it is established; it has hardly begun to be investigated. We can say virtually nothing at this point then about the acquisition of such structures. We can say only that the child gives early evidence of relying on them as organizing principles, that they appear to be relevant to early language learning (Nelson, 1974a), and that they provide initial definitional higher-order structures for organizing concepts.

A few examples of such early structures may illustrate what is meant by these terms[2] and demonstrate the appropriateness of this analysis. At the level of the concept itself, consider the following example of a child aged 18 months, 20 days who uses only single words and identifies nose, hair, eyes, mouth, and ears on demand and also produces "nose" and "eyes" appropriately. However, when asked "Where's your face?," she does not respond. When the request is changed to "Wash your face," she goes through the motions of washing, wiping her hands all over her face. "Face" here is clearly embedded in the event structure named "washing your face" and at this point cannot be responded to independently of that structure.

At a more advanced conceptual level, consider the concepts of "yesterday" and "tomorrow" as explicated by a three-year-old boy, Steven (S), in conversation with his mother (M). They are driving to nursery school:

S: This . . . remember the water was here . . . the old puddle was here when it rained tonight?
M: When it rained . . . the other day.
S: No, it rained yesterday.
M: No, it was the day before yesterday.

[2] I am indebted to Janice Gruendel for the collection of these examples, based primarily on her observations and tape-recorded dialogues with her own son. The example from Schank was reported at a Developmental Psychology Seminar at Yale, October 1975.

S: No, it was the day before . . . yest . . . yesterday. It was now yesterday!

M: It was now yesterday?

S: No, when we were . . . when it was night then . . . nighttime then it was yesterday. When we waked up . . . when we had some supper . . . then we went to bed, then it was nighttime, then the sun was out, then it was nighttime, then it rained, then we waked up, then we . . . then we goed, then we went in that puddle.

Later in the same dialogue:

M: Margie's coming tomorrow.

S: Oh, but it *was* tomorrow.

M: When will it be tomorrow? Can you tell me?

S: Yeah, when we have supper, then we go to bed. No. When we have supper, then we're going to light the fire, then we're gonna light Darren's pumpkin, then . . . then Margie's coming.

M: In the nighttime?

S: Yeah.

M: In the nighttime tonight?

S: No. Tomorrow.

In both of these excerpts the child has clearly defined the concepts yesterday and tomorrow in terms of a sequence of events, which have formed a definitional script-based concept, within which other concepts (puddles, pumpkins, Marjorie) can be inserted.

The relation of such organizations to the child's operations in the world, and the way in which knowledge in general is organized and used at this age is perhaps more apparent in the following example from Roger Schank reported from his daughter at age 2 years, 6 months:

> "Next time when you go to the market I want you to buy straws, pay for it, and put it in the package and take it home, OK?"

From this example, it appears that the differences between the 2½-year-old child's store script and the adult's is mainly that the adult does not verbalize all the parts: paying, packaging, and bringing home are all implicit in the adult's buying script, whereas they are spelled out by the child who has newly organized the parts. Schank has provided many other examples based on this child's stories which illustrate the building up of script-based knowledge in the preschool child.

Perhaps the most striking, however, is an example from Lois Bloom (1973), which illustrates the use of event structures in the formation of early concepts, as well as the power and duration of episodic memory at this age. Bloom periodically video taped sessions with her daughter Allison during her second year in a laboratory setting equipped with standard toys. At 16 months, Allison played for the first time with a particular truck, giving her baby doll a ride in the truck. Three months later, at 19 months, Allison saw the same truck again for the first time. Immediately on seeing the truck, she said, "baby," sought out the baby doll and placed it in the truck in the same way that she had previously done, at which point she said, "truck," a word that had not been in her vocabulary on the previous visit. In Bloom's (1973) words:

> Allison remembered that particular truck in terms of her previous experience with it: putting her doll into the truck three months earlier. The word "truck" was frequently used elsewhere at this time, and it occurred six times in this sample. However, Allison did not say "truck" until after she had, in a sense, reestablished the original situation (by bringing the doll to the truck), and it was the structure of the original situation that was evidently most salient to her. (pp. 81–82)

Although one could wish for a control on this observation (to be certain that asking for the baby and putting it in the truck would not have occurred to any similar object), as it stands it is a provocative illustration of the way in which concepts of novel objects are based on the events in which they are embedded.

Selection Bases

What is novel and interesting to the individual is very important to the notion of how concepts are formed, and additionally, the structure into which concepts fit is vital to establishing what is novel and interesting. A familiar object may take on new meaning in a different context, and this is as true for adults as for children. For example, a person might be very familiar with the policeman at the corner, but seeing that policeman in one's own living room gives him a new and different meaning. What is new depends upon the concepts and the organizing structures already present in the child, but what is interesting is a slightly different question. Not all new things are interesting. The child might not predict the acquisition of a new dining room table, but he might not find it particularly interesting either. Some things are interesting simply because of their salient perceptual characteristics, that is, they are big or bright or shiny or for some other reason stand out from the ground against which they are viewed. A particularly important case of perceptual salience is movement, and even very young infants are especially attracted to movement. Other things are interesting to children because they can act on them in satisfying ways, while others are interesting because they are the focus of interaction with another person. It is impossible to be more specific about the characteristics of interesting objects because, like novelty, what is interesting changes with development.

An alternative to *interest* as the motivation for conceptualization is *importance*. Something might not be intrinsically interesting to the child, but might be very important. Irritating and distasteful experiences are perhaps the best examples here: for example, medicine, getting dressed, having one's face washed all are likely to lead to conceptual organization. Another manifestation of importance is utility in a problem-solving situation. When a barrier arises which prevents a person from reaching a goal, the person usually attempts to solve the problem in some way, and in order to do so is often led or forced to form a new concept. A recent experiment by Platt (1974) demonstrated that young school children learned more about the properties of magnets (that is, they more often formed a concept of magnetic polarity) when those properties (attraction or repulsion) interfered with completing a puzzle task than when they aided the task. That is, only when the concept was important to problem solving in order to reach a goal was it generated.

These characteristics in the child-environment structure — novel, interesting, important — signal the occasion for forming a new concept. The function or relationship of the object or event that identified it as novel, interesting, or important can be specified as the initial *meaning* of the concept for the child. Elsewhere (Nelson, 1974a), I have referred to this as the functional core of the concept. The core includes relations of the thing or event in time and space and to self, others, and other objects. Not all possible relationships are included in the core, however; initially only those relationships that led to the forming of the new concept will be included. Here, the term functional does not imply conventional usage, which the child may not come to understand for many years. Rather it implies function from the point of view of the individual forming the concept, in this instance, the child. Thus, it may include what the object does, the set of its possible actions, as well as what can be done to and with it and the results of actions on it. Function is essentially a set of potential relationships and may be as primitive as "container" or as complex as "communication."

An important characteristic of this model of concept generation should be emphasized here, namely, that concepts may be formed on the basis of a single experience with a thing or event. That is, concepts do not depend on repeated experiences from which the child can extract invariant features. Rather, they depend upon a departure from prior organization of such a kind that the child is led to set up a new conceptual unit. This new concept might be very skeletal; it might contain only a small part of the information that will eventually become part of it, but it is, nonetheless, a concept and will be entered into the framework of concepts in such a way that the information it contains can be used for making new predictions within the event structure of which it is a part.

A vital contribution to prediction of new occurrences of previously formed concepts is the establishment of a set of perceptual features by which they can be identified in the future. Therefore, the process that is set off when the child meets a new, interesting, or important event must include the encoding of salient features which can be used to recognize new instances. We know, in fact, that young children tend to rely on certain features of objects for this purpose: primarily shape, contours, and internal configurations, but not color or size, although they perceive and judge both of the latter (Clark, 1973; Nelson, 1976). The use of perceptual features leads to errors of recognition when either the probabilities or the necessary conditions are poorly understood. Many errors of naming and classification by young children can be understood in these terms (Nelson, in press a).

There are then three parts to the conceptualization process: establishing conceptual frameworks (scripts), generating functional cores (concept event structure), and finding identifying attributes (perceptual features). Let us see how each of these contributes to the prediction process. The spatial and temporal frame or script enables the child to predict which things and events to expect and in what order. So long as these expectations are met she can act according to a preestablished automatic script; she does not have to give special attention to the order of events or use problem-solving skills to figure out what the situation implies. The functional core concept enables the child to predict which things to expect in a given context, and also what to expect of a given thing when it is encountered. The identifying attributes enable the child to predict the functions of a thing before they are observed or experienced. They also make it possible for the concept to be freed of its tie to context. That is, new instances can be recognized wherever they are encountered by virtue of their identifying attributes.

Subsequent Concept Formation Processes

Thus far, we have considered concepts without names, and a concept generation process with neither a teacher nor a learner, and therefore with no standard of right and wrong, correct or incorrect. Early concept formation in fact cannot be incorrect. The only errors that are possible arise when the child comes to match his prelinguistic concepts to the language terms that are used around him. I have reviewed elsewhere (Nelson, 1974, in press a) the evidence from early word learning and use for this view. Space does not permit me to expand on that here. Rather, what I want to consider is the extent to which this description can be considered a general basic process for the acquisition of knowledge that can apply to the sophisticated adult as well as to the prelinguistic child.

The discussion thus far has relied heavily on the encountering of novel events. I think it is hard to overestimate the extent to which the world of the young child is composed of novelty. The world of the adult, on the other hand, is all too familiar. It is rare that we encounter something truly novel. Leeuwenhoek looking through his microscope is perhaps the best example that comes to mind, and, indeed, the creative scientist does have to form new concepts occasionally for things observed or ideas newly formulated, which have never before been identified and which have never before been named. I would suggest that in this case, too, the functional core is established by identifying those aspects that are novel, interesting (in the light of relationships already established), and important. Identifying attributes will be isolated to the extent that they are valuable in distinguishing among concepts for future recognition. The name will be the last thing to be considered, and it will be created in order to communicate to others the nature of the discovery.

The parallel between the creative scientist and the child learner has been made before in discussions of the discovery method of teaching concepts (e.g., Bruner, 1962) and it may indeed have educational implications. At this point, however, I want to note the relation between the concept and the name that this consideration implies. Once formed, a concept can be named (by "named," I do not mean necessarily a single word, but only that a language term or terms can be invented for it). This seems obvious when we are considering a totally new concept. Concepts do not derive from names but names are given to concepts. As I have stressed above, children, especially young children, are in the business of forming new concepts, and when, and only when, they have formed a concept, can it be named. This is one reason for the claim that the child's earliest words reflect preexisting prelinguistic concepts. But what of the reverse process? Can a child learn a concept to go with a name?

This reverse process is of course what most psychological research on concept formation has always been about, from Hull (1920) to Vygotsky (1962, originally 1934) to Bruner (1957) to Bourne (1966). Considering the numbers of people, both children and adults, who have learned, one way or another, to match an appropriate concept to a nonsense word in our laboratories, it would seem that the process is at least possible. In fact, to claim otherwise would be absurd. (One could, of course, claim that the *kind* of concepts taught in our laboratories are themselves absurd, but that is a different question.) Obviously, children can and do take words and try to attach meanings to them. This is, I would suggest, however, a different and secondary event, one that takes place after the child has come to realize that names in fact imply concepts, and that therefore upon hearing a new name the reasonable thing to do is to look for the concept underlying it. The beginning of this process may be first observed among some (not all) children who toward the middle of the second year begin to ask for the name of common objects, the period that Vygotsky (1962) talked about as the realization that "everything has a name." This realization was memorialized dramatically in Helen Keller's great breakthrough to symbolism when she finally grasped that what was being spelled into her hand was the name for "water" and that all other things could have names. This is surely an important realization. Up to this point a child may have had names for some concepts; now the child realizes that all of the other names heard also refer to concepts, and sets about identifying names for those concepts already known.

A further step must be taken when a new name is heard for which the concept is not identifiable. At this point, a new concept must be formed to fit the name. How does this take place? If the concept formation process outlined above is correct, the child may be expected to apply a similar set of operations to build a concept where the process is not set off by a novel and important event, but by a novel and important name. First, the child might note the referent of the word if possible; make an assessment of what the probable function of that referent is, in terms of current understanding of contextual frames and relative importance; assume this function to be the core meaning of the word; determine what distinguishes the referent from other previously conceptualized objects, and assign those as identifying attributes. The resulting concept structure may be tested for validity the next time the word is heard. It seems probable that many of the language terms that children acquire after the initial word learning period are acquired in this way, although there is at present little evidence relative to this proposition. (It is obvious that the process described is quite different from that assumed in the traditional concept formation experiment. Experimental tests of these differences are currently underway.)

In summary, we have seen that the first concepts that are named are based on functional relations of things, and I have theorized that, when presented with a new name, the child will seek to understand the functional basis of that thing. That is, when the process proceeds from name to concept rather than from concept to name, the child will nonetheless look for the definitional functional core without which the concept cannot be understood.

It is noteworthy that Blank (1973) has designed a program for teaching concepts to preschoolers that, although not derived from this model, is exactly consonant with it. She stresses that the child must first be taught the function of a new single instance in an active situation and that only thereafter should she be presented with a range of applications of the concept in the context of negative instances. The description of this program emphasizes the similarity of the process of learning concepts from names and learning names for concepts, in contrast to Vygotsky's (1962) stress on the difference between learning a (scientific) concept from the top down and a (spontaneous) concept from the bottom up. Understanding all of the necessary components of the concept and presenting them all to the child in the most explicit form and in the most effective sequence is the key to this approach, where the most effective sequence begins with the child's own experience, in effect establishing an event structure. Obviously, most concepts to be presented in school are far more complex and abstract than simple object names, but similar principles would be expected to apply.

DEVELOPMENTAL CHANGES IN CONCEPTUAL STRUCTURE

Considerable evidence, however, supports the notion that there is a very real difference between the conceptual system of the young child and that of the older school child and adult. What is the nature of this difference and how is it to be explained? Can one underlying process explain the way that knowledge is acquired at all ages, and, if not, what needs to be added to this description? We looked at some explanations for the difference at the outset. Let me recapitulate what needs to be explained.

A primary difference between the preschool child and the older child that has been often observed is the growing reliance on hierarchical categorical structures and on the logical relationships among concepts. This is, of course, one of the basic characteristics that Piaget has proposed as an indication of the concrete operational period, and as noted earlier, it has been pinpointed by others who have been interested in conceptual development, for example Vygotsky (1962) and Bruner (1966). There is supporting experimental evidence for such a shift which can be only briefly summarized here.

Piaget's stage of concrete operations begins at about seven years and rests in part on a new understanding of the logical relations that hold within and between classes. In particular, children come to understand the relations between parts and wholes, and that a member of a subordinate class can simultaneously be a member of a superordinate class; for example, a rose can also be a flower.

Studies of free recall (see reviews by Cole, Frankel, & Sharp, 1971; Jablonski, 1974) suggest that preschool children make little use of the categorical relations between words in a list to be memorized in the sense that they neither group members of a category together in recall nor is their recall facilitated by the inclusion of such categories in comparison to unrelated lists. By eight or ten years of age, however, children have begun to utilize these categorical relations in memorizing in a way that is similar to that of adults.

In another research tradition, free word associations have shown that younger children tend to produce responses to stimulus words that are appropriate to natural or sentential contexts (thus are *syntagmatic*) while older children tend to produce responses that are *paradigmatic*, usually reflecting categorical (coordinate, superordinate) relations (see Nelson, in press b, for review). The age shift for each of these effects tends to occur somewhere around 5–8 years of age.

Thus, it would appear that we need to modify the previous description of concept generation and organization if it is to apply to the school child by adding the notion of categorical organization: that is, of hierarchical organizations of knowledge, rather than simply temporal–spatial ones. But where does this new organization come from? Does it really exist? What is its relation to the previously established event structure organized in script form? How does it influence the child's concept formation process and the nature of the concepts that are formed? What influences does schooling have on its formation?

First, it should be noted that categories do not arise de novo at school age. Some common categories may be derived from concrete episodic experiences, for example, food, clothes, furniture, vehicles, even animals, which may be observed in spatial–temporal contiguity on farms or in zoos. Indeed, preschool children give evidence of knowledge of and use of such categories when these have been studied in a habituation paradigm (Ross, in preparation; Faulkender, Wright, & Waldron, 1974) or in a grouping paradigm (Nelson, 1973a). Investigators have had problems, however, establishing that the preschool child will affirm a logical hierarchical relation of the kind that says "a dog is an animal" (e.g., Anglin, 1975). Nonetheless, recent work has shown rather clearly that not only five-year-olds (Nelson, 1974b), but even three-year-olds (research in progress) will readily name common category members of this kind when the problem is to "name all the animals you can think of." I suggest that this evidence implies that the child's first categories are derived from her episodic or script-based memory structure: grouping together things that belong together spatially or temporally. Nonetheless, establishing such categories indicates an extraction from context in some degree, as well as an ability to use words in a new context-free way.

It is tempting to conclude that the difference here is that the young child's concepts and categories are context dependent, but that is not quite accurate, because the child is not dependent upon context for the interpretation of words, concepts, or categories (although context often helps). Even children who are just beginning to talk show a remarkable ability to abstract from context in situations where they are asked to name pictures of familiar objects, for example. Thus, it is not that the concept depends upon context for its interpretation, but rather that its meaning *derives* from its context, and that it is stored in memory in terms of its usual contextual framework. Rather than context dependent then, such concepts are context derived, while the older child's categories give evidence of being general and context free.

Scribner and Cole (1973) have presented an analysis of the cognitive effects of formal schooling which provides an interesting parallel to the suggestions made here. They emphasize, following Bruner (1966), that the two principal attributes of the school are, "That language is the predominant mode of transmitting and acquiring information, and that teaching and learning occur 'out of context'" (p. 556). In regard to the latter Scribner and Cole (1973) state:

> Everyday life also presents occasions in which the child learns material through the use of language when the referents of the words are not physically present – when someone tells a story, for example, or recalls his family genealogy. But the referents to the words used are familiar, natural and social entities, and in that sense the new information can be assimilated "in context." What is special about learning out of context in the school is that the child is asked to learn material that has no natural, that is, nonsymbolic, context. A prototype for this kind of learning is mathematics. In informal learning, numbers are used to count things and are learned in connection with the particular things counted.... By contrast, when the school child is asked to learn numbers the operation has changed. He is no longer using numbers for the purpose of manipulating particular things; he is manipulating numbers qua numbers; they are themselves the things (p. 557). (Copyright 1973 by the American Association for the Advancement of Science.)

It is of considerable interest that Cole and his colleagues (Cole, Gay, Glick, & Sharp, 1971; Scribner, 1974; Sharp & Cole, 1972) in their cross-cultural research have found effects of schooling on the use of categories in free recall as well as on the production of paradigmatic responses in word association, independent of the effects of age. That is, two of the shifts in conceptual organization that are found among American children in school are also found among older African villagers, but primarily among those who have been to school. Is it possible then that the hierarchical organization to which we have given such attention both in studying children and in studying semantic memory in adults is an artifact of our educational system? It would appear that its development is at least speeded by the school experience.

CONCEPTUAL DEVELOPMENT AND ITS IMPLICATIONS FOR SCHOOLING

The major move suggested here, the developmental dimension that I would propose in place of those discarded above, is from context derived to context free. (Although no concept is independent of some context, the usage here refers to experiential context.) Note that there is a continuum involved in this move in that the first categories are experientially-based, and indeed much of Rosch's work (1973, 1975, 1976) implies that many of our familiar adult concepts are still very much context derived. It is only in later childhood that the child may become capable of constructing a context-free system within which concepts can be *logically* derived. It seems quite clear, however, that general categorical-hierarchical context-free systems are an *addition* to the spatial–temporal systems that the child works within in the preschool years, rather than a *substitute* for it. The evidence for this statement is as plain as the noses on our faces, and has been apparent in all the discussions at this conference: we all work with scripts all the time; they are not something that children abandon when they find that a general hierarchical system is more powerful.

Although memory can be sorted on any number of bases (see Posner & Warren, 1972), the types of organization that are normally relied on may be quite limited. What we seem to find is that episodic memory (that is, scripts) is characteristic of people at all ages but that preschool children tend to rely on it to the exclusion of other forms of organization. Only at school age, however, do we find fairly general ready reliance on categorical hierarchies (that is, semantic memory as it is usually understood) in verbal tasks. It seems not improbable that the preschool child can sort through memory, at least for some purposes (such as producing names of animals), but that his memory is not structured in this way. Only later will this structure be somehow added to the *primary* event structure.

The analysis of Bransford *et al.* (Chapter 2, this volume) of the shift from thinking about to thinking *in terms of* as a person acquires expertise in an area seems especially relevant here. It seems quite possible that the shift so often observed from prelogical to categorical functioning during the early school years may in fact be a manifestation of the first of a number of possible shifts in cognitive organization as a result of new expertise. That is, the school child acquires a new level of expertise in using taxonomic category systems to the extent that, at least part of the time, she begins to think *in terms of* them rather than *about* them.

What might induce this new "expert" level of organization? Scribner and Cole's (1973) analysis would indicate that the formal, general, and context-free tasks of school are relevant to its appearance, although the particular experiences that lie behind the acquisition of this kind of expertise are not now identifiable. Further research may shed light on the emergence of this type of structure. Rather than emphasizing the emergence of this system, however, I would urge that we become more aware of the continuities in process and structure in development which the present analysis has emphasized.

Indeed, one of the primary lessons that I would draw is that the young child has both concepts and a conceptual framework which are not different in kind from those of older children and adults, although the logical inferences the child draws from experience may be faulty (Piaget, 1952) and he may lack a powerful component of the educated adult system. Too often we have viewed preschool children as deficient (prelogical, preconceptual, preverbal) overlooking the real strengths and abilities that they use to understand the world.

To recapitulate those continuities: the basic process of concept formation is the same throughout development, involving the construction of a functional core meaning based on relations of the novel event to other previously known events within the conceptual system, the addition of identifying attributes which distinguish it from similar concepts, giving it a name. The process may proceed from any direction: name, attributes, relationships. Concepts are organized and interpreted in terms of larger event structures which we have called scripts, which enable the child (or adult) to make predictions about recurrent events.

From this point of view the dimensions considered earlier take on a new meaning. The complexes or preconcepts of the young child are not really different from similar concepts of the adult, but rather take their meaning and their relation to other concepts from a script-based conceptual system. Object concepts include both functional and perceptual information, but the definition of function may shift from a personally oriented event system to a hierarchical system of relations, and the perceptual attributes may become organized into a logical system of relationships in later childhood. Truly abstract concepts become possible only in later childhood as the context-free system becomes sufficiently elaborated to enable the child to derive new concepts from it alone. Finally, the specific to general hypothesis can be seen as the result of the move from an episodically based structure which derives its meaning from particular episodes to a context-free structure.

The general educational implications to be drawn from these considerations have been implicit throughout this discussion. The child brings not only a store of concepts to the school experience but also a framework within which those concepts can be understood. The framework is based on extraction of relations from temporal-spatial experiences, but it is not unique to young children: adults also rely on such organizing frameworks. Neither are the child's concepts different in kind from the adult's, although relations between concepts may be, in that they are less analytical. It would seem that the school's best strategy is to take advantage of the child's own knowledge system at the outset and to do that, it is necessary to recognize that the child's system is functional, predictive, and based on prior episodic experiences. Thus, as Scribner and Cole emphasize, the more remote the child's experience from that of the school the harder it will be to build on the old system in the school experience. Indeed, much of the child's time in school must then be spent building up new experientially based scripts, and little time or effort will be available for learning new "school" concepts.

More specific implications depend on expanding our own knowledge about how the process of building up natural and formal systems of knowledge takes place in the developing child. The cognitive transition from the preschool years to the middle school years is increasingly well documented, as illustrated here, but how and why remain open questions. We still have not solved the problem of developmental process. In addition, the many important factors not considered in this discussion, for example, those involved in strategies for acquiring knowledge and strategies for inparting it, will certainly make more complex any simple conclusions derived from these considerations of structure and function.

REFERENCES

Anglin, J. The child's first terms of reference. In S. Ehrlich & E. Tulving (Eds.), Special Issue of the *Bulletin de Psychologie* on Semantic Memory, July, 1975.

Blank, M. Concepts by principle. In *Teaching learning in the pre-school: A dialogue approach*. Columbus, Ohio: Charles Merrill, 1973.

Bloom, L. *One word at a time*. The Hague: Mouton, 1973.

Bourne, L. E., Jr. *Human conceptual behavior*. Boston: Allyn & Bacon, 1966.

Braine, M. D. S. Piaget on reasoning: A methodological critique and alternative proposals. In W. Kessen & C. Kuhlman (Eds.), *Thought in the young child, Monographs of the Society for Research in Child Development*, Vol. 27, No. 2, 1962.

Bransford, J. D., & Franks, J. J. The abstraction of linguistic ideas. *Cognitive Psychology*, 1971, 2, 331–350.

Brown, R. How shall a thing be called? *Psychological Review*, 1958, 65, 14–21.

Brown, R. *Social psychology*. New York: The Free Press, 1965.

Bruner, J. S. Going beyond the information given. In H. Gruber (Ed.), *Contemporary approaches to cognition*. Cambridge, Mass.: Harvard University Press, 1957.

Bruner, J. S. *On knowing: Essays for the left hand*. Cambridge, Mass.: Harvard University Press, 1962.

Bruner, J. S. On cognitive growth II. In J. S. Bruner, R. R. Olver, & P. H. Greenfield, *Studies in cognitive growth*. New York: Wiley, 1966.

Bruner, J. S., Goodnow, J. J., & Austin, G. A. *A study of thinking.* New York: Wiley, 1956.

Bruner, J. S., & Olver, R. R. Development of equivalence transformation in children. In J. Wright & J. Kagan (Eds.), *Basic cognitive processes in children. Monographs of the Society for Research in Child Development,* 1963, Vol. 28, No. 2, Pp. 125–142.

Clark, E. V. What's in a word? On the child's acquisition of semantics in his first language. In T. E. Moore (Ed.), *Cognitive development and the acquisition of language.* New York: Academic Press, 1973.

Cohen, L. B., & Salapatek, P. (Eds.). *Infant perception: From sensation to cognition.* New York: Academic Press, 1975.

Cole, M., Frankel, F., & Sharp, D. Development of free recall learning in children. *Developmental Psychology,* 1971, 4, 109–123.

Cole, M., Gay, J., Glick, J., & Sharp, D. *Cultural context of learning and thinking.* New York: Basic Books, 1971.

Deese, J. Meaning and the change of meaning. *American Psychologist,* 1967, 22, 641–65.

Faulkender, P. J., Wright, J. C., & Waldron, A. Generalized habituation of concept stimuli in toddlers. *Child Development,* 1974, 45, 1002–1010.

Flavell, J. H. Concept development. In P. H. Mussen (Ed.), *Carmichael's manual of child psychology,* Vol. 1, 3rd ed., New York: Wiley, 1970.

Goldstein, K. & Sheerer, M. Abstract and concrete behavior. An experimental study with special tests. *Psychological Monographs,* 1941, 53, no. 2, (whole number 239).

Hull, C. L. Quantitative aspects of the evolution of concepts. *Psychological Monographs,* 1920, 28, No. 1 (whole number 123).

Inhelder, B., & Piaget, J. *The early growth of logic in the child.* London: Routledge & Kegan Paul, 1964.

Jablonski, E. M. Free recall in children. *Psychological Bulletin,* 1974, 81, 522–539.

Kessen, W. "Stage" and "Structure" in the Study of Children. In W. Kessen and C. Kuhlman (Eds.), *Thought in the Young Child. Monographs of the Society for Research in Child Development,* Vol. 27, no. 2, 1962.

Miller, R. The use of concrete and abstract concepts by children and adults. *Cognition,* 1973, 2, 49–58.

Nelson, K. Some evidence for the cognitive primacy of categorization and its functional basis. *Merrill-Palmer Quarterly of Behavior and Development,* 1973, 19, 21–39. (a)

Nelson, K. Structure and strategy in learning to talk. *Monographs of the Society for Research in Child Development,* 1973, 38 (1–2, Serial No. 149). (b)

Nelson, K. Concept, word and sentence: Interrelationships in acquisition and development. *Psychological Review,* 1974, 81, 267–285. (a)

Nelson, K. Variations in children's concepts by age and category. *Child Development,* 1974, 45, 577–584. (b)

Nelson, K. Some attributes of adjectives used by young children. *Cognition,* 1976, 4, 13–30.

Nelson, K. The conceptual basis for naming. In J. Macnamara (Ed.), *Language learning and thought.* New York: Academic Press, in press. (a)

Nelson, K. The syntagmatic–paradigmatic shift revisited: A review of research and theory. *Psychological Bulletin,* in press. (b)

Olver, R. R., & Hornsby, J. R. On equivalence. In J. S. Bruner, R. R. Olver, & P. M. Greenfield, *Studies in cognitive growth.* New York: Wiley, 1966.

Piaget, J. *The origins of intelligence in children.* New York: Norton, 1952.

Piaget, J. *The construction of reality in the child.* New York: Basic Books, 1954.

Piaget, J. *Play, dreams and imitation in childhood.* New York: Norton, 1962.

Piaget, J. *Biology and knowledge.* Chicago: University of Chicago Press, 1971.

Platt, J. E. The initiation of children's concept-formation processes in a non-directed situation. Unpublished doctoral dissertation, Yale University, 1974.

Posner, M. I., & Keele, S. W. On the genesis of abstract ideas. *Journal of Experimental Psychology*, 1968, 77, 353–363.

Posner, M. I., & Warren, R. E. Traces, concepts and conscious constructions. In A. W. Melton & E. Martin (Eds.), *Coding processes in human memory*. Washington, D.C.: Winston, 1972.

Rescorla, L. Concept formation in word learning. Unpublished doctoral dissertation, Yale University, 1976.

Ross, G. Doctoral dissertation, Harvard University, in preparation.

Ricciuti, H. N. Object grouping and selective ordering behaviors in infants 12 to 34 months old. *Merrill-Palmer Quarterly*, 1965, 11, 129–148.

Riegel, K. F., & Rosenwald, G. C. *Structure and transformation: Developmental and historical aspects*. New York: Wiley, 1975.

Rosch, E. H. On the internal structure of perceptual and semantic categories. In T. E. Moore (Ed.), *Cognitive development and the acquisition of language*. New York: Academic Press, 1973.

Rosch, E. H. Cognitive representations of semantic categories. *Journal of Experimental Psychology: General*, 1975, 104, 192–233.

Rosch, E. H., Merris, C. B., Gray, W., Johnson, D., & Boyes-Bream, P. Basic objects in natural categories. *Cognitive Psychology*, 1976, 8, 382–439.

Saltz, E. *The cognitive bases of human learning*. Homewood, Ill.: The Dorsey Press, 1971.

Saltz, E., Soller, E., & Sigel, I. E. The development of natural language concepts. *Child Development*, 1972, 43, 1191–1202.

Schank, R. Is there a semantic memory? Unpublished manuscript, Instituto pergli studi Semantici Cognitivi, Castagnola, Switzerland, 1974.

Schank, R., & Abelson, R. P. Scripts, plans and knowledge. Paper presented at the fourth International Joint Conference on Artificial Intelligence, 1975.

Scribner, S. Developmental aspects of categorized recall in a West African society. *Cognitive Psychology*, 1974, 6, 475–494.

Scribner, S., & Cole, M. Cognitive consequences of formal and informal education. *Science*, 1973, 183, 554–559.

Sharp, D., & Cole, M. Patterns of responding in the word associations of West African children. *Child Development*, 1972, 43, 55–65.

Tulving, E. Episodic and semantic memory. In E. Tulving & W. Donaldson (Eds.), *Organization of memory*. New York: Academic, 1972.

Vygotsky, L. S. *Thought and language*. Cambridge Mass.: M.I.T. Press, 1962.

DEVELOPMENT, SCHOOLING, AND THE ACQUISITION OF KNOWLEDGE ABOUT KNOWLEDGE: COMMENTS ON CHAPTER 7 BY NELSON

Ann L. Brown

University of Illinois at Urbana-Champaign

In order to approach a topic of such scope as "development and the acquisition of knowledge," particularly in the context of a symposium on schooling, it is necessary to limit the focus of attention to a manageable realm. Nelson chose to concentrate on the development of event structures and scripts as a fundamental part of the knowledge base. This focus of attention led her to conclude that (1) "the young child has both concepts and a conceptual framework which are not different in kind from adults," and (2) "the basic process of concept formation is the same throughout development involving the construction of a functional core memory based on relations of the novel event to other previously known events within the conceptual system." In addition, the major part of her chapter is concerned with very early concept formation while the other contributors have, for the most part, been concerned with mature subjects. But there is a great deal of development that occurs between the nursery school stage and that level of functioning achieved by even low-verbal sophomores. Therefore, in order to put Nelson's contribution into developmental perspective, at least from my viewpoint, I would like to concentrate, initially on one aspect of thinking that Nelson ignores, one sensitive to developmental stage within our culture, and degree of formal schooling in other cultures. Following this, I would like to consider the effects of formal schooling on different kinds of knowing and then return to Nelson's concern with the fundamental continuity of thought throughout development.

Vygotsky (1962) described two phases in the development of knowledge, first its automatic unconscious acquisition, followed by gradual increases in active conscious control over that knowledge. I would like to concentrate my remarks on the issue of conscious control, for, whereas it may be true that the basic equilibration processes of assimilation and accommodation remain constant across the life span, as Nelson suggests, voluntary exploitation and control of the knowledge we have is an extremely sensitive index of developmental maturity. Thus, while Nelson focused on the development of the "structure" of the knowledge base, I would like to stress the problem of the executive "processes," for not only does the knowledge base undergo qualitative transformations with ontogenesis, but so does the strategic systems employed in the service of acquiring and using the knowledge base effectively.

The distinction of structure and process is a perennial problem for those interested in cognitive systems, whether human or robot, and is a particularly thorny problem for developmental psychologists. The differences between proceduralists (knowing how) and declarativists (knowing that) have been described by Winograd (1975), and I certainly do not want to become enmeshed in this problem. I would, however, like to mention that what we regard as process-like or structure-like is not only a matter of personal theoretical bias for developmentalists, but is the very essence of the problem of change itself (for an excellent discussion of this problem see Newell, 1972). For example, consider the structural features of Piagetian theory which have been described as internalized sets of cohesive rules for constructing reality. Far from being static or immutable, or object-like fixtures in the head, the structures are themselves imbued with active process-like capabilities, the operations of the intelligence. Note also that although Nelson's discussion of the development of hierarchies of organized, context-free, categorical knowledge suggests a concentration on structure, her long-term memory, far from being a passive store of organized data, is an active system in the business of prediction. From this viewpoint, it is illusory to try to establish process models which are not closely linked to structural ones and vice versa. My focus on processes is for emphasis, not because of any fundamental belief in the structure—process separation.

Thus the distinction between process and structure may have little meaning at the present state of our knowledge about knowledge, so I would like to avoid the issue by concentrating on a relatively uncontested area of process, that of executive decision making. No matter how active the modules or structures at the various levels of a knowledge hierarchy are allowed to be, in the majority of human and subhuman intelligence systems some central control processor, interpreter or executive is introduced to oversee the operations of the total system.

An essential characteristic of the central mechanism favored by many current theories is that it must be capable of performing intelligent evaluation of its own operations; for, some form of self awareness, or explicit knowledge of its own workings is essential for any efficient problem solving system (Becker, 1975; Bobrow, 1975; Bobrow & Norman, 1975). To demonstrate the complexity of the issue it seems that some basic requirements of such a control system are that it include the ability (a) to predict its own capacity limitations; (b) to be aware of its repertoire of heuristic routines and their appropriate domain of utility; (c) to identify and characterize the problem at hand; (d) to plan and schedule appropriate problem-solving routines; (e) to monitor and supervise the effectiveness of those routines it calls into service; and (f) to dynamically evaluate these operations in the face of success or failure so that termination of routines (if not self-terminating) can be strategically timed. These forms of executive decision making are perhaps the crux of efficient problem solving, for the use of an appropriate piece of knowledge, or routine to obtain knowledge at the right time and in the right place is the essence of intelligent mental operations, of cognitive maturity as we define it in our society.

In the light of this description, consider what we know about the executive function in the developing child. One of the most general characteristics of the young child is that he is less conscious of his own thought processes and less able to introspect and evaluate such processes than is the older child (Piaget, 1928). Thus, the problem of self-awareness and executive control is of central concern to those interested in the child's problem solving capacities. The general area of metacognitive development, of the child's knowledge of his own knowledge, has only recently become a topic for research and the majority of experiments have focused on metamemorial awareness (Brown, in press; Flavell & Wellman, 1977), although there is some interesting information concerning metalinguistic knowledge and metacomprehension. For this reason the majority of my examples will concern the child's growing awareness and control of his deliberate memorization skills.

Consider first what the adult knows concerning the knowledge he already has and his ability to operate on that knowledge. When faced with a question concerning what we know, how do we ascertain that we do or do not have the answer, or that it would be reasonable to attempt a search? Take the "simple" case when the material is in the knowledge base and we must estimate its accessibility. William James (1890) first drew attention to the "peculiar experience of trying to recall a forgotten name, knowing and feeling how close we are, being aware of improper matches and vainly groping in our inability to retrieve" *what we know is there.* Adults are quite accurate at predicting what is known, or have reliable feeling-of-knowing experiences (Blake, 1973; Hart, 1967), but the familiar tip-of-the-tongue phenomena does not appear to be as dramatic for young children. Not only do they fail to predict their recognition accuracy when recall has failed, the feeling-of-knowing phenomena, but they also experience difficulties with the active strategic attempts used by adults to resolve a tip-of-the-tongue experience (Brown & Lawton, in press; Wellman, 1975). It is not until the mid-grade-school years that young children can reliably indicate a distinction between what they know but cannot retrieve, and what they do not know.

The mature problem-solver not only has a reasonable estimate of the accessibility of his known facts, he is also cognizant of which facts cannot be known and which can be deduced on the basis of what he already knows. Adults know immediately that they cannot know Charles Dickens' phone number (Norman, 1973), but they arrive at this conclusion by inferential reasoning concerning other aspects of their knowledge. Not only do children know less than adults, and their knowledge is more often poorly organized, incomplete, and inconsistent, but they lack the complex systems of inferential reasoning used by adults to infer information from incomplete and contradictory knowledge bases. Consider the variety of strategies Collins and his associates (Collins, Warnock, Aiello, & Miller, 1975) describe as operative when adults must decide when something is not known, but could be inferred from the knowledge they have. Of particular interest is the lack-of-knowledge inference whereby adults reason that they probably would know something if it were true:

> The lack-of-knowledge inference involves reasoning from cases, like an induction. One kind of induction has the following form: if several objects in a class have a given property, then an object of the same class that one knows less about probably also has that property. In contrast, the lack-of-knowledge inference has the following form: if several objects in a class have a given property, then an object of the same class that one knows as much or more about probably does not have that property. Thus it turns out that the lack-of-knowledge inference is a kind of inverse of an induction. (Collins, *et al.,* 1975, p. 398)

One does not need to know too much concerning the young child's deductive reasoning capacities, his lack of understanding of the logical relations that hold between and within classes, his inability to reason by exclusion or to make transitive inferences except under the most favorable of circumstances, his high tolerance for contradictions, etc. to understand why the ability to reason from incomplete knowledge is a late developing skill, apparently trainable, or at least subject to refinement, in college populations. One major difference between the young child and the adolescent may be, as Nelson suggests, the ability to derive new concepts from a consideration of the knowledge base alone.

Next, consider what an adult knows about his ability to *deliberately* acquire new information. We have just discussed probabilistic inferences concerning what is already available in memory or can be deduced from the knowledge we have. Here, we are looking specifically at deliberate attempts to incorporate "new" information to memory. As an initial step in producing a realistic plan for remembering, the memorizer must be capable of estimating his own capacity limitations and, therefore, of knowing that a deliberate plan is needed in certain situations when capacity limitations will be overreached. Yet the very distinction between intentional and incidental learning instructions (Murphy & Brown, 1975), or a set to remember versus just-to-look-at material (Appell, Cooper, McCarrell, Sims-Knight, Yussen, & Flavell, 1972) is often beyond the metamemorial functioning of the very young child. A form of "secondary ignorance" (Brown, 1975; Sieber, 1968) appears to be operating; for, besides not knowing how to memorize efficiently, the young child does not seem to realize that he *needs* to memorize. He appears oblivious to the limitations of his memory capacity and unaware that he can make more efficient use of this limited capacity by strategic intervention (Brown, 1974, 1975; Kreutzer, Leonard, & Flavell, 1975). A simple concrete example of this state of ignorance concerning capacities is that children in the early grade school years have difficulty estimating how many items they will be able to recall from a supra-span list (Brown, Campione, & Murphy, 1974; Flavell, Friedrichs, & Hoyt, 1970; Markman, 1973). They typically overestimate their span and predict that they can remember *all* of the presented items. Examples of underestimation are extremely rare and the incidence of realistic estimation increases dramatically between kindergarten and fifth grade. If the young child is not aware of his own limitations for reproductive recall it is scarcely surprising that he fails to initiate spontaneously a plan to remedy his shortcomings.

Given that the child is sufficiently mature to realize that his capacity to acquire new information via deliberate memorization is limited, is he capable of recognizing that a plan will help him make more efficient use of this limited capacity, and in addition, capable of selecting a task appropriate, or domain-specific heuristic? Here, the argument has a tendency to become circular, for hand-in-hand with the child's lack of awareness of the need to execute a mnemonic strategy is his accompanying inability to handle such strategies effectively. It is difficult to conceive how an executive can predict the suitability or potential effectiveness of a strategy without experience actually carrying out the process in question. It does not appear to be the case, however, that once a subset of suitable routines becomes available to the child the executive control of those routines emerges full blown. There is ample evidence in the developmental literature of what has become known as production deficiencies, cases in which the child can perform certain operations if explicitly prompted, but fails to introduce them on his own volition. Quite simply, young children can do much more than they will do; it is as if they assign some function of their executive to external agents. Thus, many of the familiar mnemonic techniques, rehearsal, organization, elaboration, etc., are within the child's problem-solving capacity long before he uses them spontaneously and effectively for the purpose of remembering. Explicit prompts to use a set of operations are needed before they will be used, with the degree of explicitness needed correlated with age (Brown, in press).

Another function of an efficient executive is that of keeping track of operations employed and monitoring the effectiveness of strategic intervention. The question of whether young children have such executive control only arises late in the grade school years when they are sufficiently mature to both recognize the need for deliberate skills for remembering certain types of material and when a subset of routines, however limited, is available for control. As pointed out in the preceding section, the control of strategy utilization lags behind the acquisition of a repertoire of certain operations which could legitimately be supervised by an executive. This can best be illustrated by reference to a specific task, the recall-readiness task introduced by Flavell (Flavell *et al.*, 1970). The child is given a list (preferably supraspan) and is allowed unlimited study time in which to memorize this list. When he is sure that he can recall all the items in order, he is to indicate his readiness. Perfect monitoring of both the strength of items in memory and, therefore, the effectiveness of any strategic intervention would lead to perfect recall; the child has unlimited time. Yet, the ability to predict when a set of items can be recalled perfectly is very much a function of age, with young children quite unable to predict. Is this problem the result of failure to introduce appropriate strategic activities or failure to employ appropriate self-testing subroutines to establish whether one is ready to recall? To remedy this, we trained children in the efficient use of certain self-testing mnemonics in order to see if once the child had available a suitable mnemonic, he would spontaneously monitor its effective use. More mature subjects given the appropriate strategy improved their recall readiness efficiency and maintained this efficiency over time. Younger children, however, appeared to continue the use of the specific trained mnemonic, but were still unable to monitor the effectiveness of this activity and, therefore, to appreciate their readiness (or lack of readiness) to recall (Brown & Barclay, 1976), again illustrating the developmental lag between the use of a mnemonic strategy and the efficient monitoring of the success or failure of that operation.

One clear example of how late developing is efficient control of mnemonic subroutine has been provided by Butterfield and Belmont (1976). They were concerned with the relatively simple situation where a "cumulative rehearsal—fast finish strategy" must be introduced when changing lists of digits are to be recalled, but should be abandoned when the lists are repeated. Both the initial stabilization of a pattern and the speed with which the strategy was abandoned were developmentally sensitive. It is of interest that fifth-grade children performed inadequately on the task, and it was not until tenth grade that evidence of efficient executive control in this situation was clearly manifested. If the preadolescent has difficulty monitoring the need to employ one simple strategy, how much more difficult should be the problem of selecting between competing alternatives, scheduling their applications, terminating their operations when they fail or are no longer needed, and keeping track of what operations have been attempted and with what relative success? All these operations are necessary in more complex problem solving situations demanding executive functioning. Note also as Bransford, Nitsch, and Franks (Chapter 2, this volume) have mentioned, a desirable outcome of schooling in this domain would result not only in the efficient control of a few common strategies, but in the ability to invent new and flexible solutions for the needs of the moment. The development of such abilities, which appears to be continuous throughout the period of formal schooling, is a slow and laborious process.

One common factor in the studies quoted so far, and in others conducted in the area (see Flavell & Wellman, 1977, for an excellent review), is that all presented relatively meaningless material, out of context, for deliberate memorization. Of interest is whether the consistent pattern of metamnemonic deficiency which has emerged is restricted to such tasks, that is, is the problem of control limited to deliberate strategic intervention in the service of rote recall? While there is insufficient data to answer this question, there are three studies which suggest that the problem at least extends to somewhat more meaningful materials in an intentional recall paradigm. It is assumed that adults have little difficulty picking out the main theme of a paragraph, of knowing what is nonessential or readily inferable from a passage, etc. Yet, young children do not share this talent. After reading a brief passage they experience difficulty naming the three most important concepts (Shuy, 1974), or selecting key sentences as "notes" for future recall (Danner, 1974). In the same vein, using a procedure borrowed from Johnson (1970), we had children and adults rate prose passages for the importance of the constituent propositions to the main theme of the passage. Subsequently, new groups of subjects were tested for recall. The recall of both the adults and the children was determined by the importance ratings of the *adults*. That is, children did recall the most important elements of the story, but, unlike adults, they were not able to indicate what the important elements were. In light of the considerable emphasis in school placed on such activities as précis writing, making outlines of the main events, selecting important points for extra study, etc., the failure of third- to fifth-grade subjects to indicate the salient points is somewhat interesting (Brown & Smiley, 1977). It also suggests that the child's problems with estimating the difficulty of a task are not restricted to "meaningless materials."

As a final general point, I would like to mention the problem of transfer. A large section of the developmental literature has been concerned with training studies where specific mnemonic and metamnemonic deficiencies have been identified and steps taken to remedy these deficiencies by deliberate intervention. Studies of this nature are legion (see Brown, 1974; Campione & Brown, 1974, 1977, for a full review). Of interest here is the common finding that careful training routinely produces improved performance in immature subjects; however, evidence of retention over time or without specific promptings is somewhat scanty, and evidence of generalization to new situations is almost entirely lacking. The problem of transfer is of central concern to educators and experimentalists alike; for without evidence of broad generalization the efficiency of any training program must be questioned. Transfer of training involves executive functions, for the executive must judge the range of utility of a trained strategy, and the ability to apply a suitable heuristic in new situations is the essence of executive control. As we have seen, such executive functioning does not come easily to the young child.

In keeping with the title of the volume, I would like to address the issue of the effects of formal schooling on the development of mnemonic skills and their control. It is interesting to note that the period of development discussed in this paper, from the first emergence of the child's awareness of himself as an active agent in knowing, to the establishment of the complex executive functions exhibited by high school and college students, coincides exactly with the period of formal education in most Western societies. Does this suggest that formal education is in some way implicated, that we have a case of educational rather than maturational development? The only meaningful way to consider such a question is by reference to cultures where the degree of formal schooling and chronological age are not hopelessly confounded as they are in America. Using this ploy, Nelson has already pointed out that the formation of context-free semantic hierarchies may very well be an outcome of our educational system.

While the complexity of education—task interactions prohibits any sweeping generalizations about the effects of schooling, a consideration of the cross-cultural literature on cognitive development does reveal some persistent findings relevant to the problems discussed in this contribution. First, let me reemphasize that, constrained by the available literature, I have concentrated on the emergence and control of specific skills for remembering new information and for deducing facts on the basis of old information by probabilistic reasoning. I would like to argue that the development of the subset of skills under consideration is not only influenced by formal education, but is very largely the product of schooling as we know it. Here I am greatly indebted to the work of Michael Cole, Sylvia Scribner and their associates (Cole & Scribner, 1975a, b, 1977; Scribner & Cole, 1973) who have pointed out that schools represent the major cultural institution in technological societies where remembering as a distinct activity or specialized skill, in and for itself, in isolation from possible applications, is routinely undertaken. Outside the school setting, in unschooled populations, including that of the preschool child, such activities are rarely if ever encountered (Brown, 1975). Deliberate remembering as an end in itself rather than as a means to achieve a meaningful goal is very much a school-inspired activity.

It should not seem surprising, therefore, that one of the consistent differences between schooled and unschooled populations rests in the ability to deal with the kinds of mnemonic skills for deliberate memorizing I have described here. Several years of formal schooling seem to be necessary before the emergence of spontaneous attempts to organize, rehearse, categorize, etc. for the purpose of remembering. As Wagner (1974) points out, "higher mnemonic strategies in memory may do more than lag by several years" in unschooled populations, for without formal schooling "such skills may not develop at all." Note, however, the interesting exception of the complex mnemonics used by narrative singers to maintain and transmit epic poems (Brown, 1975; Colby & Cole, 1973; Cole & Scribner, 1977).

The second general finding which distinguishes schooled from unschooled populations concerns the problem of transfer. Scribner and Cole (1973) suggest that one cognitive characteristic of unschooled populations is that they tend to treat *traditional* learning and memory tasks as independent, each as a new problem. In short, there appears to be a conspicuous absence of learning to learn such problems. Schooled populations, however, show a marked tendency to treat such problems as instances of a general class. The application of common operations and rules to a universe of similar learning tasks appears to be an outcome of formal schooling. As we have seen, applying a domain-specific rule appropriately is a clear example of executive functioning, at least of the kind we build into our children and our machines.

One final piece of cross-cultural evidence I would like to introduce concerns the emergence of formal operations of deductive reasoning. I will limit my comment to the simple case of operating on material in the absence of empirical support. I know of no cross-cultural or developmental studies similar to the example raised by Collins (Chapter 10, this volume) regarding the ability to operate on material already in the knowledge base, to predict what can be known. Yet, there is one relevant area which has been studied developmentally and cross culturally. Following Piaget (1929), Osherson and Markman (1975) considered the metalinguistic ability of children to evaluate contradictions and tautologies. Faced with sentences of the form: "either it is raining outside or it is not," or the "chip (hidden) in my hand is blue or it is not blue" young children indiscriminately sought empirical support for the truth value of the statement. The children did not recognize the nonempirical nature of the simple contradictions, or at least were unwilling to evaluate these sentences in the absence of empirical evidence. A similar example of the need for empirical support to evaluate language comes from Scribner's (1974) studies of comprehension of classical syllogism among schooled and unschooled Kpelle villagers. Given problems such as "All Kpelle men are rice farmers. Mr. Smith (Western name) is not a rice farmer. Is he a Kpelle man?", unschooled villagers refused to consider the problem if they had not met Mr. Smith. They failed to grasp the fact that the task involved logical implications determined solely by the structural relations between the stated propositions, independent of their factual status. Again, on the basis of the scanty evidence it would appear that certain forms of logical thinking in response to traditional academic problem-solving situations, far from being the natural outcome of maturation are very much dependent on the intervention of formal schooling. In support of this position Piaget (1972) has recently suggested that under some cultural conditions formal propositional thinking may not emerge at all.

Even this brief consideration of cognitive development in cultural perspective suggests that much of what we regard as the normal course of development is, if not actually an outcome of formal schooling, at least greatly influenced by the process. Let me hasten to add that unschooled populations should not be regarded as cognitively immature, or in any way comparable to preschool children in our society, in terms of their level of mental operations or intelligence, for Cole and Scribner have repeatedly demonstrated the richness of intellectual life among "primitive" peoples (Cole & Scribner, 1975b; Scribner, 1974); see also the discussion of nonliterate memory by Olson (Chapter 3, this volume) and by Havelock (1963, 1971). While I do not have time to discuss this issue here, the available literature to date would suggest that what we regard as intelligence is very much an outcome of societal values; for it is not that unschooled populations do not think, reason, or remember, but that they do not always think, reason, and remember in the same way that we do.

At this point let me return to Nelson's contribution. Nelson has emphasized the fundamental continuity of concept formation throughout life and I would argue that her concentration on the scripts of early childhood is responsible for this conclusion. Nelson's description of a script for organizing the interaction of a number of different concepts around an action or a goal is very similar to Cole and Scribner's (1977) description of a natural type of memory concerned with personally experienced scenes or events which lend organization and predictability to the world around us. Nelson points out that context-derived event structures and scripts involving actually experienced, meaningful and repetitive sequences in space and time are the important organizing structures for young children. There is, however, some evidence that they may be the dominant form of knowing in both the elderly in our society (Denney, 1974) and unschooled young adults in other societies (Cole & Scribner, 1977). Thus, I would like to take up Nelson's point that the later emerging context-free categorical organizations are an addition to, and not a replacement for, the basic spatiotemporal scripts. Just as the elaborate skills for deliberately remembering are added to the "automatic" knowing of childhood (Brown, 1975) so the context-free conceptual system described by Nelson is an addition, a form of specialized skill grafted onto the more basic script structure.

At the risk of overstating my case, I would like to argue that the demands of a technological society exert a powerful influence on the course of cognitive growth. There is evidence that even minor changes in nonliterate societies, such as converting to a cash economy (Cole & Scribner, 1977), or collective farming (Luria, 1971) are reflected in the modes of thinking of the people. Formal schooling is a more potent shaper of cognitive development and not only do we foster the development of certain forms of knowing in our children, but we use these ways of knowing as the definition of intelligence. But much of what we regard as intelligent thinking is an outcome of a specialized set of educational experiences which are discontinuous from those encountered in everyday life, experiences which promote different modes of learning and knowing.

So, like Nelson, I would conclude that there is a fundamental continuity to human conceptual development; for, the basic way of knowing consists of the formation of increasingly rich event structures and scripts which allow interpretation of the novel, prediction of the familiar and an organizational structure for a personal universe. Some of the many effects of formal schooling are to create new ways of knowing tailored to the needs of a technological society, which include context-free systems of knowledge and elaborate skills for deliberately acquiring and using knowledge, divorced from social—contextual support, decontextualized in Bransford's *et al.* sense (1976; Chapter 2, this volume). The ability to manipulate knowledge for new purposes, to derive new concepts on the basis of the knowledge structure itself, without additional empirical support, indeed, the entire system of propositional thinking of formal operations, may also be largely determined by the specific type of experiences fostered in a traditional school setting. When these formal systems of knowing are the subjects of study, powerful effects of age will be found in this culture, contaminated as the measure is with degree of formal education. In addition, clear differences between schooled and unschooled populations in other societies would be expected. When the methods of knowing described by Nelson are considered, there will be little evidence of a developmental discontinuity within our society, and qualitative differences between schooled and unschooled populations would not be expected. Without the intervention of formal schooling differences between adults and children reflect the increasing richness and diversity of human experience across the life span rather than fundamentally different modes of thought.

REFERENCES

Appell, L. F., Cooper, R. G., McCarrell, N., Sims-Knight, J., Yussen, S. R., & Flavell, J. H. The development of the distinction between perceiving and memorizing. *Child Development,* 1972, **43,** 1365—1381.

Becker, J. D. Reflections on the formal description of behavior. In D. G. Bobrow & A. Collins (Eds.), *Representation and understanding: Studies in cognitive science.* New York: Academic Press, 1975. Pp. 83—102.

Blake, M. Prediction of recognition when recall fails: Exploring the feeling of knowing phenomena. *Journal of Verbal Learning and Verbal Behavior,* 1973, **12,** 311—319.

Bobrow, D. G. Dimensions of representation. In D. G. Bobrow & A. Collins (Eds.), *Representation and understanding: Studies in cognitive science.* New York: Academic Press, 1975. Pp. 1—34.

Bobrow, D. G. & Norman, D. A. Some principles of memory schemata. In D. G. Bobrow & A. Collins (Eds.), *Representation and understanding: Studies in cognitive science.* New York: Academic Press, 1975. Pp. 131—149.

Brown, A. L. The role of strategic behavior in retardate memory. In N. R. Ellis (Ed.), *International review of research in mental retardation* (Vol. 1), New York: Academic Press, 1974. Pp. 55–111.

Brown, A. L. The development of memory: Knowing, knowing about knowing, and knowing how to know. In H. W. Reese (Ed.), *Advances in child development and behavior* (Vol. 10). New York: Academic Press, 1975. Pp. 103–152.

Brown, A. L. Knowing when, where and how to remember: A problem of metacognition. In R. Glaser (Ed.), *Advances in instructional psychology* (Vol. 1). Hillsdale, N. J.: Lawrence Erlbaum Associates, in press.

Brown, A. L., & Barclay, C. R. The effects of training specific mnemonics on the metamnemonic efficiency of retarded children. *Child Development,* 1976, 47, 71–80.

Brown, A. L., Campione, J. C., & Murphy, M. D. Some experiments on metamemory in the retarded. Paper presented at a meeting of the American Psychological Association, New Orleans, August 1974.

Brown, A. L., & Lawton, S. C. The feeling of knowing experience in educable retarded children. *Developmental Psychology,* in press.

Brown, A. L., & Smiley, S. S. Rating the importance of structural units of prose passages: A problem of metacognitive development, *Child Development,* 1977, in press.

Butterfield, E. C., & Belmont, J. M. Assessing and improving the cognitive function of mentally retarded people. In I. Bailer & M. Sternlicht (Eds.), *Psychological issues in mental retardation.* Chicago: Aldine, 1976, in press.

Campione, J. C., & Brown, A. L. The effects of contextual changes and degree of component mastery on transfer of training. In H. W. Reese (Ed.), *Advances in child development and behavior* (Vol. 9). New York: Academic Press, 1974. Pp. 69–114.

Campione, J. C., & Brown, A. L., Memory in the retarded child. In R. V. Kail, Jr. & J. W. Hagen (Eds.), *Perspectives on the development of memory and cognition.* Hillsdale, N.J.: Lawrence Erlbaum Associates, 1977.

Colby, B., & Cole, M. Culture, memory, and narrative. In R. Horton & R. Finnegan (Eds.), *Modes of thought: Essays on thinking in western and nonwestern societies.* London: Faber & Faber, 1973. Pp. 63–91.

Cole, M., & Scribner, S. Theorizing about socialization of cognition. *Ethos,* 1975, 3, 249–268. (a)

Cole, M., & Scribner, S. Developmental theories applied to cross-cultural cognitive research. Paper presented at the New York Academy of Sciences, October, 1975. (b)

Cole, M., & Scribner, S. Cross-cultural studies of memory and cognition. In R. V. Kail, Jr. & J. W. Hagen (Eds.), *Perspective on the development of memory and cognition.* Hillsdale, N. J.: Lawrence Erlbaum Associates, 1977.

Collins, A., Warnock, E., Aiello, N., & Miller, M. Reasoning from incomplete knowledge. In D. G. Bobrow & A. Collins (Eds.), *Representation and understanding: Studies in cognitive science.* New York: Academic Press, 1975. Pp. 383–415.

Danner, F. W. Children's understanding of intersentence organization in the recall of short descriptive passages. Unpublished doctoral dissertation. University of Minnesota, 1974.

Denney, N. W. Evidence for developmental changes in categorization criteria. *Human Development,* 1974, 17, 41–53.

Flavell, J. H., Friedrichs, A. G., & Hoyt, J. D. Developmental changes in memorization processes. *Cognitive Psychology,* 1970, 1, 324–340.

Flavell, J. H., & Wellman, H. M. Metamemory. In R. V. Kail, Jr. & J. W. Hagen (Eds.), *Perspectives on the development of memory and cognition.* Hillsdale, N. J.: Lawrence Erlbaum Associates, 1977.

Hart, J. T. Memory and memory monitoring processes. *Journal of Verbal Learning and Verbal Behavior,* 1967, 6, 685–691.

Havelock, E. A. *Preface to Plato.* Cambridge: Harvard University Press, 1963.

Havelock, E. A. *Prologue to Greek literacy.* Cincinnati: University of Cincinnati Press, 1971.

James, W. *The principles of psychology* (Vol. 1). New York: Holt, 1890.

Johnson, R. E. Recall of prose as a function of the structural importance of the linguistic unit. *Journal of Verbal Learning and Verbal Behavior,* 1970, 9, 12–20.

Kreutzer, M. A., Leonard, C., & Flavell, J. H. An interview study of children's knowledge about memory. *Monographs of the Society for Research in Child Development,* 1975, 40 (Serial number 159).

Luria, A. R. Towards the problem of the historical nature of psychological processes. *International Journal of Psychology,* 1971, 6, 259–272.

Markman, E. M. *Factors affecting the young child's ability to monitor his memory.* Unpublished doctoral dissertation, University of Pennsylvania, 1973.

Murphy, M. D., & Brown, A. L. Incidental learning in preschool children as a function of level of cognitive analysis. *Journal of Experimental Child Psychology,* 1975, 19, 509–523.

Nelson, K. Concept, word and sentence. Interrelations in acquisition and development. *Psychological Review,* 1974, 81, 267–285.

Newell, A. A note on process-structure distinctions in developmental psychology. In S. Farnham-Diggory (Ed.), *Information processing in children.* New York: Academic Press, 1972. Pp. 125–139.

Norman, D. A. Memory, knowledge and the answering of questions. In R. L. Solso (Ed.), *Contemporary issues in cognitive psychology: The Loyola Symposium.* Washington, D.C.: Winston, 1973.

Osherson, D. N. & Markman, E. Language and the ability to evaluate contradictions and tautologies. *Cognition,* 1975, 3(3), 213–226.

Piaget, J. *Judgment and reasoning in the child.* New York: Harcourt, 1928.

Piaget, J. *The child's conception of the world.* London: Routledge & Kegan Paul, 1929.

Piaget, J. Intellectual evolution from adolescence to adulthood. *Human Development* 1972, 15, 1–12.

Scribner, S. Recall of classical syllogisms: A cross-cultural investigation of error on logical problems. In R. Falmagne (Ed.), *Reasoning: Representation and process in children and adults.* Hillsdale, N.J.: Lawrence Erlbaum Associates, 1975.

Scribner, S., & Cole, M. Cognitive consequences of formal and informal education. *Science,* 1973, 182, 553–559.

Shuy, R. W. Pragmatics: Still another contribution of linguistics to reading. Paper presented at the Western Washington State College Symposium on Reading, Bellingham, Washington. October 1974.

Sieber, J. Secondary ignorance. Paper presented at the UNESCO International Conference on Learning and the Education Processes, Stockholm, August, 1968.

Vygotsky, L. S. *Thought and language.* Cambridge, Mass.: M.I.T. Press, 1962.

Wagner, D. A. The development of short-term and incidental memory: A cross-cultural study. *Child Development,* 1974, 45, 389–396.

Wellman, H. M. The development of memory monitoring: The feeling of knowing experience. Unpublished doctoral dissertation. University of Minnesota, 1975.

Winograd, T. Frame representations and the declarative/procedural controversy. In D. G. Bobrow & A. Collins (Eds.), *Represenation and understanding: Studies in cognitive science.* New York: Academic Press, 1975. Pp. 185–210.

OPEN DISCUSSION
ON THE CONTRIBUTIONS
BY NELSON AND BROWN

Nelson: Let me open by thanking Dr. Brown for adding to the argument and, in particular, for emphasizing strategies and problem-solving skills. I agree that is where development is really at in terms of the school-age child.

Olson: I would like to say a word about decontextualization. It is a problem that has intrigued me, too. The thing that now seems to me to be the case is that it is perhaps better not to think of the knowledge as decontextualized. Rather, it is assigned to a new context, that context being the formalized, linguistic system. For example, the concept of "cup" is no longer just related to the activities of using that object, but rather more or less to the definite dictionary definitions of the concept, "cup", relative to other concepts in that semantic vein, and so on. So that it is just a new context rather than decontextualization.

Nelson: In fact, that is the way I had conceived of it, as a new context. When I speak of context free, I mean free from the spatial-temporal context in which it had been previously embedded. Now it would be conceived within a new context or framework which would be categorical in one sense, or linguistic, or however you choose to characterize it.

Resnick: I think I fundamentally agree with Dr. Brown's praise of schools. However, I might point out that as far as I know, there is no way of disassociating the general technological culture from the school culture. I know of no technological culture that does not put heavy emphasis on schooling. It is possible that it is the technological culture that demands the schooling and the kinds of cognitive behavior we are talking about, not that the schooling produces it in the absence of the technological culture.

There is some evidence for example that just the degree of commercialization and the degree of urbanization of an African town will affect the rate at which concrete operations are acquired and the likelihood of formal operations show-ing up at all. That is even without schools.

Hunt: The trend toward technological culture and the trend in schooling toward emphasizing social adjustment rather than emphasizing formal, abstract thought, could be quite dangerous to development. You see, many people in the culture can really react to a very good technology, not to a nineteenth century technology, but to a very good technology, as if it were magic. I simply ask how many of you really know how your car starts? By that, I do not mean that you can recite words to me that you do not understand. How many of you really understand why the car starts, and how many of you start a car using the same logic that the Hopi did to make it rain? It is different if you have technology that basically does not work, or that works marginally. For example, in the early twentieth century a car owner had a much better idea of how a car worked, because he damn well better, than he needs to have today.

Broudy: I am going to try and reinforce this. To use a product it is not necessary to possess the rationality that entered into the making of it. Karl Mannheim pointed that out in the 1930s, that the functional rationality of a system does not entail the substantive rationality of the members of that system. The better your technology, the more trouble free it is, the lower the cognitive demand on the user, if he chooses not to understand it. The best refrigerator is the one the consumer has to know nothing about. Extend that to the use of technology to deliver ideas, opinions, and tastes, many of which are produced at a fairly high level of quality by any standard. When Eric Severeid speaks, whatever I may think about Severeid, I dare say that his opinions are better considered, and more rationally founded, than those of most of the people who are listening to him. Nevertheless, to adopt his opinions requires no preparation. It does not even require too much criticism. Therefore, as the necessity to make up one's own mind, to be critical, to make up one's own taste, to be authentic, diminishes, there is a danger of the diminished mind. The point is that you can have a pretty good life ready made whether it is foods, clothing, ideas, and there are no great sanctions against such a life.

Hunt: If you put this in a schooling context, you can sense the seriousness of the problem. For example, there are calculators available which automatically compute variance. The *concept* of variance to a statistics student becomes "Press the second function, and then press the X." We are using technology now not just to reduce physical labor, but to reduce mental labor. Various other uses of computing technology are good examples of that. Talk to an advertising execu-tive and find out how little they know about the Nielson ratings by which they live. The bad thing is that they do not understand the limitations of the system on which they are making decisions. They are making them like the Hopi made decisions about rain. The extent to which people are taught this in the schools could very well have an effect upon their ability to deal with logical structures.

Petrie: We have paid the appropriate lip service to the importance of the logical ways of thinking; there are these other alternatives, but obviously they are less important than the rational ones. A part of the cultural challenge to academia in the last ten years said it is just lip service. The prepackaged, nonacademic culture is where it is at. I think that however much we may be committed to our abstract, logical, rational, modes of thought, the culture is actually suggesting to us that we are going to have to do more than just be committed to them. We are going to have to show how they have any kind of bearing on the rest of the world. Higher education is in for some tough times precisely because we are not very good at showing that to the people who get fairly good opinions from Eric Severeid. To those people the alternatives are *real* alternatives.

8

Attitudes, Beliefs, and Information Acquisition

Robert S. Wyer, Jr.

University of Illinois at Urbana-Champaign

GENERAL CONSIDERATIONS

It is a unique experience for me to discuss something with practical implications. Certainly, there is little danger that my personal research will ever be criticized for being unduly concerned with matters of social relevance. It has, therefore, been worthwhile for me to consider the possible implications of my own and related work for the important issues of concern in this conference.

Definitions and Concepts

Before beginning to discuss the role of attitudes in the acquisition of knowledge, I should perhaps be explicit about what I personally mean by "attitude," and what I mean by "knowledge." My conception of an attitude is somewhat nontraditional. That is, I view it as nothing more than the judgment of a person, object or concept along an evaluative dimension favorable—unfavorable, good—bad, *et al*).

Such a judgment may be subject to the same laws as other types of judgments (for some evidence of this, see Wyer, 1975). This conception differs from that proposed elsewhere in that it does not require the assumption that an attitude is accompanied by any underlying affective state or level of emotional involvement. Nor does it assume a priori that an attitude is related either to other cognitions or to overt behavior. These relations may often exist. In fact, the evaluation of an object may often occupy a central position in the interrelated set of cognitions a person has about that object, in that it both affects and is affected by a large number of other cognitions. However, the existence of these relations, and of the relations among attitudes, internal (unobserved) affective responses, and overt behavior, are matters of empirical investigation, and are not embodied in the definition of an attitude itself. As I have pointed out elsewhere (Wyer, 1973, 1974a), it can sometimes be misleading to segregate attitudes from other cognitions and to assume a priori that they are governed by qualitatively different cognitive processes.

"Knowledge" may refer to two general things. First, it may refer to the body of intellectual and motor skills a person has acquired through learning. The acquisition of skills is obviously important, and deserves more attention than can be given here. Although I will touch briefly upon certain factors that may stimulate behavior necessary to acquire intellectual and motor skills, a general consideration of these matters is unfortunately beyond the scope of this discussion.

"Knowledge" may also refer to information, that is, to a collection of propositions, each of which is held to be true with a certain probability. To this extent, knowledge about an object may be conceptualized as simply a set of beliefs. These beliefs are of course interconnected. For example, the belief that inner-city schools are of generally poor quality, and the belief that urban public-school systems do not have adequate financial support, may be connected by the conditional belief that *if* urban school systems do not have adequate financial support, inner-city schools will be of poor quality. Note that the three beliefs in combination comprise a syllogism of the form $[A; if A, then B; B]$. It seems reasonable to suppose that such syllogistically-related beliefs are common in a subject's cognitive system. The implications of this possibility will be considered presently.

While knowledge may be acquired in many ways, a primary way in educational settings is through a written or oral communication. Such a communication may consist of a series of ostensibly factual statements or opinions, usually centered around a general proposition or conclusion. To this extent, it resembles a "persuasive" message of the form often used in research on belief and opinion change.

From the perspective outlined above, an important aspect of the question of how attitudes are related to the acquisition of knowledge concerns the manner in which evaluative judgments of an object affect the formation of beliefs about the object. On the other hand, beliefs formed on the basis of information about an object may be related not only to attitudes toward the object itself, but also to attitudes toward the source of the information presented, the situational context in which the information is received, and in some instances, the recipient himself. These various relations have been the major focus of research and theory on belief and attitude change for several years. While this work has generally been conducted within the confines of the social psychology laboratory, it may have implications for the processes of acquiring information in more natural settings, as I will attempt to point out.

The relation of attitudes to the acquisition of knowledge may of course be bidirectional. For example, one can consider both the effect of attitudes upon the acquisition of knowledge about the object, and the effect of acquiring knowledge about an object upon evaluative judgments of it. The theoretical and empirical issues underlying a consideration of these effects differ. However, so do the practical merits of these considerations. The effect of acquiring knowledge upon attitudes is undoubtedly of value to propagandists, political candidates, professors who would like to place their graduate students in good jobs, and students who wish to make themselves appear more attractive to their dates. However, I am not sure that the development of attitudes is or should be an objective of the educational system unless the attitude of concern is toward education or toward the acquisition of knowledge itself. In addition, I am unconvinced that general attitudes toward an object are particularly useful predictors of behavior toward the object, a conviction also held by Fishbein and Ajzen (1975) and others. Thus, although there has been much research on the effects of information upon evaluative judgments, to which I personally have contributed more than my share (see Wyer, 1974a), I will focus most of my attention upon the possible *effects* of attitudes upon information acquisition.

To provide a framework for this discussion, it may be useful to consider two general questions related to the acquisition process itself. One concerns the mediating effects of reception and counterarguing upon beliefs in the conclusions drawn from new information. The second concerns the indirect effects of new information bearing upon one belief upon other, unmentioned but related beliefs.

A Conceptual Model of Informational Influence

Here and throughout our discussion, we will assume that the information to be acquired is presented in a series of written or oral statements which, if true, provide evidence in support of some more general conclusion. Two general factors underlie the influence of such a communication upon a person's beliefs in either the information presented or the conclusion to be drawn: his reception and comprehension of the information contained in the communication, and his acceptance of its contents as true. (The latter is, of course, contingent upon whether the contents of the communication can be discredited either through reasoning or through recourse to previously acquired information.) Although the individual effects of these factors upon information acquisition may seem self-evident, their combined effects are less so. It seems reasonable to suppose that a person will be influenced by a communication to the extent he receives the information contained in it, but cannot effectively refute its implications (see McGuire, 1968a). This suggests the simple equation

$$P_I = P_R(1 - P_{CA}), \tag{1}$$

where P_I is the probability of being influenced by a given piece of information (of changing a belief in the event or relation described in the information), P_R is the probability of receiving and comprehending it, and P_{CA} is the probability of counterarguing it effectively, or refuting its validity. (For a more general analysis of informational influence from which this equation can be derived, see Wyer, 1974a.)[1]

There are interesting implications of this simple equation. For example, it predicts that if factors simultaneously affect both reception and counterarguing, they may have a curvilinear effect upon the influence of the message. To see this, suppose that both reception and counterarguing increase with some characteristic X, such that P_R and P_{CA} are both equal to .1 when X is low, both equal to .5 when X is moderate, and both equal to .9 when X is high. Then, according to Equation 1, the likelihood of influence (P_I) should increase from .09 to .25 as X increases from low to moderate, but should decrease again back to .09 as X increases from moderate to high.

This simple equation helps to conceptualize the combined effects of many individual difference variables and situational variables in terms of their mediating effects upon reception and counterarguing. Attitudinal variables are of course among these. To give a concrete example, suppose a message is presented to persons who vary both in intelligence and in their initial attitudes toward the viewpoint being expressed. It seems likely that the ability to receive and comprehend the message and the ability to counterargue it effectively will both increase with intelligence. However, whether or not a person will *try* to refute the contents of the message will depend upon whether the information opposes his initial opinion. Among persons whose initial views differ from the position advocated in the communication, the likelihood of receiving a communication and the likelihood of counterarguing it effectively should both increase with intelligence. Thus, as suggested by our previous analysis, the communication should have greater influence on those of moderate intelligence than on those of either very high or very low intelligence. However, now consider persons with no previously formed beliefs about the issue. The likelihood that these persons will counterargue the communication may be low, regardless of their ability, since they have little motivation to do so. The influence of the communication on these persons should be simply a function of their ability to receive and comprehend its contents (P_R), and therefore should consistently increase with their intelligence. In summary, then, this line of reasoning predicts that the impact of information that runs counter to an initial position should be greatest

---

[1] The extention of this equation, which is a mathematical tautology, takes into account the probabilities of yielding to a communication given that one does and does not counterargue effectively, and thus allows for the consideration of tendencies to comply overtly with the implications of information without underlying acceptance, evaluation apprehension effects, etc. Equation (1) is based upon the simplifying assumption that these conditional probabilities are equal to 0 and 1, respectively.

when one is of moderate ability, while the impact of information that does not oppose an initial view should be greatest when one is of high ability.

Equation 1 does not directly take into account certain factors to be considered in our discussion, such as the interpretation of the information presented or the tendency to adopt publically a position with which one privately does not agree (see Footnote 1). Nevertheless, it is of considerable value in conceptualizing many of the phenomena to be considered in this paper, as we shall see.

Indirect Effects of Information

To the extent that the information presented in a communication is accepted as valid, it is likely to have implications for other, unmentioned beliefs to which the information is directly relevant. For example, a communication that defends the proposition that Darwin's theory of evolution is true may not only affect the belief in this proposition, but also may affect the belief that the Bible should be interpreted literally. This may occur even though the latter proposition is not mentioned in the communication presented. The magnitude of these indirect effects of information may of course depend upon beliefs that the unmentioned proposition (that the Bible should be interpreted literally) is more apt to be true if the first is true (that is, if Darwin's theory is correct) than if it is not.

The effects described above can theoretically be described by the equation

$$P_B = P_A P_{B/A} + P_{A'} P_{B/A'},$$ (2)

where A and B are the two propositions being related, P_B is the belief (in units of probability) that B is true, P_A and $P_{A'}$ are beliefs that A is and is not true, respectively, and $P_{B/A}$ and $P_{B/A'}$ are conditional beliefs that B is true *if A* is and is not true, respectively. Note that the two products on the right side of the equation are essentially beliefs in two mutually exclusive sets of premises, [A; if A, then B] and [not A; if not A, then B], each with the same conclusion B.

Substantial evidence has accumulated to suggest that this equation, which is basically an extension of McGuire's (1960) model of cognitive organization, provides a reasonably accurate quantitative description of the manner in which syllogistically-related beliefs are interconnected and the manner in which information that changes one belief (say, P_A) will affect beliefs in others (say, P_B); for a review, see Wyer (1975). Several considerations related to the application of this formulation should be noted, however. First, it seems obvious that for a communication bearing upon A to affect beliefs in B, the various beliefs and their relationship must be salient to the recipient. In some instances, A and B may be so strongly associated that a consideration of A (for example, "the world is becoming overpopulated") automatically elicits a consideration of B (for example, "birth control practices should be encouraged"). In other instances, however, two beliefs may be related, but are seldom thought of together, and thus become cognitively segregated. To this extent, information about A may have little effect upon beliefs in B unless this latter proposition is called to the recipient's attention at the time the information is presented.

On the other hand, it seems likely that the implications of new information will be resisted if its acceptance would require a major cognitive reorganization, that is, if it would require a change in a large number of other logically related beliefs in order to maintain consistency among them. To this extent, information bearing upon a proposition A will have less direct influence upon beliefs in this proposition when its relation to other beliefs is salient than when it is not. Therefore, to summarize this line of reasoning, making related beliefs salient to a recipient of information should increase the indirect effect of the information upon these beliefs, but should decrease the effect of the information upon the beliefs to which it directly pertains.

Although indirect effects of information may indeed occur, the cognitive work required to produce these effects obviously does not take place instantaneously. Rather, it may take time for the implications of new information to "filter down" to all other beliefs upon which they bear (McGuire, 1960, 1968b). The fact that cognitive reorganization does take place over a period of time is suggested by the abundant evidence for the "Socratic" effect, that is, the tendency for beliefs to become more internally consistent, that is, more closely related in the manner described by Equation (2) once they have been made salient in temporal proximity (Henninger, 1975; Rosen & Wyer, 1972; Wyer, 1974b). It seems reasonable that new information bearing upon a proposition A will produce a temporary inconsistency between the belief in this proposition and beliefs in other related propositions (say, B), and that this inconsistency may take time to be eliminated. This could be done in several ways. First, the belief that B is true may change to a level consistent with the initially induced change in belief that A is true. Second, the belief in A may return to its original level. Third, beliefs in the relevance of A to B (that is, the beliefs that B is likely to be true given that A is or is not true) may shift. These various effects may occur simultaneously. It seems likely that the extent to which these alternative methods of inconsistency resolution are used will depend upon the degree of commitment to each of the beliefs involved, and the interconnectedness with other beliefs in a cognitive system. However, this possibility has not been systematically investigated (for some evidence of commitment effects, see Holt, 1970).

In any event, calling attention to these matters makes salient the fact that the effects of new information are often widespread, and that to understand these effects, one must consider factors other than simply the recall and acceptance of the material itself. Moreover, the extent to which the information is accepted may depend greatly upon its implications for beliefs in other, unmentioned propositions.

Effects of information salience upon cognitive organization. As we noted, there is substantial evidence that beliefs may be modified simply by making salient previously formed cognitions that have implications for these beliefs (Rosen & Wyer, 1972; Wyer, 1974b). If this is true, and if different sets of cognitions have different implications for a certain belief, this belief should be able to be changed by simply manipulating the particular set of cognitions that is salient to a person at the time he reports it. This possibility has been the focus of a series of studies by Salancik, one of which (Salancik, 1974) is of particular relevance to behavior and attitudes in an educational setting. Students in a class completed one of two types of open-ended statements about their normal classroom activities. Statements of one type were completed following the phrase "because I" (for example, "I generally raise my hand in a classroom because I . . ."). Statements of the other type were completed following the phrase "in order to" (that is, "I generally raise my hand in a classroom in order to . . ."). Salancik reasoned that completing the first type of statement would make salient intrinsic motives for engaging in the behavior described (for example, ". . . because I want to learn"), while completing the second would make salient extrinsic motives for the behavior (for example, ". . . in order to let the teacher know I am paying attention"). After completing one or the other set of statements subjects reported how much they enjoyed the course. The enjoyment reported by subjects who were given the extrinsic set was correlated .94 with course grades; in marked contrast, the enjoyment reported by subjects given the intrinsic set was correlated −.16 with course grades. Presumably, subjects given the two sets generated different sets of previously formed cognitions in responding to the open-ended questions and these cognitions served as a basis for their subsequent enjoyment ratings.

With these considerations in mind, let us finally turn to the role of attitudes in the acquisition of information. As I have noted, a general consideration of the role of attitudes in the information acquisition process must take into account the effect not only of attitudes toward the object to which the information directly pertains, but also of attitudes toward the source of the information, toward the situation in which the information is presented, and toward the recipient of the information. The possible effects of evaluative responses to each type of element will be discussed in turn.

ATTITUDES TOWARD THE OBJECT

The evaluation of an object or concept may affect any of several interrelated aspects of information acquisition: the seeking and receiving of information, the interpretation of the information, and its acceptance as valid. Rather than get bogged down in a detailed discussion of the abundant theory and research on the nature of these effects, I will focus upon a few of the more general issues that seem most relevant to the issues at hand.

Effects upon Information Seeking and Receiving

The effect of a person's attitude toward an object upon his tendency to seek and attend to information about the object has been studied extensively. It was originally hypothesized that persons tend to seek and attend to information that supports their attitudes toward the issues to which the information pertains, and to avoid opposing or dissonant information. However, based upon a comprehensive review of research on this question, Freedman and Sears (1965) concluded that if this tendency exists at all, it is very weak, and that its effect is often overridden by the effects of other factors. Two of these are the utility of the information in accomplishing some anticipated future objective, and the redundancy of the anticipated information with information one has already acquired. Thus, if a person is unfamiliar with both arguments that support and arguments that oppose his preconceived attitude, he may exhibit greater preference for supportive arguments, perhaps because they are useful to him in defending his position publically. On the other hand, if a person already has ample information about one side of the issue but not the other, he will show preference for the information supporting the position with which he is unfamiliar, regardless of whether it supports or opposes his present attitude.

Effects upon the Organization and Recall of Information

While there is little evidence that previously formed evaluations of an object have substantial effects upon the *reception* of information, there is indirect evidence that it affects the manner in which information is organized once it has been received, and therefore the manner in which it is recalled. McGuire (1960) reported a strong positive correlation between beliefs in the validity of a proposition and judgments that the event or relation described in the proposition is desirable. This correlation suggests either a tendency for persons to believe that if something is desirable, it is likely to be true ("wishful thinking"), or to believe, somewhat religiously, that if something is true, it is likely to be desirable.

McGuire went on to postulate that when syllogistically related beliefs become cognitively segregated, wishful thinking may give rise to inconsistencies among them. For example, if the conclusion of a syllogism is considerably more desirable than the premises, and if these beliefs are not considered in combination, a person will come to believe this conclusion more strongly than would be expected on the basis of their beliefs in the premises. On the other hand, once the person's beliefs in the premises and conclusion are made salient to him in temporal proximity, he should become aware of any inconsistencies that exist, and should modify one or more beliefs to make them more internally consistent. The previously cited evidence for the "Socratic effect" supports this possibility.

However, it may be premature to conclude that cognitive distortions of the sort described above are produced by evaluative cognitions alone. The decrease in the effect of wishful thinking identified by McGuire may reflect an attempt to resolve inconsistencies in the implications of two different sets of premises for the same conclusion. To give a simple example, consider two sets of premises, one of which is nonevaluative (for example, "I study hard; if I study hard, I will graduate from college") and the other of which is evaluative (for example, "graduation from college is desirable; if graduation from college is desirable, I will graduate from college"). Beliefs in the two sets of premises may not be equally strong, and thus may have different implications for the conclusion. If the beliefs involved have not recently been considered in combination, the belief in the conclusion (in this case, the belief that I will graduate from college) may be somewhat inconsistent with beliefs in *both* sets of premises. Thus, if the first, nonevaluative set is made salient in conjunction with the conclusion, these cognitions will tend to become more organized in a manner consistent with these premises, and the effect of wishful thinking will appear to decrease. However, by the same token, if the second set of (evaluative) premises is made salient in combination with the conclusion, the belief in the conclusion may be modified to make it more consistent with beliefs in *these* premises, and thus more inconsistent with the *non*evaluative beliefs (that is, the effect of wishful thinking would appear to *increase*).

Effects upon the Interpretation of New Information

While previously formed beliefs and attitudes undoubtedly provide a context for interpreting new information, the nature of these contextual effects is surprisingly unclear. This is especially true with regard to evaluative judgments. The extent to which a person's attitude toward a concept affects his judgment of the evaluative implications of new information pertaining to the concept has been a traditional concern in social psychology for many years, largely as a result of the stimulation provided by Sherif and Hovland's (1961) theory of assimilation and contrast. This theory, which is basically a theory of social judgment, predicts that if the implications of a piece of information for a position on an issue are relatively similar to those of its context, it will be "assimilated," or perceived as more similar to its context; however, if the position advocated in the information is relatively discrepant from its context, it will be "contrasted," or judged as even more discrepant. Thus, suppose a previously formed attitude toward an issue provides a "context" for evaluating the implications of new information about the issue. To this extent, information that advocates a position not too far removed from one's own attitude will be interpreted as more similar to this attitude than it is objectively, while information that advocates a position discrepant from his attitude will be contrasted, or perceived to be more opposed to one's own position than it is objectively.

While this hypothesis is quite intriguing, only the second, "contrast" portion of the hypothesis has received strong support. That is, there appears to be a general tendency for persons to judge a communication as more strongly opposed to a given position when one's own position on the issue is favorable than when it is unfavorable. However, there is little evidence for an assimilation effect. Based upon a critical analysis of the research on these effects, Upshaw (1969) concluded that the results of most of the research to date could be interpreted in terms of the effect of tendencies by subjects to use one's own attitude as a scale "anchor," or standard of comparison relative to which attitude-relevant stimuli are judged.

However, a factor overlooked both by Upshaw and by Sherif and Hovland is the possible tendency for subjects to interpret a piece of information about an object as consistent in its descriptive implications with previous information acquired about the object. Semantic material may have a variety of denotative implications, not all of which apply at any given time. When a person receives verbal information about an object with which he is already familiar, he may ignore interpretations that are inconsistent in meaning with those of the information he has already acquired, and his judgment of this information may be some composite of only those interpretations that remain.

Some evidence supporting this possibility was obtained by Wyer and Schwartz (1969). In this study, subjects rated test communications along an evaluative dimension after being exposed either to a set of context communications with consistently positive values along the dimension or to a set of communications with consistently negative values along the dimension. In some cases, the stimuli had little semantic content (for example, photographs of either high or low quality, or cartoons that were either funny or not funny). Here, contrast effects occurred; that is, stimuli were judged more positively when the quality of the stimuli preceding them was poor than when it was high. However, in other cases, the context and test stimuli required some semantic integration (for example, statements favorable or unfavorable to or statements about social issues varying in liberalness or conservatism). In these cases, assimilation effects occurred; that is, statements were judged as more positive (for example, more favorable toward Negroes or more liberal) when the series of statements preceding them had positive values than when they had negative values. In combination, these data suggest that contrast effects of the sort hypothesized by Upshaw occur, but are overridden by assimilation effects resulting from attempts to reinterpret the descriptive implications of information in a manner consistent with those of information one has previously acquired.

One might expect the assimilation effects described above to occur only when there is reason to reinterpret the information to eliminate inconsistencies in meaning. For example, it should be more likely when the statements presented were ostensibly all made by a single person than when they were made by different persons. While this contingency was found in the domain of statements about social issues, assimilation effects on judgments of statements about blacks were pronounced even when these statements ostensibly came from different sources. Apparently in some domains, previously acquired information may establish an interpretative set that leads persons to be selectively sensitive to alternative interpretations of the information presented, even when there is no obvious need to reconcile the implications of the information with the context information.

The preceding study has interesting implications for the effect of one's own attitudes upon the interpretation of new information. Suppose a person's initial attitude is based upon previously acquired semantic material (that is, if it is a composite of the implications of specific descriptive information acquired about the object), and that the new information presented him is also semantic in nature. In such a case, he should judge this latter information to be similar in its evaluative implications to his attitude. However, suppose the information upon which a person's attitude is based, or the new information presented, is not semantic in nature. Then, contrast effects may occur. To give a concrete example, I may interpret someone's statement about a program for integrating public schools to be more favorable if I personally have a favorable opinion of the program than if I do not, based upon previous information I have acquired about it. However, suppose I learn of someone's evaluative judgment of the Rolling Stones. I may interpret this judgment as more unfavorable if I am a Stones fan than if I am not, based upon my (nonverbal) contact with their music.

It is important to note that the effects described above are not unique to the processing of material with evaluative implications. Attempts to reconcile the descriptive implications of new information with those of previously acquired information may affect judgments along many dimensions. Evidence that persons' previously formed beliefs affect their interpretation of nonevaluative material and the conclusions drawn from it, is suggested in research on syllogistic inference dating back at least to Janis and Frick (1943). In a more recent study of the effects of previously formed beliefs upon syllogistic inference processes (Wyer, 1976), we found that persons' judgments of the implications of individual statements were affected by their a priori beliefs that these statements were true or false, even when they were given explicit instructions to disregard their previously formed beliefs in making these judgments. Apparently persons have a very difficult time divorcing their previously formed beliefs from their interpretation of new information.

The interpretation of new information may be affected not only by previously formed beliefs about specific objects and concepts, but also by more general beliefs about the nature of one's world and the laws that govern it. For example, we have already speculated that persons often appear to believe in an ideal world in which good events are more apt to occur than unpleasant ones. A similar notion has been suggested by Lerner and Simmons (1966), who postulate that persons tend to believe in a "just world." As a result of this general belief, persons may judge others not only to get what they deserve, but also to deserve what they get. This possibility has many implications. For example, the victim of an accident may be held more responsible for it, and may be disparaged to a greater extent regardless of his responsibility, if the accident is severe than if it is mild (Walster, 1966). It is interesting to speculate about the implications of this for student's interpretation of history. That is, the more devastating a war, the more likely it is that the loser will be disparaged and the winner judged to be on the side of the angels.

There are undoubtedly other general beliefs about the nature of our world that persons bring to bear upon their interpretation of new information. Moreover, there may be individual differences in the extent to which these beliefs are held. In a factor analysis of Rotter's I/E scale, Collins (1974) identified four different general beliefs that are held to greater or lesser extent: the belief that the world is just or unjust, that it is easy or difficult, that it is predictable or unpredictable, and that it is politically responsive or unresponsive. These general beliefs could all affect persons' interpretation of information and the judgments based upon it. Such possibilities remain to be investigated.

Effects upon the Acceptance of Information

Our discussion so far has been focused upon the effects of evaluative and nonevaluative cognitions upon the reception and comprehension of new information, that is, upon P_R as defined in our general model of informational influence. An equally important concern is with the effects of previously formed judgments of an object upon P_{CA}, or the likelihood of effectively refuting the validity of the new information presented. A consideration of these effects may sometimes be irrelevant to the acquisition of information in an educational setting for several reasons. For example, the tendency to counterargue is partially a function of situational set. That is, persons may not put forth the energy to counterargue unless they are motivated to do so, either because the issues involved are important to them, or because there are external situational pressures upon them to perform this cognitive work. In many educational settings, these conditions may not exist. Rather, students in a classroom may adopt a "reception" set; that is, they may view their task as one of simply assimilating new information without evaluating it critically, and storing it in memory where it can be later recalled and regurgitated on an examination. To this extent, they may respond passively to the information presented, P_{CA} may be low, and they may be more influenced (see Equation 1).

Under the assumption that educational situations do not *always* induce such an overwhelming reception set that tendencies to counterargue are entirely eliminated, certain considerations may be worth mention. First, the tendency to counterargue a communication is a function of both the motivation to do so and the ability to do so. As we have already noted, the motivation to counterargue is apt to be less when the information presented does not contradict the recipient's previously formed beliefs and opinions. The ability to do so may depend upon two things; the availability of information to use in refuting the arguments presented in the communication, and the practice one has had in counterarguing. McGuire (1964) has shown that a person's beliefs in cultural truisms (for example, propositions such as "Persons should brush their teeth daily," that are typically assumed to be unquestionably true despite little factural basis for this assumption) are very vulnerable to attack unless the recipient has either previously been exposed to information refuting arguments against the truism, or has had practice in refuting these arguments himself. In other words, an extreme initial opinion is not enough to make a person resistant to influence when the underlying basis for this opinion is unclear, and when the person has had no practice in refuting arguments against it.

Two of McGuire's findings have particularly important implications. First, persons who had either received information *supporting* the truism to be attacked, or had been given practice in preparing communications in support of arguments why it was true, were no less resistant to subsequent attack than were persons who had simply been exposed to the attack without warning. In terms of our general model, this is not too surprising, since neither the information presented nor the practice provided would affect the ability to *counterargue* effectively. However, it has important implications for education, since it suggests that information supporting a point of view will not be successful in warding off subsequent attacks by others; rather, persons must be exposed to arguments *against* the position to be attacked and then must be given either new information that will help them *refute* these arguments or practice in using old information effectively.

On the other hand, McGuire found that persons' resistance to persuasion was increased by exposing them to refutations of arguments against the proposition even when these arguments differed from those contained in the impending attack. Moreover, merely exposing persons to arguments against the proposition, *without* accompanying these arguments with refutations, also increased resistance to persuasion provided a period of time had elapsed between their exposure to these arguments and the onset of the attack. McGuire argued that when recipients have been exposed to an argument against their initial point of view, they become aware of their potential vulnerability and therefore are stimulated to bolster their defenses in the time interval before the attack occurs. This "innoculation effect" is also important educationally, since it suggests that we need not be afraid of exposing students to points of view that are considered to be invalid, and to criticisms of a position that is considered either socially or educationally undesirable. In fact, exposure to these points of view may increase, rather than decrease, resistance to subsequent attacks on the more desirable position.

Summary

To summarize our discussion thus far, there seems to be little evidence that previously formed attitudes and opinions affect the attention paid to new information bearing upon these opinions; rather, the critical determinants of one's attention to new information appears to be its redundancy with previous information one has acquired and its utility in attaining his objectives. Previously formed opinions may have more effect upon the interpretation of new information; however, the nature of this influence may depend largely upon the type of information upon which these opinions are based. Finally, initial attitudes and opinions may affect one's motivation to refute arguments against new information that contradict these prior beliefs. However, they do not affect the amount of influence that actually occurs; this depends upon the information one has available and the practice one has had, that help him to refute specific arguments against this belief. (Caution should, of course, be taken in applying these conclusions to the acquisition of information in an educational setting in which recipients do not have a set to counterargue, but only to assimilate information without evaluating it.)

ATTITUDES TOWARD THE SOURCE OF INFORMATION

The extent to which the influence of a communication depends upon characteristics of its source has been considered in a variety of theoretical and empirical contexts, ranging from the early work on persuasion by Kelman, Hovland and others (e.g., Kelman & Hovland, 1953), through various applications of cognitive consistency theory (Heider, 1958; Osgood & Tannenbaum, 1955), to the more recent work on social power (Schopler, 1965). However, beyond the fairly commonplace finding that communication impact increases with the extent to which its source is held in high regard, surprisingly little is known about the dynamics of these effects. I see two reasons for this. First, with few exceptions, we have not sufficiently distinguished between the various criteria upon which attitudes toward a source may be based; rather, we have implicitly assumed that the general goodness of the source, regardless of *why* he is good, is a sufficient determinant of his influence. Second, we have not adequately attended to the effects of source characteristics upon different components of the information acquisition process. A detailed discussion of these issues is beyond the scope of this paper, and moreover would be redundant with McGuire's excellent analyses of these effects in the *Handbook of Social*

Psychology (1969). However, certain issues relevant to these considerations may be worth noting briefly.

Differentiation of Source Characteristics

Many factors may contribute to the degree to which a person is held in high regard:

1. personal likeableness: the extent to which he is valued as a friend or is believed to have personal qualities relevant to favorable interpersonal relations.
2. prestige or status: the extent to which the source holds a position of high social status.
3. power: the extent to which the source controls resources or events considered to be desirable or undesirable by the recipient.
4. expertise: the extent to which the source is intelligent and knowledgeable about the issues to which the communication pertains.
5. impartiality: the extent to which the source has no vested interest in the issue to which the communication pertains or, alternatively, has no interest in persuading the recipient to accept the position advocated in the communication.

It seems likely that in many instances, a communication from a source with any one of these attributes will have more influence than will the same communication from a source without it. However, the reasons for the effects of these attributes, and the conditions under which they occur, may vary. Moreover, the various characteristics are not independent. For example, a manipulation of a source's prestige may affect perceptions of his impartiality or expertise. Or, as McGuire notes, source descriptions that increase a source's expertise may decrease his apparent similarity to the recipient, and therefore may decrease his likeableness (Byrne, 1971). Thus, the interpretation of different specific manipulations of source characteristics is often difficult.

The different effects of source characteristics are exemplified in an early study by Kelman (1958). Students at an all-Black university listened to a speech advocating segregation of colleges. The speech was attributed in one case to a wealthy alumnus who was in a position to allocate funds both to the college as a whole and to individual students, in a second case, to a student body president at a neighboring Black university; and in a third case, to a well-known specialist in Black history. Although communications from all three sources had effects, the conditions under which these effects occurred differed markedly. Specifically, communications attributed to the alumnus had an influence only when recipients believed that the source might have access to their reported opinions. This suggests that in this case, no true change in beliefs occurred. Communications from the student leader had an influence even in the absence of surveillance by the source; however, their effects dissipated over time. The communication had an enduring effect only when it was attributed to the expert in black history. Clearly, source favorableness is not enough to induce real and permanent effects of a communication; the basis of attitude must also be considered.

A clearer understanding of the possible effects of source variables upon communication impact may potentially be gained by considering their effects upon the processes assumed to mediate informational influence. Before discussing representative research on the effects of source variables upon the influence of information, let us consider each of these processes in turn, and note briefly how each source characteristic may bear upon it.

Hypothetical Effects of Source Characteristics upon Reception, Interpretation and Counterarguing

Reception and recall. Although attention to a communication might be expected to depend upon the nature of its source, there is little evidence of this in laboratory situations (see Hovland & Weiss, 1951). The failure to obtain this evidence may be attributable in part to poor measures of reception, which typically are insensitive to differences in comprehension of the material. It could also be a result of the particular manipulation of source characteristics used. Finally, it may be a consequence of situational set. That is, in the laboratory, where the information is ostensibly being presented for some purpose of interest to the experimenter, the situational stress to be a "good" subject and attend to the information may override tendencies that exist in nonlaboratory situations to pay differential attention to information from different sources.

Indeed, it would be somewhat surprising if in the absence of such situational pressures, the various factors assumed to affect source evaluations did not contribute differentially to reception. Certainly the information from various sources should be regarded as differentially useful. Moreover, the difference in perceived utility of information from an expert and that of information from a novice is likely to be greater than the difference in perceived utility of information from persons differing in friendship status or in objectivity. Indeed, information from one's enemies, or from persons low in social status, may often be regarded as quite interesting to the extent one has not frequently been exposed to such information. In any event, more work must be done to make a convincing case that source characteristics do not affect information reception outside the laboratory.

Interpretation of information. The conditions under which the source of a piece of information will affect the interpretation of the information have also not been clearly identified. A statement that public schools should be segregated seems likely to be interpreted as less favorable to blacks if it is attributed to a leader of the Ku Klux Klan than if it is attributed to a leader of a black separatist organization. A question arises as to whether these different judgments are due to different interpretations of the statement per se, or to differences in direct responses to the source. In other words, both the descriptive content of a statement and the general opinion attributed to the source may combine *additively* to affect judgments of the statement. However, this hypothesis seems implausible as a general rule. For one thing, it would imply that *any* statement, regardless of its relation to the issue at hand, would be judged as having different implications for the issue, depending upon the nature of its source. (For example, it would imply that the statement "the moon is yellow" would also be interpreted as less favorable to blacks if attributed to the Klansman than if attributed to the black separatist.) It seems more likely to suppose that when a source has already been identified with a position on the issue at hand through various statements he has made, recipients of new information from him will attempt to interpret it in a manner that is maximally consistent in its semantic implications with the source's previous statements, and their judgments of this information will reflect this effect. The previously cited data reported by myself and Schwartz are consistent with this interpretation.

Even though the content of previous communications from a source is unknown, it may often be inferred on the basis of a general description of the source along dimensions assumed to affect attitudes toward him. The nature of these effects and their relation to specific source characteristics are unclear, however. For example, while indications of source bias clearly have implications for the position the source is apt to have taken in the past, indications of source expertise may not. Recipients may attribute different a priori opinions to likeable persons than to dislikeable ones; however, this may be only with respect to certain matters relevant to interpersonal relations. Differences in social status are more likely to produce differences in the interpretation of messages, but only to the extent that status is confounded with attributions of bias. Unfortunately, little information on these matters is available. However, it seems reasonable to suppose that a source's favorableness does not affect the interpretation of information unless it has implications for the opinion held by the source on the issue to which the information pertains.

Source effects on the interpretation of a message may of course not occur if the issue is unfamiliar to the recipient, or if the recipient has no indication of previous statements the source has made on the topic. Such was the case in a study by Tannenbaum (1967). Subjects each received two communications, one from a favorable source and another from an unfavorable source, each of which either favored or opposed the concept of teaching machines. The design made it possible to separate the effects of the source's opinion per se[2] and the effect of

[2] Tannenbaum assumes that a favorably evaluated source who favors a position, and an unfavorably evaluated source who opposes the position, will both increase beliefs in the position advocated in the communication, whereas a favorable source who opposes the position and an unfavorable source who favors it will decrease beliefs in the position.

communication content. If the interpretation of the message was affected by the characteristics of its source, these effects should be interactive. However, while the statistical analyses required to test this possibility were not performed, the effects appear to be nearly independent (for details, see Wyer, 1974a). Independent effects of source and communication content are also suggested in the series of studies on the "sleeper effect" (Hovland & Weiss, 1951; Kelman & Hovland, 1953). These studies provide no evidence that a source has any permanent effect upon communication impact, contrary to expectations based upon the hypothesis that the source affected the manner in which the information was interpreted at the time it was initially received.

Counterarguing. The tendency to refute arguments contained in a communication seems likely to increase with the extent to which its source is perceived as either biased or low in expertise, since in both cases there is some a priori reason to believe that the information presented may be invalid. The manner in which other source characteristics affect counterarguing is less obvious, however. Source prestige and likeableness may affect counterarguing tendencies to the extent that prestige is confounded with apparent differences in bias or expertise in the areas to which the communication pertains. On the other hand, it is conceivable that agreement with a low status source may be considered undesirable, and that information from such a source may stimulate counterarguing for this reason. The anticipation of agreement with disliked sources may also create discomfort (Sampson & Insko, 1964) and lead to counterarguing. To this extent, the effects of source characteristics on tendencies to counterargue may be quite general, although the reasons for engaging in this counterarguing differ.

Representative Research on Source Effects

As we implied earlier, few studies have attempted to separate the effects of different source characteristics upon communication influence, let alone to investigate their effects upon different subprocesses involved in information acquisition. What evidence is available, however, suggests that the most important of these characteristics is expertise. A brief summary of this evidence may serve to demonstrate this.

Expertise and bias. Based upon a review of the research conducted by Hovland and his colleagues, McGuire (1969) concluded that descriptions of a source conveying different degrees of bias affected the influence of a communication only when these different levels of bias were implicitly confounded with expertise. In instances in which the expertise of the source was relatively high, communications from a disinterested source were judged fairer than those from a source with vested interest in the position being advocated, but produced no greater attitude change (see Hovland & Mandell, 1952). McGuire also concludes that situational factors that convey intent by the communicator to persuade the recipient to accept the position advocated also have surprisingly little effect. In combination, these considerations suggest that suspiciousness of bias alone does not induce the counterarguing necessary to decrease the influence of the communication presented, contrary to our speculations in the previous section. However, the effect of persuasive intent may be more pronounced after a period of time has elapsed between the expression of persuasive intent and the presentation of the message (Freedman & Sears, 1965). Information about the vested interest of the communicator may therefore stimulate recipients to bolster their defenses against the impending communication, but this preparation, and thus its effect upon communication impact, takes time to occur, and thus is often not detected.

Expertise, likeableness, and prestige. The effect of attraction to the source upon the influence of a communication is also unclear because of its frequent confounding with attributions of expertise. That is, friends may be attributed greater expertise and competence than enemies (Sherif, White, & Harvey, 1955) and thus their influence may be in part attributable to this latter characteristic rather than to likeableness per se. Aronson and Golden (1962) found that prejudiced elementary school subjects were more influenced by a communication from a White source than by one from a Negro even though they judged the two sources to be equally intelligent. This result suggests that attractiveness may have an effect independent of expertise. However, it is also possible that prejudiced subjects interpreted the position advocated by a white to be more socially desirable, and thus conformed more publically to this position without any greater underlying opinion change. A similar interpretation could be given to Kelman's (1958) finding that although subjects at first adopted the position advocated by a student leader when a communication from him was presented, this effect did not persist over time. That is, subjects may have taken the leader's opinion as an indication of a socially desirable position, but reverted to their original position once they had had the opportunity to discuss the issue with their peers.

More recently, Eagly and Chaiken (1975) found that communications from a source who disparaged undergraduate students (thus inducing greater dislike for him) had less influence than communications from a source who praised undergraduates. However, the issues involved pertained to venereal disease and to unemployment among college graduates. It seems likely that sources who seem irrationally to derogate undergraduates are attributed less expertise and knowledge about matters related to undergraduate problems than sources who are sympathetic to undergraduates. Thus, the source effect in this study could also be mediated by differences in attributed expertise. In general, therefore, there is little clear evidence that likeableness per se induces greater communication impact.

In summary, despite all of the *possible* effects of source variables described above, the only characteristic that seems empirically to have a clear and pronounced effect upon the influence of communication is expertise. That is, provided a recipient has some incentive to receive the communication, it appears to make little difference whether or not the source is attractive, prestigious, or biased, provided he is perceived to have knowledge of the subject matter being discussed. While other factors may initially affect a person's verbal report of his belief in the position advocated in the communication, these effects do not appear to reflect a change in his underlying beliefs, and thus are apt to decrease substantially over time.

Counteracting Source Effects

The preceding discussion does not make explicit whether differences in expertise affect attention to the communication, differential counterarguing, or what. A series of studies by Tannenbaum (1967) bear indirectly upon this question, and also provide insight into procedures for counteracting source effects. In these studies, several techniques were used either to dissociate the source from the communication (by presenting statements from the source denying he had ever generated the message) or to discredit the source by calling his competence into question. When these techniques were used before the communication was presented, the effect of the message was substantially decreased, and was often not effective at all. However, when the technique was used *after* the communication was received, the influence of the communication was hardly diminished. This suggests that the initial description of the source as credible increased recipients' attention to the communication, and thus led the information content to have a substantial effect, an effect that was maintained even after the source was later discredited or dissociated from the message. However, when the source was discredited or dissociated from the message *before* the message was received, recipients appeared to pay little attention to the message, and thus were not influenced by it. While these results are provocative, their generalizability should be treated with caution. As we have noted, if the information is expected by the recipient to be useful to him (a condition that did not clearly exist in Tannenbaum's studies), the effects of discrediting the source or dissociating him from the message may not be so pronounced.

ATTITUDES TOWARD THE SITUATION

Attitudes toward aspects of the situation in which a communication is presented may affect its influence in two ways. First, the favorableness of the situation may affect a recipient's motivation to receive the information and to comply overtly with its implications. Second, evaluative reactions to aspects of the situation *other* than the message could also distract the recipient from attending to and evaluating the contents of the message. Let us consider each possible effect in turn.

Effects on Motivation to Receive and Accept the Communication

The possibility that persons may behave in a situation in ways they think will comply with others' expectancies is widely accepted. Moreover, the hypothesis that this tendency is likely to increase with the pleasantness of the situation for the recipient is hardly profound. However, fairly subtle situational cues may affect a person's attitude toward the situation, and therefore may affect his behavior. For an example, let me borrow from an experimental situation constructed by Insko and Cialdini (1969). That is, compare the effectiveness of two alternative strategies for teaching a person to make one of two verbal responses: (a) approval for choosing the desired response coupled with neither approval nor disapproval for choosing the undesired one, and (b) disapproval for making the undesired response with neither approval nor disapproval for choosing the desired one. The information provided about which alternative is desirable is the same in both cases. However, approval for desirable responses has greater effect. Why? Inski and Cialdini argue that the reinforcing agent is liked more by the recipient in the approval condition than in the disapproval condition, and thus the recipient's motivation to manifest the correct behavior is greater.

The implications of this analysis for the acquisition of information are fairly clear. For example, a person who receives a communication from another may often assume that he is expected both to attend to the communication and to accept its implications. Thus, situational factors that increase his desire to comply with these expectancies may increase P_R but decrease P_{CA}, thus increasing the influence of the message. However, consider conditions in which the recipient is implicitly expected to evaluate the content of the communication critically. In these conditions, situational factors that increase compliance with these expectancies would increase *both* P_R and P_{CA}. Thus, according to Equation (1), they would have a nonmonotonic effect upon the impact of the information; that is, the influence of the information may be greater at moderate levels of situational attractiveness than at either very high or very low levels.

It is important to note that the factors that increase the motivation to manifest certain behaviors in a *particular* situation may not necessarily increase the desire to manifest the behavior in *other* situations. Indeed, there are some reasons to expect that although situational pressures or incentives may increase compliance with expectancies of another in the situation, they may actually have the opposite effect upon responses made in the absence of these situational factors. For example, Brehm (1966) has argued that perceived restrictions upon freedom of choice induce reactance, and thus increase noncompliance in the absence of surveillance. More recently, Lepper, Green, and Nisbett (1973) have postulated that extrinsic rewards for engaging in a behavior decrease subjects' self-perceptions that they are intrinsically motivated to engage in it, and therefore decrease their tendency to do so when these rewards are no longer available.

The interpretation of this phenomenon is somewhat controversial (see Reiss & Sushinsky, 1975). However, its existence is sufficient to raise questions about the enduring effects of situational variables that provide extrinsic motivation to engage in an activity. For example, giving children praise and gold stars for reading in a classroom may increase their desire to read in the classroom, but may actually decrease their tendency to read outside the social situation, where praise and gold stars are unlikely to be forthcoming.

Effects on Distraction

Situational characteristics may often adversely affect the acquisition of information in a communication by preventing the recipient from concentrating upon its contents. While distraction may be created by external stimuli such as noise and other persons in the situation who capture the recipient's attention, it may also result from internal factors such as arousal. The predicted effects of distraction upon the impact of a communication have been analyzed in detail elsewhere (Wyer, 1974a) and are considered here only briefly with relation to Equation (1).

It seems reasonable to suppose that as distraction increases, the likelihood of receiving and comprehending a communication (P_R) and of counterarguing it effectively (P_{CA}) will both decrease. However, to this extent, the effect of distraction on informational influence may be nonmonotonic. For example, suppose that in the absence of distraction, the probabilities of receiving and counterarguing are both high $(P_R = P_{CA} = .9)$, and so the likelihood of being influenced is low $(P_I = .09)$. If a given amount of distraction decreases reception and counterarguing to a moderate level $(P_R = P_{CA} = .5)$, it may increase the influence of the communication $(P_I = .25)$; however, a further increase in distraction may have a deleterious effect $(P_R = P_{CA} = .1; P_I = .09)$.

Application of this analysis in specific situations is difficult for several reasons. First, the particular level of distraction induced in any given instance is hard to specify a priori. Second, the magnitude and direction of distraction effects depend upon the initial levels of P_R and P_{CA}, that is, the extent to which the information will be comprehended and refuted in the absence of distraction. If, for example, the information is such that counterarguing is unlikely to occur in any case, distraction will serve only to decrease reception, and thus should have a deleterious effect. If, on the other hand, the material is apt to inspire counterarguing, or if recipients are required to evaluate the material critically, the effect of distraction may depend upon situational factors such as the intrinsic difficulty of the material to understand, whether the arguments contained in it are easy or hard to refute, and the general ability of the recipient. For example, suppose the communication is easy to understand and refute in the absence of distraction. In this case, the initial levels of P_R should be high, and consequently, the introduction of a moderate level of distraction should increase the impact of this information, as noted above. However, suppose the material is difficult to understand but hard to refute, so that the initial levels of reception and counterarguing in the absence of distraction is only moderate (for example $P_R = P_{CA} = .5$), then, the introduction of distraction should have a deleterious effect. Research reported by Regan and Cheng (1973) support these speculations.

Equation (1) is useful for conceptualizing the possible effects of a variety of distracting situational variables upon information influence. For example, a person may be more apt to be distracted from attending to and evaluating the information presented him when he is in the company of friends than when he is alone or with persons he does not know. Suppose the presence of friends induces a moderate amount of distraction. Then, applying the above reasoning, their presence should increase the influence of information that is easy to understand and refute, but should decrease the impact of more complex and cogent material.

The model is also useful to consider in predicting the effects of unpleasant aspects of a situation such as threat of punishment, coercion, or the possibility of being unfavorably evaluated. Such aspects may create arousal, or internal "noise," and therefore may have a distracting effect. If the information to be presented is easy, or if recipients have high ability, Equation 1 predicts that a moderate amount of arousal will increase the impact of the information. However, if the material is complex, or if recipients have moderate ability, the introduction of arousal may decrease the impact of the message.

The above analysis has obvious implications for information acquisition in educational settings. However, one must keep in mind the educational objectives of presenting the information to be acquired. If the objective is to have the recipient learn a lot of material without evaluating its validity, or if critical evaluation of the material is not at issue, clearly distraction of any kind is inadvisable. The effects above apply only to conditions in which the educational objective, or the by-product of the educational process, is to convince the recipient that conclusions to be drawn from the information he is receiving are valid.

ATTITUDES TOWARD ONESELF

The effect of attitudes toward oneself, or alternatively self-esteem, upon behavior has been a popular but not particularly productive area of interest. This lack of productiveness may be due in part to the failure to analyze self-relevant attitudes along dimensions that are relevant and irrelevant to the particular behavior of concern. Some persons may in fact have a self-perception of themselves as either universally worthy or as universally unworthy. However, it seems more likely that a person's self-evaluation will depend substantially upon the dimension of judgment. In any event, there are at least two ways in which self-relevant attitudes may affect the acquisition of knowledge. One is through their mediating effects upon the reception and acceptance of information in a communication. A second is through their effects upon the active pursuit of knowledge and the acquisition of skills. Let us consider each briefly.

Effects upon Reception and Acceptance of Information

It is reasonable to suppose that if a person feels incapable of refuting the contents of a communication, he may not attempt to counterargue it. On the other hand, if the person also feels incapable of understanding the communication, he may not attempt to read it carefully, and his reception may be low as well. To the extent that self-esteem affects both one's belief that he can understand the communication and his belief that he can effectively refute its contents, it may therefore be related nonmonotonically to communication impact; that is, this impact may be greater on persons whose self-esteem is moderate than on those whose self-esteem is either high or low. This hypothesis assumes that the recipient is motivated to engage in the counterarguing, either because of situational demands or because the information presented contradicts his previously formed beliefs. If this motivation does not exist, self-esteem may primarily affect reception without affecting the tendency to counterargue; to this extent, there should be a positive monotonic relation between self esteem and communication influence.

Little research bears directly upon this general hypothesis. However, the extensive research by Leventhal and his colleagues on the effects of fear-arousing communications (for a summary, see Leventhal, 1970) is indirectly relevant. Leventhal hypothesizes that when fear-arousing material accompanies a communication which describes a potential danger (tetanus, lung cancer, etc.) and a means of avoiding it (getting an innoculation, not smoking, etc.), it will increase the acceptance of the communication by persons who feel able to engage in the danger-reducing behavior, but will decrease its acceptance by persons who feel unable to cope with the danger. For example, a communication advocating the proposition that smoking caused lung cancer will have greater effect upon nonsmokers' beliefs in the proposition when it is accompanied by vivid descriptions of the horrors of lung cancer, whereas it will have less effect upon the beliefs of smokers when accompanied by these descriptions. While the results of research conducted by Leventhal and his colleagues are not entirely consistent, they seem generally in accord with this hypothesis.

There are several interpretations of these findings (see Janis, 1967; Leventhal, 1970; McGuire, 1968a; Wyer, 1974a). The one most closely allied with the considerations outlined in this paper is based upon the hypothesis that fear-provoking material generates internal noise, and thus interferes with both reception and counterarguing. To this extent, it should increase the influence of a persuasive communication up to a point, and then decrease communication impact as it becomes more intense. However, the amount of fear engendered by any given amount of fear-related material will be less for persons who feel able to cope with the danger than for persons who feel unable to cope. To this extent, fear content should be more apt to increase the impact of a communication upon copers than upon noncopers, as Leventhal finds.

The above predictions may hold only if the recipient perceives himself to be potentially vulnerable to the danger described in the message. If this is not the case, the motivation to counterargue the contents of the message may be low, and its influence may be simply a function of reception. Berkowitz and Cottingham's (1960) finding, that fear-arousing material pertaining to automobile safety increased beliefs in the use of safety belts by persons who rarely used automobiles but not among persons who used them frequently, is consistent with this prediction. When recipients were not personally vulnerable, the fear-arousing material may have served primarily to increase interest in the communication, and thus increased rather than decreased reception without affecting counterarguing tendencies.

The preceding discussion makes salient the need to specify clearly the dimensions along which self-esteem differences occur if one is to predict its effects, and to take into account whether motivation to counterargue is likely to exist. Qualitatively different results would be expected, depending upon whether the recipient's low self-esteem results from his perceived inability to understand the communication, his perception that he is incapable of refuting its contents, or his belief that he cannot deal effectively with its implications for behavior.

Effects upon Persistence in the Acquisition of Skills

Throughout most of this paper we have concentrated upon the acquisition of information in a written or oral communication. In a broader sense, however, the acquisition of knowledge also includes the development of skills, often acquired through practice. Perhaps the most intriguing body of literature with implications for the effects of self-evaluations has grown out of the attribution literature on the mediating effects of self-attributions upon responses to success and failure. The thesis underlying this research is that a person's perseverance following success or failure depends upon whether he attributes these outcomes to himself (for example, to ability or effort) or to external factors (for example, to task difficulty or luck). Moreover, it depends upon whether he attributes them to stable characteristics that are difficult to change (inherent ability or task difficulty) or to transient characteristics that may not exist on subsequent trials of the task (luck or effort).

For example, it seems reasonable that a person is less likely to try to perform better following failure if he attributes his failure on the task either to task difficulty or to his inherent lack of ability on the task than if he attributes his poor performance to lack of effort. Data reported by Dweck and Repucci

(1973) support this hypothesis. In a later study, Dweck (1975) identified children with extreme reactions to failure (that is, those who in the opinion of their teachers expected to fail and gave up easily. She then exposed these children to 25 days of either (a) success-only training, in which they received only success experiences in performing a series of problems, or (b) success with interpolated failure, in which they were given the impression that they had failed through lack of effort. Children who received success-only training performed less well on the test problems as the training progressed. However, children who had failed, but attributed it to lack of effort either maintained or increased their performance on test problems. This suggests that an alteration of self-attributions can reverse well-established responses to failure, while simply providing more frequent success experience cannot do so.

In the absence of direct information about their reasons for failing, persons may use two indirect sources of information in interpreting their performance: the success or failure of other persons on similar tasks, and their own previous history of success or failure in achievement activity. In combination, these factors may have interesting effects. For example, if a person fails on a particular task but is told that others have failed as well, he may attribute his failure to task difficulty, regardless of his past personal history of success or failure on other achievement tasks. However, if he fails but is told that others have succeeded, he may attribute his failure to lack of effort (an unstable characteristic) if this outcome is discrepant from those he has typically received in other achievement tasks, but to lack of ability (a stable characteristic) if this outcome is consistent with his past experience. Assuming that attributions of failure to lack of effort increase persistence while attributions of failure to lack of ability decrease persistence, this reasoning has interesting implications. Specifically, information that others have succeeded should increase a person's persistence following failure if he has had a past history of success (for evidence, see Wortman, Panciera, Shusterman, & Hibscher, 1976); however, this information may decrease a person's persistence if he has had a past history of failure.

While the above considerations suggest that perseverence following failure is mediated by self-attributions concerning the reasons for failing, these attributions may not have an effect unless situational conditions arise that make them salient. A study by Dweck and Gilliard (1976) is of interest in this regard. In this study, fifth graders were exposed to a series of failure trials, but were asked to state their expectancies for success either (a) before every trial, (b) before only the first trial, or (c) not at all. Males' persistence over the series of trials increased with the frequency with which verbal expectancy statements were made. However, females' persistence decreased. It seems reasonable to assume that students' statements of their expectancies were mediated by their attributions of past performance to either oneself or the task. If this assumption is correct, these data suggest that males typically attribute their failure to lack of effort, and thus making these attributions salient causes them to work hard. In contrast, females are apt to attribute their failure to lack of ability or task difficulty, and thus forcing them to make these attributions decreases their persistence.

While the studies described above are only representative, they suggest some very important areas of future research with clear implications for the educational process. At the most general level, this research makes salient that the persistence in acquiring skills and information is not simply a function of previous success and failure. Rather, it depends upon the interpretation given to these outcomes. Moreover, these interpretations are affected not only by the consistency of past outcomes with present ones, but by the situational context in which the task is performed. Finally, the effect of past success and failure may be greater when students are in a situation in which there is a need to make self-referent judgments and thus their self-attributions are salient. The implications of these notions are well worth pursuing.

CONCLUDING REMARKS

We have covered a lot of ground in our discussion of the role of attitudes in information acquisition. On the basis of this discussion, however, it appears that this role is not very important. While attitudes toward the concept to which information pertains appears to have some influence upon the manner in which this information is interpreted and organized in memory, this influence may not be inherently any different from the influence of previously formed, nonevaluative cognitions with which the implications of new information may be incompatible. While attitudes toward the source of the information may sometimes appear to affect the influence of this information, this may be due largely to the mediating effect these attitudes have upon attributions of expertise. Factors that engender favorable or unfavorable attitudes toward the situation in which information is presented may have influence, but this is primarily because of their effect upon the recipient's concentration upon this information. Finally, while self-evaluations may affect informational influence and also the acquisition of skills, this is most likely to be true only insofar as these evaluations pertain to specific attributes that are relevant either to the reception and critical evaluation of the information presented, or to performance on the task being administered. Thus, while our discussion has hopefully provided some insight into the factors that may affect the acquisition of knowledge, a consideration of attitudes per se has not helped us very much in gaining this insight.

Many of the specific conclusions drawn in this contribution may pertain only to conditions in which the information to be acquired is likely to be evaluated critically by recipients rather than accepted without question. Whether these conditions exist may depend heavily upon the type of material contained in the communication as well as the situational context in which it is presented. In generalizing the implications of our analyses to educational settings, these factors must of course be considered. Nevertheless, the approach we have taken in analyzing information acquisition processes may be useful in assessing the extent of this generalizeability, and therefore may be of heuristic value.

ACKNOWLEDGMENTS

Work related to the preparation of this contribution was supported by National Science Foundation Grant SOC73-05684.

REFERENCES

Aronson, E., & Golden, B. W. The effect of relevant and irrelevant aspects of credibility on attitude change. *Journal of Personality,* 1962, **30,** 135–146.

Berkowtiz, L., & Cottingham, D. R. The interest value and relevance of fear-arousing communications. *Journal of Abnormal and Social Psychology,* 1960, **14,** 23–31.

Brehm, J. W. *A theory of psychological reactance.* New York: Academic Press, 1966.

Byrne, D. *The attraction paradigm.* New York: Academic Press, 1971.

Collins, B. E. Four components of the Rotter Internal-External scale; Belief in a difficult world, a just world, a predictable world, and a politically responsive world. *Journal of Personality and Social Psychology,* 1974, **29,** 381–391.

Dweck, C. S. The role of expectations and attributions in the alleviation of learned helplessness. *Journal of Personality and Social Psychology,* 1975, **31,** 674–685.

Dweck, C. S., & Gilliard, D. Expectancy statements as determinants of reactions to failure: Sex differences in persistence and expectancy change. *Journal of Personality and Social Psychology,* 1976,

Dweck, C. S., & Repucci, N. D. Learned helplessness and reinforcement responsibility in children. *Journal of Personality and Social Psychology,* 1973, **25,** 109–116.

Eagly, A. H., & Chaiken, S. An attribution analysis of the effect of communicator characteristics on opinion change: The case of communicator attractiveness. *Journal of Personality and Social Psychology,* 1975, **32,** 136–144.

Fishbein, M. A., & Ajzen, I. *Belief, attitude, intention and behavior: An introduction to theory and research.* Reading, Mass.: Addison-Wesley, 1975.

Freedman, J. L., & Sears, D. O. Selective exposure. In L. Berkowtiz (Ed.), *Advances in experimental social psychology,* Vol. 2. New York: Academic Press, 1965.

Heider, F. *The psychology of interpersonal relations.* New York: Wiley, 1958.

Henninger, M. An information processing approach to the "Socratic effect." Unpublished master's thesis, University of Illinois, 1975.

Holt, L. Resistance to persuasion on explicit beliefs as a function of commitment to and desirability of logically related beliefs. *Journal of Personality and Social Psychology,* 1970, **16,** 571–583.

Hovland, C. I., & Mandell, W. An experimental comparison of conclusion-drawing by the communicator and by the audience. *Journal of Abnormal and Social Psychology,* 1952, **47,** 581–588.

Hovland, C. I., & Weiss, W. The influence of source credibility on communication effectiveness. *Public Opinion Quarterly,* 1951, **15,** 635–650.

Insko, C. A., & Cialdini, R. B. A test of three interpretations of attitudinal verbal reinforcement. *Journal of Personality and Social Psychology*, 1969, **12**, 333—341.

Janis, I. L. Effects of fear arousal on attitude change: Recent developments in theory and experimental research. In L. Berkowitz (Ed.), *Advances in experimental social psychology*. Vol. 3. New York: Academic Press, 1967.

Janis, I. L., & Frick, F. The relationship between attitudes toward conclusions and errors in judging the logical validity of syllogisms. *Journal of Experimental Psychology*, 1943, **33**, 73—77.

Kelman, H. C. Compliance, identification and internationalization: Three processes of attitude change. *Journal of Conflict Resolution*, 1958, **2**, 51—60.

Kelman, H. C., & Hovland, C. I. "Reinstatement" of the communicator in delayed measurement of opinion change. *Journal of Abnormal and Social Psychology*, 1953, **48**, 327—335.

Lepper, M., Green, D., & Nisbett, R. E. Undermining children's intrinsic interest with extrinsic reward: A test of the "overjustification" hypothesis. *Journal of Personality and Social Psychology*, 1973, **28**,

Lerner, M. J., & Simmons, C. H. Observer's reaction to the "innocent victim": Compassion or rejection? *Journal of Personality and Social Psychology*, 1966, **4**, 203—210.

Leventhal, H. Findings and theory in the study of fear communications. In L. Berkowitz (Ed.), *Advances in experimental social psychology*, Vol. 5. New York: Academic Press, 1970.

McGuire, W. J. A syllogistic analysis of cognitive relationships. In M. J. Rosenberg, C. I. Hovland, W. J. McGuire, R. P. Abelson, & J. W. Brehm, *Attitude organization and change*. New Haven: Yale University Press, 1960.

McGuire, W. J. Inducing resistance to persuasion: Some contemporary approaches. In L. Berkowitz (Ed.), *Advances in experimental social psychology*, Vol. 1. New York: Academic Press, 1964.

McGuire, W. J. Personality and susceptibility to social influence. In E. F. Borgatta & W. W. Lambert (Eds.), *Handbook of personality theory and research*. Chicago: Rand McNally, 1968. (a)

McGuire, W. J. Theory of the structure of human thought. In R. P. Abelson *et al.* (Eds.), *Theories of cognitive consistency: A sourcebook*. Chicago: Rand McNally, 1968. (b)

McGuire, W. J. The nature of attitudes and attitude change. In G. Linfzey & E. Aronson (Eds.), *Handbook of social psychology*, Vol. 3 (2nd ed.). Reading, Mass.: Addison-Wesley, 1969.

Osgood, C., & Tannenbaum, P. The principle of congruity in the prediction of attitude change. *Psychological Review*, 1955, **62**, 42—55.

Regan, D. T., & Chen, J. Distraction and attitude change: A resolution. *Journal of Experimental Social Psychology*, 1973, **9**, 138—147.

Reiss, S., & Sushinsky, L. W. Overjustification, competing responses and the acquisition of intrinsic interest. *Journal of Personality and Social Psychology*, 1975, **31**, 1116—1125.

Rosen, N. A., & Wyer, R. S. Some further evidence for the "Socratic effect" sing a subjective probability model of cognitive organization. *Journal of Personality and Social Psychology*, 1972, **24**, 420—424.

Salancik, J. R. Inference of one's attitude from behavior recalled under linguistically manipulated cognitive sets. *Journal of Experimental Social Psychology*, 1974, **10**, 415—427.

Sampson, E. E., & Insko, C. A. Cognitive consistency and performance in the autokinetic situation. *Journal of Abnormal and Social Psychology*, 1964, **68**, 184—192.

Schopler, J. Social power. In L. Berkowitz (Ed.), *Advances in experimental social psychology*, Vol. 2. New York: Academic Press, 1965.

Sherif, M., & Hovland, C. *Social judgment*. New Haven: Yale University Press, 1961.

Sherif, M., White, B. J., & Harvey, O. J. Status in experimentally produced groups. *American Journal of Sociology,* 1955, **60**, 370–379.

Tannenbaum, P. H. The congruity principle revisited: Studies in the reduction, induction and generalization of persuasion. In L. Berkowitz (Ed.), *Advances in experimental social psychology,* Vol. 3. New York: New York: Academic Press, 1967.

Upshaw, H. S. The personal reference scale: An approach to social judgment. In L. Berkowitz (Ed.), *Advances in experimental social psychology,* vol. 4. New York: Academic Press, 1969.

Walster, E. The assignment of responsibility for an accident. *Journal of Personality and Social Psychology,* 1966, **3**, 73–79.

Wortman, C., Panciera, L., Shusterman, L., & Hibscher, J. Attributions of causality and reactions to uncontrollable outcomes. *Journal of Experimental Social Psychology,* 1976,

Wyer, R. S. Category ratings as "subjective expected values": Implications for attitude formation and change. *Psychological Review,* 1973, **80**, 446–467.

Wyer, R. S. *Cognitive organization and change: An information-processing approach.* Hillsdale, N.J.: Lawrence Erlbaum Associates, 1974.   (a)

Wyer, R. S. Some implications of the "Socratic effect" for alternative models of cognitive consistency. *Journal of Personality,* 1974, **42**, 399–419.   (b)

Wyer, R. S. The role of probabilistic and syllogistic reasoning in cognitive organization and social inference. In M. Kaplan & S. Schwartz (Eds.), *Human judgment and decision processes.* New York: Academic Press. 1975.

Wyer, R. S. The effects of previously formed beliefs on syllogistic inference processes. *Journal of Personality and Social Psychology,* 1976,

Wyer, R. S., & Schwartz, S. Some contingencies in the effects of the source of a communication upon the evaluation of that communication. *Journal of Personality and Social Psychology,* 1969, **11**, 1–9.

COMMENTS ON
CHAPTER 8 BY WYER

Carolyn Wood Sherif

The Pennsylvania State University

Wyer has performed yeoman's service in outlining major points in the process of acquiring information at which the person's attitudes toward various aspects of the total acquisition context may affect that process. In treating the acquisition process relative to "schooling," he has emphasized appropriately that the material to be acquired and its semantic content are only parts of the total context. It may be noteworthy that he included the person's self, as object of attitudes. Until recently, such notions have led many psychologists to start slamming closet doors. Later in this commentary, I shall attempt to indicate that opening closet doors may do more than reveal psychology's metaphysical skeletons. On the contrary, we may find many of the problems central to our understanding of schooling and knowledge acquisition stored in such inauspicious locations.

Wyer is to be commended for stressing one such problem sorely neglected until recent years, namely *selectivity* in reception, processing, and recall. Although central to the theorizing of such diverse figures as Wundt and William James, selectivity or "attention" has been accorded far too little research effort.

I want to emphasize Wyer's introductory caution against artificial "segregation" of the psychology of attitudes from the psychology of cognition in general, including any a priori assumptions that "they (attitudes) are governed by qualitatively different cognitive processes" (page 260). In the past, the psychology of cognition has been enormously handicapped by such assumptions, which are relics of old mind—body formulations that assigned to mind the intellective functions of "knowing" and to body the ultimate driving forces, hence the problems of motivation, as well as emotions or affectivity. As a consequence, many a psychologist has presented theoretical schemes that purported to handle the problems of cognition—learning—intellectual processes, but included the escape clause "if the organism is properly motivated." If the organism is not, such grand schemes have little better to offer practitioners concerned with schooling and the acquisition of knowledge than such old saws as, "Well, you can lead a horse to water, but you can't make him drink."

For the newly awakened and self-consciously "cognitive" psychologists of today, one route to avoid the hoary and philosophically unacceptable segregation of Mind from Body, of cognition from motivation and affectivity, is the broad path toward understanding of evaluation. As Wyer stated: "The evaluation of an object may often occupy a central position in the interrelated set of cognitions a person has about that object, in that it both affects and is affected by a large number of other cognitions" (page 259). I agree with Dr. Wyer's implication that the study of cognition and the study of attitudes will both gain enormously if their common meeting ground becomes the further exploration of evaluative judgment or, more generally, social judgment. Whether we consider social discrimination, social categorization, social comparison, social choice, or decision making, we find that social judgments are invariably and inevitably evaluative at the same time. As Wyer and I both recognize, these suggestions are not new, having a long tradition in both the psychology of attitudes and the psychology of judgment (e.g. Sherif, 1936; Sherif & Cantril, 1945, 1947; Sherif & Hovland, 1961; Sherif, Sherif, & Nebergall, 1965; Volkmann, 1951).

Wyer has joined a considerable number of social psychologists who recognize that a person's endorsements of highly generalized belief statements are not "particularly useful" as the sole predictors of that person's actions toward the object of belief in a specific situation. Unfortunately, time does not permit me to pursue the issues that have led to this recognition nor the problems that it concerns, but I have delivered my own opinions on them recently and regard the issues as critical (Sherif, 1976, Chapter 9).

Wyer's exact wording of the foregoing point is particularly interesting. He stated: "I am unconvinced that general attitudes toward an object are particularly useful predictors of behavior toward the object . . ." (page 261). Later, however, he makes a plea for further study of the effects of "general beliefs" about the nature of the world in interpretations of new information. In research practice, what he terms "general attitudes" have invariably been inferred from the person's endorsement of general belief statements, using procedures developed by Thurstone, Likert, Guttman, and others. Something is amiss here. How can he reject the principal methods for studying "general attitudes," yet call for further study of "general beliefs"?

Wyer began by defining an attitude as "an evaluative judgment," a definition he termed "somewhat nontraditional." He then defined *information* as "a collection of propositions, each of which is held to be true with a certain probability" (page 260). The latter were termed "beliefs," presumably earning that status when some criterion probability level is reached. When the possible dimensions representing evaluation are expanded, it becomes obvious that acceptance—rejection as well as agreement—disagreement are also evaluative dimensions. The individual makes an evaluative judgment when he or she rates an object, belief, or action as good–bad, etc. and/or accepts–rejects, agrees–disagrees with it in some degree. Is this a "nontraditional" definition?

The "operational definition" of an attitude as an evaluative judgment represents a deeply entrenched tradition of more than four decades. It was precisely that "operational definition" of attitude in questionnaires or attitude tests that LaPiere (1934) criticized so sharply in a paper frequently cited in controversies over what Wyer calls "general attitudes." LaPiere (1934) criticized the use of "a verbal response to a symbolic situation" as a "reflection of a 'social attitude',", a practice which he characterized as "to entirely disregard the definition commonly given for the phrase 'attitude' " (p. 237). In terms of that definition, LaPiere was explicit that a person's attitude "must, in the main, be derived from a study of humans behaving in actual social situations" (p. 237). Unfortunately, there is not time here to pursue what LaPiere's words imply for research practice, except to note that they point toward the more contemporary emphasis upon the use of a combination of methods and techniques to collect the data from which we make so bold as to infer that a person has an attitude.

LaPiere's paper reveals the longevity of the tradition within which we must place Wyer's definition of attitude ("an evaluative judgment" with belief as another evaluative judgment, this time about the truth of a proposition). The most significant growth of the tradition was not in the laboratory or in scientific circles at all, but in the rise of the opinion survey as a thriving commercial enterprise, starting in the late 1930s. Spurred by governmental interest in opinion survey techniques, especially during World War II, research into opinions and opinion change then entered academic laboratories. It gained new respectability, particularly under such prestigious programs as Carl I. Hovland's Communications Research Program at Yale starting in the 1940s. Shortly, vast amounts of research poured from laboratories all over the country on opinions or evaluative judgments rendered under a variety of experimental conditions.

If you examine that vast research literature, you will find that the terms "opinion" and "attitude" became virtually interchangeable in the reports of many psychologists. Yet, an opinion is an evaluative judgment. Wyer's definition is altogether appropriate for a great bulk of research literature presented under the labels of attitude, attitude change, cognitive dissonance, and attribution theory from the 1940s to the present. However, it was not often recognized that the odd coupling between the shy laboratory, modestly pursuing "basic research" into opinions, and the blatantly commercial enterprise studying "public opinion" had very little to do with the problems that made the concept "attitude" important in social psychology in the first place.

The concept of attitude was introduced early into social psychology as a tool for dealing with those critical problems concerning relationships between psychological functioning and the social environment in which the individual develops and lives, the social environment being defined not only with reference to social objects and the behavior of other persons, but also to those patterned structures and events that are variously referred to as human groups (family, friends, work groups, religious groups, etc.), institutions, social values, ideologies, technology and, more generally, to aspects of the society and culture. While the particular focus of early investigations varied, the questions invariably inquired into regularities in behavior and in psychological processes that were contingent upon or were reactions to regularities in the social environment.

Among the earlier theorists were Thomas and Znaniecki (1918), asking how the Polish peasant transported to the United States retained personal ties to social values predominant in the peasant culture in Poland; Emory Bogardus (1925) wondering whether the discriminatory social practices in immigration and in other phases of living toward varied groups of immigrants and native Americans (e.g. Blacks, Mexican-Americans, American Indians) would be reflected in the decisions made by individual Americans about associating with their representatives in social situations varying in social distance; Katz and Braly (1933) inquiring into the consensus of Princeton students on what all "those other kinds of people" were like and finding these "highly educated" young men reflecting the supercilious and degrading stereotypes toward less privileged groups prevalent at that time; Katz & F. H. Allport (1931) predicting that the distributions of endorsements by students' about religious beliefs would represent a J-shaped curve conforming to the central tenets of their religious groups; E. L. Horowitz (1936) discovering to his astonishment that white children by elementary school age preferred white companions over black ones consistently across three methods of choice, whether they grew up in New York City or Tennessee; Sherif and Cantril (1945, 1947) proposing that the major directions and outlines of personal identity were composed from the individual's past experiences as members and aspirants to membership in diverse reference groups.

All of these early investigators used evaluative judgments, among other evidence, for making inferences about the person's attitudes. However, their search was for regularities, consistencies, patterns in the individual's behaviors that indicate the directionality of the individual's relationship to some aspect of the society and culture. The notion of equating attitude with an evaluative judgment would have struck them as ridiculous.

My purpose in dragging out the history of the attitude concept in social psychology is not merely pedantic, but practical as well. Having chosen to define attitude as an evaluative judgment and beliefs as evaluative judgments concerning the truth of propositions, Wyer proceeded to survey research evidence to which those definitions led him. His conclusions are tenable in terms of the definitions with which he started and the research evidence they led him to survey: The role of attitudes in information acquisition" is not very important," and the effects of attitudes toward the source of information reflects "the mediating effects these attitudes have upon attributions of expertise."

However, in terms of the attitude concept that developed to handle the problem of the individual—group—society relationship and research related to it,

Wyer's conclusions are astounding. Surely, they will surprise the classroom teacher who finds that his love of Shakespeare arouses the students to laughter, to the coach who finds that a player who is flunking out of school because of poor reading has memorized all the rules of the game and the records of players since 1900, to the navy commander who finds that he simply cannot communicate information to dissident black sailors on board, to the dental expert who finds that all his data on the value of fluoridation for dental health has utterly failed to put over a local campaign to fluoridate the water supply, to a representative of the United States when he attempts to bring "facts" into controversies over whether Zionism or United States policy is racist, to a woman who attempts to inform men about the sexism of their behavior toward her.

All such individuals, and every one of us who work in education, have real problems involving the interaction of people's attitudes, the information presented, and the social context in which it is presented. We can take small comfort from Wyer's conclusion that we really have very small problems, or that the problem is no different than those in which a teacher tries to teach addition in a numerical system, base three, to pupils who know a numerical system, base ten. If this be the case, I cannot help but wonder why Wyer expresses concern over whether "the development of attitudes is or should be an objective of the educational system unless the attitude of concern is toward education or toward the acquisition of knowledge itself" (page 261). No matter how much knowledge may affect attitude, he tells us that the resulting attitudes play a rather unimportant role in acquiring information. More seriously, his concern would seem to imply that the vast institutions of schooling in which children and young adults spend so much of their waking hours do *not* affect attitude formation by their very existence. As an important part of society, every educational system does influence attitude formation, both deliberately and unwittingly.

The remainder of this discussion is devoted to those concerned that there are some serious problems in knowledge acquisition that have something to do with attitudes. Historically and theoretically, attitude has been a concept referring to psychological structure that is inferred from a person's behaviors in relevant situations. An attitude is inferred from a set of acquired or learned behaviors that are selectively, more or less consistently and characteristically directed *toward* or *against* specified classes of objects, persons, situations, events, groups, institutions, and social values (including beliefs about the world). Behaviors directed *toward* include approaching, persistently trying to gain, and other actions as well as explicit judgments of preference, choice, favoring, accepting, or desiring. Behaviors directed *against* include avoidance, invidious discrimination, aggression, or attempts to eliminate as well as explicit judgments of rejection, discarding, not accepting, disdaining, or abhorring.

Whether explicit or not, the behaviors in question invariably imply a process of evaluative judgment, that is, of sizing up the situation and its various parts against some standards and simultaneously evaluating them. But an evaluative judgment need not imply an attitude. Human beings give opinions and render evaluative verdicts at the drop of a hat, even on matters that they have never heard of. For a researcher with the aura of "science" who might evaluate *them* on whether or how they respond, most research subjects in the past have been willing to oblige the request for opinions on the widest range of topics, whether they gave a damn about them or not. (Of course, all this may be changing, at least insofar as the public opinion survey is concerned, as researchers find more people reluctant or refusing to participate.)

Although the concept "attitude" implies subjective experience, attitudes can only be inferred from behaviors and can be studied scientifically only when their referent is known. Formed during interaction in a social environment, attitudes do not imply that the person *has* something or other, as implied when some psychologists refer to a trait, a state or a disposition to respond. An attitude refers to a *relationship* between a person (subject) and an object. That object can also be studied independently of the person having the attitude, even when it is as intangible as a belief. Its history can be traced by historians. Its existence as a social fact can be affirmed through study of consensus by other members of the culture or group.

Since the person is one pole of the subject—object relationship, it is not surprising that the relationship is not neutral. It has directionality toward or away from the object that is the earmark of motivated behavior. Like any motivated behavior, it is accompanied by emotional or affective arousal, in varying degrees. Such directionality and arousal are especially striking when the attitude object is related to the particular brand of "Thou shalts" and "Thou shalt nots" prevailing in the individual's reference groups, in terms of which self-worth and self-esteem are assessed. Finally, with linguistic development, the subject—object relationship embodied in attitude becomes a conceptual structure consisting of categories that simultaneously slice the domain of objects in question and evaluate their contents differentially (Sherif, Sherif, & Nebergall, 1965; Sherif & Sherif, 1969). Needless to say, attitudinal structures are not readily or lightly subject to change with the whims of the moment or circumstances, though change they do over time and in response to altered social contexts.

To the extent that the person's attitude is stable, the various categories included in it may be more broadly characterized as comprising a *latitude of acceptance* for objects that the person seeks, prefers, accepts, or even evaluates as "ideal" and a *latitude of rejection* for those objects in the same domain that the person prefers to avoid, reject, find objectionable, or even abhor. When the individual is not forced by a researcher to evaluate every single item in that object domain, we have found in our research that he or she frequently prefers neither to accept or to reject certain objects or categories of objects, that is, prefers to remain noncommittal. You will note that I did not say remain "neutral," for neutrality is not defined either by the procedures we have used nor by the significance that I shall attach to what is *not* explicitly evaluated. It is in part because the *latitude of noncommitment* can yield so much information about a person's attitude that it is misleading to equate attitude with an opinion or evaluative judgment.

The study of attitudinal structure through the relationships among lattitudes of acceptance, rejection, and noncommitment relative to a domain or class of objects was introduced by Sherif (1960), Sherif (1963) and Sherif & Hovland (1961) in the process of developing what Wyer correctly calls a theory of social judgment (page 267). He neglects to mention that it is also a theory of attitudes. From the earliest research (Hovland & Sherif, 1952; Sherif & Hovland, 1953) to more recent surveys of research findings (Sherif & Sherif, 1967, 1969; Sherif *et al.*, 1973; Sherif, 1976), a primary intent of the work has been to develop methods and techniques in studying attitudes that provide more information about their structure than the traditional methods, all of which yield a sum or average of scale values assigned to the individual's several evaluative judgments. While such composite scores may be useful for certain research purposes, their interpretative value with regard to the *structure* of a person's attitude is virtually nil, regardless of which method one considers. In particular, none of the conventional methods yields more than a tenuous hint about an elusive property that every theorist or researcher, including Wyer, introduces someplace along the line to qualify theoretical statements on attitudes. The property to which I refer is variously labeled attitude intensity, strength, salience, importance, commitment or, as I prefer, personal involvement. (I have reluctantly abandoned the term ego involvement after a struggle of nearly three decades has convinced me of the power of labels. Even though the Greek work "ego" was used by others before and after Freud, I have become too weary of explaining that the term "ego involvement," first introduced by Sherif in 1936, has nothing in common with the Freudian ego.)

As it turns out, research investigating the latitudes of acceptance, rejection, and noncommitment has shown that the structure of a person's attitude is related to the degree of that person's involvement in his or her own preferred position in the object domain. In the earlier research, these relationships were discovered through correlations between the relative sizes, or ranges of the lattitudes and the relative extremity of positions upheld on sociopolitical issues (Sherif & Hovland, 1961; Sherif, Sherif, & Nebergall, 1965). Typically, though not always, persons upholding extreme positions were more highly involved. During the last ten years, sufficient data have accumulated to state with considerable confidence the relationships between attitude structure and degree of personal involvement, regardless of the extremity of the stand adopted by the person and for object domains as dissimilar from sociopolitical attitudes as monetary expenditures, clothing and hair styles, children's toys, and religious convictions. Furthermore, the relationships hold across two entirely different procedures for ascertaining the person's latitudes of acceptance, rejection, and noncommitment, procedures we have called, respectively, the Method of Ordered Alternatives and the Own Categories Procedure (mainly because people kept mixing up the two procedures). The relationships are as follows:

> The more personally involved the individual is in the acceptable objects in the domain, the greater is the latitude of rejection relative to the latitudes of acceptance and noncommitment. Specifically, the highly involved person's latitude of rejection is greater than acceptances and noncommitments combined, the latitude of noncommitment approaching zero. The less involved person, when given the opportunity to refrain from evaluating everything, exhibits a broad latitude of noncommitment. A moderately involved person is likely to exhibit latitudes of acceptance, rejection, and noncommitment approximately equal in size or scope.

As a correlate of the foregoing relationships, the individual who is presented with a large number of objects or verbal items and asked to categorize them on the basis of similarity, without mention of their possible acceptability or objectionableness, uses significantly fewer categories when the object domain is highly involving than when it is not. This generalization holds when the person generates his or her own categories provided the entire range of the object domain is included. It does not hold when the series presented for judgment falls entirely within the person's acceptable latitude (Sherif, 1963). The use of few categories is typically accompanied by lumping together a disproportionate number of items into a single category that includes all those objectionable to the person, which outcome typifies the broadened latitude of rejection of the highly involved person.

Furthermore, in such a "free sort" or "own categories" procedure, the use of only two or three categories by the highly involved person and the piling up of objectionable items are dependent upon the presentation of a large number of ambiguously worded or denotatively unstructured items. These ambiguous items are subject to the assimilation-contrast effects to which Wyer referred (pages 267–269). Wyer is mistaken in attributing neglect of ambiguity to Sherif and Hovland. From their earliest research on assimilation-contrast effects, stimulus structure was central in their theory. Wyer attributes to Upshaw a summary conclusion concerning the interpretation of research on assimilation-contrast effects that, in fact, is exactly the Sherif–Hovland interpretation. That summary conclusion may clarify why I must take issue with his closing remarks on the role of attitudes in information acquisition.

You will recall that conclusion: assimilation-contrast effects can be interpreted as systematic variations in the judgments of particular stimuli toward or away from "one's own attitude as a scale 'anchor,' or standard of comparison" (page 268). Such systematic variations, or "displacements" if you prefer, are not confined to the case when the individual's "own position" serves as anchor or standard for comparison. When the person has no attitude, stimulus anchors or standards produce such effects, depending on the relationship between the standards and stimulus to be judged. In fact, they were observed in psychophysical judgments of lifted weights and numerosity made in categorical terms before they were called assimilation-contrast effects (see Volkmann, 1951).

In judgments of verbal belief statements of the kind used in many traditional attitude scales, such systematic variations have been obtained relative to the person's own stand in many studies (Sherif & Sherif, 1969), some using paired comparison judgments (e.g., Dawes, Singer, & Lemon, 1972) as well as categorical judgments analyzed through the method of successive intervals, and ratio judgments (Fraser & Stacey, 1973). In such research, the individual makes judgments of an entire series of verbal belief statements. Both assimilation and contrast effects have been well and extensively documented when (a) a large number of denotatively ambiguous statements is included and (b) the person rendering ostensibly "objective" judgments is highly involved in the matter at hand. Such a person cannot help evaluating at the same time. Assimilation-contrast effects occur relative to the person's own stand whether the person's attitude is favorable to one extreme or to the other extreme, thus unfavorable to the opposite extreme (see Eiser, 1971; Vaughan in Sherif, Sherif & Nebergall, 1965).

In view of these strong statements, one may properly wonder how a conscientious scholar like Wyer could have spent so much space on the alleged lack of evidence for assimilation effects. The answer is simple: The lack has been alleged in several authoritative sources on the basis of a single study (1957) concerning judgment of a single complex message. In subsequent research, we reported a post hoc finding that denotatively ambiguous messages advocating a moderate position on a political issue were contrasted by highly involved advocates with own positions discrepant from the message, but assimilated by less involved persons with positions similarly discrepant (Sherif, Sherif, & Nebergall, 1965). To the best of my knowledge, that finding was ignored in all of the authoritative sources Wyer cited. I can cite additional references pronouncing that assimilation effects, but not contrast effects, are more frequently demonstrated. Such assimilation effects predominate when the person is not very involved.

Therefore, let me set the record straight by referring to a recent doctoral dissertation (Kearney, 1975), in which women with the same own positions on the issue of legalized abortion were presented messages discrepant from their own positions, but only moderately opposed to their own side of the controversy. Judgments of the position represented in the messages were made by active partisans on both sides of the issue in the field, as well as by women with comparable positions in a laboratory experiment.

In brief, the findings were as follows: To the degree that involvement in one's own position is high, moderately discrepant opposed messages are sharply contrasted, that is seen as extremely opposed to one's position, even though independently assessed as moderate and, in fact, viewed as moderate by partisans of the same side. With identical own positions, less involved persons assimilate the same messages to their own position, judging them near their own side of the issue.

When Kearney introduced a message at the *extreme* opposite to the person's own side as an additional anchor for judgment of the moderately opposed message, this message context had no significant effect on the judgments of the most involved, active partisans on either side. The extreme opposite context did significantly affect the judgments of the more and less involved laboratory subjects, reducing the contrast effect for the more involved women and enhancing the assimilation effect for those less involved.

In terms of a general theory of social judgment, which Wyer advocates, the findings are quite consistent. What does high personal involvement mean? First, it means that the person's own position will be more salient as an anchor than that of the less-involved person, who in turn will be more attentive to environmental anchors, such as standards introduced by a researcher or other context effects. Second, it means that the range of positions that the highly involved person has already rejected, categorically, is quite broad, hence that information only slightly discrepant from his or her own position is likely to fall within that objectionable latitude. The less involved person, on the other hand, has a broader latitude of noncommitment: the "mind is not made up" and assimilation can occur more readily over a wider range of discrepant messages.

Several years ago, Carl Hovland (1959) found that he could reconcile apparently contradictory findings on attitude change obtained in the laboratory and in field research chiefly by noting that laboratory studies typically employed topics of little concern to the subjects and segregated them from interaction with anyone else. Field studies, on the other hand, were undertaken more typically when the topic at hand was of some social importance and often concerned topics highly involving to many people who, in turn, were free to interact with one another. Similarly, I believe that you will find that most of the research that Wyer cites was laboratory research on topics of indeterminate or low involvement for the subjects. Thus, neither the confusion nor the conclusions should be a great surprise.

What personal involvement of an attitude does is to provide a salient internal anchor, greater consistency or coherence to the person's behaviors, and less responsiveness to transitory situational factors. True, as Wyer stated, attitudes pertain to other people and to structural aspects of situations themselves. All attitudes are not toward informational material or its object. Therefore, it is by no means essential that it is the information that is reinterpreted, misinterpreted, or ignored. To some people involved in schooling, it is the school situation, or the teachers, or the other students, or the task engaged in that become the focus of personal involvement, for good or for bad.

With these possibilities in mind, let me comment briefly on a few points at which Wyer's discussion suffers from the particular definition of attitude he employs and the lack of systematic concern with personal involvement. First, let me urge caution in accepting the conclusion that attention paid to new information bearing on one's attitudes is little affected by previously formed attitudes (page 266). Both here and in discussing selectivity in recall, Wyer falls into the trap set by most of the research that he cites in assuming that selectivity always operates in the direction of one's own position on an issue. It is simply not true that opposing information is always avoided. But when the person is highly involved in a position, it is *not* always the case that he or she avoids exposure to redundant materials, as found in research he cites. People do listen, read, and watch redundant materials, which is one reason why "information campaigns fail" if they are intended chiefly to persuade opponents (Hyman & Sheatsley, 1947). But people also selectively expose themselves to opponents' views at times, even when their utility is not immediately obvious (Diab, 1967); they may want to know "what the opponents are up to." These are selective effects of attitudes on attention to information, whether they supply information supportive to one's attitude or opposed to it. As stated earlier, I would certainly agree that this entire problem is grossly neglected. I hope that the issue of personal involvement will be systematically introduced into research on selective attention.

Similarly, I trust that a consideration of personal involvement in selective recall of information might lead to different conclusions than those based on McGuire's relatively uninvolving exercises in syllogistic reasoning. One of the best supported conclusions in the research literature on selectivity in recall is that materials personally involving to the individual are recalled better than materials that are not (Smith & Jamieson, 1972). Spiro and I (1975) recently found support for this conclusion and for the suggestive notion that highly involved persons selectively recall proportionally more imbalanced than balanced structures relevant to their attitudes. Particularly in selective recall, Hovland's critique of the limitations of the laboratory through its segregation of the person from interacting with others would seem relevant as well. Spiro's (1975) more recent research on recall suggests that such interactions may decisively affect the recall process.

It may also be wise to caution against placing too heavy an emphasis on the concept of "counterarguments" generated by the individual alone in analysis of information acquisition. The concept is based on research into truisms or beliefs that were not very involving. In the course of life, the individual is seldom isolated and at the mercy of a single authority figure (for example, a researcher) to stimulate him or her to develop counterarguments or to provide refuting arguments. If the matter at hand is at all important, he or she is likely to take up the matter with friends, family, or associates. Or, if the person is highly involved, high confidence and certainty may obviate the need for counterarguments at all. The truth value assigned to propositions is highly correlated with their similarity to one's strongly held positions (Sherif & Jackman, 1969). Socratic dialogues are more likely to occur where Socrates found them, between two persons, than inside one hard skull where the mind is "made up."

When Wyer discusses attitudes toward the source of information, I begin to get the feeling that we are entering a never-never land in which all information is conveyed by total strangers who vary in possessing expertise, attractiveness, likableness, prestige, and the like, by virtue of natural endowment. This never-never land is not of Wyer's making. I have the feeling that he was almost as uncomfortable in it as I.

At one point, he cites a study by Sherif, White, and Harvey (1955) that showed a positive relationship between status in a group and other members' evaluations of competence in throwing a ball at a target. Then he proceeds to suggest that school pupils may have been more influenced by a white than a black source because the former was more attractive. Doesn't status figure here at all? Still earlier, we read that differences in social status only produce differences in message interpretation when "confounded with attributions of bias." Then, we get the solemn conclusion that "attitudes toward the source . . . may sometimes appear to affect the influence of . . . information" but that "this may be due largely to the mediating effect these attitudes have upon attributions of expertise" (page 285). Does anyone want to charge that ex-President Nixon lost credibility because he lost his expertise at being president? Did his expertise at lying have anything to do with it? What will happen if, as seems possible, many people lose faith in society's "experts?" Will attitudes toward sources of information cease to have any influence?

While I am sure that many people involved in conveying information would dearly love to think that "expertise" is all that counts in the last analysis, let us put the matter in some perspective: In dealing with attitudes towards sources of information, we are not dealing with abstract variables but *relationships among human beings* as these affect the person's evaluative judgments of the sources' credibility, expertise, attractiveness, etc. The individual's involvement in the human relationship and in the matter at hand are both inevitably in question as such evaluations are made, whether as "confounders" or "mediators," or in all likelihood, as major anchors for the evaluations. If you doubt this at all, try to remember where, when, and from whom you first gained information about sexual relationships. Next, consider how you reacted to your first sex education lecture by some "expert." Now recall your first pornographic movie, if you saw one. Let us not remove sources of information from the context of human groups and social institutions in which they are almost invariably found.

I suspect that Wyer is most nearly correct when he discusses the role of the source in interpretation of information (page 274). He suggests that we make judgments about the sources' attitudes and assimilate subsequent statements toward that evaluation. His supporting evidence pertains to effects of a preceding stimulus context. Fortunately, Rodgers (in Sherif *et al.*, 1973) found that Wyer's expectation was supported when both the source and the receiver of information have highly involved positions. As Wyer predicted, the effects occurred only on issues that were highly involving, not on those of little concern to their group. In this case, the groups were the Students for a Democratic Society and the Young Americans for Freedom. Issues were chosen that were highly involving for each group, but some were less involving to each group. Specifically, the SDS was much involved on the Vietnam war and the status of blacks. The YAF was hung up on the issue of the gold drain from the U.S. and the war, but not highly involved in the race issue.

Rodgers presented ten well-known political figures, asking the students to judge the credibility of each on each issue, and then to locate their own positions on each issue and the position taken by each political figure. For comparison, introductory sociology students made the same judgments. As you might suspect, the positions taken by communicators who were judged as *not* credible were located remotely from the students' own positions, but not to the same extent on the different issues. In fact, SDS members located communicators *not* credible to them close by their own position on the gold drain issue, despite the fact that they used almost the entire scale to separate themselves from not credible sources on the war and race issues. Conversely, the YAF members judged a great gap between themselves and *not* credible communicators on the gold issue and the war issue, but closed it when making judgments on the race issue. Naturally, the gaps were much smaller for communicators judged credible and for the less involved sociology students on all issues and communicators.

I will close by suggesting that attitudes that are involving are attitudes linking self and others, hence include self as object quite as much as the measures of "self-esteem" whose use Wyer finds "not particularly productive" (page 281). I agree with his evaluation of that research at present. With Gecas (1972), I believe that a person's self-regard or self-worth varies depending upon the reference group context in which it is assessed, and the importance of the matter at hand in their eyes, as well as one's own. Although the concept of personal involvement and degrees thereof implies more comprehensive organization or structure than the concept of attitude alone, I have not been able to insert notions about the structure of the self system here (see Sherif, 1976, Chapters 7—10). I would like to point out, however, that the self system is a product of development and interaction in a social context, hence, amenable to study in those terms.

In fact, cognitive psychologists might find exploration of the self system a congenial path toward uniting the conceptual—motivation—affective aspects of cognitive processes. As a start, Luis Escovar (1975) recently completed a doctoral investigation comparing the classifications of boys and girls from three through nine years of age. He used a "free sort" (own categories) method, often used in developmental study of classification, presenting two carefully standardized sets of pictures for sorting: one of familiar household objects and one of children's toys. Some of the toys had previously been judged as traditionally masculine or traditionally feminine, while others were ambiguous or indeterminate as to sex role appropriateness in traditional terms.

The household objects were presented as familiar, but not personally involving to the children, in order to compare the number of categories used by children of various ages with reports in the classification literature of a definite age trend during this period toward the generation of fewer categories with age. This trend in fact was found, the number of categories decreasing from about ten to about six, on the average. In contrast, the children used significantly fewer categories for the same number of toys at the youngest age (only about three categories, on the average), and these did not change in number with age.

In categorizing the toys, what did change with age was the significantly increasing tendency toward preference for same sex toys and rejection of other sex toys, particularly among boys. Girls were by and large categorizing as traditional girls by age 3—4.

I do not interpret these findings as showing altogether different psychological laws governing classification of toys and of household objects. On the contrary, they simply suggest that toys are highly involving objects for very young children, that they have already formed a ready set of evaluative categories for dealing with them, and that what they accept and reject starts approaching the cultural norms prescribed for their self-identification as boy or girl quite early. Household objects, though familiar and commonly appearing together in different location in the house, are simply not a matter for classificatory concern until the child has developed conceptually to think of "living room things," "bedroom things," "kitchen things," etc. Even then, the desires and expectations for self enter into the picture hardly at all; the self is not placed into one of the categories to be compared with others.

If the social psychology of attitudes can ever get itself together by relating the person's evaluative judgments and actions to significant boundary conditions in human relationships, in social institutions, in groups, in social values, and ideologies, we may know something worthwhile to contribute to serious discussions on schooling and the acquisition of knowledge. Meanwhile, I suggest that all conclusions about the role of attitudes be coupled with a question: How personally involving are the matters at hand, the interpersonal relationships, and the situational context for the people? Then we can turn to other problems that should be addressed in any examination of schooling and people, including the query made years ago by the now-departed sociologist Robert Lynd. He entitled a book addressed to problems of the relationship between social sciences and society with this provocative question: *Knowledge for What*?

REFERENCES

Bogardus, E. S. Measuring social distances. *Journal of Applied Sociology*, 1925, 9, 299—308.

Dawes, R. M., Singer, D., & Lemon, F. An experimental analysis of contrast effect and its implications for intergroup communication and indirect assessment of attitude. *Journal of Personality and Social Psychology*, 1972, 21, 281—295.

Diab, L. Measurement of social attitudes: Problems and prospects. In C. W. Sherif & M. Sherif (Eds.), *Attitude, ego involvement and change.* New York: Wiley, 1967.

Eiser, J. R. Enhancement of contrast in the absolute judgment of attitude statements. *Journal of Personality and Social Psychology*, 1971, 17, 1—10.

Escovar, L. A. Categorization of social stimuli by young children: A study of social cognitive development. Ph.D. dissertation, The Pennsylvania State University, University Park, 1975.

Fraser, R. S., & Stacey, B. G. A psychophysical investigation of the influence of attitude on the judgment of social stimuli. *British Journal of Social and Clinical Psychology*, 1973, **12**, 337–352.

Gecas, V. Parental behavior and contextual variations in adolescent self esteem. *Sociometry*, 1972, **35**, 332–345.

Horowitz, E. L. The development of attitudes toward Negroes. *Archives of Psychology*, 1936, No. 194.

Hovland, C. I. Reconciling conflicting results derived from experimental and survey studies of attitude change. *American Psychologist*, 1959, **14**, 8–17.

Hovland, C. I., & Sherif, M. Judgmental phenomena and scales of attitude measurement: Item displacement in Thurstone scales. *Journal of Abnormal and Social Psychology*, 1952, **47**, 822–832.

Hyman, H. H., & Sheatsley, P. B. Some reasons why information campaigns fail. *Public Opinion Quarterly*, 1947, **11**, 412–423.

Katz, D., & Allport, F. H. *Students' attitudes.* Syracuse, N.Y.: Craftsman Press, 1931.

Katz, D., & Braly, K. W. Racial stereotypes of 100 college students. *Journal of Abnormal and Social Psychology*, 1933, **28**, 280–290.

Kearney, H. R. Personal involvement and communication context in social judgment of a controversial issue. Ph.D. dissertation, The Pennsylvania State University, University Park, 1975.

LaPiere, R. T. Attitudes versus actions. *Social Forces*, 1934, **13**, 230–237.

Sherif, C. W. Social categorization as a function of latitude of acceptance and series range. *Journal of Abnormal and Social Psychology*, 1963, **67**, 148–156.

Sherif, C. W. *Orientation in social psychology.* New York: Harper and Row, 1976.

Sherif, C. W., & Jackman, N. R. Judgments of truth by participants in collective controversy. *Public Opinion Quarterly*, 1969, **30**, 173–186.

Sherif, C. W., Kelly, M., Rodgers, H. L., Jr., Sarup, G., & Tittler, B. I. Personal involvement, social judgment and action. *Journal of Personality and Social Psychology*, 1973, **27**, 311–328.

Sherif, C. W., Sherif, M., & Nebergall, R. E. *Attitude and attitude change: The social judgment-involvement approach.* Philadelphia: W. B. Saunders, 1965.

Sherif, C. W. & Sherif, M. (Eds.). *Attitude, ego-involvement and change.* New York: Wiley, 1967. Greenwood Press, 1976.

Sherif, M. *The psychology of social norms.* New York: Harper & Row, 1936.

Sherif, M. Some needed concepts in the study of attitude. In J. Peatman & E. L. Hartley (Eds.), *Festschrift for Gardner Murphy.* New York: Harper & Row, 1960.

Sherif, M., & Cantril, H. The psychology of "attitudes." Part 1. *Psychological Review*, 1945, **52**, 295–317; Part 2, *Psychological Review*, 1946, **53**, 1–24.

Sherif, M., & Cantril, H. *The psychology of ego-involvements.* New York: Wiley, 1947.

Sherif, M., & Hovland, C. I. Judgmental phenomena and scales of attitude measurement: Placement of items with individual choice of number of categories. *Journal of Abnormal and Social Psychology*, 1953, **48**, 135–141.

Sherif, M., & Hovland, C. I. *Social judgment. Assimilation and contrast effects in communication and attitude change.* New Haven, Conn.: Yale University Press, 1961.

Sherif, M. & Sherif, C. W. *Social psychology.* New York: Harper and Row, 1969.

Smith, S. S. & Jamieson, B. D. Effects of attitude and ego-involvement on the learning and retention of controversial material. *Journal of Personality and Social Psychology*, 1972, **22**, 303–310.

Spiro, R. J. Inferential reconstruction in memory for connected discourse. (Tech. Report No. 2), Urbana, Ill.: Laboratory for Cognitive Studies in Education, 1975.

Spiro, R. J. & Sherif, C. W. Consistency and relativity in recall with differing ego-involvement. *British Journal of Social and Clinical Psychology*, 1975, **14**, 351–361.

Thomas, W. I., & Znaniecki, F. *The Polish peasant in Europe and America*. Boston: R. G. Badger, 1918–1920. 5 vols. Reprinted, New York: Dover, 1958.

Volkmann, J. Scales of judgment and their implication for social psychology. In J. H. Rohrer & M. Sherif (Eds.), *Social psychology at the crossroads*. New York: Harper and Row, 1951.

OPEN DISCUSSION
ON THE CONTRIBUTIONS
BY WYER AND SHERIF

Ortony: I would like some clarification on the claims made about the relationship between knowledge and belief. I think the idea that belief is knowledge about the probable degree of truth of something is an absolute nonstarter. How do social psychologists relate knowledge and belief?

Wyer: I do not distinguish between knowledge and beliefs within this context. I define knowledge as a set of propositions, each of which is held to be true with some subjective probability.

Ortony: You do not think that you can put probabilities both along the dimension of knowledge and along the dimension of belief?

Wyer: I think that some things, like my belief that the light is up there, are held to be true with a probability of one. But I think of a probability estimate as being the unit of analysis, an estimate of the likelihood that an object is a member of some kind of a category (for example, true or false).

Petrie: I understand that your belief is probably one that there is a light up there, but is there a light up there or isn't there? Is your belief true? That question makes sense, and insofar as it makes sense it points to another dimension of problems beyond *what* your belief is.

Wyer: It does not make sense to me as a psychologist. All I know is that I hold something to be true with some probability. Whether it is true or not is irrelevant to my understanding of how my cognitions are interrelated. I have difficulty semantically with the statement a "belief is true." I have a belief about a proposition, and the belief *is* the estimate that the proposition is true.

Spiro: This argument seems to be proceeding at two different levels. Dr. Petrie is making an epistemological argument for the necessity of distinguishing between beliefs and their objective truth value. I do not think Dr. Wyer would disagree with the necessity for that distinction. However, he is only concerned, in the context of his paper, with the cognitive consequences of beliefs. From his perspective, it is irrelevant whether a belief is true. For the kinds of phenomena Dr. Wyer is interested in, all that matters is what is going on in the individual's mind. If an individual's belief is shown to be false, then the relevant probabilities are adjusted. Furthermore, Dr. Wyer's position does not require individuals to fail to attempt to validate their beliefs.

Wyer: I agree with that.

Sherif: I agree Dr. Wyer's position has been clarified. I would like to add a perspective from another social psychologist on the larger issue raised by this discussion. Relationships between environmental events (studied independently of a particular individual's perception of them or propositions about them) and psychological concepts (including beliefs) have to be tackled if there is to be anything scientific about psychology. "Scientific experimental psychology" has been based on this premise since its inception late in the nineteenth century. The so-called "illusions" in visual perception cannot be understood otherwise, for example, the Müller–Lyer illusion. Individuals hold beliefs with probabilities near 1.0 that have little support from environmental events or little likelihood of being invalidated on such a basis. They assign low levels of probability to other propositions that are demonstrably true by independent criteria. Social psychology becomes both subjectivist and ethnocentric unless it makes independent checks on beliefs and other definitions of knowledge, including knowledge about social facts.

Wyer: The relation between subjective estimates of the likelihood that something is true and the objective probability that it is true, and the factors that affect this relation, are of course interesting areas of empirical investigation. However, I do not see that the last observation is particularly relevant to the issues of concern here. I think we are getting off the track.

Rothkopf: Changing the subject, there are discrepancies between what people say and what they do. Take the antismoking programs that produce considerable attitude change (as conventionally measured), with little actual change in smoking behavior. This has led some people to say that there is something fundamentally wrong with the methods used by people who study attitudes, opinions, beliefs, etc. What they are measuring is a verbal system that is deceptive. It is controlled by many secondary factors and has very little relationship with what people do in important situations.

Wyer: It is a question of definitions. It does not bother me to say that there is not a relationship in some instances between a verbal statement and some other sort of behavior, any more than it bothers me to say that any other two types of behavior are unrelated. In order to say that a given verbal statement is related to some other behavior I need a theory, or it becomes an empirical question. I am perfectly happy to ask about the conditions under which the statement, "I think smoking is bad" is related to some other behavior pertaining to smoking. Sometimes these two things are related and sometimes they are not. Where we get into hangups, and I think this is a fuzzy notion that has pervaded psychology through the years, is with the fact that attitudes are supposed on a priori grounds to be related to behavior. Now if *you* want to define the attitude as the behavior, that is fine. That is not the way I define an attitude. I define an attitude as the judgment, and then it becomes an empirical question or a theoretical question as to whether it is related to some other behavior.

Sherif: I would like to respond to this, because I do not agree with Dr. Wyer and I do agree with Dr. Rothkopf. I think that a good many psychologists have been getting away with murder for years. I think that if the attitude concept is to have any meaning at all, then it has to be related, not necessarily to any particular behavior or any particular evaluative judgment or verbal statement that you may choose to pick at a given time and in a given situation, but to certain paradigms, certain regularities, certain consistencies in people's actions toward classes of objects. This is what the attitude problem was defined as originally. There is a tradition in psychology that says just be operational, just call attitudes what my test studies. We have heard that before from psychologists. "Intelligence is just what my test measures." This is the approach that leads to the position where you have to say things like "what we are studying does not have anything to do with the way people act."

Now, if one has a notion of attitude like the one I offered, you have a framework for relating attitudes to behavior. We have some recent studies (e.g., Sherif *et al.*, 1973, which was mentioned in my paper) relating to various kinds of important actions that a person can take in specific situations relative to their level of personal involvement. People who are more involved are more likely to behave consistently with their attitudes.

Wyer: When we talk about acceptance and rejection, we are talking about verbal statements. You give a person a statement. You ask, "Do you agree with that?"; "Which is your most preferred statement?"; "What are all the other statements that you will accept or reject?" That is how Dr. Sherif defines attitudes. I do not see that that is particularly different from my concern with verbal statements.

The other question that I have has to do again with the relationship between attitudes and behavior. If we want to define an attitude as something that both involves a value judgment or opinion and some other behavior, it seems to me we add more problems than we eliminate. What do you do with a person who says he likes to smoke and does not smoke? Does he have an attitude? If so, what is it? You can find some people who say they like to smoke, and smoke; some people say they like to smoke and do not; and there are all the other possible combinations.

Sherif: I would like to add one more thing here. Dr. Wyer feels happy with equating an evaluative judgment rendered on a good—bad or like—dislike dimension with an attitude. I do not, but that does not mean that I would not use evaluative judgments as data. However, there is a difference in research methodology in the studies that I have described and those that Dr. Wyer has described.

Evaluative judgment is never, in the research I have described, the sole basis for inferring the person's attitude. We do look at a person's actions, and we look at the pattern of evaluative judgments and their consistency. Furthermore, as I tried to point out, you can learn something fascinating when you do not look at what the person evaluates at all, but look at what the person does *not* evaluate. The latitude of noncommitment, as it turns out, is one of the most revealing things in terms of how important attitudes are for the individual. There are big differences in methodology here, and I would never be so bold as to infer that someone had an attitude using *one* method.

Wyer: I think the thing with any definition is whether it is useful, whether it generates certain types of questions that are empirically testable and interesting. I think we differ primarily in how useful we have found one way of looking at it as opposed to another.

I do want to say one other thing about predicting behavior. It turns out that people like Marty Fishbein have done very well in predicting behavioral intent. Basically, what he is arguing is that we have had a lot of trouble because we have not specified the attitude object. There may be little relation between a person's statement that he dislikes cigarettes and his behavior of smoking or not smoking. But what we are interested in is the attitude towards the *behavior* itself. In fact, there is a very substantial relationship between the statement, "I am not going to smoke" and the actual behavior of not smoking. But you cannot predict that from responses to any attitude statement about liking *cigarettes*. Anyway, people are doing a good job of predicting behavior by simply identifying what one wants to be able to predict and the information needed in order to do it, in a commonsensical way. If we are interested in predicting behavior, we can do it, and we do not necessarily have to use the word attitude.

REFERENCES

Sherif, C. W., Kelly, M., Rodgers, H. L., Jr., Sarup, G., & Tittler, B. I. Personal involvement, social judgment and action. *Journal of Personality and Social Psychology*, 1973, 27, 311–328.

9
We Know Who Knows, but Why?

Earl Hunt

The University of Washington

There is an apocryphal story about a student who sued Columbia University because the university had taken his tuition and had not given him wisdom. Columbia replied that they had agreed only to expose him to knowledge. I used to think this was a fine reply, but now I am not so sure. The educated person should be able to correlate the present with the past; both the past of personal experience and the vicarious past through which we know our culture. It is not enough to select the knowledge to be learned. It must be displayed in such a way that it can be acquired. It is the business of psychology to provide some hints about how we can ensure that information presented does indeed get into the head, how it is organized when it gets there, and how it can be fetched upon demand. What we really want to know is how variations in information presentation today will affect information use then, twenty, and thirty years later. It is easier to do research on short term memory. Therefore, some of this paper will be quite speculative.

I assume that most education now and in the future will rely upon combining linguistic information with physical (usually visual) models of the world. The student will be required to correlate his or her representations of memorial, linguistic, and visual information in order to be understood. A televised film of an attempt on Gerald Ford's life can call to mind representations of Brutus killing Caesar and Charlotte Corday killing Marat, although I have not witnessed any of these events. When I find similarities and differences between these representations I am displaying my ability to handle "academic knowledge." No one disputes this, but it brings me to a more controversial fact.

We can predict who will be good and who will be poor at manipulating academic knowledge. We can do this by use of the psychometric device called a "verbal intelligence test." It is not wise to dispute the fact that such predictions can be made, for there is a mountain of evidence to support the assertion (Cleary *et al.*, 1975; Willerman, 1975; and many others). It is the mechanism of prediction which is in doubt. On its face, the verbal intelligence test is a test of knowledge about the (mostly white, middle class) world. One of its most useful subtests is a simple vocabulary test. Since words are arbitrary, what could be more culture bound? But knowledge builds on knowledge. One interpretation of the predictive power of the test is that it measures the extent to which one has acquired that knowledge which will be useful in ascending the next rung of the academic ladder ... including rungs in the armed service and industrial academies. A second interpretation of the predictive power of the test is that it measures the ability to acquire and use meaningful information. This stronger assertion views the knowledge displayed during the test session itself and the future performance in an educational program as both being reflections of an underlying ability to process certain types of information.

Tempers run strong in this controversy, so I want it to be clear where I stand ... firmly on both sides of the issue. Certainly beyond the age of five, and maybe before that, most of our knowledge is acquired in the context of prior knowledge. A test that measures the knowledge base acquired prior to entering into any training course will be, if it taps relevant knowledge, a good predictor of success. Some areas of knowledge are relevant to a wide variety of training programs. Language, including vocabulary, has perhaps the widest span of relevance and thus a measure of linguistic knowledge will be a good predictor of educational success in many settings. Part of the accuracy of the intelligence test is due to this. I also believe that some training programs strain the information processing capacities of the students. There exists a substantial body of experimental work which has convinced me that individuals vary considerably in their capability to perform certain basic information processing acts. Whether this variation is sufficient to make a difference in information acquisition in the normal educational setting is very much an unresolved issue. In this chapter, I suggest a conceptual framework for thinking about how individual differences in information processing may affect the acquisition of knowledge. I hope my speculations point the way toward further research.

Any discussion of individual differences must proceed within the context of a general framework for discussing thinking. I espouse a rather limited view of man, as an information storing and retrieving system. These ideas are by no means unique, and have been presented elsewhere (Hunt, 1971, 1973; Hunt & Poltrock, 1974), so I shall not go into great detail. The basic postulates of the theoretical approach are:

1. Information storage is a process of recoding into progressively more complex, meaningful units. At any point in this process attention may be directed toward the storing of information at a particular level, with implications for how that information will be stored and how it can be retrieved later.

2. The process of recoding requires that information be held in active "short term" memory (STM) for varying periods of time. The information in STM

may be held in a variety of codes, including codes dependent upon particular sensory systems (i.e., images).

3. It is possible to alter the codes in STM.

4. There exists a permanent storage system, "long term memory" (LTM), of codes which cannot be changed.

5. The code altering processes in (2) and (3) above depend upon a pattern recognition mechanism in which STM is recognized as being in a state appropriate for the application of a transformation stored in LTM. (To take a simple example, the pattern A may be replaced by the acoustic code A. At a deeper level, 3+2 can be recorded as 5.)

Very many people have argued for some or all of these postulates, and I shall make no attempt to cite the relevant literature. The major contribution which I and my colleagues have made, and this is not unique either, is our contention that the processes involved in Points (1)–(5) are reflected in individual differences in information processing. Our evidence has been presented in a series of experimental reports (Hunt, Frost, & Lunneborg, 1973; Hunt, Lunneborg, & Lewis, 1975; Love & Hunt, 1975; Lunneborg, 1975) and a theoretically oriented literature review (Hunt & Lansman, 1975). Generally, we have found that there are consistent individual differences in a variety of information processing tasks and that some of these differences are nontrivially related to differences in intelligence as measured by conventional psychometric tests. This has suggested to us that differences in psychometric intelligence do not simply reflect differential exposure to knowledge.

In our previous work, we did not grapple with the fact that performance on a conventional verbal test is obviously a function of previously acquired knowledge. Instead, we made vague statements about how it was reasonable to suppose that small differences in information processing could be amplified into large differences in acquired knowledge. A most unflattering way to describe our position would be to say that we took psychometricians to task for not having a theory of the process of intelligence, and then proceeded to make the same error. In this paper, I shall attempt to correct the situation, by considering a model of a situation which is fundamental to knowledge acquisition and relating it to our own work.

COMPREHENDING LINGUISTIC DESCRIPTIONS

Suppose that you were to be presented with a display of some sort and a linguistic statement describing it, and were asked if the description was accurate. How would you proceed? Carpenter and Just's (1975) *constituent comparison model* has been developed to deal with such situations. Their original concern was with data from studies which involved very simple statements and displays, and most of the illustrations of the model will be taken from such applications.

The model can be elaborated to apply to more complex situations, including educational applications (Just & Carpenter, 1976).

It is assumed that knowledge from both lingusitic and nonlinguistic sources is coded internally in a propositional form.[1] Propositions consist of strings containing three types of symbols; predicates, their arguments, and polarity markers. Thus, the sentence

(1) The dots are not red.

would be represented in STM by a string of symbols equivalent to

(2) NEG (RED (DOTS)).

Terms such as RED and DOTS are tokens pointing to the associated LTM concepts, and not the concepts themselves. This is important because it means that any comparison between two terms in STM (e.g., RED and BLUE) will require retrieval and comparison of the associated concepts.

Information from nonlinguistic sources, such as pictures or images generated from LTM, are similarly assumed to be codes in propositional form.

When two representations are to be compared, the sequence of actions is postulated to be equivalent to the "flow chart" depicted in Fig. 1. Beginning with the innermost components, the propositions are compared, component by component, until all components have been matched or until a mismatch occurs. Thus in comparing

(3a) The apples are not green = NEG (GREEN (APPLES))

to

(3b) The apples are red = AFFIRM (RED (APPLES)),

the first mismatch would occur in comparing RED and GREEN. When a mismatch occurs, a response index (initially set to TRUE) has its truth value changed. The two mismatched components are marked "checked," so that they will match in subsequent comparisons, and the process begins anew *at the original innermost component.*[2] The algorithm terminates when the comparison sequence is completed without a mismatch. At this point the current value of the response index should indicate whether or not the two representations match.

---

[1] Acceptance of the notion of a propositional form of memory representation does not force one to deny the subjective experience of imagery. The propositional representation could provide the LTM directions for generating a STM image.

[2] Intuitively, the process of beginning anew at the start is the most unlikely step in the theory. Carpenter and Just argue for its plausibility on the grounds that the assumption removes the need for a placeholder in STM. The assumption is used heavily in accounting for the data which Carpenter and Just cite to support their model.

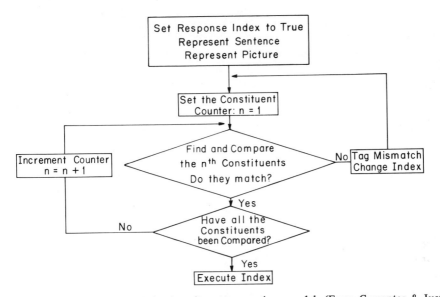

FIG. 1 A flow diagram of the constituent comparison model. (From Carpenter & Just, 1975, Fig. 1.)

To illustrate, consider the steps involved in comparing the sentence "The plus is not below the star" to the picture of a plus above a star. The picture would be coded as

(4) $\binom{*}{+}$ = AFFIRM (ABOVE (PLUS,STAR))

and the sentence as

(5) The plus is not below the star = NEG (BELOW (PLUS,STAR)).

Initially the predicates ABOVE and BELOW would mismatch,[3] causing the response index to be reset from TRUE to FALSE. Subsequently, a mismatch would occur in the comparison of AFFIRM and NEG. The response index would be reset to TRUE and the process initiated again. This time it would complete, after a total of three scans, and the response TRUE would be made.

Most of the evidence for the constituent comparison model is drawn from studies of the time required to verify sentences in simple situations, such as those just given. It should be clear from the example that Sentence (5) would require fewer scanning operations than the equally correct sentence

(6) It is not true that plus is not above star = NEG (NEG (ABOVE (PLUS,STAR))).

---

[3] It can be argued that BELOW is a marked form of ABOVE and should be coded NEG (ABOVE (X,Y)). The simpler coding has been chosen for purposes of illustration.

On the other hand, Example (4) should be verifiable in fewer scanning operations than Sentence (5). Carpenter and Just have collected an impressive amount of evidence to support their assertion that the time to verify a statement is a linear function of the number of scanning operations predicated by the model.

The exact form of the nonlinguistic stimulus to be compared to the sentence does not seem to matter. While the model was originally proposed to explain results obtained by Clark and Chase (1972) in the sentence-picture comparison just illustrated, Just (1974) has applied it to sentences about semantic memory, as in verifying the statement that "All elephants are mammals." Carpenter and Just (1975) and Just and Carpenter (1975) list several other areas of application. It must be admitted that the documentation is not as detailed as the documentation for the original sentence comprehension paradigm, but it is certainly sufficient to show that the constituent-comparison model should be regarded seriously.

The flow chart presented in Fig. 1 treats the act of searching STM as a primitive process. Carpenter and Just (1975) point out that STM searching is, in fact, based on still more primitive operations of addressing and pattern matching: "There are a number of suboperations in the find and compare operator, most of which can be classified as "find" and only one of which is "compare . . ." (p. 56) and ". . . most of the processing time in sentence verification may be consumed by retrieving and positioning the appropriate constituents and keeping track of one's place . . ." (p. 56).

How does this reasoning relate to individual differences? Adult intellectual performance is dependent on both possession of appropriate knowledge and the ability to recognize which known facts are relevant to the current situation. When an adult acquires new information, that information is incorporated into a complex framework of old information. In both cases, the adult is required to compare representations of the current and the past situations. Language plays an important part in this process. We all talk to ourselves to describe what is going on. The constituent comparison model is a general description of the psychology of this act. To the extent that the comparison process is a limiting feature in performance, individuals who possess capacities for information processing which are important in the model would be more effective. This does not address the question of what representations a person has available. To the extent that problem solving is limited by knowledge itself, the constituent comparison model is not relevant. It becomes relevant when we are concerned with the process rather than the product of knowledge acquisition.

It would be nice if this picture could be supported by directly relevant experiments. This is not possible now, because most of the experiments were designed independently of the theory. There is a great deal of tangentially relevant evidence, the "previously gathered data" for which constituent comparison is proposed as an umbrella.

RESEARCH ON INDIVIDUAL DIFFERENCES

Verifying negatively worded sentences about simple pictures takes longer than verifying corresponding positively worded sentences. Given the picture ($^*_+$), "plus is above star" is understood more rapidly than "star is not above plus," even after allowing for the greater length of the second sentence (Clark & Chase, 1972). Carpenter and Just argue that the difference beween the two verification times is due to the requirement for additional scan and comparison operations in the latter case. Examples (4)–(6) illustrate this. Hunt *et al* (1975) found that university students with relatively high verbal intelligence test scores (high verbals) showed a small difference in verification times between positively and negatively worded sentences, while students with relatively low scores (relative to the general university level) (low verbals) showed a larger difference. This is what one would expect if high verbals are more efficient at executing the addressing, scanning, and comparison operations.

Some added support for this conclusion is provided by several studies using Baddeley's (1968) procedure for rapid assessment of verbal intelligence. Baddeley developed a test in which the subject is asked to indicate whether or not a simple sentence is true of an immediately following pair of letters, for example,

(7) These letters are identical.   A B True___ False___.

The score on the test is the number of such sentences correctly verified or rejected in a fixed time period. In a rather small study, Baddeley found that the test score had a correlation of .59 with the verbal intelligence test scores of a group of soldiers in the British Army. Subsequent work by Rose (Note 3) and our own laboratory has shown similar results using samples of university and high school students.

While the results by Hunt and colleagues provide a direct test of the relation between verbal intelligence and a basic measure of the Carpenter and Just model, the results using the Baddeley procedure admit of an alternative explanation. It could be argued that high verbals do well simply because they are faster readers. A variant of the Baddeley procedure could be developed in which the subject verified blocks of sentences, with different proportions of negatively and positively worded propositions within each block. The difference in number of sentences verified in different blocks could be used to calculate the time required for the constituent scan operation. As Baddeley's test can be completed in a matter of minutes this might prove to be an efficient way of measuring individual information processing parameters.

The observation that those with high verbal intelligence comprehend sentences rapidly is not a tautology. Sentence comprehension involving such simple elements places demands on rapid information processing, but all those tested can be presumed to have the appropriate knowledge.

Let us look next at a series of studies involving individual differences in tasks that seem to tap processes underlying the constituent comparison operation itself. Constituent comparison involves a scan of two propositional representations to find and compare corresponding components. Memory scanning has been studied directly using a paradigm originally developed by Sternberg (1966) and since utilized by many others. The sequence of events is

1. A small series of n items (letters, digits, or words) is presented, one at a time. This is called the *memory set*.
2. A *probe item* is presented.
3. The subject indicates whether the probe item was or was not a member of the memory set.

The dependent variable is the time between presentation of the probe item and the subject's response. This is called the *reaction time* (RT). For memory sets of size six or less, RT is a linear function of the size of the memory set. The slope of the function is usually regarded as a measure of the rate of information processing in short term memory.[4]

Sternberg (1975) has observed that strong individual differences in slope have been displayed within many studies using this paradigm, but that in general there has been no consistent relationship displayed between scanning rate and other individual difference variables. The conclusion is certainly true for those studies which use "normal adult" populations. This is a serious embarassment for our ideas. There ought to be relationships between scan rates and measures of intellectual performance.

There are two excuses for the theory. One is that the differences between information processing capabilities of normal subjects in the scanning task are not great enough to display the relationship except in a very large study. This is a serious point, for Lunneborg (1975) has found that the range of information processing in university students is considerably restricted relative to that in high school students. The second excuse is that the Sternberg paradigm may not provide a scanning task sufficiently complex to demonstrate individual differences. Consider any task involving k scans. Suppose individuals i and j carry out these tasks with scan rates s_i and s_j, respectively. The difference in their performance on the task will be proportional to $k(s_i - s_j)$. If k is small the effect may be masked by the noise level of the data.

When we study extreme groups it appears that scanning rate is related to intellectual ability. Mental retardates show scan rates markedly above those of normal controls. Within mentally retarded populations, those with a history of

---

[4] Sternberg argued that the scanning process is a serial one in which each item in STM is compared with the probe item in turn. Subsequent theoretical analyses have called into question this interpretation of the data. Nevertheless, it appears that in all the models yet proposed the slope of the function relating RT to memory set size can be treated as an approximate measure of the rate of information processing in memory scanning.

encephalitic infection, and thus possible brain damage, show unusually high scan rates (Harris & Fleer, 1974). At the other end of the mental scale, Hunt and Love (1972) report a case study of a highly skilled memorizer who relied almost exclusively upon verbal coding. He had a scan rate of 10 msec. per digit, better than twice as fast as the scan rate reported for college subjects using comparable material (Cavanaugh, 1972). The absolute comparison of the scan rates involved is striking. Some typical results are shown in Fig. 2.

In one of our series of studies we (Hunt *et al*, 1975) compared the performance of high verbal and low verbal college students using a complex scanning task. The subjects solved "simple" arithmetic problems made difficult by replacing the integers with code mapping digits into other overlearned lists: the days of the week, months of the year, or the alphabet. Each problem was simple, then,

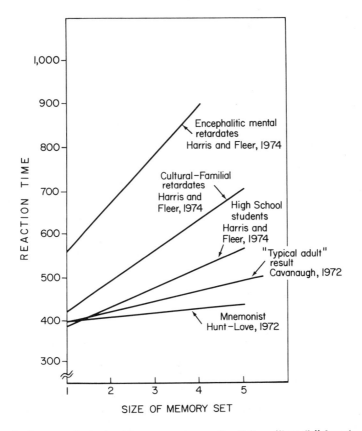

FIG. 2 Some results in short term memory scan for digits — "best fit" functions.

in the computing used, but complex in the scanning required. For instance, an easy problem was

(8) If Monday is 1 and Sunday is 7, what is Tuesday plus Wednesday? (Friday).

This can be compared to the hard problem

(9) What is May plus October?   (March).

The problems require the subject to scan down a list to find the operands, and then scan along the list to find the answer. Scanning must restart at the beginning of the list when a carry is encountered. Individual reaction times (RT) were well fitted to a model expressing RT as a linear function of parameters stating the base, the amount of scanning required, and the presence or absence of a carry. The magnitude of the parameters was generally larger for subjects in the "low verbal" group, indicating that as the problems became more complex, the disparity between low and high verbal performance increased.

It appears that there is indeed a relation between STM scanning and verbal intelligence. Scanning alone, however, does not appear to be predictive of verbal reasoning ability within the population of well educated adults. Whether or not it would show a stronger relation to intellectual performance in children, where acquired knowledge is presumably a less powerful contributor to variations in performance, is an open question.

What does it mean to compare two items in STM? We assume, as do most others, that STM does not contain items of information per se, but rather that it contains pointers to associated LTM concepts. Scanning and comparing, then, must involve going back and fourth from place holders in STM to the associated LTM concepts. This adds another step to the sentence comprehension process (and to many other tasks), the step of associating a pattern in STM with LTM information about it. Within the scanning paradigm, it does not appear to be possible to adduce a measure of STM–LTM interplay. In order to do so, we move to a slightly different paradigm.

Hunt *et al* (1973, 1975) measured the time required to associate a pattern with LTM information about it by use of a modification of Posner and Mitchell's (1967) "name identification-physical identification" task. The subject is shown two letters which are either different in both their name and physical shape (e.g., A–B), or are identical in both (e.g., A–A), or are physically disparate but have the same name (e.g., A–a). The task is to indicate whether or not the letters have the same name. Posner *et al* (1969) have provided evidence that the difference between the RT required to identify a name-identical pair (A–a above) and a physically identical pair (A–A above), may be interpreted as partly due to the time required to access the name code of the physical pattern. In university students typical times for name access vary from 60 to more than 100 msecs. Hunt *et al*, in several experiments using modifications of the basic paradigm, found that high verbal students were 25–30% faster in name code arousal than were low verbal students. It is important to realize that the low verbals in these studies were low relative to the university average. Our best guess is that they are at about the average verbal intelligence of the proverbial man in the street (Hunt *et al*, 1975).

What can we conclude? We are confident that there are substantial individual differences in the handling of information in short term memory. These differences are related to psychometric measures of verbal intelligence. In the population of university students, the correlations range from .20 to .40. Presumably the relations would be higher in the general population, but we have no direct evidence for this.

It is unlikely that the relationship between basic information processing variables and intelligence test performance is due to the operation of those variables while a person is taking an intelligence test. Test performance in young adults is probably due, for the most part, to the presence or absence of specific knowledge, including knowledge about how to solve problems. The information processing abilities more probably exert their influence by influencing the process of knowledge comprehension itself. The Carpenter and Just constituent comparison model is suggested as a description of how that influence is exerted.

EXTENSIONS

Why acquire information unless it can be used later? Several current theories of long term memory assume that information in LTM is stored as a set of propositions. Information retrieval is seen as a problem in matching the propositional representations of current and past stimuli. (See, for example, the models proposed by Anderson & Bower, 1973; Kintsch, 1974; Norman & Rumelhart, 1975). The time required to retrieve information will be an increasing function of the number of propositions to be matched, especially if the logical relationships between the propositions require that they be retrieved in series. To be consistent with our other studies, the time to retrieve information should be positively correlated with other measures of constituent comparison speed and should have a low, positive relation to verbal intelligence.

A recent study in our laboratory addressed the latter point. Forty-five high-school students participated in a two-day long term memory experiment. On the first day, the subjects memorized twenty two propositions, each of which took one of the following forms:

	Form	Example
	X is the Y.	Ann is the writer.
(10)	Y is in Z.	The writer is in the park.
	Anyone in Z can W.	Anyone in the park can smell the flowers.

The following day the subjects answered "yes–no" questions about these facts. The questions varied in the number of facts which had to be recalled in order to give the correct answer. For instance, given Example (10), the question

	Form	Example
(11)	Is X the Y?	Is Ann the writer?

can be answered by recalling one fact, while

	Form	Example
(12)	Can X do W?	Can Ann smell the flowers?

requires that three facts be retrieved. The relation between RT for question answering and the number of facts required is shown in Fig. 3. Over 90% of the variance is accounted for by the linear component, although there is a significant quadratic effect. The relationship is regular in individual cases as well. Furthermore, the slope of the linear component had a correlation of −.34 with scores on a verbal reasoning test. Note that this is an example of a situation in which significant performance differences are related to verbal intelligence, although preperformance knowledge was under the experimenter's control.

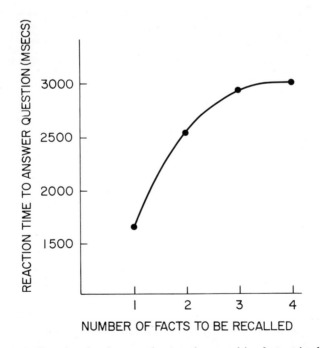

FIG. 3   Reaction time in answering questions requiring fact retrieval.

All the studies cited have assumed that linguistic and nonlinguistic stimuli are somehow translated into a propositional representation. The process of this transformation has been ignored. We know that the transformation of linguistic stimuli into the appropriate propositional form can be tortuous. We do not know the extent to which skill in making this transformation is an individual difference variable with significant implications for performance. Similarly, the translation from nonlinguistic stimuli into propositional form may involve considerable manipulation of the stimulus image. This has been shown on logical grounds alone by Artificial Intelligence research on computer vision (Winston, 1975), where it has been shown that a number of alterations in a visual image are needed before an appropriate propositional description can be computed. These manipulations are dictated by the problem constraints, and not by the characteristics of the computing machinery used, so somehow humans must go through logically equivalent operations. It has long been known that people differ in their ability to manipulate visual images. Recent work by Shepard and his colleagues (see especially the review by Cooper & Shepard, 1973) has demonstrated the existence of a sharp demarcation between good and poor image manipulators. This ability appears to be related to the psychometric factor "visualization ability" and may be a partially genetic trait. There is some evidence for sex linkage (Yen, 1975). The facts seem fairly well established. We need some theoretical model to relate the manipulation of visual and linguistic stimuli to each other.

QUESTIONS FOR THEORY AND PRACTICE

Verbal intelligence test scores are statistically related to knowledge acquisition and use in formal educational settings. We have found that verbal intelligence is also related to the speed of information processing in a variety of tasks involving scanning and selection of information in short and long term memory. In the present paper the constituent comparison model has been suggested as a way of conceptualizing the relationship between these findings. The reasoning is summarized in Fig. 4. Our present knowledge is presumed to result from information exposure and processing in the past. Our present performance, including performance on the intelligence test, is an amalgamation of knowledge and information processing capacity. Presumably the older we grow, the more knowledge becomes important and the less information processing plays the key role. Why solve anew, problems you have solved before? The ability to relate linguistic and nonlinguistic information to each other in a short time does not appear to be a major factor in adult human information processing at any one instant. It exerts its effect cumulatively, over the long period of time in which we acquire the information that we need at the moment of the test.

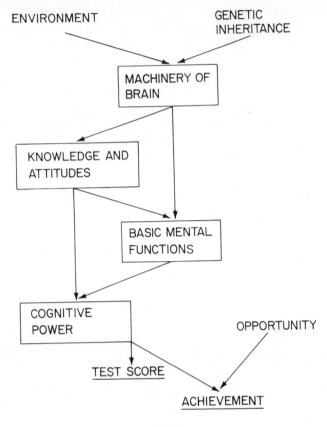

FIG. 4

The evidence presented here is consistent, but far from conclusive. There are a number of research questions within the theory itself which remain to be answered.

1. Associations have been shown between various measures of information processing and verbal intelligence test scores. How do the information processing measures relate to each other? Are the relations sensible in the light of the constituent comparison model?

2. Problem solving requires selection as well as comparison of representations. The ability to select an appropriate representation appears to be one of the most important distinctions between successful and unsuccessful problem solvers, at least in situations in which both groups are composed of highly intelligent subjects (Bloom & Broder, 1950). A simulation study of how people establish representations from a written description of a problem has shown that they are very much guided by the surface structure of the text (Simon & Hayes, in press).

This suggests that subjects capable of developing several alternative representations in a short time will be more capable problem solvers. We have little direct evidence that this is or is not so.

3. How do the relative contributions of information processing and knowledge change as the tasks and the subjects change? Presumably in young children, information processing plays a greater role and acquired knowledge less, but the balance shifts as we age. Is this in any way related to Horn and Cattell's distinction between fluid and crystallized intelligence (Horn, 1968; Cattell, 1971)?

Research demonstrating that "intelligence really means something" is sometimes interpreted as a message that there is nothing the educator can do; the smart will get smarter and the stupider will not. As a matter of fact, I believe that educators who overlook individual differences in information processing are not acting wisely or in the best interests of their students. However, I do not believe that educators should be either dismayed or scornful of our findings. Information processing involves more than a capacity, it involves a strategy, and strategies can be learned. To cite one commercially successful venture which should have arisen from educational research, but did not, the techniques for success through memory which are advocated by Lorayne and Lucas (1974) are all strategies for knowledge acquisition which can be learned, and which are compatible with the ideas about memory which have been expressed here. When you memorize for later recall you have to find a representation which can be organized in the context of previous information, and in a manner that can be cued when it is time to recall. Lorayne and Lucas' techniques are instructions for how to do this. It is likely that people who are "really super" in execution of these techniques are superior information processors (Hunt & Love, 1972; Love & Hunt, 1975). But everyone can learn to be better than they are without training. If a teacher is given a careful analysis of a student's information processing capacities, it ought to be possible for the teacher to develop a training program to improve the student's skill at memorizing useful information. We spend too much time showing children (and other students) what to learn and what problems to solve. Perhaps we should spend some time on individual development of memory and problem-solving processes. After all, physical educators regularly prescribe different training regimens for the needs of their athletes. Should not mental educators do as well?

ACKNOWLEDGMENTS

Preparation of this paper was supported by the National Institute of Mental Health, grant no. MH21795, for the University of Washington (Earl Hunt, principal investigator). I am happy to acknowledge the several discussions I have had with Clifford Lunneborg and Steven Poltrock on topics related to those discussed here.

REFERENCES

Anderson, J., & Bower, G. *Human associative memory*. New York: Academic Press, 1973.

Baddeley, A. D. A 3 minute reasoning test based on grammatical transformations. *Psychonomic Science*, 1968, **10**, 341–342.

Bloom, B., & Broder, L. *The problem solving processes of college students*. Chicago: University of Chicago Press, 1950.

Carpenter, P., & Just, M. Sentence comprehension: A psycholinguistic model of verification. *Psychological Review*, 1975, **82**, 45–73.

Cattell, R. *Abilities: Their structure, growth, and action*. Boston: Houghton-Mifflin, 1971.

Cavanaugh, J. Relation between the immediate memory span and the memory search rate. *Psychological Review*, 1972, **79**, 525–530.

Clark, H., & Chase, W. On the process of comparing sentences against pictures. *Cognitive Psychology*, 1972, **3**, 474–517.

Cleary, T., Humphreys, L., Kendrick, S., & Wassman, A. Educational uses of tests with disadvantaged students. *American Psychologist*, 1975, **30**, 15–41.

Cooper, L., & Shepard, R. Chronometric studies of the rotation of mental images. In W. Chase (Ed.), *Visual information processing*. New York: Academic Press, 1973.

Harris, G. J., & Fleer, R. E. High speed memory scanning in mental retardates: Evidence for a central processing deficit. *Journal of Experimental Child Psychology*, 1974, **17**, 452–459.

Horn, J. Organization of abilities and the development of intelligence. *Psychological Review*, 1968, **75**, 242–259.

Hunt, E. What kind of computer is man? *Cognitive Psychology*, 1971, **2**, 57–97.

Hunt, E. The memory we must have. In R. Schank & K. Colby (Eds.), *Computer models of thought and language*. San Francisco: Freeman, 1973.

Hunt, E., Frost, N., & Lunneborg, C. Individual differences in cognition: A new approach to intelligence. In G. Bower (Ed.), *Advances in learning and motivation*, Vol. 7. New York: Academic Press, 1973.

Hunt, E. & Lansman, M. Cognitive theory applied to individual differences. In W. Estes (Ed.), *Handbook of learning and cognitive processes*, Vol. 1: *Introduction to concepts and issues*. Hillsdale, N.J.: Lawrence Erlbaum Associates, 1975.

Hunt, E., & Love, T. How good can memory be? In A. Melton & E. Martin (Eds.), *Coding processes in human memory*. Washington: Winston, 1972.

Hunt, E., Lunneborg, C., & Lewis, J. What does it mean to be high verbal? *Cognitive Psychology*, 1975, 7, 1944–227.

Hunt, E., & Poltrock, S. The mechanics of thought. In B. Kantowitz (Ed.), *Human information processing*. Hillsdale, N.J.: Lawrence Erlbaum Associates, 1974.

Just, M. A. Comprehending quantified sentences: The relation between sentence–picture and semantic memory verification. *Cognitive Psychology*, 1974, **6**, 216–236.

Just, M. A., & Carpenter, P. A. Verbal comprehension in instructional situations. In D. Klahr (Ed.), *Cognition and instruction*. Hillsdale, N.J.: Lawrence Erlbaum Associates, 1976.

Kintsch, W. *The representation of meaning in memory*. Hillsdale, N.J.: Erlbaum Associates, 1974.

Lorayne, H., & Lucas, J. *The memory book*. New York: Stein & Day, 1974.

Love, T., & Hunt, E. Information processing characteristics of very good memorizers. Technical Report, Department of Psychology, University of Washington, October 1975.

Lunneborg, C. Choice reaction time and psychometric performance revisited. University of Washington Educational Assessment Center Report, 76–7, October 1975.

Norman, D., & Rumelhart, D. *Explorations in cognition*. San Francisco: Freeman, 1975.

Posner, M., & Mitchell, R. F. Chronometric analysis of classification. *Psychological Review*, 1967, 74, 392–409.

Posner, M., Boies, S., Eichelman, W., & Taylor, R. Retention of visual and name codes of single letters. *Journal of Experimental Psychology*, 1969, 79, No. 1, pt. 2, 1–16.

Rose, A. Human information processing: An assessment and research battery. Technical Report No. 46 for the Air Force Office of Scientific Research, University of Michigan Human Performance Center, January 1974.

Simon, H., & Hayes, J. R. The understanding process. Problem isomorphs. *Cognitive Psychology*, 1976, 8, 165–190.

Sternberg, S. High speed scanning in human memory. *Science*, 1966, 153, 652–654.

Sternberg, S. Memory scanning: New findings and current controversies. *Quarterly Journal of Experimental Psychology*, 1975, 27, 1–32.

Willerman, L. Individual and group differences. In W. Holtzman (Ed.), *Personalized Psychology*. New York: Harper, 1975.

Winston, P. *The psychology of computer vision*. New York: McGraw-Hill, 1975.

Yen, W. Sex linked major gene influences on selected types of spatial performance. *Behavior Genetics*, 1975 (in press).

INDIVIDUAL DIFFERENCES
IN INFORMATION PROCESSING:
COMMENTS ON CHAPTER 9 BY HUNT

Mary Lou Koran

University of Florida

It is encouraging to note the growing interest of cognitive psychologists, such as Dr. Hunt, in cognitive processes in relation to individual differences. Research in the basic psychology of individual differences and of learning has never been systematically combined. Yet there is increasing evidence brought forth in Hunt's work, as well as the research of others, to believe that each discipline can contribute to advancing understanding in the other, and that a more unified science of psychology may emerge from a systematic combination of the two.

From a theoretical perspective, the incorporation of individual differences into learning research and theory is important for determining construct validity for both aptitude and learning measures and for determining more explicitly the individual parameters within which more general principles of learning might be expected to be applicable. Practical interest arises from the possibility that such information can be used to adapt instruction to individual students. As Hunt has noted, if physical educators are able to regularly prescribe different regimens for the needs of their athletes, shouldn't other educators do as well?

It can be argued that all attempts to individualize instruction rest explicitly or implicitly on hypothesized interactions between aptitude and treatment variables (Snow, Shuell, & Marshalek, 1975). The search for aptitude X treatment interactions (ATI) has been the subject of many studies in recent years and a wide variety of findings now exist to suggest that aptitudes often interact with instructional variables, that is, relate differently to learning outcomes under different instructional methods (Cronbach & Snow, in press). The bulk of the evidence indicates interactions for a vaguely defined "general ability" and absence of interactions with more specialized abilities. While some of these results are plausible, few are well understood or, as of yet, applicable in practice. In addition the relative difficulty of obtaining hypothesized results in ATI research has led some researchers to the conclusion that the approach is of little theoretical or practical value.

The initial thrust of ATI research may have been ineffective because it generally failed to recognize that the theory underlying this research must consider the cognitive processes assumed to be correlated with aptitudes and induced by treatments, and the possibility that common processes underlie both kinds of variables. While information-processing models have had little application to ATI research thus far, research such as Hunt's suggests that such models in combination with laboratory experimentation may provide ideas about possible underlying and connecting mechanisms between aptitude tests and learning tasks. Represented in newly understood or newly designed aptitude measures these ideas might be further examined in more complex instructional research in which practically useful ATI may be assessed. Linked with sound theories of information processing and individual difference variables it is even conceivable that the earlier studies of the effects of more global variables can be replicated in more sophisticated fashion (DiVesta, 1975).

INFORMATION-PROCESSING MODELS
AS A THEORETICAL FRAMEWORK

While current information-processing models, such as the constituent comparison model, appear to provide a reasonable starting point, there is clearly much to be done before work on basic information-processing phenomena in learning reaches theoretical conceptions adequate for characterizing school learning.

Current information-processing models typically specify one or more parameters representing particular processing steps. These variables typically represent the speed, efficiency, or capacity of operations in particular steps. Hunt has been primarily concerned with individual differences arising from such processing steps. However, it is conceivable that individual differences may arise from several sources in addition to parameter variation on particular steps (Snow, Shuell, & Marshalek, 1975). Individuals may also differ in the sequence each pursues through a common set of steps or in the kinds of alternative steps or routes through which information is processed. The idea that there is a dual coding and processing system in memory and cognition provides an example of such variables. An additional source of individual differences might lie in summative emergent properties of the model since some measures might reflect a combination of other sources. While laboratory tasks and test items are often repetitive and noncumulative, we are ultimately concerned with individual differences in school learning which is generally cumulative. Previous knowledge and skills are closely associated with present learning, and instruction is usually designed to capitalize on this. However, repetitive laboratory tasks may also have cumulative properties such as continuing practice yielding a consistent strategy or persistent errors producing a change in strategy. Similarly, retention and transfer differences operate across trials or tasks in both laboratory and school learning (Snow, Shuell, & Marshalek, 1975).

While simple models may provide parsimonious starting points, they can be expected to be too simple in their account of individual differences in instructional learning. Thus, research in this field should attempt to recognize and distinguish clearly the various sources of individual differences within information processing models and to use such process variables in analyzing aptitude and task variables, and their interactions.

In view of the variety of aptitude and processing constructs which may be examined in current information processing models, the concept of construct validity and the importance of multitrait–multimethod designs (Campbell & Fiske, 1959) should be considered. The models currently studied in experimental cognitive psychology tend to be quite task specific. A variety of parameters and processing constructs have been derived from this work, each of which may have greater or lesser relevance to specific school learning tasks. While cognitive processes will necessarily be task specific to some extent, interest should focus primarily on processes that are generalizable beyond any one particular laboratory task. Thus, a given process should be demonstrable through measurement in independent tasks or at least correlated significantly with measures arising outside of the immediate processing task. Hunt attempts to focus on such generalizable processes in his use of a model believed to be fundamental in knowledge acquisition and his efforts to conceptualize the relationships between previous findings in terms of it.

Similarly, parsimonious interpretations of results also make it desirable to work with rather broad abilities and employ more specific interpretations only as forced to do so by the data. The use of hierarchic models of ability organization tend to promote such parsimony. Given a correlation between verbal or quantitative ability and some learning measure, for example, it cannot be determined that the relationship involves the special ability alone unless it can be shown that a more general ability cannot account for the result. The ultimate objective with respect to both the ability measures used in research on cognitive processes, as well as the process measures themselves, is to determine the minimum number of the most general constructs needed to account for individual differences in cognitive processes in learning (Snow, Shuell, & Marshalek, 1975).

It is of interest to note in this regard that for the purposes of this paper Hunt has restricted himself to the use of verbal ability scores, although presumably the quantitative scores from the Washington Precollege Battery would also be available. In employing a hierarchic model of ability organization, if both verbal and quantitative ability are related to learning outcomes in a similar manner, this would imply that a more general ability rather than verbal ability alone underlies the relationship. Although this information was not provided, it would certainly be of interest to examine the strength of these relationships. In previous work of Hunt's (Hunt, Frost, & Lunneborg, 1973) both verbal and quantitative abilities were shown to be related to particular model parameters in a similar fashion, and in some cases quantitative ability appeared to moderate the relation between verbal ability and the particular parameters considered (Snow, Shuell, & Marshalek, 1975). Such relationships are of potential importance and deserve consideration.

It is also important to recognize that a construct like verbal ability may have many parameters. Verbal ability measures, especially those used in college admissions tests such as the Washington Precollege Battery are usually composities of vocabulary, English usage, spelling, reading comprehension, and verbal reasoning, which may involve such processes as encoding speed, order preservation, and rapid memory search, as well as retrieval from long-term memory. Which combination of components accounts for which proportion of variance in a particular learning task may be difficult to determine and may also be expected to vary from task to task. Thus, verbal ability may be differently constituted, depending on the task. While laboratory tasks may study the effects of specific components of verbal ability in isolation, it is likely that more complex instructional tasks in school learning situations may deal with a number of components simultaneously. Thus, findings based on laboratory tasks are likely to suggest ideas regarding mechanisms for adapting instruction rather than provide direct generalizations to instructional situations.

EXTENSIONS TO INSTRUCTIONAL SETTINGS

In considering the application of information regarding individual differences in information processing to school learning, Hunt has observed that information processing involves more than a capacity, it involves a strategy and strategies can be learned. Ultimately if a teacher is given a careful analysis of a student's information processing capacities, it ought to be possible for the teacher to develop a training program aimed at the improvement of memory and problem solving approaches. This certainly represents one important use to which such information could be put. However there are at least two additional models for using such information (Salomon, 1972).

Some aptitudes, processes, or strategies are formed through years of cumulative experience, and deficiencies in such skills or habits may be difficult to overcome. In such cases, analysis of students' information processing capacities can be utilized to design instruction which compensates for a particular deficiency by providing for the learner what he cannot provide for himself. Conversely, such information can also be used to design instruction which capitalizes on strongly developed characteristics of the learner.

In a general sense, high-ability subjects may be expected to perform best when instructional treatments allow them to do more of the information processing work themselves, thus capitalizing on strongly developed skills. Lower-ability subjects may need treatments that compensate for learner processing deficiencies by processing critical aspects of the instruction for the learner (Snow, Shuell, & Marshalek, 1975). A study by Cromer (1970), for example, has shown that printing sentences in phrase segments allowed those readers unable to integrate separate meanings in sentences to reach the comprehension levels of good readers. Presumably segmenting the sentences into meaningful chunks compensated for the readers inability to do so. In contrast, good readers did best with conventional sentences, whereas fragmenting sentences tended to disrupt their processing. Thus, conventional sentences capitalized on processing skills already possessed by good readers, but segmented sentences appeared to circumvent certain processing weaknesses of poor readers.

It should be noted that since most aptitude test items are selected on the basis of their predictive power in our rather uniform educational programs rather than on their relationship to observed or hypothesized intellectual processes, such aptitude constructs may not be the most productive dimensions for measuring those individual differences that do interact with different ways of learning. Although Hunt has been primarily concerned with verbal ability, there are likely to be many aspects of human ability that have been largely untapped by conventional testing, but may be predictive of scholastic performance under different instructional methods. It is possible that alternative instructional treatments might be designed around distinctions such as Cattell's fluid and crystallized intelligence. Hunt has posed the question, "How do the relative contributions of information processing and knowledge change as the tasks and subjects change?," and suggests that Cattell's distinction between fluid and crystallized intelligence may be related. It is possible that closer analysis of fluid and crystallized intelligence may suggest mechanisms for capitalizing on alternative aspects of general ability. At the present time there is virtually no theoretical understanding of what might constitute desirable instructional features for those whose fluid and crystallized abilities are discrepant.

Similarly, Jensen's (1970) investigation of Level I versus Level II abilities suggests that some learners should be taught by instructional techniques that can utilize abilities manifested in rote learning while others should be taught in a conceptual or meaningful way reminding us that memory factors have repeatedly separated off in research on aptitude tests. Traditional school methods appear to be ill adapted to students who are high in Level I but low in Level II abilities. Moreover, Jenson (1970) has stated:

> At present we do not know how to teach Level I ability. Although Level I is manifested in rote learning it is not advocated that simple notions of rote learning be the model for instruction. Instructional techniques that can utilize the abilities that are manifested in rote learning are needed, but this does not necessarily imply that instruction consist of rote learning per se. We also need to find out to what extent Level II abilities can be acquired or stimulated by appropriate instruction to children who possess good Level I ability but are relatively low on Level II. (p. 190)

It would appear that exploration of individual differences in relation to various information processing models may prove extremely useful in providing answers to such questions.

While Hunt thus far has focused on individual differences in cognitive abilities, it should also be noted that information processing analysis need not be limited to cognitive abilities as individual difference variables. It is widely recognized, for example, that stylistic or personality variables can have both interfering and facilitating effects on cognitive processes. The research from which this conclusion is drawn, however, typically has not indicated which cognitive processes are affected or precisely how they are affected. Thus, these studies generally fail to indicate any specific ways in which persons could be treated or situations modified in order to maximize learning. Information processing models could conceivably be used in analyzing the influences of individual differences in noncognitive variables on cognitive processes involved in problem solving. A glimpse of this kind of analysis is provided in a study by Seiber (1969), who hypothesized that the debilitating effect of anxiety on problem solving resulted from its effect on short-term memory. Therefore, treatments providing memory support were expected to primarily benefit highly anxious learners. This expectation was supported. Depending on whether treatment and interaction effects occur that satisfy a reasonable model of information processing, this approach may permit a highly satisfactory construct explanation to be made concerning the specific ways in which noncognitive variables influence cognitive processes which in turn affect response to varying instructional methods.

SUMMARY

In brief, systematic investigation of individual differences in cognition appear now to hold the promise of making unique contributions to both the basic psychology of individual differences and of learning, and of helping to build a more unified science of psychology. Both theory and practice alike may be expected to benefit as a result. While current information-processing models such as the constituent comparison model appear to provide reasonable starting points for examining possible underlying and connecting mechanisms between aptitude and learning measures, there is much to be done before work on basic information-processing phenomena in learning reaches a theoretical conception adequate for conceptualizing school learning. Findings based on laboratory analysis of individual differences in cognition are likely to provide ideas regarding mechanisms for adapting instruction to individual differences rather than to provide direct generalizations to instructional situations. Represented in newly designed aptitude measures and instructional tasks, these ideas might then be examined in more complex instructional research in which practically useful aptitude–treatment interactions may be assessed.

REFERENCES

Campbell, D. T., & Fiske, D. W. Convergent and discriminant validation by the multitrait–multimethod matrix. *Psychological Bulletin,* 1959, *56,* 81–105.

Cromer, W. Difference model: A new explanation for some reading difficulties. *Journal of Educational Psychology,* 1970, *61,* 471–483.

Cronbach, L. J., & Snow, R. E. *Aptitudes and instructional methods.* New York: Appleton-Century-Crofts, in press.

DiVesta, F. J. Trait–Treatment interactions, cognitive processes and research on communication media. *A V Communication Review,* 1975, *23,* 185–194.

Hunt, E., Frost, N., & Lunneborg, C. Individual differences in cognition: A new approach to intelligence. In G. H. Bower (Ed.), *The psychology of learning and motivation,* Vol. 7. New York: Academic Press, 1973.

Jensen, A. R. Hierarchical theories of mental ability. In W. B. Dockrell (Ed.), *On intelligence.* London: Methuen, 1970.

Salomon, G. Heuristics models for the generation of aptitude-treatment interaction hypotheses. *Review of Educational Research,* 1972, *42,* 327–343.

Sieber, J. E. A paradigm for experimental modification of the effects of test anxiety on cognitive processes. *American Educational Research Journal,* 1969, *6,* 46–61.

Snow, R. E., Shuell, T. J., & Marshalek, B. Individual differences in learning related processes: A prospectus. Unpublished manuscript, Stanford University, 1975.

OPEN DISCUSSION
ON THE CONTRIBUTIONS
BY HUNT AND KORAN

Berliner: I see your results as similar to other findings for timed performance tests. The correlation you found is not surprising. What is it you see as unique in what you are doing?

Hunt: I think I see in much of what we are doing a verification of things which we have all believed, but which we have not had very much evidence for believing. First, the unique contribution is that we are now taking these performance tests and we are relating them to parameters which have a theoretical meaning. Let me give you an example from another source. Suppose I were to take the correlations of various aspects of motor car performance. I would never need to know about carburetors and axles and things like that. I could observe the external performance of various cars, take a bunch of measures, correlate them, and I would come up with factor loadings and such. However, those factor loadings would be a lousy description of a car. For some purposes, for example, for the purposes of predicting how the car would perform in traffic, they might work. But in terms of understanding the car in any sort of scientific sense, I would rather know about gears, axles, and compression ratios.

I cannot look inside the skull, but I am talking about parameters which have a theoretical interpretation, and about relationships between the gross performance and the theoretical parameters. That is the big difference between what I am doing and what the performance tests are doing. If I were to do all those correlations with cars, I would find that a number of measures were correlated. In fact, I would probably come out with a first principal factor that I could label "m" and call "motoric." My point is that there is no reason that the various parameter estimates that we are dealing with will be orthogonal in the statistical sense. They can be quite separate components and not reflect any underlying, general factor, just as weight of a vehicle and the width of the axle are related. There is no reason in engineering that that has to be the case. It would be possible to design a car that was long, narrow, and heavy, but they are not designed that way for a Darwinian reason: they would not survive on the market. It may be that the correlation between these different patterns and parameters produce a better human being in terms of efficiency in some way, but that is a separate question.

Anderson: I am concerned about the criterion in your speed of access study. I would want to be very, very careful in your research to make sure I got a measure of vocabulary which I knew was a "power test" in the traditional psychometric sense, otherwise you do have a tautology.

Hunt: We are careful about that. We also take tests of simple motor perfor-mance because a great concern is that we are measuring finger-pushing time. First, we are not measuring finger-pushing time in the experimental tests. So if we are just measuring time to get through an item, and writing speed, for instance, then that has to be correlated with these internal events in the experimental test because it has quite clearly ruled out motor points.

The other thing, which is something that I think all psychometricians should be worried about, is that Clifton Lunneburg (1975) has recently done a couple of studies in which he has found that motor reaction times are indeed correlated to psychometric performance. That is, simple time to press a button is correlated with many of the tests which psychometricians are now using, including tests of the French Kit. What I think happened historically is that we started out being very careful to get motor response time out, and then, as the tests evolved, we stopped checking motor response time because we all knew it was out. But it has crept back in.

Anderson: At least you did deal with that problem in some of your studies. Then a good, one-line summary of what you are saying is that slow people are literally slow. There is an educational movement which is based on just such an assumption. The way you get over the difficulty, and prevent the cumulative deficit in knowledge is by giving slow people more time. Then their crystalized capability at the end could approximate that of the fast person. Now, I do not know to what extent in the long run these hopes will be realized, but there are some at least surface appearances that programs like the Keller Plan and Individually Prescribed Instruction work.

Hunt: In general, I know of very few studies which indicate that, when initial learning is controlled, anything else very interesting happens. Once you have got it, you have got it. So I would agree with what you said, and that is what we should certainly do. However, let me become pessimistic again, and this is something that the schools can do nothing about. Let us go back to the "Ann is the writer" studies. The measure there is the speed with which you get informa-tion out. It is *in* with probability one. Everybody gets those one line questions right. If that is the case, what I am saying is that retrieval is also a problem of intelligence. Slow people are slow at retrieving. As long as you are dealing with the school situation, you can, by controlling the input, get substantial gains in getting information in (providing you can maintain the motivation of those people, which is another issue). However, in this society, if you are going to be bright, you have got to be able to solve a detective mystery before Kojak does. And Kojak has only got 50 min. So what I am saying is, yes, I am sure that the schools can help, but if a slow person is caught in a situation where the information is coming at him, and at that time the information is not under his control, the slow person is in trouble.

Brown: What about studies that have shown 160% improvement in short-term memory as a function of 10 min of training in retarded populations? You say here that you are very pessimistic about training, but you have not considered the fact that training is dramatic in certain cases.

Hunt: As your work well demonstrates, you can get dramatic improvement in retardates, but it is from a very, very low base.

Brown: How about Belmont and Butterfield (1971), where they show educable children behaving like college students? I am not happy with the argument that seems to be emerging which is that since our training has failed, we should give up training, when we have not really tried training people yet.

Hunt: No, I am certainly not saying that. I am saying, and this is very clear in my paper, that I think you should have training. However, you should not have any illusion that training is going to eliminate individual differences unless you intentionally set out to avoid having that training for those who are proficient.

Brown: One can structure the situation to take into consideration problems that certain populations have. I would have thought that is the whole individual difference approach.

Hunt: Then you get into a philosophical argument. What I am trying to say is individual differences is a variance argument. You are talking about raising a mean of the population. You should always raise the mean as high as you can. What I am saying is that once you raise that mean, I think the variances are still going to be there.

Royer: Am I correct in assuming that you are saying that there is a correlation between retrieval time from long term memory and the verbal ability test, and that retrieval time is *not* accounted for by short-term memory differences?

Hunt: No, I have not said that.

Royer: Then is the correlation accounted for by short-term memory?

Hunt: Statistically? I cannot answer that. I know of no data that can answer that. We have a study underway now directed to that.

Royer: What would be your guess about that?

Hunt: Absolutely no guess. That is a very basic question for cognitive theory, because it gets to the question of whether there is a progressive recoding or whether there are discrete stages. This is a matter of some theoretical debate which is one of the reasons that we are doing the study, but I have no guesses whatsoever on that.

Olson: I have absolutely no quarrel with the evidence that there is this systematic regularity in how people retrieve information and so on. What alarms me is the conjecture you add that this may, in fact, be a measure of mechanics, and the implicit assumption that the mechanics may be genetic. The reason that I think it is dangerous to call this mechanics is that I do not think it is established that this is really something that underlies everything else. The way I would see what you have done is to have created a couple of items which would make suitable additions to IQ tests, if you were really interested in that sort of thing. I think what is happening with IQ tests, though, is that people are coming to see them as reflecting a very narrow stripe of competence, mainly a competence to work with linguistically categorized information, arbitrarily organized to serve a particular set of culturally valued functions, but not really estimating the power of the central nervous system. For example, I would imagine that people from other traditions who were not so verbally or literately organized would have an immense amount of difficulty with these kinds of tasks. That would not say anything about their hardware; it would indicate that is not their cup of tea, for whatever reason.

Hunt: I think there are about five different things you said there, some of which I certainly did not say. Let me be clear about what I did not say, first. I know of *no* studies which give any evidence on the genetic question at all. That is absolutely open. There is no data for which that argument can be maintained. I ought to also say that whenever somebody says "genetics," you kind of hear racism lurking in the background. Genetics and racism are two separate things. You can have genetic patterns which have nothing to do with race.

I do think that there is a mechanics component to this. Reliable variance can be produced between individuals in mental tests in which knowledge (where knowledge is defined as the probability of recall of information, not the speed of recall) is not a factor at all.

As far as what would be done in another culture, your conjecture is as good as mine. You stated your conjecture eloquently. Mine happens to be completely different, but we have no data on which to decide the issue one way or the other.

REFERENCES

Belmont, J. M., & Butterfield, E. C. Learning strategies as determinants of memory deficiencies. *Cognitive Psychology*, 1971, 2, 411–420.

Lunneburg, C. Choice reaction time and psychometric performance revisited. University of Washington Educational Assessment Center Report 76-7, October 1975.

10
Processes in Acquiring Knowledge

Allan Collins

Bolt Beranek and Newman Inc.

The purpose of education must always be twofold: to teach a variety of knowledge and to teach the skills necessary for applying that knowledge to new problems or situations. These twin goals are perhaps achieved most successfully through what is usually called the Socratic method of teaching. The Socratic method originated in the Meno dialogue of Plato (1924), but the method has reappeared in different guises throughout history (e.g., the inquiry method, the case method) as it has been applied to different kinds of knowledge. The central notion is to force the student to reason for himself, to derive general principles from specific cases, and to apply the general principles that have been learned to new cases.

In the Socratic method the student learns three kinds of things: (1) specific information about a variety of cases; (2) the causal dependencies or principles that underlie these cases; and (3) a variety of reasoning skills. These include such abilities as forming hypotheses, testing hypotheses, distinguishing between necessary and sufficient conditions, making uncertain predictions, determining the reliability or limitation of these predictions, and asking the right questions when there is not enough information to make a prediction.

The objective of this chapter is to define in precise terms what the Socratic method is and how in fact it accomplishes these goals. To this end, I have examined a variety of dialogues involving the Socratic method and tried to formalize the tutoring strategy used in these dialogues as pattern-action rules or production rules (Newell & Simon, 1972), which take the form "If in situation X, do Y." The purpose of writing the rules as productions is to express the theory in a procedural formalism that is independent of the particular content. I will also try to specify the reasoning skills that each particular production rule is designed to elicit.

What is the use of such a theory? The specific use I see is in developing an intelligent CAI system (Brown & Burton, 1975; Collins, Warnock, Aiello, &

Miller, 1975; Goldstein & Papert, in press) that can apply as many of these strategies as possible in tutoring causal knowledge and reasoning. Heretofore the Socratic method has not been considered viable for education generally, because it is a one-on-one teaching strategy (though R. C. Anderson points out it can be used very successfully in a class). However, the developing technology for building intelligent CAI systems may make it possible to teach many more students with such a tutoring strategy.

More generally the reason for trying to specify the Socratic method is to move it from the domain of folk wisdom to science. By attempting to formulate the Socratic method as a set of strategies, other theorists have something specific to challenge or revise. Once science has something to chew on, it will inevitably grind the thing into shape.

A THEORY OF SOCRATIC TUTORING

While in one sense the Socratic method is a single approach that involves teaching the student to reason from cases, in another sense it is made up of a variety of specific strategies that good teachers hit upon in the course of their teaching. Some hit upon one set, some upon another, though there is usually some overlap. There is little need for teachers to verbalize these strategies, since their application only depends on an intuitive feel as to how to use them. If they are taught, they are usually taught by example. So there is no very specific body of knowledge about the Socratic method, and hence there is no theory to be extended and refined. In fact until computers provided us with formalisms for expressing "process models," it is unlikely that anyone would have thought of constructing a specific theory about such a thing as the Socratic method.

In order to develop a computational theory of the Socratic method, I have been looking at a variety of dialogues. These included some dialogues that I conducted myself to teach causal dependencies about geography (Collins *et al.*, 1975), several hypothetical dialogues developed by Anderson (1972) to illustrate aspects of the Socratic method, and several dialogues produced by the Socratic system developed by Feurzeig (Feurzeig, Munter, Swets, & Breen, 1964; Swets & Feurzeig, 1965). The objective is to extract from these dialogues most of the specific strategies that occur and phrase them as production rules. There is no guarantee of exhaustiveness in this approach, but it should be possible to capture the major strategies.

The production rules are formulated in terms of the functional dependencies in knowledge and general situations that occur in a dialogue. Different rules can often be used in the same situation and sometimes application of one can be delayed until after application of another. Similarly, sometimes one rule is a natural follow-up to another rule. So what is not apparent in the enumeration of the rules is the structure of interactions between different rules. This requires a

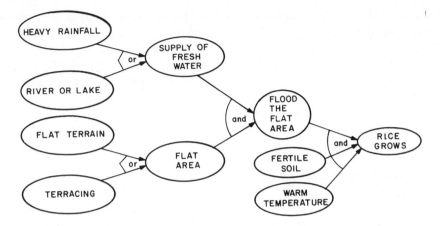

FIG. 1 A student's analysis of the causal factors affecting rice growing.

second-order theory of teaching strategy that incorporates a notion of what rules are most appropriate to invoke in different situations.

In order to explain the terminology used in the rules that will be presented, it is helpful to consider an example. Figure 1 shows the causal dependencies derived by a student in one of the dialogues that I conducted on rice growing (Collins *et al.*, 1975). Rice growing is the *dependent variable*, and in this case it is treated as having two possible *values*: either you can grow rice or you cannot. Unlike rice growing, which the student treated as a threshold function, many dependent variables are treated as continuous functions (e.g., a place is colder or warmer), where there is a continuous range of values.

During the course of the dialogue the student identified four principal *factors* affecting rice growing: fresh water, a flat area, fertile soil, and warm temperature. These were configured as shown in the diagram. The factors (or *functional determinants*) such as heavy rainfall or flat terrain are linked to rice growing through chains with various *intermediate steps.* In fact any node in a chain can be considered as a factor. The diagram itself represents only a top-level description, and any *node* or *link* in the diagram can be expanded indefinitely. Causal links expand into intermediate steps, so that for example "irrigation" can be considered an intermediate node on the chain from "river or lake" to "supply of fresh water."

Given the dependencies in the diagram, it is apparent that a factor like heavy rainfall is neither *necessary* nor *sufficient* for rice growing. It is not necessary because obtaining a supply of fresh water (which is a necessary factor) can also be satisfied by irrigation from a river or lake. It is not sufficient because other factors, such as a warm temperature, are required. When prior nodes are connected into a node by an "or," any of the prior nodes is sufficient and none is necessary with respect to that node. For example, either heavy rainfall or a river or a lake is a sufficient source for fresh water, but none of these is necessary for fresh water. In contrast, when prior nodes are connected into a node by an "and," all of the prior nodes are necessary and none is sufficient with respect to that node. For example, fresh water is necessary to flood a flat area, but is not sufficient. Though heavy rainfall is sufficient as a source of fresh water, it is not sufficient for growing rice, because of the "ands" in the causal structure between rainfall and rice. By moving down any of the chains, one gets to a higher level of abstraction. But it is not always helpful to know only the most general causes (i.e., the nodes immediately prior to the dependent variable), because the information available about a particular case is often restricted to specific factors further back in the causal structure.

There are different kinds of dependent variables: some vary continuously as do temperature or rainfall, and some vary discretely. For example, different diseases can be regarded as different values on a single dimension of what is wrong with a patient. Wheat, rice, and corn can be regarded as different values on a dimension of what grain can be grown in a given region. There are several differences between the discrete and continuous cases. First, in the discrete case there may be more or less than one of the values for the dependent variable present (e.g., a patient may have more than one disease or no disease at all), whereas in the continuous case there can only be one value. Second, in the discrete case different causal factors may be *relevant* for the prediction of different values on the dependent variable (what factors are relevant for predicting mumps may be different from cancer), whereas in the continuous case the same factors are always relevant or irrelevant for making a prediction.

There is a third difference that cuts across the discrete—continuous distinction. In cases such as medical diagnosis or electronic troubleshooting, the causality runs from the dependent variable to the functional determinants (e.g., the disease causes the symptoms), whereas in cases like grain growing or temperature the causality runs from the functional determinants to the dependent variable. In the case of identifying a letter from its features there is no causality in either direction, but still different letters can be treated as values of the dependent variable and the features as different factors. Despite these differences in the domains of knowledge studied, it turns out the tutoring strategies can be characterized in a single framework.

I have listed below the rules (or important strategies) derived so far, as well as brief explanations of why they are effective strategies. Examples of each are given in terms of the causal factors for average temperature or for growing rice. More examples will occur in the following section where the rules are illustrated by some of the actual dialogues from which they were derived.

Rule 1:   Ask about a known case.
If
(1) it is the start of a dialogue, or
(2) there is no other strategy to invoke,

then

(3) pick a well-known case and ask what the value of the dependent variable is for that case, or

(4) ask the student if he knows a case with a particular value of the dependent variable.

Example: Ask the student "Do they grow rice in China?" or "Do you know any place where rice is grown?"

Reason for use: It brings out any well-known facts the student knows about such as rice growing in China.

Rule 2: Ask for any factors.

If

(1) a student asserts that a case has a particular value of the dependent variable, then

(2) ask the student why.

Example: If a student says they grow rice in China, ask why.

Reason for Use: This determines what causal factors or chains the student knows about.

Rule 3: Ask for intermediate factors.

If

(1) the student gives as an explanation a factor that is not an immediate cause in the causal chain,

then

(2) ask for the intermediate steps.

Example: If the student mentions monsoons in China, as a reason for rice growing, ask "Why do monsoons make it possible to grow rice in China?"

Reason for Use: This insures that the student understands the steps in the causal chain, for example, that rice needs to be flooded.

Rule 4: Ask for prior factors.

If

(1) the student gives as an explanation a factor on a causal chain in which there are also prior factors,

then

(2) ask the student for the prior factors.

Example: If the student mentions water as a factor in growing rice, ask him "What do you need to have enough water?"

Reason for Use: Same as Rule 3.

Rule 5: Form a general rule for an insufficient factor.

If

(1) the student gives as an explanation one or more factors that are not sufficient,

then

(2) formulate a general rule asserting that the factor given is sufficient and ask the student if the rule is true.

Example: If the student gives water as the reason they grow rice in China, ask him "Do you think any place with enough water can grow rice?"

Reason for Use: This forces the student to pay attention to other causal factors.

Rule 6: *Pick a counterexample for an insufficient factor.*

If

(1) the student gives as an explanation one or more factors that are not sufficient, or

(2) agrees to the general rule in Rule 5,

then

(3) pick a counterexample that has the right value of the factor(s) given, but the wrong value of the dependent variable, and

(4) ask what the value of the dependent variable is for that case, or

(5) ask why the causal dependence does not hold for that case.

Example: If a student gives water as the reason they grow rice in China or agrees that any place with enough water can grow rice, pick a place like Ireland where there is enough water and ask "Do they grow rice in Ireland?" or "Why don't they grow rice in Ireland?"

Reason for Use: Same as Rule 5.

Rule 7: *Form a general rule for an unnecessary factor.*

If

(1) the student gives as an explanation one or more factors that are not necessary,

then

(2) formulate a general rule asserting that the factor is necessary and ask the student if the rule is true.

Example: If a student says rainfall is a reason for growing rice, ask "Do you think it is necessary to have heavy rainfall in order to grow rice?"

Reason for Use: This forces the student to consider the necessity of a particular factor.

Rule 8: *Pick a counterexample for an unnecessary factor.*

If

(1) the student gives as an explanation one or more factors that are not necessary, or

(2) the student agrees to the general rule in Rule 7,

then

(3) pick a counterexample with the wrong value of the factor and the correct value of the dependent variable, and

(4) ask the student what the value of the dependent variable is for that case, or
(5) ask why the causal dependence does not hold in that case.

Example: If the student gives rainfall as a reason for growing rice, ask "Do you think they can grow rice in Egypt?" or "Why do they grow rice in Egypt when they don't have much rainfall?"

Reason for Use: Same as Rule 7.

Rule 9: *Pick a case with an extreme value.*

If
(1) the student is missing a particular factor,
then
(2) pick a case with an extreme value of that factor and ask why the dependent variable has a particular value in that case.

Example: If the student has not mentioned temperature with respect to rice growing, ask "Why don't they grow rice in Alaska?"

Reason for Use: This forces the student to pay attention to any factor he is ignoring.

Rule 10: *Pose a misleading question.*

If
(1) there is a case in which a secondary factor overrides the primary factors,
then
(2) pose a misleading question to the student, based on the fact that the value of the dependent variable is different from what would be predicted from the primary factors above, or
(3) pose a misleading choice as to the dependent variable between two cases in which consideration of the primary factors alone leads to the wrong prediction.

Example: Because the tree cover in the Amazon jungle keeps the temperature down to a high of about 85 degrees, ask the student "Do you think the temperatures in the Amazon jungle reach a 100 degrees?" or "Do you think it gets hotter in the Amazon jungle or Texas?"

Reason for Use: This forces the student to learn about common exceptions, about secondary factors, and about the limitations of general rules.

Rule 11: *Specify how the variable depends on a given factor.*

If
(1) the student mentions a factor, but does not specify how the dependent variable varies with that factor, or
(2) only partially specifies the relationship,
then
(3) ask him to specify the relationship more precisely, or
(4) suggest a possible relationship to him.

Example: Ask the student "Can you say how temperature depends on latitude?" or "Does average temperature increase linearly the further south you go?"

Reason for Use: This forces the student to specify more precisely the functional relation between the factor in question and the dependent variable.

Rule 12:   *Probe for a necessary factor.*

If

(1) a student makes a wrong prediction of the dependent variable because he has not identified one or more necessary factors,

then

(2) tell him he is wrong, and ask him to formulate a hypothesis about another factor that is necessary.

Example: If a student thinks they can grow rice in Ireland because of the heavy rainfall, point out they cannot grow rice there and ask "Can you make a hypothesis about what other factor is necessary for rice growing?"

Reason for Use: This forces the student to use hypothesis formation as a systematic strategy for dealing with unexplained problems.

Rule 13:   *Probe for a sufficient factor.*

If

(1) a student makes a wrong prediction of the dependent variable because he treats a factor as necessary when it is not,

then

(2) tell him he is wrong, and ask him to formulate a hypothesis about another factor that might be sufficient.

Example: If a student thinks they cannot grow rice in Egypt because there is little rain, point out they can grow rice there and ask "Can you think of what other factor makes it possible to grow rice there?"

Reason for Use: Same as Rule 12.

Rule 14:   *Probe for differences between two cases.*

If

(1) a student cannot think of a factor that could account for different values of the dependent variable between two cases,

then

(2) ask him to consider what the differences are between the two cases that might account for the difference in the dependent variable.

Example: If a student cannot think of why they can grow rice in China but not in Alaska, ask what the differences are between China and Alaska that might account for the difference in rice growing.

Reason for Use: Same as Rule 12.

Rule 15: Request a test of the hypothesis about a factor.

If

(1) the student has formulated a hypothesis about how the dependent variable is related to a particular factor,

then

(2) ask him how it could be tested.

Example: Ask the student "If you want to test whether distance from the ocean affects temperature, would you compare the temperature in January for St. Louis with Washington, D.C. or Atlanta?"

Reason for Use: By getting the student to test hypotheses, it forces him to learn to control other factors that might affect the variable.

Rule 16: Ask for a prediction about an unknown case.

If

(1) a student has identified all the primary factors that affect the dependent variable,

then

(2) pick a case that is either hypothetical or unlikely to be known and ask the student to predict the likely value of the variable for that case.

Example: If the student has identified the factors that affect rice growing, then ask "Do you think they can grow rice in Florida?"

Reason for Use: This forces the student to use the factors he has accumulated in a predictive way.

Rule 17: Ask what are the relevant factors to consider.

If

(1) the student cannot make a prediction,

then

(2) ask the student what are the relevant factors to consider.

Example: Ask the student "If you cannot predict whether they grow rice in Florida, what factors do you need to consider?"

Reason for Use: This teaches the student to ask the right questions in trying to make reasonable predictions about new cases.

Rule 18: Question a prediction made without enough information.

If

(1) a student makes a prediction as to the value of the dependent variable on the basis of some set of factors, and

(2) there is another value consistent with that set of factors,

then

(3) ask the student why not the other value.

Example: If the student predicts they grow wheat in Nigeria because it is fertile and warm, ask him why not rice.

Reason for Use: This forces the student not to jump to conclusions without enough information.

Rule 19:   *Point out irrelevant factors.*
If
(1) the student asks about the value of an irrelevant factor in trying to make a prediction,
then
(2) point out the factor is irrelevant, or
(3) ask whether the irrelevant factor affects the dependent variable.

Example: If the student asks whether Denver or Salt Lake City is further west in trying to decide which has the colder temperature, then point out that longitude does not matter, or ask whether longitude affects temperature.

Reason for Use: This forces the student to learn what is irrelevant, as well as what is relevant, in making any decision.

Rule 20:   *Point out an inconsistent prediction.*
If
(1) a student makes a prediction about the dependent variable which is inconsistent with any of the values of the factors discussed,
then
(2) point out the inconsistency, or
(3) ask whether the value of the factor discussed is consistent with his prediction about the dependent variable.

Example: If the student predicts they grow rice in Spain after the dryness of the climate has been discussed, either point out that a dry climate is incompatible with rice growing unless there is irrigation, or ask how he thinks they can grow rice when the climate is so dry.

Reason for Use: This reminds the student to consider all the relevant factors in making a prediction, and insures he understands the relation between the factor and the dependent variable.

Rule 21:   *Ask for consideration of a possible value.*
If
(1) there is a value of the dependent variable that has not been considered and which either is consistent with several factors or important to consider a priori,
then
(2) ask the student to consider that value.

Example: If the student has not considered rice as a possible grain in Nigeria, ask him to consider it.

Reason for Use: This forces the student to actively consider alternatives in making any prediction.

Rule 22:   Test for consistency with a given hypothesis.

If

(1) a particular value of the dependent variable is being considered, and

(2) the values of one or more relevant factors have been discussed, but

(3) whether these values are consistent with the particular value of the dependent variable has not been discussed,

then

(4) pick one or more of the factors that are consistent with the dependent variable and ask if they are consistent, or

(5) pick one or more of the factors that are inconsistent with the dependent variable and ask if they are consistent.

Example: If the hot climate and rainfall in Java has been discussed, the student can be asked "Is the heavy rainfall in Java consistent with growing wheat?" or "Is the hot climate and heavy rainfall consistent with growing rice?"

Reason for Use: This tests whether the student understands the functional relations between the various factors and the dependent variable.

Rule 23:   Ask for consideration of relevant factors.

If

(1) a student makes a wrong prediction in a particular case, or

(2) cannot make a prediction,

then

(3) pick the most relevant factor not discussed and

(4) ask the student what the value of that factor is for the particular case.

Example: If the student predicts that the average temperature is very hot in Buenos Aires, ask if he knows what the latitude of Buenos Aires is.

Reason for Use: This forces the student to consider relevant factors in making a prediction, and elicits whether a mistake is due to wrong information about a case, or a mistake about how the dependent variable varies with different factors.

Rule 24:   Trace the consequences of a general rule.[1]

If

(1) a student agrees to a general rule such as Rule 5 or Rule 7,

then

(2) ask if he agrees with the consequences of that rule in a particular case.

---

[1] Rule 24 was added after the paper was completed and the comments by Lauren Resnick were written. This rule was needed to encompass the tracing of consequences by the tutor in Table 4 (lines 19, 21, 23, and 25). To the degree there is a grouping of the rules, it would be most appropriately grouped with Rules 5 through 8.

Example: If the student states that it is necessary to have flat terrain to grow rice, then point out that since they do not have flat terrain in Japan, they must not grow much rice and so must import most of the rice they eat.

Reason for Use: Same as Rule 5 or Rule 7.

DATA ON WHICH THE THEORY IS BASED

In this section I have included segments of some of the dialogues I have been looking at in order to specify the various tutoring strategies used in the Socratic method. Each rule from the previous section that is used in one of the dialogues is indicated in parentheses. Often the tutor is not applying one of the tutoring strategies but answering a student's question or further specifying a question. Sometimes, however, he may be applying a strategy that has not yet been incorporated into the theory, through ignorance or oversight.

Tables 1 and 2 show fragments of two of the dialogues I conducted to teach different causal interdependencies in geography (Collins *et al.*, 1975). These dialogues show heavy use of the counterexample strategies (Rules 6 and 8) and the strategies directed toward getting the student to make predictions using the factors he accumulated. The student appeared to be learning a great deal in these dialogues, as is detailed in Collins *et al.* (1975).

Table 1 includes fragments from a dialogue about grain growing (in particular, rice, wheat, and corn) conducted with a rather sophisticated student. The beginning section of Table 1 (lines 1–10) illustrates the use of both counterexample strategies. In one case (line 5) the tutor chose Washington and Oregon because they have a lot of water, but no rice; in the other case (line 9) he chose Japan because it is mountainous, but has rice. In the first case enough water was not sufficient for growing rice; in the second case flat land was not necessary for growing rice.

The next three segments of Table 1 show the tutor asking for predictions about unknown cases (lines 11, 13, and 15) after the student had developed the structure of causality about rice growing depicted in Fig. 1. In the last case the student incorrectly predicted that wheat is grown in Nigeria, so the tutor asked him to consider the relevant factors one by one. After doing this the student changed his prediction to rice, which was correct.

Table 2 shows the middle of a dialogue on population density with a less sophisticated student than the one above. To get this student to think about the relevant factors, it was often necessary to use a strategy of picking a case which has an extreme wrong value on one of the factors that affects the dependent variable (i.e., population density). Thus, northern Africa (line 1) was chosen to elicit discussion about water, Tibet (line 12) to elicit discussion about mountains, and Alaska (line 18) to elicit discussion about cold climate. The extreme

TABLE 1

Fragments of a Dialogue on Growing Grain[a]

---

1 T: Where in North America do you think rice might be grown? (Rule 1: Ask about a known case)

2 S: Louisiana.

3 T: Why there? (Rule 2: Ask for any factors)

4 S: Places where there is a lot of water. I think rice requires the ability to selectively flood fields.

5 T: O.K. Do you think there's a lot of rice in, say, Washington and Oregon? (Rule 6: Pick a counterexample for an insufficient factor)

6 S: Aha, I don't think so.

7 T: Why? (Rule 2: Ask for any factors)

8 S: There's a lot of water up there too, but there's two reasons. First the climate isn't conducive, and second, I don't think the land is flat enough. You've got to have flat land so you can flood a lot of it, unless you terrace it.

9 T: What about Japan? (Rule 8: Pick a counterexample for an unnecessary factor)

10 S: Yeah, well they have this elaborate technology I suppose for terracing land so they can flood it selectively even though it's tilted overall.

                    (section omitted)

11 T: Do you think they might grow rice in Florida? (Rule 16: Ask for a prediction about an unknown case)

12 S: Yeah, I guess they could, if there were an adequate fresh water supply. Certainly a nice, big, flat area.

                    (section omitted)

13 T: What kind of grains do you think they grow in Africa, and where, then? (Pause) Well where would they grow rice if they grew it anywhere? (Rule 16 again)

14 S: If they grew it anywhere, I suppose they'd grow it in the Nile region, and they'd grow it in the tropics where there was an adequate terrain for it.

                    (section omitted)

15 T: What do you think they live on (in West Africa)? (Rule 16 again)

16 S: I guess they grow some kind of grain in West Africa.

17 T: What kind is most likely?

18 S: Wheat.

19 T: You think wheat is the most likely grain?

20 S: Wheat or some combination of wheat and rice if they can grow it, and I suppose they could. I don't really know much about the geography there, but I suppose there are places, like Nigeria is pretty damn fertile.

---

continued

TABLE 1 *(continued)*

---

21 T: O.K. its fertile but what other qualities? Is the temperature warm or cold? (Rule 23: Ask for consideration of different factors)

22 S: Yeah, the climate's temperate and . . .

23 T: Do they have rain or not? (Rule 23 again)

24 S: Yeah.

25 T: They have a lot of rain. O.K. What do those kind of configurations predict as far as grain? (Rule 16 again)

26 S: Rice.

---

[a]After Collins *et al*. (1975).

value in each case forced the student to pay attention to a relevant factor she was ignoring.

In the discussion about Alaska, the tutor's probing for various intermediate and prior factors led the student to construct a somewhat complex network of causal interconnections. In particular, the student suggested that cold climate leads to low population density by three causal chains: one through agricultural problems, one through fuel needs, and one through people's desire not to settle in cold climates. Earlier two other factors, dryness and mountains, had been causally linked to agricultural problems. This illustrates the complex interconnections that can occur among causal chains.

Table 3 is a hypothetical dialogue developed by Anderson (1972) to illustrate the power of the Socratic method as a teaching strategy. What is most important about the teaching strategies in this dialogue is the way they force the student to use hypothesis formation and testing as systematic strategies for reasoning about causal dependencies.

In Table 3 the initial question by the tutor was designed to entrap the student into saying that Newfoundland is colder than Montana, because its latitude is further north, when in fact Newfoundland is warmer, because of the ocean. A similar kind of entrapment occurred in one of my dialogues, in which the question was designed to elicit a wrong prediction about the value of the dependent variable:

(T) Is it very hot along the coast here? (Points to Peruvian Coast near the equator.) (Rule 10: Pose a misleading question where a secondary factor overrides the primary factor.)

(S) I don't remember.

(T) No. It turns out there's a very cold current coming up along the coast; and it bumps against Peru, and tends to make the coastal area cooler, although it's near the equator.

TABLE 2

Fragments from the Middle of a Dialogue on Population Density[a]

---

1 T: In Northern Africa is there a large population density there? (Rule 9: Pick a case with an extreme wrong value)

2 S: In Northern Africa? I think there is.

3 T: Well there is in the Nile valley, but elsewhere there is not. Do you have any idea why not? (Rule 12: Probe for a necessary factor)

4 S: Because it's not good for cultivating purposes?

5 T: It's not good for agriculture?

6 S: Yeah.

7 T: And do you know why? (Rule 4: Ask for prior factors)

8 S: Why?

9 T: Why is the farming at a disadvantage?

10 S: Because it's dry.

11 T: Right.

(section omitted)

12 T: Do you know why there is sparse population in Tibet now? (Rule 9 again)

13 S: Because its desert?

14 T: No.

15 S: No? I don't know. Oh you said it was mountainous.

16 T: Very mountainous.

17 S: So it isn't good farmland.

18 T: OK. It's very tough to farm when you have mountains there. You only have valleys to farm in. O.K. Now do you think its very dense in Alaska? (Rule 9 again)

19 S: No.

20 T: Why? (Rule 2: Ask for any factors)

21 S: I would imagine because of the cold.

22 T: The cold climate. And why does a cold climate ... ? (Rule 3: Ask for intermediate factors)

23 S: There again you would have the problem of farming and agriculture.

24 T: O.K. And are there possibly other reasons why a cold climate leads to low density? (Rule 3 again)

25 S: Yeah. You would use up more heat and fuel. They wouldn't think of it as a desirable place to locate.

---

[a]After Collins *et al.* (1975).

TABLE 3

A Hypothetical Dialogue by R.C. Anderson (1972)

---

1 T: Which is likely to have the coldest winter days, Newfoundland or Montana? (Rule 10: Pose a misleading choice where a secondary factor overrides the primary factor)

2 S: Newfoundland.

3 T: Please give your reasons for answering Newfoundland. (Rule 2: Ask for any factors)

4 S: Newfoundland is further north.

5 T: Yes, Newfoundland is further north than Montana. Are you arguing, then, that if you take any two places in the Northern Hemisphere, the one which is further north will have the lower average winter temperature? (Rule 5: Formulate a general rule for an insufficient factor)

6 S: Yes, I guess so.

7 T: I'll tell you now that Montana has lower average winter temperatures than Newfoundland. Does this fact cause you to change your reasoning? (Rule 12: Ask for another necessary factor)

8 S: Yes.

9 T: In what way?

10 S: Being further north isn't as important as I thought.

11 T: Please try to be more precise. Would you, for instance, say that if you take any two places in the Northern Hemisphere, the one furthest south has the colder winter temperatures? (Rule 11: Specify the relationship between a factor and the variable)

12 S: No, I wouldn't say that.

13 T: What would you say? (Rule 11 again)

14 S: I'm not sure.

15 T: Would you say that how far north a place is has no effect on temperature? (Rule 11 again)

16 S: No, I know it has some effect.

17 T: Yes, you're right. Distance north does affect temperature, so what do you conclude? (Rule 12 again)

18 S: I don't understand the question.

19 T: You know that how far north a place is situated, is one factor that affects the temperature. Yet, you also know that, even though it is further north, Newfoundland has higher average winter temperatures than Montana. What must this mean? (Rule 12 again)

20 S: Some other factor besides north-south distance must also affect temperature.

21 T: Yes! Right! What could this factor be?

22 S: I don't have any idea.

---

continued

TABLE 3 (*continued*)

---

23 T: Why don't you look at your map of North America. Do you see any differences between Montana and Newfoundland? (Rule 14: Ask for differences between two cases)

24 S: Montana is in the centre of the country. Newfoundland is on the ocean.

25 T: What do you mean by "in the centre of the country?"

26 S: It's a long way from the ocean.

27 T: Do you suppose that distance from the ocean affects temperature?

28 S: I'm not sure. It would just be a guess.

29 T: True! The name for such a guess is hypothesis. Supposing the hypothesis were correct, what exactly would you predict? (Rule 11 again)

30 S: The further a place is from the ocean, the lower the temperature will be in the winter.

31 T: How could you test your hypothesis? (Rule 15: Ask for a test of hypothesis about a factor)

32 S: By comparing temperatures of places different distances from the ocean.

33 T: Very good. Let's do that. Suppose we take St. Louis, Missouri. Which would be best to compare, Atlanta, Georgia, or Washington, D.C.? (Rule 15 again)

34 S: I'm not sure.

35 T: Why don't you look at your map? Maybe that will help you decide.

36 S: I would pick Washington.

37 T: Why?

38 S: Because it's at the same latitude as St. Louis.

39 T: Why is that important?

40 S: Well, if Atlanta were warmer, I wouldn't know whether it was because it was nearer the ocean or further south.

41 T: Good thinking.

Like the counterexample and extreme value strategies this strategy involves the careful selection of cases to bring up certain factors.

In line 5 the tutor formulated a general rule, which was incorrect, by suggesting that the insufficient factor (latitude) mentioned by the student was sufficient to determine the dependent variable temperature (Rule 5). This strategy is an alternative to selecting a counterexample by Rule 6 ("London is further north than New York and yet it's warmer") or telling the student he is wrong and asking for another factor that affects temperature (Rule 12). Though it did not occur in any of the dialogues, there must also be the possibility of formulating a general rule (Rule 7) by asserting that an unnecessary factor the student mentions is necessary.

When the student agreed to the general rule, the tutor pointed out the error (line 7) and started a series of questions designed to force the student to figure out that distance from the ocean affects temperature. By applying Rule 12 in line 7 and again in lines 17 and 19, the tutor tried to get the student to hypothesize another factor that might account for his error in prediction. In lines 11, 13, and 15 he tried to test the student's understanding of the relation between latitude and temperature (Rule 11). Finally, in line 23 he asked the student to consider what differences between the two cases might account for the effect on the dependent variable (Rule 14), and this succeeded in eliciting distance from the ocean.

The tutor then tried to get the student to test the hypothesis he had formulated; first by asking a very general question (line 31), and then a quite specific question (line 33). In lines 35, 37, and 39 the tutor appears to be using variations of several of the rules (Rules 14, 2, and 4, respectively) with a dependent variable something like "good versus bad comparison in order to test the effect of distance from the ocean," but it is not clear to me how to fit the rules above, or any other rules, to the three questions. This failure suggests that the rules as presently formulated are too close to the surface structure of the dialogue.

The hypothetical dialogue by Anderson in Table 4 illustrates the use of the Socratic strategy for tutoring moral causation. It shows an extended use of two

TABLE 4

A Hypothetical Dialogue by R. C. Anderson (1972)

---

1 T: If you'd been alive during the American Revolution, which side would you have been on? (Rule 1: Ask about the value of the dependent variable for a known case)

2 S: The American side.

3 T: Why? (Rule 2: Ask for any factors)

4 S: They were fighting for their rights.

5 T: You admire people who fight for their rights. Is that true? (Rule 5: Formulate a general rule for an insufficient factor)

6 S: Yes.

7 T: How about the young men who broke into the draft office and burned the records? Do you admire them? (Rule 6: Pick a counterexample to the general rule)

8 S: No, what they did was wrong.

9 T: I thought you said you admired people who fight for their rights (Rule 20: Point out an inconsistent prediction); so why don't you admire the draft resistors? (Rule 21: Ask for consideration of a possible value)

---

continued

TABLE 4 *(continued)*

---

10 S: I do admire them in a certain sense, but what they did was wrong.

11 T: What was wrong about it? (Rule 4: Ask for prior factors)

12 S: They broke the law.

13 T: Why is that wrong? (Rule 3: Ask for intermediate factors)

14 S: It's obvious. If everyone broke the law there would be chaos.

15 T: You are saying that what the draft resistors did was wrong because they broke the law. The American revolutionaries broke the laws, too. Therefore, to be consistent, you would have to say that what they did was wrong. (Rule 6: Pick a counterexample for an insufficient factor)

16 S: That was different. Those were unjust laws. They didn't recognize the authority of the government of that time.

17 T: The draft resistors say that the war in Viet Nam is immoral. They say that they have the right, in fact a moral obligation, to defy the laws that support this war. (Rule 6 again).

18 S: I don't think Viet Nam is such a good thing, but you just can't have individuals deciding which laws they are going to obey.

19 T: So, you would say the American revolutionaries should have followed the law. (Rule 24: Trace the consequences of a general rule)

20 S: Yes, I guess so.

21 T: If they had obediently followed all the laws we might not have had the American Revolution. Is that right? (Rule 24 again)

22 S: Yes.

23 T: They should have obeyed the laws even if they believed they were unjust. Is that right? (Rule 24 again)

24 S: I'm not sure. I suppose I have to say yes.

25 T: In other words what the American revolutionaries did was wrong. That's true isn't it? (Rule 24 again)

26 S: No, damn it. They were in the right. They were fighting for their liberty. They didn't have any voice in the government. There was taxation without representation.

27 T: So you would say that people do have a right to disobey laws if they don't have a voice in the government? (Rule 5: Formulate a general rule for an insufficient factor)

28 S: Yes.

29 T: The draft resistors don't have a voice in the government. According to what you have said, this means they do have a right to disobey the draft laws. Is that true? (Rule 6 again)

30 S: No. We have a democracy. The President and Congress are elected by the people. Therefore, the draft resistors are represented. They do have a voice.

---

similar cases to elicit causal factors that can account for the student's assertion that the cases differ on the dependent variable (i.e., whether the rebels should be admired or not). A similar extended comparison of two cases occurred in a dialogue on population density (Collins *et al.*, 1975) in which the comparison was between Java with high density and other Indonesian islands with low density. Comparison of cases is intrinsic to the Socratic strategy, and similar cases that have different values for the dependent variable usually require the most extensive elaboration of the underlying causal structure to explain.

Figure 2 shows the causal structure that was derived by the student during the dialogue. I have depicted it here to help explain how the Socratic rules were applied in this dialogue fragment. There are two aspects of the diagram that differ from Fig. 1: the explanation link and the disenabling link, both of which relate causal links to other nodes. In a more detailed representation these two kinds of links would be attached to causal nodes with antecedent and consequent links (see Norman, Rumelhart, & the LNR Research Group, 1975). The explanation link is a formalism to allow for expansion of any causal link into its intermediate steps, which the student was forced to do by one of the teacher's questions. The notion of disenablement derives from Abelson (1973), and was necessary to characterize the way the student treated certain concepts as negating other causal dependencies.

The dialogue starts with the teacher picking a well-known case, the American revolution, and asking for the value of the dependent variable "which side to support." The student said he would support the American side, because they fought for their rights. This established the first causal dependency in Fig. 2. In

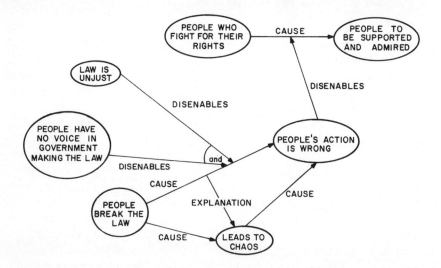

FIG. 2   The causal structure built up by the student during the dialogue in Table 4.

line 5, as in the earlier dialogue, the tutor formulated the student's explanation as a general rule, altering slightly the dependent variable from "support" to "admire." Again the student agreed with the general principle, but instead of telling the student he was wrong, the tutor responded with a counterexample. He chose as a counterexample a group of people the student was not likely to admire, but who were fighting for their rights. In order to deal with this counterexample the student declared that the causal dependency above was disenabled when the people's actions were wrong. This established the first disenablement in Fig. 2.

The tutor further elaborated the student's causal structure by several "why" questions that established the notion that breaking the law leads to actions being wrong. Then the tutor in line 15 brought up the American revolutionaries as a counterexample, because they too broke the law, though the student did not regard their actions as wrong. To deal with this counterexample, the student developed the disenablement that unjust laws are all right to break. Then the tutor in line 17 returned again to the draft resistors as a counterexample, because they too broke what they considered to be unjust laws. At this point the student temporarily gave up the disenablement he had proposed. But in tracing the consequences of the causal structure built up (lines 19–25), he realized that another disenabling condition ("the people having no voice in the government" together with "unjust laws") will differentiate the American revolutionaries from draft resistors. Thus the dialogue ended with a partial victory by the student and the development of a complicated causal structure.

Tables 5 and 6 show two short dialogues using the Socratic system (Swets & Feurzeig, 1965): in the first the student tries to identify the disease of a patient given various symptoms and in the second he tries to identify a random letter of the alphabet given various features. This was a CAI system developed to force the student to reason with causal dependencies he had already learned, such as goes on in medical diagnosis. This system is particularly rich in strategies for dealing with predictions by the student, and, in particular, forcing him to consider relevant factors, to ignore irrelevant factors, and to consider alternative hypotheses.

Table 5 is from the middle of a dialogue in which the student had earlier collected a large amount of data about the particular case. The fragment starts out by testing the student's ability to make a prediction about the dependent variable for this case, in which the correct solution is unknown. There are two rather nice strategies that occurred after this. One strategy (line 9) involved asking the student to consider a hypothesis about the dependent variable other than the one generated by the student himself. The other strategy (lines 5, 7, and 11) involved asking the student to consider whether various symptoms (or factors) were consistent with the value of the dependent variable being considered. Both of these strategies tested the student's knowledge of how different factors relate to different values of the dependent variable.

TABLE 5

Dialogue with the Socratic System on Medical Diagnosis[a]

---

1 T: We've got a fair amount of information – at least enough to raise some, perhaps several, diagnostic possibilities. Have you any in mind? (Rule 16: Ask for a prediction about an unknown case)

2 S: Yes.

3 T: Name one.

4 S: Pulmonary infarction.

5 T: Fine. Pleural pain, dyspnea, fever, and the physical exam signs and symptoms are certainly consistent with pulmonary infarction. Do you think that shaking chills and the presence of rusty sputum further support this diagnosis? (Rule 22: Test for consistency with a given hypothesis)

6 S: No.

7 T: Right. Though the white count is consistent, isn't it? (Rule 22 again)

8 S: No.

9 T: Wrong. The white count is consistent. This should further support your diagnosis. We've considered one possibility. Do you have another diagnosis in mind? (Rule 16 again)

10 S: No.

11 T: In that case I'd like to talk about viral pneumonia. (Rule 21: Ask for consideration of a possible value). The tachycardia, high WBC, elevated respiratory rate, shaking chills, bloody sputum, and severe pleural pain all lend weight to that diagnosis – right? (Rule 22: Test for inconsistency with a given hypothesis)

12 S: Yes.

13 T: You're way off base. There's not an iota of truth to any part of what I just said; in fact, the opposite of what I said is true. You'd better review some elementary medicine, doctor.

---

[a]After Swets and Feurzeig (1965). (Copyright 1965 by the American Association for the Advancement of Science.)

In Table 6 three other strategies occurred which teach important reasoning skills. One strategy (lines 9 and 11) questions any predictions that are made without enough information. Another strategy (line 13) questions the student if he asks about information that is irrelevant to predicting the value of the dependent variable. The third strategy (line 17) points out when a prediction is inconsistent with the factors that have been discussed. These three strategies stress the skills of asking the right questions and not jumping to a conclusion too quickly.

CONCLUSIONS

The theory has taken the shape it currently has because of the particular dialogues that were available to me for analysis. There is a need to look at a wider range of dialogues, such as the Meno itself, in order to obtain a more complete set of rules. Furthermore, because I have not seen enough instances of each rule, the characterizations of the rules that exist are not likely to be in the most general form possible.

TABLE 6

A Dialogue with the Socratic System to Identify a Letter[a]

---

1 T: Start when ready.

2 S: CURVES?

3 T: One.

4 S: LOOSE ENDS?

5 T: Two.

6 S: OBLIQUES?

7 T: Zero.

8 S: C.

9 T: You don't have enough information yet to get the right answer. How do you know it isn't J, for example? (Rule 18: Question a prediction made without enough information)

10 S: J.

11 T: You don't have enough information yet. How do you know it isn't C, for example? (Rule 18 again)

12 S: HORIZONTALS?

13 T: Zero. That was a wasted question. It did not eliminate any possibilities. (Rule 19: Point our irrelevant factors)

14 S: VERTICALS?

15 T: Zero. Good question.

16 S: G.

17 T: Wrong. Your guess is inconsistent with the information you've been given. You must have forgotten that the right letter hasn't any horizontal lines. The letter you guessed can't be right – it has too many loose ends. (Rule 20: Point out an inconsistent prediction)

---

[a]After Swets and Feurzeig (1965). (Copyright 1965 by the American Association for the Advancement of Science.)

As the rules developed a general structure began to emerge. The first set of rules (Rules 1–15) teaches the student to formulate general principles from specific, known cases, while the second set (Rules 16–23) teaches the student to apply general principles that he has learned (abstracted) to unknown cases. Further, within the first set there is a structure among the three kinds of "Why" questions that ask for factors (Rules 2, 3, and 4). There is also a parallel structure between the three kinds of rules for handling unnecessary versus insufficient factors (i.e., Rules 5, 6, and 12 parallel Rules 7, 8, and 13). Where such structure emerges, it is possible to specify rules (as was done for Rules 7 and 13) even though they have not occurred in the data.

In order to make the theory in any sense a complete theory, it is clearly necessary to pursue the search for greater structure through further data analysis. In particular, the lack of any structure among the rules for applying known principles to unknown cases emphasizes their tentative nature. One important possibility is that there may be one-to-one correspondence between the formulation rules (Rules 1–15) and the application rules (Rules 16–23). In fact, Rule 1 in this sense corresponds to Rule 16; one asks about the dependent variable for a known case and the other for an unknown case. Trying to construct such a correspondence will turn up obvious omissions in the data-based theory presented here. For example, because there is a rule (Rule 19) for handling irrelevant factors among the application rules, it suggests there must be some such rule in the formulation rules, though there is none currently. Though the theory's origin is mired in inelegant data, it may yet find elegance through structure.

ACKNOWLEDGMENTS

This research was sponsored by the Personnel and Training Research Programs, Psychological Sciences Division, Office of Naval Research, under Contract No. N00014-76C-0083, Contract Authority Identification Number, NR 154-379. I would like to thank Marilyn Jager Adams, Nelleke Aiello, John Seely Brown, and Ira Goldstein for valiantly trying to transform the ideas in the paper into a coherent shape.

REFERENCES

Abelson, R. P. The structure of belief systems. In R. C. Schank & K. M. Colby (Eds.), *Computer models of thought and language.* San Francisco: Freeman, 1973.

Anderson, R. C. Structure and function of a Socratic teacher. Lecture given at the University of Leeds, June, 1972.

Brown, J. S., & Burton, R. R. Multiple representations of knowledge for tutorial reasoning. In D. G. Bobrow & A. Collins (Eds.), *Representation and understanding: Studies in cognitive science.* New York: Academic Press, 1975.

Collins, A., Warnock, E. H., Aiello, N., & Miller, M. L. Reasoning from incomplete knowledge. In D. G. Bobrow & A. Collins (Eds.), *Representation and understanding: Studies in cognitive science.* New York: Academic Press, 1975.

Goldstein, I., & Papert, S. Artificial intelligence, language and the study of knowledge. *Cognitive Science,* in press.

Feurzeig, W., Munter, P., Swets, J., & Breen, M. Computer-aided teaching in medical diagnosis. *Journal of Medical Education,* 1964, 39, 746–755.

Newell, A., & Simon, H. A. *Human problem solving.* Englewood Cliffs, N. J.: Prentice-Hall, 1972.

Norman, D. A., & Rumelhart, D. E., & the LNR Research Group. *Explorations in cognition.* San Francisco: Freeman, 1975.

Plato. *Laches, Protagoras, Meno, and Euthydemus* (W. R. M. Lamb, trans.). Cambridge, Mass.: Harvard University Press, 1924.

Swets, J. A., & Feurzeig, W. Computer-aided instruction. *Science,* 1965, 150, 572–576.

HOLDING AN INSTRUCTIONAL CONVERSATION: COMMENTS ON CHAPTER 10 BY COLLINS

Lauren B. Resnick

University of Pittsburgh

Collins proposes that we consider conversations between a tutor and a student — interactions that he calls Socratic dialogues — as an important method of teaching. He further proposes that we study such conversations empirically to uncover their regular features, particularly those that characterize the tutor's behavior. I find both proposals captivating. The dialogues that Collins analyzes show us students and teachers engaged in sophisticated and important kinds of intellectual behavior. The students are displaying a particular form of problem solving: using information they do have to make reasonable propositions about things they do not yet know. The tutors are attempting, with varying degrees of success, to foster this kind of reasoning. Collins is thus studying what Broudy (see Chapter 1) calls associative and interpretive forms of knowing, rather than the simply replicative. I think there can be little quarrel with the validity of this kind of thinking and knowing as a major goal of education.

An instructional conversation differs from other kinds of conversations in that one member (the teacher) holds the intention of modifying the knowledge or skill of the other. The teacher's actions in the course of such a conversation are guided in large part by judgments concerning the kind of statements and questions that will bring about the desired modifications. Whether or not dialogues of this kind are accurately labeled "Socratic," in the Platonic sense of the word, seems not really relevant to the psychological and practical importance of the work at hand. Over the years the term "Socratic" has been adopted by many people who have chosen to teach in a dialogue form. What Collins has done is simply to accept this very general usage of the term. We could as well erase the term "Socratic" and talk about dialogue teaching or instructional conversation. That is what this work is really about, and I think we would do best not to quarrel over whether some example is or is not Socratic in form or substance.

By focussing on the empirical analysis of instructional dialogues, Collins takes us beyond broad prescriptions for what might improve the quality of education. He promises a psychological theory that will account for behavior in dialogue situations. Beyond that he promises a practical set of rules for constructing effective instructional programs. To what extent does the work to date seem to fulfill those promises? How good is it, or is it likely to become, as an instructional theory?

To answer these questions, I must begin with a distinction between two kinds of instructional theory. Bruner (1964) has called our attention to the differences in form and function of two kinds of psychological theory, descriptive and prescriptive. A descriptive theory is one that attempts to tell us what it is that people naturally do. It attempts to account for behavior as observed. It is not, however, concerned with guiding intervention. That is the role of a prescriptive theory. A prescriptive theory is concerned with specifying what one ought to do in order to optimize some desired outcome. It is a theory for designers, for those who seek to modify competence. A descriptive theory might describe regularities in peoples' behavior in some instructional situation. A prescriptive theory would seek to specify what should be done, and under what conditions, to help someone learn. Prescriptive theories require, as a base, reasonably well developed descriptive theories that can account for how learners acquire and use knowledge. But prescriptive theories themselves will take different forms than descriptive, and their adequacy must be judged according to different criteria.

Collins' work has both descriptive and prescriptive aspects. In its current form, it is quite clearly only descriptive. What is actually reported here is an attempt, using existing protocols, to find some economical set of rules that can describe the observed instructional interactions. However, Collins claims for his work a long-term prescriptive goal. In fact, he opened by saying that he hopes eventually to build a CAI system that will be effective for conversational or tutorial instruction. Such a system would in itself constitute a rather complete prescriptive theory for instruction since it would, of necessity, specify what to do and when, with considerably more exactitude than we normally demand in planning for human instructional interactions. Thus, Collins' work appears to be both descriptive and prescriptive in intent, and assessment of it must take both of these goals into account.

A Descriptive Theory of Instructional Conversations

Let us begin by considering the work according to criteria relevant to descriptive theories. In the case of a descriptive theory, we will be satisfied to the extent that it is able to account for relevant data with a reasonable degree of economy. Thus, we would judge Collins' work to be successfully completed when new protocols could be successfully accounted for without adding new rules. A successful theory would also require significantly fewer rules than there are sentences in the average set of protocols. Thus, economy and scope of applicability are the main criteria for a descriptive theory of dialogue teaching. Let us attempt to apply these criteria to Collins' work.

We cannot judge Collins' work on the scope of applicability criterion at this time since there is no specification of how many or what kinds of dialogue protocols are accounted for. We are given, in the paper, only some sample protocols. In any case, since the work is in a relatively early phase, it would be premature to assess its scope. Many more protocols will have to be analyzed before the generality of Collins' rules can be estimated. The criterion of economy is more suitable for consideration at the present time.

At first glance, Collins' theory does not seem very economical. Twenty-three rules are given, and these involve complex descriptions of conditions. It is possible, however, that the verbal presentation, heavily tied to specific examples, masks some economy and regularity. To find out, I developed a chart that laid out the essential content of the rules in three categories. The first category was the condition, that is, what the student has just done. These are what Collins lists as the "If" portions of his rules. The second category is the action, something that the tutor should do. The third category is the reason for the action. Wherever I thought that conditions, actions, or reasons were identical — even if Collins' wording for them was different — I gave them the same code.[1] For example, I coded the conditions for Rules 3 and 4 identically as, "Student gives factors that are not sufficient." I also coded the reasons for Rules 5, 6, 7, 8, and 9 as, "Force attention to other causal factors." With these codings I found that a total of 16 conditions, 17 actions, and 11 reasons would combine to form Collins' 23 rules. While this is some reduction over 23 completely independent rules, it is not an elegantly simple account of dialogue behavior. Perhaps, however, elegant simplicity is too strong a criterion for a theory dealing with behavior as complex as dialogues. It seems, then, that the best we can say at the moment is that Collins' theory may be on the road to meeting a criterion of descriptive economy. We cannot tell for certain, however, until the rules are applied to many more dialogues.

A Prescriptive Theory of Instructional Conversations

A prescriptive theory must "work" — in two practical senses of the term. First, the rules of the theory should enable one to produce dialogues that look like the real ones. The CAI effort that is the eventual goal of Collins' research will

[1] I may have misinterpreted Collins' English statements or incorrectly treated two actions or two reasons as equivalent. That possibility, of course, makes my attempt less than absolutely reliable. Nevertheless, it seems useful as a "first-pass" method for assessing Collins' general approach.

provide a strong test of that meaning of working. We do not have the data before us now, but the total research and development program, if carried through to conclusion, does provide a built-in test. The second meaning of working has to do with whether the dialogues that are produced using these prescriptive rules help anybody learn anything. Collins might produce, for example, dialogues that match the real-life ones quite well; yet they might be quite useless educationally if they did not promote some important kind of learning.

Do the rules prescribe dialogues? Once the coding described in the preceding section was completed, it became possible to draw up a schematic representation of Collins' rules in a form that could help to answer this question. A portion of that representation is shown in Fig. 1. The first line should be read as, "Any time a student does A (gives dependent value for a case), the tutor should do a (ask for an explanation), in order to z (find out what causal factors the student knows)." The important feature of this Figure is that it shows the lack of a one-to-one match between conditions and actions. Two conditions sometimes lead to the same action (e.g., C and D both lead to the $c-e$ action); and sometimes a given condition leads to more than one action (e.g., C leads to three different actions). With respect to prescriptive power, convergences (two conditions leading to the same action) pose no problems. But the divergences do. If the theory is to be used prescriptively, it cannot tolerate very well rules that do not fully specify which action should follow upon a given condition.

There is, within Collins' rules themselves, a possible solution to this difficulty. The "reasons" shown at the right in Fig. 1 do not function prescriptively. They describe why a condition-action pairing might be useful; but they do not constrain the choice of action. Suppose we were to assume that the "reasons" actually function as goals that the tutor holds at any given moment. The reasons would then move to the left hand side of the production rule and become part of the condition specifying a particular action. Figure 2 shows what happens. The first rule would be read as, "If your goal is to find out the causal factors the student knows (z) and the student has just given a value for a particular case (A), then ask for an explanation (a). The second rule reads, "If your goal is to find out the causal factors the student knows (z) and the student has just given a cause that is not the only one in the causal chain (B), then ask the student for intermediate steps of the independent variable (b)." The next two rules show the power of the goal in directing action. They say that if your goal is to force attention to other causal factors (y) and the student has given factors that are not sufficient (C), then either formulate a general rule and ask if it is true ($c-e$) or give a counterexample and ask for an explanation ($d-a$). If, however, your goal is to find out causal factors a student knows and understands (z), then, given the same behavior by the student (C), you would pick a factor and ask if it would be true ($r-e$).

The effect of this shift from post-hoc reasons to conditional goals is to reduce the number of action choices for any particular situation, although not to

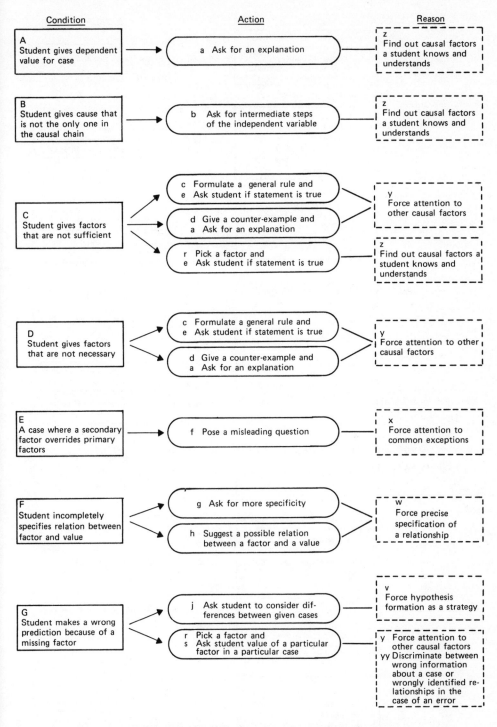

FIG. 1 Schematic representation of a subset of Collins' rules.

369

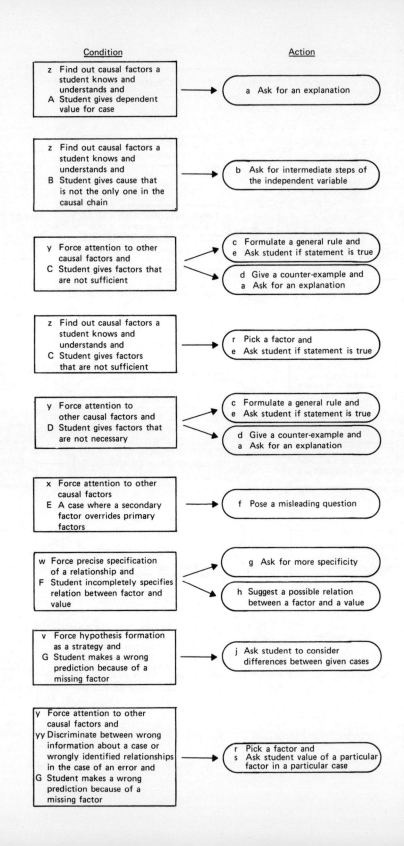

eliminate them completely. In this new form, Collins' system appears to be closer to a truly prescriptive theory. It does largely specify what the instructor should do, under conditions that include both the student's responses and the instructor's own intent. It is possible that indeterminacy might eventually be eliminated completely by a theory that also assumed that some "history" of the conversation was kept in mind by the instructor and used to decide among alternative actions. For example, it seems likely that instructors in dialogue situations seek to vary the kinds of questions they pose within any brief time span. If one assumed an ordered memory of, say, the last five actions taken, and a general rule of avoiding the most recent actions taken, some of the remaining action choices might disappear. Similar memories might be assumed for student responses so that the condition side of a rule contained not only the student's immediate response but enough about his already demonstrated knowledge or reasoning skill to suggest a particular action to the tutor.

My point here is not to either defend or attack the rules as Collins has presented them, or to defend any particular set of goals or expanded conditions. Rather, it is to suggest that goals of some kind — perhaps not identical to the "reasons" Collins has given for his rules — do function to guide tutorial dialogues, and that decisions concerning particular actions are probably not based only on immediate student responses but on at least a brief history of the student's and the tutor's actions during the dialogue itself. At least this is a proposition worth investigation. If my hypothesis is correct, then building such assumptions into the theory would enrich it as a descriptive theory. Perhaps more important, assumptions and working structures of this kind are probably necessary for the theory to function prescriptively at all.

Do the dialogues teach? Let us turn now to the second criterion for a good prescriptive theory. Assuming that dialogue actions are prescribed, do they teach anything? The answer, of course, is that we do not know at this time. There is nothing in Collins' data, nor could there be at this stage of his work, that could possibly tell us whether, in fact, doing the things specified by his rules will produce students who are good thinkers, reasoners, and users of knowledge. What data would be needed to answer such questions? The best data would be protocols of individual students in the course of a long dialogue sequence, preferably taking place over many weeks or months. Given such protocols, one might begin to determine whether students who participate in these kinds of dialogues begin to act differently — to be more specific, complete and logical about causal relations, for example. The same kinds of analyses of the students' forms of thinking that Collins has begun here for tutors might be conducted. By plotting changes in students' responses over time, it should be possible, even-

FIG. 2   Schematic representation of rules with reasons functioning as goals and forming part of the condition.

tually, to learn whether tutorial instruction, as prescribed by Collins' theory, produces thinkers who are capable of high-level forms of interpretation and reasoning.

Conclusion

It will be of the greatest interest to me to follow Collins' work as it develops. Scientific concern with reasoning and problem solving as outcomes of the instructional process is badly needed. Collins' attempt to systematically analyze instructional dialogues is, as far as I know, unique. The challenge of eventually building an automated dialogue teaching system is enormous. It is an outcome that may not be realized for a long time. Yet it is striking that the attempt itself, forcing attention as it does to the details of natural dialogues, will almost certainly yield greater understanding of the process as it occurs between human actors. This is, then, one of the sharpest illustrations I have encountered of the power of a prescriptive goal to enhance descriptive science. We would do well to look for more such examples as we seek to understand and develop the relationship between scientific research and the practice of education.

ACKNOWLEDGMENTS

Preparation of this paper was supported by the Learning Research and Development Center, supported in part as a research and development center by funds from the National Institute of Education (NIE), United States Department of Health, Education, and Welfare. The opinions expressed do not necessarily reflect the position or policy of NIE, and no official endorsement should be inferred.

REFERENCES

Bruner, J. S. Some theorems on instruction illustrated with reference to mathematics. In E. R. Hilgard (Ed.), *Theories of learning and instruction. The 63rd Yearbook of the NSSE, Part I.* Chicago: University of Chicago Press, 1964.

OPEN DISCUSSION
ON THE CONTRIBUTIONS
BY COLLINS AND RESNICK

Collins: I would like to discuss the variability in the rules as I wrote them. You have different tutors who do different things in the same situation. As far as prescriptive statements, what I had in mind was applying a particular rule depending on what was done recently. In the case where you have two possible actions in the same situation, which is where the rules as written are not well specified or deterministic, one can add additional constraints like "I did this last time; let's do something different." But I think Dr. Resnick's suggestion of having a goal in mind is even better.

Petrie: What I think this approach does is to take the very first step towards putting the production function into a cybernetic context. What you have is the condition viewed in light of the goal.

Collins: As a descriptive theory, though, it is very hard to discern the teacher's goals, so it is hard to put into the characterization what he or she was intending. However, viewed as a prescriptive theory, I agree.

Bransford: I want to comment on the ambiguity about whether it is important to base this work on a theory of semantic memory. It seems to me there is a difference between a computer description or theory of what people do and a computer as a model of how people know and grow. Your purpose here is to build a dialogue expert for tutoring, in the form of a computer. Your method seems to be to look at what good dialog tutors do in order to help people learn. The method is to prompt learners to do things in order to clarify and go beyond what they know right now. I want to argue that the method is to help them remodel their system. I do not think they just store what they heard or that kind of thing. Does this method help them do things that just telling them the information in some form could not do?

Now suppose you want to teach *teachers* to be dialogue experts, instead of building a computer as a dialogue expert. What I want to argue is that teachers do not work like computers. People do not. You cannot simply teach them the rules and have them store those and then use them in a system like a production system. They may begin with rules in a conscious manner, but gradually what they do is remodel their perspective so they think in terms of them rather than about them. Hopefully they will never be locked into a single set of strategies. Like a good detective or doctor does not simply work off a checklist, the teacher should be able to go beyond. I think that if you can build an explicit model of what you are doing, let us say as a teacher trying to learn a dialogue, you can use that to help clarify what you are doing and go beyond it. But I think there is a real difference between the computer as a model for helping you know what to do to help people go beyond, and a computer as a model of what you know, when, in fact, you have learned something.

Collins: If this were a comprehensive theory, which it is not, I am not sure whether people would go beyond or not. The reason is that I am not sure whether this is a top level or not. In other words, is there some higher meta-principle in which the rules can be characterized? That is the issue you are raising, and I just have no sense of whether this is the top level.

In one of the dialogues I taught, it is clear I was developing new strategies as I went along, in order to deal with a less sophisticated student. This is what Dr. Bransford meant by the teacher going beyond his initial set of strategies. It may be possible, however, to similarly characterize a set of higher-level generative strategies that specify how a teacher, when faced with difficulties by the student, can create new teaching strategies. These, of course, would be very difficult rules to write or even to develop a formalism to express. Though researchers in "artificial intelligence" have not yet spent much effort in trying to develop mechanisms to capture these higher-order processes, it does not mean that this is impossible. These are perhaps the most important human capabilities, and admittedly we should try harder to simulate the flexibility and growth that impresses Dr. Bransford about people.

11

The Acquisition of Knowledge in the Classroom

David C. Berliner

Far West Laboratory for Educational Research and Development

Barak Rosenshine

University of Illinois at Urbana—Champaign

A description of how knowledge is acquired in the classroom must, at a minimum, focus on the curriculum to be taught, the method by which information is communicated, and the teacher's role in fostering the acquisition of knowledge and skills so that classroom instruction is interesting, comprehensible, and pleasant. An examination of these three areas leads to some simple beliefs about how students learn in classrooms, particularly classrooms at the primary grades.

THE CURRICULUM TO BE TAUGHT

The question of what is to be taught is usually answered, at a general level, by the guidelines set forth by State Curriculum Committees. At a more specific level, the issue is settled by commercial publishers. The curriculum materials *in use*, to a large degree, define the knowledge to be acquired by students and, thus, define for the teacher what it is that is to be taught. Curriculum evaluation studies may, therefore, provide some insight into how these bodies of knowledge are acquired by students.

Walker and Schaffarzick (1974) examined over twenty studies that compared students exposed to different curricula in the same subject area. Usually, these were "horse races," comparing an innovative curriculum with a traditional curriculum. The most interesting part of their review was a comparison of results where the achievement tests of knowledge acquired from the different curriculum were analyzed by the content bias of those tests. Table 1 presents these findings.

These data make clear that "Innovative groups are overwhelmingly superior on tests biased in their direction, and traditional groups do noticeably, but not overwhelmingly, better on tests biased their way." (Walker & Schaffarzick, 1974, pp. 92–93). In one of the curriculum studies reviewed, in which a new math textbook (SMSG) was compared with a traditional textbook, it was found that the new math textbook was associated with increased student achievement on tests measuring comprehension of mathematics and with lower student performance on tests measuring computational ability. Conversely, the traditional textbook was associated with increased performance on tests of computational skills and lower performance on tests of mathematical comprehension (Wilson, Cahen, & Begle, 1970). And in an international study of mathematics achievement, it was concluded that, in general, there is a striking relationship between the national emphasis on particular curriculum areas, as rated by teachers within a country, and the student's achievement in that country (Husén, 1967).

TABLE 1

Comparisons of Innovative and Traditional Curriculum[a]

		Results		
Content bias of the tests	Number of independent comparisons	Innovative curriculum superior to traditional curriculum	Traditional curriculum superior to innovative curriculum	Innovative curriculum equal to traditional curriculum
Test of knowledge acquired favored the innovative curriculum	52	44	1	7
Test of knowledge acquired favored the traditional curriculum	30	5	9	16
Content bias of the tests could not be determined	16	4	3	9

[a]After Walker and Schaffarzick (1974, p. 92).

The conclusion that can be drawn from these reports is that one curriculum is intrinsically neither "better" nor "worse" than another, but rather that different curricula are associated with differing patterns of acquiring knowledge. What knowledge is acquired depends on the *coverage* and *emphasis* of the curriculum in use. When curricula differ, they will produce different outcomes. When curricula have common areas of concern, they will show parity, producing outcomes of equal magnitudes for those areas which were given similar coverage and emphasis.

This brief and highly selective review of curriculum evaluation leads to the conclusion that different curricula have *equipotentiality* for inducing knowledge acquisition in the classroom. Data gathered at the classroom level indicate that for differing curricula whose coverage and content emphasis are reasonably similar, the amount and types of knowledge acquired will be roughly equivalent when measured by nonbiased achievement tests.

These results, however, do not in any way imply that individual students acquire their knowledge in similar ways in differing curricula. Differing curricula require different teaching processes (e.g., inductive versus deductive methods) or can be classified as relatively structured or unstructured. These kinds of curriculum differences interact with student characteristics when analysis of curriculum outcomes includes individual student data. For example, Chastain (1970) found three clear-cut aptitude—treatment interactions where treatment was a curriculum. These interactions are presented in Table 2. Student outcomes are shown to vary in the different curricula when verbal ability is taken into account. Overall mean differences between curricula are not evident.

TABLE 2

Treatment Means on Three Measures of Outcome in Two Curriculum Areas for Different Levels of Verbal Ability[a]

Tests of acquired knowledge	Initial verbal ability	Means in foreign language curriculum	
		Audio-lingual habit theory	Cognitive code learning theory
Listening comprehension	High	15.80	20.00
	Low	17.69	14.33
Speaking analysis	High	35.00	40.62
	Low	41.62	34.00
Language aptitude	High	25.50	22.31
	Low	18.55	27.60

[a]After Chastain (1970).

Another curriculum study that analyzed data using the student as the unit of analysis examined the whole-word and linguistic (decoding) methods of teaching initial reading (Stallings & Keepes, 1970). Disordinal interactions were found between certain aptitudes measured by the Illinois Test of Psycholinguistic Abilities (ITPA) and student outcomes. In some cases, the whole-word method led to superior student acquisition of knowledge and skills in beginning reading, and in other cases, the linguistic method demonstrated superiority, depending upon the students' ITPA aptitudes.

The conclusion to be drawn from this line of research is that differing curricula have *differential potentiality* for inducing the acquisition of knowledge when the student is used as the unit of analysis. The concepts of equipotentiality and differential potentiality for inducing student acquisition of knowledge, depending upon the unit of analysis in the research study, are also useful for examining the teaching methods used to communicate the information to be acquired by students.

THE METHOD OF COMMUNICATION

Teachers have a choice of method when presenting curriculum. These methods are recurrent instructional activities, applicable to various subject matters, and include: (1) patterned teacher behavior (e.g., lecturing, discussion, recitation), (2) delivery systems for curriculum (e.g., film, computer assisted instruction, written discourse), and (3) organizational structures for promoting learning (e.g., cross-age tutoring, independent study, Keller plan).

Since teachers can usually choose the method by which they communicate information, an examination of the effects teaching methods have on knowledge acquisition is in order. In one major review, Dubin and Taveggia (1968) reanalyzed the data from nearly 100 studies that had compared variations of lecture and discussion methods at the college level. These investigators were able to make 88 comparisons between traditional lecture and traditional discussion methods, as reported in 36 experimental studies. Of these comparisons, 51% favored the lecture method and 49% favored the discussion method. In their work, they also standardized the criterion test scores from these studies, making them comparable from study to study. The differences between average test performance following exposure to lecture or discussion methods, across studies, was very close to zero.

Similar results were found in Dubin and Taveggia in reviewing comparisons of (a) lecture and lecture-discussion methods in 7 studies, (b) discussion and lecture-discussion methods in 3 studies, (c) lecture methods and supervised independent study methods in 14 studies, and (d) lecture—discussion methods and supervised independent study methods in 9 studies. The general conclusion was that teaching methods do not differ in effectiveness as measured by achievement on final examinations. However, in most school learning studies, there is an "equalizer" effect. That is, most studies of school learning with mature learners involve learning from written discourse (the text) as well as learning from lecture, discussion, CAI, etc. Students who know they will take a final examination compensate for any inadequacies in the method by which they are taught by relying heavily on the textbook. Thus, it is hard to uncover differences between teaching methods when the textbook is common to the different methods and helps to equalize achievement.

In another review of the effectiveness of different teaching methods for the acquisition of knowledge, Jamison, Suppes, and Wells (1974) examined instructional radio as a teaching method. Their conclusions indicate that instructional radio, supplemented with appropriate printed material, can be used to teach almost any subject as effectively as any of the other typical classroom teaching methods. Instructional radio was not uniquely "better" or "worse" than the other methods. Their review of programmed instruction revealed that it was generally as effective as traditional instructional methods. Overall, neither traditional instruction or programmed instruction showed great differences in effectiveness when compared with each other. In their examination of CAI they concluded that, "As in other methods of instruction surveyed in this report, no simple uniform conclusions can be drawn about the effectiveness of CAI" (Jamison et al., 1974, p. 55).

Chu and Schramm (1967) were able to make 421 comparisons of instructional television with traditional methods of instruction. Their results were as follows: In 308 comparisons, there was no significant difference between methods; in 63 comparisons, instructional television appeared to be more effective; in 50 comparisons, traditional teaching methods seemed more effective. Once again the equipotentiality of teaching methods is noted when the level of aggregation is the class.

In general, there is sufficient evidence to talk about the approximate equivalence of teaching methods when the acquisition of knowledge is used as a criterion. This in no way means that different teaching methods are equivalent in other ways. For example, it seems reasonable to conclude that programmed instruction may result in a decrease in the amount of time required for a student to achieve specific educational goals. This is an important efficiency factor. At the elementary school level, CAI has been shown to be an important supplement to traditional instruction, but associated with this teaching method are increased monetary expenditures for installing computer equipment and programs. Achievement may not be enhanced through the use of small group discussions, but the attitudes of the students participating in the discussions are often quite positive. And the motivation of students playing instructional games is obvious to any observer. Thus, many considerations enter into a choice of teaching method.

It is also important to remember that different teaching methods are likely to have differential potentiality for affecting knowledge acquisition when the student is the unit of analysis and student aptitudes are taken into account. Dowaliby and Schumer (1973) examined the relationship of anxiety to student performance in lecture versus discussion-oriented teaching methods. High anxious students performed better than low anxious students in the teacher-centered lecture situation. Students low in anxiety performed better than students high in anxiety in the student-centered discussion situation. In another study, Doty (1967) compared three different types of teaching methods: two structured methods, conventional lecture and audio-taped lecture; and one unstructured method, small-group discussion. She found that if social needs of students were high, achievement was high when the lecture and discussion methods were used ($r = .40$ and $.65$, respectively). But the higher the social needs of students, the poorer their performance when audio-taped lectures were used ($r = -.53$). When creativity of the student was examined, it was found that the correlations between creativity and achievement in conventional lecture and audio-taped lecture were negative ($r = -.21$ and $-.16$, respectively). But when the teaching method used was small group instruction, the correlation between creativity and achievement was $.37$. Thus it must be remembered that, although one teaching method may not be superior to another when class averages are examined, individual students with particular aptitudes may very well perform differently, depending on which teaching method is used for instruction. At the level of the individual student, teaching methods have differential potential for affecting knowledge acquisition.

The Effects of Curriculum and Methods on Knowledge Acquisition

The fact that socially significant amounts of knowledge are acquired regardless of the curriculum or teaching method chosen for instruction has important implications. It means that at some level yet to be understood, the information value of the material presented in the various curricula and methods is often equivalent (see Olson, 1972), at least when the class is the unit of analysis. Perhaps information that is conveyed by the various curricula and teaching methods is coded, stored, and retrieved from memory in similar ways by different people, no matter how the information was first obtained. How else can one explain that different students exposed primarily to only one teaching method or curriculum correctly classify a piece of obsidian as igneous in origin? One student may have learned his earth science through programmed instruction, another student may have learned through lecture, and another from textbooks. In one case, the curriculum may have used a process approach relying heavily on discovery by the student, and in another case, a more didactic and deductive curriculum may have been used. In each case, *symbol* systems were used and information transferred. For other students, acquisition of knowledge about earth science may have been enhanced by observing a discussion leader classify rocks. Still others may have watched a film on rock classification in which relevant cues on how to classify were highlighted by film techniques. In these ways, *iconic* representations of the information may have been established. Still other students may have gained *enactive* representations of the requisite knowledge when a tutor brought in specimens of particular rocks for handling, or, in the course of a classroom discussion or recitation, the teacher passed ou· mineral samples to be examined. To use a metaphor from Chomsky, it could be said that although the surface structure of the information being presented appeared to be quite different, at some level yet to be understood, the deep structure of the information presented to students was similar. *All* curricula and methods allowed *some* students to derive sufficient understanding of the origins of rocks to display appropriate acquisition of knowledge.

Information is presented in numerous forms and with varying degrees of efficiency to the learner who must attend, rehearse, code, store, generalize, and retrieve it. New kinds of concepts are needed to describe the nature of the learning that goes on when the deep structure of information is processed in the mind of the learner. Attneave (1974) attempted to do this when he suggested that we must posit the existence of language-like representational structures, whose elements have word-like status that provide meaning to all forms of our experience. To use another metaphor, there must be an elemental internal language which provides meaning for a student's symbolic, iconic, and enactive classroom experiences, much as a computer's machine language processes information from FORTRAN, ALGOL, or COBOL entry languages. At this elemental level of information processing, surface differences among the various curricula and teaching methods disappear. Thus, it should be anticipated that knowledge acquisition by students of similar ability levels will be roughly equivalent, at least when the content and emphasis of the curricula and methods are similar and the class is the unit of analysis.

THE TEACHER'S ROLE IN KNOWLEDGE ACQUISITION

It is no longer acceptable to take seriously those who minimize the impact of the teacher on the students' acquisition of knowledge (e.g., Coleman *et al.*, 1966; Heath & Nielson, 1974; Jencks *et al.*, 1972; Mosteller & Moynihan, 1972). Even if the percentage of variance in student outcomes accounted for by teacher behavior was merely around 20%, as is often suggested by these authors, that estimate is an annual rate. Over 12 years of schooling, enormous teacher effects on students would accrue.

Flawed though it may be, an emerging body of literature dealing particularly with children from low income families at the primary grades indicates that teacher behavior focused on direct instruction results in increased acquisition of student knowledge and skills. Teachers apparently do make a difference, particularly if they act in accordance with some of the commonsense principles that are used by instructional technologists. The data to be presented will warm the hearts of the Council for Basic Education, which for years, has stressed the importance of direct instruction.

Direct Instruction

Direct instruction means a set of teaching behaviors that focus on academic matters in which goals are clear to students, time allocated for instruction is sufficient and continuous, content coverage is extensive, student performance is monitored, questions are at a low cognitive level producing many correct responses, and feedback to students is immediate and academically oriented. The teacher controls instructional goals, choosing material appropriate for the student's ability level, and pacing the instructional episode. Interaction is characterized as structured but not authoritarian. Rather, learning takes place in a convivial academic atmosphere. These components of direct instruction will be described in greater detail.

Goal setting. A recent study assigned anthropological ethnographers to 20 more effective and 20 less effective classrooms at the second and fifth grades (Tikunoff, Berliner, & Rist, 1975). Effectiveness had been determined by measuring 200 teachers' ability to provide instruction in experimental teaching units. These teaching units were specially constructed two-week-long curriculum packages in reading and mathematics with common objectives, materials, pretests, and posttests. The amount of time each lesson was taught was controlled. The most effective and least effective teachers were chosen for the ethnographic analysis. The ethnographers carefully prepared protocols of reading and mathematics lessons during one week of instruction in each classroom. Neither the ethnographers nor the raters who analysed the protocols knew the measured effectiveness of the teachers. The analysis of the protocols of the less effective teachers, and personal observation, revealed that in many classrooms, the goals of instruction are not clear. That is, many children simply do not know what is expected of them. For example, lessons in two-column addition were given without a structuring statement linking the material to be learned to previous lessons, and without any statement of the expected outcome of the instructional episode. Seatwork often occurs without the students knowing what they are responsible for mastering. Teacher statements of the lesson's objectives or of an advance organizer for a lesson are rare. Structuring, defined primarily as the teacher's preparation of students for a particular lesson, distinguished the more effective teachers from the less effective teachers in the protocols describing second grade reading, second grade mathematics, fifth grade reading and fifth grade mathematics. Structuring, or goal setting, appears related to knowledge acquisition in the classroom and is part of an environment characterized as direct instruction.

Time allocation. Wiley and Harnischfeger (1974) examined the average number of hours of schooling for students in schools (average daily attendance X length of school day X length of school year). Variation by school was dramatically associated with the acquisition of verbal and mathematical knowledge as measured by tests of verbal ability, reading comprehension, and mathematics. Similarly, studies by Bond and Dykstra (1967), Harris and Serwer (1966), and Harris, Morrison, Serwer, and Gold (1968) all report negative correlations between teacher absences or student absences and achievement.

Stalling's (1975) evaluation of 150 Follow-Through classes revealed similar data. "Out of a possible 340 correlations between reading achievement and classroom processes, 118 were significantly related at the .05 level. Of these, the most strongly correlated variables suggest that the length of the school day and the average time a child spent engaged in a reading activity were related to high reading scores in both first and third grade" (Stalling, 1975, p. 6). And in reviewing her data on mathematics achievement, she noted: "Out of a possible 340 correlations between math achievement and classroom processes, 108 were significantly related at the .05 level. Of these, the most strongly correlated variables suggest that, as in reading, the length of the school day and the average length of time each child spent in math activities were related to higher math scores in both First and Third grades" (Stalling, 1975, pp. 6–7). In this national sample, the length of the school day varied as much as two hours per day between schools. Instructional time appears to be a powerful factor in accounting for acquisition of knowledge in the classroom.

Following up the variable of time has led us to observe classroom allocations of time from the teachers' and the students' standpoint. A reliable measure of time allocation by the teacher is easy to obtain. Typically, a teacher in the primary grades allocates 50–100 min a day to reading, and 30–50 min a day to mathematics. From an analysis of teaching protocols taken in the classes of more and less effective teachers, it was noted that when teachers become fixed by their time allocation, starting and ending lessons by the clock rather than on the basis of student behaviors, or when teachers rushed students for any reason, they appeared to be less effective in helping students achieve in academic areas (Tikunoff, Berliner, & Rist, 1975). Also, if the teacher engaged in abrupt shifts during the time allocated for a particular subject, such as switching from individual instruction in reading to behavior management, then to reading the principal's message, and then to large group instruction in reading, they were less effective teachers (Tikunoff, Berliner, & Rist, 1975). Immature learners cannot thrive when "choppy" or "disjointed" lessons occur within a given period of instructional time.

While the teacher is allocating and using time wisely or unwisely, what is the student doing about allocating his or her own time? The variable called active learning time (synonyms are engagement, attention, and on-task behavior) is easily coded. Every time a student is apparently on-task during a teacher's allocated time for a lesson, a stop watch can be run. When the student is apparently off task (looking out the window, going to the restroom, doodling, talking, etc.), the observer can stop accumulating time. Recently, in a suburban school, one of us clocked a typical child's active learning time during 45 min of seatwork on decoding skills that had been allocated by the teacher. The child was engaged with the learning task 3½ min. During a subsequent teacher-led small group meeting for developing reading skills lasting 25 min, the child was apparently engaged for 20 min.

To understand the process by which knowledge is acquired in the classroom, one must, at a minimum, be able to describe the duration of the treatment. The typical 180 days of schooling must be reduced by teacher and student absences due to illness, strikes, busing difficulties, parent conferences, etc. This result must be multiplied by the number of minutes per day allocated for instruction in a subject by a teacher. The new figure must be adjusted for the number of minutes a student allocates to active learning time. After this is done, one is likely to find that academically oriented instructional activity accounts for a trivial amount of the total activities during the school year at the primary grades. Data from McDonald *et al.* (1975) provide estimates that the median hours of on-task reading and mathematics instruction for second and fifth grade students is well under 70 hours per school year. Within-class and between-class variation is, however, quite large. Given this state of affairs, even slight increases in active learning time would appear to be logically related to increased student acquisition of knowledge. Data from many sources are accumulating to support this proposition (Bloom, 1974).

It may be concluded that at the primary grades more academic knowledge is acquired by students in classes in which (1) the schools and teachers have allocated more time for academic instruction; (2) the time used for lessons is continuous rather than disjointed; (3) teachers are activity oriented rather than bound by the clock as a guide for the length of the lessons; and (4) students are actively involved in the instructional episode so that differences between the teachers' and the students' allocation of time are minimized.

Academic focus.   Time is, of course, an empty vehicle. It must be filled. To produce academic outcomes, it must be filled with academic activities. For example, Stallings and Kaskowitz (1974) studied process variables related to reading and mathematics outcomes in first and third grade Follow-Through classes. Table 3 presents selected samples from their data. The conclusions are as expected. Academic activities are positively related to the acquisition of reading and mathematics knowledge. Nonacademic classroom activities are negatively

TABLE 3

Correlations between Classroom Process Variables and Student Achievement[a]

| | Grade and subject | | | |
| | First-grade classes (N = 108) | | Third-grade classes (N = 58) | |
Variables	Math achievement	Reading achievement	Math achievement	Reading achievement
Approximate number of children involved in mathematics	.35	.29	.60	.31
Approximate number of children involved in reading	.32	.40	.50	.32
Percent of instances in which an academic activity occurs	.21	.35	.59	.42
Total academic verbal interactions	.41	.42	.50	.29
Number of activities concerned with numbers, math, or arithmetic	.29	.26	.59	.33
Number of activities concerned with reading, alphabet or language development	.18	.40	.40	.23
Number of activities concerned with arts and crafts	−.23	−.29	−.26	−.03
Number of activities concerned with music, story telling and dancing	−.03	−.16	−.52	−.39
Amount of active play	−.26	−.23	−.29	−.10
Amount of classroom management	−.33	−.23	−.10	−.17

[a] After Stallings and Kaskowitz (1974).

385

related to the acquisition of reading and mathematics knowledge, and, of course, when classroom management problems are frequent, achievement is lower. As Rosenshine (1976) notes for the Follow-Through data as a whole,

> ... there was *no* nonacademic activity which yielded positive correlations with reading and mathematics achievement. This finding is somewhat surprising, since it has frequently been argued that some of these other activities contribute to reading achievement by motivating students or by providing additional stimulation or practice. Such indirect enhancement was not evident in this study. (p. 345)

Content coverage.   The academic focus of classroom time is not unlike the opportunity-to-learn variable so important in Carroll's (1963) theory, and a basis for the innovative mastery learning and Keller plan programs which generally work well. The academic focus provides for content coverage and emphasis, the two powerful variables that emerged from the analyses of the effects of curriculum on the acquisition of knowledge. On this issue, studies by Armento (1975), Chang and Raths (1971), Rosenshine (1968), and Shutes (1969), all found significant relationships between their assessment of the content covered by teachers and student achievement. Moreover, for Armento and Rosenshine, the correlations between the content that was covered and student achievement were larger than those obtained for any other teacher behavior variables.

McDonald's (1975) data from almost 100 second- and fifth-grade classrooms also support these findings:

> ... at both the second and fifth grade, the *amount of mathematics covered* is a critical factor. This result should not be surprising. Mathematics is an organized body of content, and tests constructed to measure what students learn in mathematics are organized around this content. If students have not been taught ... some ... concept or procedure, they simply do not do well on those portions of the test relevant to that topic. Teaching procedures which maximize the range of content covered are teaching procedures likely to be effective (p. 27)

Monitoring student activities.   Although data is not always consistent within and between studies, there is a trend in the data pointing toward the need for adult monitoring of student progress. Some results from the observations of Stallings and Kaskowitz (1974), presented in Table 4, provide pertinent information. One implication of this table is that independent seatwork or independent small group work is an inappropriate organizational structure for elementary school classrooms, while large group instructional settings appear to be more conducive to acquisition of reading and mathematics knowledge. Such is the opinion of Rosenshine (1976): "The results do not support 'individualizing' and provide support, particularly in the third grade, for the use of large groups" (pp. 353–354). But Rosenshine recognizes that these data also imply that when a teacher or other adult can monitor student activities (e.g., large group instruction versus independent seat work), achievement is higher.

It was previously noted that one student was actively engaged for 3½ min out of the 45 min of independent seatwork allocated to her by the teacher. This

TABLE 4

Correlations between Grouping Practices and Student Achievement[a]

| | Grade and subject | | | |
| | First-grade classes | | Third-grade classes | |
Grouping practice	Math achievement	Reading achievement	Math achievement	Reading achievement
Small group of children working independently in math	-.14	-.22	-.46	-.41
Small group of children working independently in reading	-.26	-.19	-.23	-.23
Teacher with large group	.07	.15	.47	.54
Large group of children with any adult	.10	.09	.42	.48

[a]After Stallings and Kaskowitz (1974).

provides an estimate of approximately 8% apparent utilization of time. In small group work, *with the teacher*, 20 of 25 min was recorded as engaged time. This represents a utilization level of about 80% of the allocated time. The difference in utilized time is parsimoniously accounted for by the presence or absence of a monitor of student activities.

Soar (1973) also studied grouping patterns in elementary school Follow-Through classes and found similar evidence. He discovered that when students worked in a group under adult supervision, correlations with achievement were positive and often significant. On the other hand, when small groups met without an adult, correlations between this organizational pattern and achievement were negative and often significant. A simple fact of life may be inferred from the studies cited: Many students do not engage in on-task academic behavior when a teacher or other adult is not monitoring their academic activities.

Individualized instructional programs make extensive use of independent seatwork activities. Before advocates of individualized programs rise in righteous indignation at the interpretations of the data given above, let us hasten to note that some teacher training that accompanies individualized programs prepares the teacher to deal with these facts. Pittsburg's Individually Prescribed Instruction (IPI) emphasizes the need for a "traveling teacher" or "traveling aide," someone who is constantly monitoring each student's classroom behavior. Alas, in the implementation of many individualized programs, students' independent seatwork or independent small group work is monitored infrequently. Lower levels of acquired knowledge will result for students in classrooms where these kinds of instructional procedures are normative.

Questioning. Table 5 from Stallings and Kaskowitz (1974) presents data that is substantiated in other studies. Open ended questions, that is, questions high in the Bloom Taxonomy, are negatively related to student achievement. So are nonacademic questions. Only academically focused direct questions at lower levels of the Bloom Taxonomy resulted in increased acquisition of knowledge by students. Using a similar sample of low income students, Soar (1973) also found that factors with high loadings from variables such as convergent questions, drill, or questions that have single answers, usually correlated positively with achievement. Factors with loadings from variables like divergent questions and open-ended questions usually correlated negatively with achievement.

Despite Piaget's theory, which cautions against the use of higher cognitive questions with preoperational or concrete operational children, there has been an emphasis on training teachers to use higher order questions. Recent experimental work, along with the correlational data presented, may reverse that trend. Two well-designed experiments have demonstrated that the percentage of cognitive questions asked by teachers per lesson has *no* discernable effect on elementary school students' acquisition of knowledge (Gall, Ward, Berliner,

TABLE 5

Correlations between Adult Questioning and Student Achievement[a]

| | Grade and subject | | | |
| | First-grade classes | | Third-grade classes | |
Variable	Math achievement	Reading achievement	Math achievement	Reading achievement
Adult academic commands, requests, and direct questions to groups of children	.10	.29	.54	.51
Adult academic commands, requests, and direct questions to individual children	.23	.29	.30	.10
Adult nonacademic commands, requests, and direct questions to individual children	-.31	-.25	-.47	-.37
Adult open-ended questions to children	-.03	-.11	-.35	-.31

[a]After Stallings and Kaskowitz (1974).

Cahen, Crown, Elashoff, Stanton, & Winne, 1975; Program on Teacher Effectiveness, 1975).

Rosenshine (1976) has brought together data on the association with achievement of the kinds of student responses made to teacher questions. As might be expected, academic responses are positively correlated with outcomes; nonacademic responses, and responses to open-ended questions are negatively correlated with outcome measures. Brophy and Evertson (1974) also examined student responding and detected an interesting interaction. For lower socioeconomic status students, the percent of correct answers was positively correlated with achievement while for higher socioeconomic status children, the percent of wrong answers was a positive predictor. As with curriculum and teaching methods, there are main effects and interactions, depending upon whether the class or the student is the unit of analysis.

Feedback.   Combining studies reviewed in Rosenshine (1971) and Dunkin and Biddle (1974), Gage and Berliner (1975) found 14 studies on the relationship between teacher praise and student achievement. Eight of these studies yielded positive correlations with achievement while six studies yielded negative correlations with achievement. No clear relationship between feedback in the form of praise and student acquisition of knowledge was discernable from these studies. When combining studies of feedback in the form of a teacher's criticism of students, Gage and Berliner (1975) found thirteen studies that yielded negative relationships with student achievement and three studies that yielded positive relationships with student achievement. Frequent criticism by teachers would appear to be a negative predictor of student achievement.

Stallings and Kaskowitz (1974) also studied praise and criticism and their data help to refine the conclusions drawn about these feedback dimensions. They catagorized praise or criticism as academic or nonacademic in focus (e.g., praise for reading work versus praise for working well in groups; or, criticism for mathematics performance versus criticism for music activities). The relationship with student achievement is generally positive for *both* praise and criticism when such feedback is focused on academic activities. The relationship of both these teacher-feedback dimensions to student achievement is mixed or negative when given for nonacademic student behaviors.

It appears that feedback to students, whether praise or criticism, helps students acquire knowledge, providing the feedback is academically focused. This is consistent with the idea that a direct instructional emphasis in the classroom is a major determinant of student achievement.

Once again, a distinction must be made between the class and the student as units of analysis. At the classroom level, feedback dimensions appear to have similar effects when academically focussed, but at the student level of analysis, praise and criticism seem to have different effects on different types of students. As one example of this, introverts and extroverts appear to respond very differently to praise and criticism (Forlano & Axelrod, 1937; Thompson & Hunnicutt, 1944).

Atmosphere. An environment that stresses academic achievement, making use of many of the components of direct instruction mentioned above, need not be authoritarian, coercive, or aversive. Among the characteristics of the more effective classrooms reported by ethnographers were "conviviality," "coopera- tion," "democracy," and "warmth." Less effective classrooms showed more evidence of "belittling" and "shaming" of students and of teachers' use of "sarcasm." The ethnographic protocols were also analysed for competitiveness, but this variable did *not* distinguish between more effective and less effective teachers. The ethnographic analysis also confirmed an obvious fact: In classes where behavior management problems exist, a warm atmosphere cannot develop, and direct instruction cannot take place. Classes that are out-of-control are invariably classes where little academic student learning takes place (Tikunoff, Berliner, & Rist, 1975).

The above description of effective classroom teaching, in which the successful classroom environment is characterized by a press toward academic achievement, appears to be an unusually simple way to explain the acquisition of knowledge in the classroom. Teaching behavior which is not directly aimed at furthering academic achievement of the kind measured by standardized achievement tests, will not result in much growth in knowledge as measured by those kinds of tests. Teachers who make a difference in students' achievement are those who put students into contact with curriculum materials and find ways to keep them in contact with the knowledge to be acquired through their choice of teaching method.

Though it may be easy to dismiss the data presented as nothing but common sense, it is clear from our observations of classrooms that common sense is not necessarily common practice. And even these simple descriptions of successful environments for classroom learning are complicated by the fact that data are not consistent within and between studies. Moveover, when we try to explore how individual students process the information to be acquire – their ability to encode, retrieve, decode, and transfer information – the classroom becomes a very complex environment in which to work.

Studying Classroom Learning

By addressing the molar environment characterized as direct instruction, and with highly selected data relating components of that environment to student achievement, this paper avoided the problems that arise when classroom teaching is approached in a more molecular fashion. Studies which attempt to examine single skills or particular behaviors of teachers and relate those variables to student outcomes have some incredible inadequacies (see Berliner, 1975).

Some of these problems relate to the issue of appropriateness of teacher behavior, the unit of analysis for the independent variable, problems pertaining to the stability of teacher behavior, and problems of construct validation. (We will not discuss the equally befuddling problems associated with the criterion measure used to assess student achievement and the statistical methods used to measure change in students' performance.)

Appropriateness. Many studies of the acquisition of knowledge in the classroom count or rate behavior and do not deal with the crucial question of appropriateness of teacher behavior, a qualitative dimension with which it is difficult to come to grips. When observing in a classroom, one becomes acutely aware of the difference between a higher cognitive question asked after a train of thought is running out, and the same type of question asked after a series of lower cognitive questions have been used to establish a foundation from which to explore higher order ideas. Teachers sometimes ask inane questions. Teachers have been seen responding to student initiated questions with irrelevant information. Teachers sometimes achieve a high rate of probing student responses to questions, seemingly without regard for the student or the kind of initial response given to the question. Some students are embarrassed by the probing; with other students, the probes occurred at inappropriate times, and sometimes probes were not used when the situation seemed to cry out for them. At other times, the teachers' probing questions may have been as skillful as Socrates', but only their frequency was recorded. Before we can adequately assess how particular teacher activities contribute to a student's acquisition of knowledge and skills, we must learn to deal with this qualitative dimension where value judgments about appropriate use of skills enters into our description of classroom phenomena.

The unit of analysis for the independent variable. Another problem one becomes acutely aware of in studying teacher effectiveness is the problem of the unit of analysis for chacterizing the independent variable. Is a single teacher question the unit of interest? Is a question, along with the wait-time which follows, the unit of interest? Or does a teacher question, wait-time, and student answer make up the unit which best characterizes the independent variable? Teachers often follow strategies of long duration. Teachers may conduct an inductive lesson where the meaningful unit of analysis may be a one hour or one week episode that is concerned with the conservation of matter. The individual questions, reinforcers, probes, and student responses may be trivial aspects of the overall episode. Until we have adequate conceptions of the unit of analysis for our independent variables, we may need to remain at a more molar level for describing classroom processes.

Stability of teacher behavior. When describing a "good" teacher, many people use a term such as "flexible." Such teachers are expected to change methods, techniques, and styles to suit particular students, curriculum areas, time of day, etc. That is, the standard of excellence in teaching commonly held implies a teacher whose behavior is inherently unstable. Needless to say, this poses a problem for an observer trying to understand a teacher's customary and usual ways of teaching. A recent review of the stability of teacher behavior (Shavelson & Dempsey, 1975) pointed out that many of the skills and behaviors that have been studied in research on teacher effectiveness are unstable over occasions. A rather large number of low and even negative stability coefficients were found. This means that the independent variables in many studies of teacher effectiveness were often not fair indicators of a teacher's typical behavior. Researchers seem so eager to capture variables for data analysis with rating scales and frequency counts, that they apparently forget to check if their methodology is appropriate to the phenomena they are interested in studying!

Construct validation. Scientific understanding of any phenomena requires a descriptive language which uses concepts having common meaning among the scientists working in the same area. Among researchers on teacher effectiveness, this criterion is not currently being met. A concept such as "warmth" does not have the same meaning from study to study. A teacher's warmth may be measured by self-report, student report, observer rating, frequency count of smiles, percentage of gestures regarded as affectionate, or anything else that can be thought of. If these various imprecise and imperfect measures of warmth were intercorrelated, one could perhaps begin to understand the construct which is now so glibly used but so poorly defined. Extensive construct validation must take place in research on teaching or else the impreciseness of the language used to describe phenomena of interest will retard the empirical study of teaching indefinitely.

For all of these and other reasons, the more organismic description of the environment which affects student achievement in classrooms seems more useful. Across many studies, using different observation instruments and different statistical techniques, a convergence around the concept of direct instruction is evident, but this promising concept also will need more clear and precise definition if it is to be useful in future research on classroom learning.

CONCLUSION

Major factors in the process of knowledge acquisition in the classroom are the content and emphasis of the curriculum in use and the content coverage and emphasis given through the teaching methods employed. The classroom behavior of a successful teacher is characterized by direct instruction, whereby students are brought into contact with the curriculum materials and kept in contact with them until the requisite knowledge is acquired. At the primary grades, direct instruction includes goal setting, allocation of sufficient time to reach goals, appropriate choice of curriculum materials, use of teaching methods and teaching behaviors to achieve high levels of active learning time, provision of an academic focus, and the monitoring of student activities during the allocated instructional time. The successful teacher asks direct questions and provides positive and negative feedback to students on academic matters. The atmosphere for successful direct instruction is warm and student behavioral problems are low in frequency.

In general, studies of isolated teacher skills and behavior in natural classroom environments have not provided much information about how knowledge is acquired in the classroom. This will continue until investigators engaged in research on teaching have learned how to work with concepts of appropriateness, define a unit of analysis for the study of teaching, obtain stable estimates of teacher behavior over occasions, and perform extensive construct validation.

If today's schools are failing to provide students the knowledge and skills they need, as many criticis contend, some of the blame may be placed on the failiure of educators to understand a very simple fact. That is, almost all teacher behaviors that increase a classes engagement with the content of almost any curriculum, communicated to students through almost any teaching method, will increase student achievement. Complexity only arises when we focus on individual students who may need different curriculum, specially chosen teaching methods, and exposure to a unique set of teaching behaviors in order to optimize their learning. Thus, the factors related to knowledge acquisition in the classroom may be viewed as both disarmingly simple, and frightfully complex, at the same time.

ACKNOWLEDGMENTS

Work on this paper was supported, in part, by the United States Navy Personnel Research and Development Center, and, in part, by the California Commission for Teacher Preparation and Licensing (through funds provided by the National Institute of Education). The opinions expressed in this publication do not necessarily reflect the position or policy of any of the above mentioned agencies, and no official endorsement by them should be inferred. Dr. Maragaret Bierly, California State University at Chico, helped in the development of this contribution.

REFERENCES

Armento, B. Correlates of teacher effectiveness in social studies. Unpublished doctoral dissertation, Indiana University, Bloomington, Indiana, 1975.

Attneave, F. How do you know? *American Psychologist*, 1974, 29, 493–499.

Berliner, D. C. Impediments to the study of teacher effectiveness, Technical Report No. 75-11-3. San Francisco, California: Far West Laboratory for Educational Research and Development, November, 1975.

Bloom, B. S. Time and learning. *American Psychologist*, 1974, 29, 682–688.

Bond, G. L., & Dykstra, R. The cooperation research programme in first grade reading instruction. *Reading Research Quarterly*, 1967, **2**, 1–42.

Brophy, J. E., and Evertson, C. M. Process-product correlations in the Texas teacher effectiveness study: Final Report. Austin, Texas: University of Texas, 1974.

Carroll, J. B. A model of school learning. *Teachers College Record*, 1963, **64**, 723–732.

Chang, S. S., & Raths, J. The schools contribution to the cumulating deficit. *Journal of Educational Research*, 1971, **64**, 272–276.

Chastain, K. D. A methodological study comparing the audio-lingual habit theory and the cognitive code-learning theory: A continuation. *Modern Language Journal*, 1970, **54**, 257–266.

Chu, G. C., & Schramm, W. Learning from television: *What the research says*. Stanford, California: Institute for Communication Research, 1967.

Coleman, J. S., et al. *Equality of educational opportunity*. Washington, D.C.: U.S. Government Printing Office, 1966.

Doty, B. A. Teaching method effectiveness in relation to certain student characteristics. *Journal of Educational Research*, 1967, **60**, 363–365.

Dowaliby, F. J., & Schumer, H. Teacher-centered versus student-centered mode of college classroom instruction as related to manifest anxiety. *Journal of Educational Psychology*, 1973, **65**, 125–132.

Dubin, R., & Taveggia, T. C. *The teaching-learning paradox: A comparative analysis of college teaching methods*. Eugene, Oregon: Center for Advanced Study of Educational Administration, University of Oregon, 1968.

Dunkin, M. J., & Biddle, B. J. *The study of teaching*. New York: Holt, Rinehardt and Winston, 1974.

Forlano, G., & Axelrod, H. D. The effect of repeated praise or blame on performance of introverts and extroverts. *Journal of Educational Psychology*, 1937, **28**, 90–100.

Gage, N. L., & Berliner, D. C. *Educational Psychology*. Chicago, Illinois: Rand McNally, 1975.

Gall, M. D., Ward, B. A., Berliner, D. C., Cahen, L. S., Crown, K. A., Elashoff, J. D., Stanton, G. C., & Winne, P. H. The effects of teacher use of questioning techniques on student achievement and attitude. San Francisco, California: Far West Laboratory for Educational Research and Development, August, 1975.

Harris, A. J., Morrison, C., Serwer, B. L., & Gold, L. *A continuation of the CRAFT Project: Comparing reading approaches with disadvantaged urban negro children in primary grades*. New York: Division of Teacher Education of the City University of New York, 1968. (U.S. Office of Education Project No. 5-0570-2-12-1). ERIC ED: 010 297.

Harris, A. J., & Serwer, B. *Comparison of reading approaches in first grade teaching with disadvantaged children*. (the CRAFT project). New York: City Univeristy of New York, 1966. (U.S. Office of Education Cooperative Research Project No. 2677.)

Heath, R. W., & Nielson, M. A. The research basis for performance-based teacher education. *Review of Educational Research*, 1974, **44**, 463–483.

Husén, T. *International study of achievement in mathematics: Comparison of twelve countries*, Vols. I and II. New York: Wiley, 1967.

Jamison, D., Suppes, P., & Wells, S. The effectiveness of alternative instructional media: A survey. *Review of Educational Research*, 1974, **44**, 1–68.

Jencks, C. et al. *Inequality: A resassessment of family and schooling in america*. New York: Basic Books, 1972.

McDonald, F. J. Research on teaching and its implications for policy making. Report on phase II of the beginning teacher evaluation study. Paper presented at the conference on Research on Teacher Effects: An examination by policy-makers and researchers, Sponsored by the National Institute of Education, at the School of Education, University of Texas, Austin, Texas, November, 1975.

McDonald, F. J., Elias, P., Stone, M., Wheeler, P., Lambert, N., Calfee, R., Sandoval, J., Ekstrom, R., & Lockheed, M. Final report on phase II beginning teacher evaluation study. Prepared for the California Commission for Teacher Preparation and Licensing, Sacramento, California. Princeton, New Jersey: Educational Testing Service, 1975.

Mosteller, F., & Moynihan, D. P. *On equality of educational opportunity.* New York: Vintage Books, 1972.

Olson, D. R. On a theory of instruction: Why different forms of instruction result in similar knowledge. *Interchange*, 1972, 3, 9–24.

Program on Teacher Effectiveness. Preliminary report of a factorially designed experiment on teacher structuring, soliciting and reacting. Occassional Paper No. 7. Stanford, California: Stanford Center for Research and Development in Teaching, October, 1975.

Rosenshine, B. Objectively measured behavioral predictors of effectiveness in explaining. In N. L. Gage, M. Belgard, D. Dell, J. E. Hiller, B. Rosenshine, & W. R. Unrah (Eds.), *Explorations of the teacher's effectiveness in explaining.* Technical report No. 4. Stanford, California: Stanford Center for Research and Development in Teaching, 1968. ERIC ED 028 147.

Rosenshine, B. Classroom Instruction. In N. L. Gage (Ed.), *The psychology of teaching methods. Seventy-fifth yearbook of the National Society for the Study of Education.* Chicago: University of Chicago Press, 1976.

Rosenshine, B. *Teaching behaviors and student achievement.* London, England: National Foundation for Educational Research, 1971.

Shavelson, R., & Demsey, N. Generalizability of measures of teacher effectiveness and teaching process. Technical Report No. 75-4-2. San Francisco, California: Far West Laboratory for Educational Research and Development, May, 1975.

Shutes, R. E. Verbal behaviors and instructional effectiveness. Unpublished doctoral dissertation, Stanford University, Stanford, California, 1969.

Soar, R. S. Follow-Through classroom process measurement and pupil growth (1970–71): Final Report, Gainesville, Florida: College of Education, University of Florida, 1973.

Stallings, J. A. Relationships between classroom instructional practices and child development. Paper presented at the annual meetings of the American Education Research Association, Washington, D.C., April, 1975.

Stallings, J. A., & Keepes, B. D. Student aptitudes and methods of teaching beginning reading: A predictive instrument for determining interaction patterns. Final Report, Contract No. OEG-9-70-0005, Project No. 9-I-009, U.S. Office of Education, 1970.

Stallings, J. A., & Kaskowitz, D. *Follow-Through classroom observation evaluation, 1972–1973.* Menlo Park, California: Stanford Research Institute, 1974.

Thompson, G. G., & Hunnicutt, C. W. The effect of repeated praise or blame on the work achievement of "introverts and extroverts." *Journal of Educational Psychology*, 1944, 35, 257–266.

Tikunoff, W., Berliner, D. C., & Rist, R. C. *An ethnographic study of the forty classrooms of the Beginning Teacher Evaluation Study known sample.* Technical Report No. 75-10-5, San Francisco, California: Far West Laboratory for Educational Research and Development, October, 1975.

Walker, D. F., & Schaffarzick, J. Comparing curricula. *Review of Educational Research*, 1974, 44, 83–112.

Wiley, D. E., & Harnischfeger, A. Explosion of a myth: Quantity of schooling and exposure to instruction, major educational vehicles. *Educational Researcher*, 1974, 3, 7–12.

Wilson, J. W., Cahen, L. S., & Begle, E. G. *Reports of the National Longitudinal Study of Mathematics Ability*, Vol. 10. Stanford, California: Stanford University Press, 1970.

COMMENTS ON CHAPTER 11
BY BERLINER AND ROSENSHINE

Philip W. Jackson

The University of Chicago

I begin with a statement written 21 years ago by Irving Lorge. Near the conclusion of an article entitled, "If they know not, teach," Lorge (1954) writes:

> During the last thirty years, a considerable amount of effort has been expended in attempts to evaluate the various methods of teaching in order to find a "best", or at least a better method. Much reliance has been placed on experimental studies of contrasting methods such as, Is the lecture method better than individualized conferences? or Is the discussion method superior to recitation? . . . It would be happy indeed, if there were a clear answer on the relative value of the different methods studied. Unfortunately, this is not so. The experimental literature allows every teacher to find support for any method. . . . Hence variation in methods is more likely to attain all of the goals for more of the students. No method is really superior to any other: Variety in method is the spice of teaching, as well as of life [pp. 165–168].

Here, then, was the state of the art as seen by a major figure in educational research a generation ago. Oddly enough, we seem not to have progressed very far since then, as Berliner and Rosenshine's review of the literature makes abundantly clear. Indeed, our chief advance seems to be that of moving the null hypothesis a shade closer to being hailed as the one and only educational law!

Lest we feel too depressed, however, by this lack of progress, we should hasten to take heart from one of Berliner and Rosenshine's main points. With a flick of a word he manages to change our normal gloom over "no significant difference" into something resembling cheer. Now, instead of concluding that nothing works better than anything else, we are encouraged to look upon different curricula and different teaching methods as having "equipotentiality." This advice strikes me as a beautiful example of the power of positive thinking!

They go on, however, to suggest that there is "differential potentiality" among teaching methods when different types of students, rather than entire classes, are employed as the units of analysis. In other words, certain methods might work better than others with certain students. This belief, which borders on being a truism, has led to the burgeoning of studies that seek to discover the subtle interactions between educational methods, on the one hand, and pupil charac-teristics, on the other, studies that have come to be referred to by the three-letter abbreviation ATI, standing for "attribute-treatment interaction."

Clearly, I am not equally optimistic about where such a line of research will take us. I am more skeptical than they. The ATI studies that I have read to date leave me, I regret to report, rather underwhelmed. Moreover, I am despairing of the future. I see little chance of tomorrow's ATI studies doing much in the way of transforming classroom teaching practices.

I am led to this gloomy forecast not only because attribute-treatment interac-tions appear to be very elusive phenomena, but also because the likelihood of our doing anything about them, once they are discovered, is also very slim. For example, of what possible value, in a practical setting, is the knowledge that introverts, as a group, gain more from lectures than do extroverts or vice versa? Can you imagine teachers or school administrators trying to match their students with the proper kinds of methods? Picture the testing program, the scheduling difficulties, and the staffing problems that would ensue.

Or, take, as another example, the reported interaction between scores on tests of manifest anxiety and the capacity to benefit from various teaching methods. Would we be able to group students on the basis of anxiety scores, even if they did interact with instructional treatment? I doubt it. I cannot imagine even an intellectually enlightened community sitting still for such a practice. If we now have difficulty justifying ability groupings in our schools, think of the uproar that would be triggered by an announcement that we were now going to lump together all the high-anxious or low-anxious pupils. In sum, the flimsiness of the findings, together with the practical, administrative, and political problems that any action dictated by those findings would entail, leave me very skeptical about the future of ATI research, at least insofar as it promises to be of help to classroom teachers. Unfortunately, it is highly probable that such research will continue, at least in the near future, to consume a lot of our monies and energies if for no other reason than that it has become the fashionable mode of framing research questions among a group of prominent educational leaders; leaders, in my opinion, who should know better.

There follow a few brief and almost random reactions to other portions of Berliner and Rosenshine's contribution.

To begin, I agree that a renewed look at on-task time in classrooms (I prefer the old-fashioned term "attention") is long overdue. Such a look would doubt-lessly reveal a surprising amount of off-task activity, or inattention. I would hope, however, that we do not rely too heavily for that estimate on the single statistic that Berliner and Rosenshine themselves supply, the one that was reportedly derived from an observational study of a single "typical" pupil. That datum, you will recall, leads to the conclusion that the typical child in an elementary school classroom spends only 3 min out of every 45 doing what he is supposed to be doing. Such a shocking statistic statistic may turn out to be true, of course, but before we start reporting it in published articles and passing it out to the media, it would be nice to have a firmer foundation for our pronouncements, including means and variances based on a much larger sample.

Another "finding" that gives me pause has to do with the discovery that low-level questioning by the teacher, aimed at factual recall, seems to pay off in achievement better than higher-level questioning, aimed at critical evaluation, conceptual synthesis, etc. Before such a finding is transformed into educational advice, I would want to have a very close look at the achievement tests used as criterion measures. If the test items largely call for low-level informational recall, as I suspect they might, then it would not be too surprising to find that a similar form of questioning by the teacher provides a good rehearsal for the test itself. Again, before we start encouraging teachers to give up their attempts to engage the higher mental processes of their students, we need much more careful study, including an item-by-item analysis of our criterion measures.

Another of my misgivings has to do with the research on the teacher's role in knowledge acquisition reviewed in Berliner and Rosenshine's chapter. I am unimpressed by the bulk of that research. Let me explain why.

Suppose we were to interview a group of eight students who had done poorly on a test of mathematics achievement. Imagine each student being asked why he or she did so poorly, with the following results:

STUDENT 1: "Well, the teacher never made the assignments clear, so I never knew what to do."

STUDENT 2: "To be truthful, I was absent most of the year. I was sick. I just rarely attended class."

STUDENT 3: "In my room we only had math once a month. No wonder I did so poorly!"

STUDENT 4: "The teacher told jokes most of the time in math class. He just never got around to teaching us anything."

STUDENT 5: "The teacher never took us beyond the times table. We spent almost all year on two's and four's."

STUDENT 6: "Well, the teacher gave us seatwork most of the time. But then she never checked on what we did, so we just goofed off."

STUDENT 7: "Our teacher never bothered to question us about what we knew. When he did ask questions, they seemed nonsensical."

STUDENT 8: "Our teacher never did anything but nag us about what we were doing wrong all year. I got discouraged and gave up."

Though we might not trust the veracity of reports such as these — they do sound a bit more like excuses than explanations — if we did assume them to be true, the question is whether they sound at all reasonable as explanations. That is, if the described conditions actually existed, would we be surprised to find the student in question doing poorly on a mathematics achievement test? I suspect we would not.

Now, what I have done should be obvious. I have taken the major findings of the research on the teacher's role in knowledge acquisition as reported in the Berliner and Rosenshine contribution and presented them, somewhat more starkly and with a bit of poetic license, as issuing from the mouths of students. I use this rhetorical device merely to suggest that such research has added very little to our workaday understanding. Indeed, it seems yet to have caught up with common sense.

In the wake of all these negative comments, I feel obliged to throw in a word or two in defense of observational research in classrooms, for I do believe there is a lot to be learned there, a lot that will be of direct benefit to teachers. But, if we truly want to help teachers, which I think we should, we must first consider what they need to know in order to do a better job. Do they need to know that students with high or low scores on test X will benefit if they, the teachers, adopt method A? Is that the form of knowledge that will help them? I doubt it. Yet, it is knowledge in that form that we as researchers commonly seek.

I suspect we would be of greater help to teachers than we presently are if we could develop ways of aiding teachers to develop an increased awareness of their own actions. As an observer in classrooms, I have discovered that many, if not most, teachers have a very limited perception of their own teaching behavior. They typically give grossly inaccurate estimates, for example, of the frequency and distribution of their own interchanges with students. Such blindspots are understandable, perhaps, for teaching is such an engrossing activity that it is difficult to step back and watch oneself engaged in the act. Nonetheless, it seems reasonable to assume that the greater the teacher's awareness of his own actions, the greater the likelihood that he can control or change those actions to suit his pedagogical intentions.

One obvious way of increasing the teacher's self-awareness is by having an outside observer in the classroom who will report to the teacher on what he sees. Unfortunately, this is not a very practical alternative for most teachers, for there simply are not enough outside observers to go around. Consequently, there is a need to develop techniques that will enable teachers to move toward such a goal on their own. This is neither the time nor the place to conjecture on what such techniques might be, but a fleeting reference to one of my own experiences as an observer should help to clarify what I have in mind.

It is obvious to even a casual observer that teachers in elementary school classrooms do not spend equal amounts of time in each portion of the room. If, for example, you were to divide the classroom into quadrants and chart the teacher's movements, you would find that the probability of locating the teacher in any one of the four sections was not the same for each section. The presence of the teacher is rarer, in other words, in some parts of the room than others. Interestingly enough, however, teachers are not always fully conscious of how their physical presence or absence affects what is going on in the room and their perception of it.

In one classroom in which I was observing a few years back, I noticed that the teacher tended to inhabit one quadrant of the room about 65% of the time, and another, diagonally opposite, about 15% of the time. The heavily frequented quadrant, incidentally, was where a group of house plants were kept, and this teacher, being a plant lover, liked to spend time tending them. The quadrant of the room rarely frequented by the teacher contained an upright piano. A tally of the teacher's interactions with the students whose desks were in these two quadrants revealed, as might be expected, that the students in the "plant" quadrant had more dealings with the teacher than did those in the "piano" quadrant.

At the end of one school day I made an unusual request of the teacher. "Tomorrow," I explained, "I would like you to do something that may sound a bit odd. Whenever you are freely moving about the room, try to head for the piano. Don't make a big deal of it, but whenever the idea crosses your mind, move toward the piano." The teacher agreed to comply, and on the next day she did indeed do so.

What happened, as you might guess, was a dramatic reversal of the teacher's typical interaction pattern. On the day in question the pupils in the "piano" quadrant received a much larger share of the teacher's time and talk than they had previously. More important, however, was the teacher's own response to the events of the day. After the children had gone home she conveyed her reactions with enthusiasm. "My goodness," she said, "I hadn't realized how far behind Elaine (whose desk was in the "piano" quadrant) has fallen in her workbook assignments. I must give her more help than she has been getting. And did you notice how talkative Sidney (another "piano" student) was today?" And so on. In short, as the teacher's interaction pattern changed, so did her perception of her students, and all of this the result of a simple suggestion aimed at dislodging the teacher from her normal grooves of action.

The example may be inconsequential but the idea, I believe, is not. There are doubtlessly many self-help techniques that classroom observers could develop if they put their minds to it, techniques that would help to make teachers more aware of what they are doing. We might not want to dignify such efforts with the word "research," but I suspect they would do more to improve teaching then would an equal amount of energy devoted to yet another batch of ATI studies.

Finally, a word about Berliner and Rosenshine's concluding paradox. They end the paper, you will recall, with the following sentence: "Thus the factors related to knowledge acquisition in the classroom may be viewed as both disarmingly simple and frightfully complex at the same time." I puzzled over that sentence.

How, I asked myself, could the same thing be disarmingly simple and frightfully complex at one and the same time? My answer is that it cannot. I conclude, therefore, that Berliner and Rosenshine must be talking about two different things. And I think I know what they are.

What is disarmingly simple, I suspect, is the advice we have to give teachers on the basis of what we have learned to date about the teaching and learning process. What is frightfully complex is our emerging understanding, in a theoretical or scientific sense, of how and why things work as they do. The simple and complex, therefore, are attached to quite different domains of intellectual concerns. As researchers, who are often tempted to slip into the role of advice givers, we would do well to keep the distinction in mind.

REFERENCE

Lorge, I. "If they know not, teach," *Teachers College Record*, 1954, 56, 165–168.

OPEN DISCUSSION
ON THE CONTRIBUTIONS BY BERLINER
AND ROSENSHINE AND JACKSON

Koran: I do not understand the type of action research Dr. Jackson is suggesting. The example he provided about self-awareness rests, at least implicitly, on the idea that somebody is performing some behavior which is a mistake; if he becomes aware, it will change in a direction which is going to influence some kind of student behavior. It seems to me that that assumption has to rest on the kind of research that Dr. Berliner has been talking about. What is the basis for making a choice about what things you want to make them aware of?

Jackson: Well, I do not know how to answer that, except that I am in favor of heightened awareness in general. The distribution of teacher actions among students is an important variable in determining what happens in classroom situations. If the teacher never interacts with the kids, and does not know that he or she is forgetting to, awareness of it gives the teacher an added degree of potential.

Anderson: Implicit here is the notion of some framework which allows one to judge that some goals and actions are better than others. That is Dr. Koran's point.

Berliner: The teacher's self-awareness may have other than academic outcomes associated with it, for example, attitudinal outcomes that are very important, but are not the outcomes I am talking about. The concern is whether you want academic achievement as we normally measure it, and I am willing to say that anything involving the teacher's self-awareness that furthers direct instruction is what I would personally recommend.

Carter: It seems, historically, that there have been a number of people who have suggested that teaching is an art. Other people have thought that was not true, with Skinner most notable among them. He attempts, by systematizing what goes on in instruction, to make the teacher a much less influential variable. In listening to what Dr. Berliner said, I am not sure that I see much in there that would disabuse someone of the notion that teaching is an art. Whatever makes a good teacher a good teacher involves certain variables that may not be amenable to training as we would like to think. Could you take those people that your studies indicated were ineffective teachers, for instance, and make them, through some training, effective? If so, how would you do that?

Berliner: You certainly have to be able to put children into contact with the curriculum material. That is what Skinner focused on. The less effective teachers in the study we were working on simply were not getting the kids into contact, they were not organized to do so. One of the first commonsensical things I would do is just what Dr. Jackson did with his teachers. I would try to increase awareness. "Did you know that you broke the chain of logic in that spelling lesson because you attended to the behavior problems over here? The kids lost where you were going. Why don't you see if you can find ways to keep your time allocation continuous rather than disjointed?" It seems that immature learners need a continuous flow. I think that many of the things that would increase the effectiveness of teachers, whether they view themselves as artists or instructional designers, are in this constellation of activities I called direct instruction.

12

Schooling and
the Relevance of Research:
General Discussion

Robert M. Gagné

Florida State University

We have been afforded the opportunity of hearing and discussing some important ideas about the kinds of knowledge to be learned in schools, and about the ways in which they are learned. Many of these ideas are quite novel, and are of the sort that open up new horizons of thought about human learning and human information processing. At the same time, the contributors have tried to give serious attention to questions about the relation of their work to some sort of ultimate application pertaining to instruction as it might be designed to occur in schools.

For those of us who come into direct contact with schools and their personnel, and who try to suggest the kinds of transformations which are necessary for practical application of research findings, the ideas we have heard are a treasure trove. This is so, not because the means of application to schooling have been made apparent in concrete terms — in many instances, such means remain quite obscure — but, rather, because in most instances the ideas which have been discussed require us to adopt new frames of reference for conceiving of human learning as it may occur within the organized situations of training programs or schooling programs. And since many of us who try to interpret and apply research knowledge are often led to the conviction that currently existing methods of schooling are seriously maladaptive, new frameworks for thought about human learning cannot fail to be welcome. New prototypes of learning, several of which we have heard about, may in good time make possible the design of new and better models of schooling.

Following this line of thought, I am inclined to frame my remarks within two major categories. The first consists of some comments that are suggested by the question, What implications are there that would incline us toward the questioning and revaluing of schooling goals and methods, or of assumptions that underlie these goals and methods? The second is the reverse of this. Given the existence of educational systems and their programs, along with the current goals of these systems, are there implications which might call for the questioning and revaluing of the objectives of research on human learning? I believe that relevance should be a two-way street. Communication is needed from research findings to the design of practical programs of instruction. Of at least equal importance, communication is needed from the procedures of schooling to the formulation of research goals.

THE QUESTIONING OF OLDER PROTOTYPES

Several of the chapters, either explicitly or implicitly, have called into question some prototypes of human learning, or of school learning, which are "old" in the sense of being familiar. This questioning was apparently done, not for the purpose of destroying useful ideas, but rather because the possibility was seen that the key ideas involved in a given prototype may have outlived their usefulness — they may no longer make good predictions, or give satisfying explanations, of the phenomena the author wishes to account for.

Surely one of the most fundamental questions about prototypes of school learning has been posed by Harry Broudy. He reminds us that the goals of instruction with which we are most familiar consist of the learning of knowledge that is replicative, "knowing that"; and knowledge that is applicative, "knowing how." We do tend to consider these two kinds of knowledge as being important as educational outcomes, and those who design instruction are equally concerned with the *distinction* between them. There is, after all, much evidence that knowledge of facts and generalizations does not necessarily lead to "knowing how," as in exhibiting rule-governed performance. And it is equally evident that being able to perform some symbol-mediated performance (which I usually call "intellectual skill") does not insure that the individual is able to talk about it, that is, to state the verbal propositions that describe or communicate the nature of the performance.

Broudy suggests, however, that if these types of knowing represent the goals of school education, schooling is a failure. I think this may be arguing from extreme cases, since it seems to me that plenty of examples exist in which "knowing that" is useful in everyday life, and plenty of others in which "knowing how" is necessary for a good life, if not for actual survival. Nevertheless, Broudy's other kind of knowledge, *tacit knowledge*, knowledge at the associative level, or "knowing with," has much to recommend it as a badly needed kind for inclusion in the goals of schooling. Should this become *the*, or even *a*, major goal for schooling, we should need to deal with *contexts* of facts and skills, rather than with the facts and skills themselves as learning outcomes.

How are we to know what are the contexts of the knowledge of an educated person? Obviously, this is not as easy as knowing how to measure knowledge or intellectual skills. Broudy's suggestion for psychologists, as I understand it, is that they try to study this problem directly. This would mean finding out what an educated person remembers about American history, for example, or what has become of the poetry he memorized in high school. The question would be not how much is directly remembered (although that is of incidental interest) but what kind of *context* has been formed from the scraps that remain. Investigation could certainly be made of these questions, and such studies would appear worthwhile.

However we may be affected by Broudy's suggestion, the fact remains that many of the presentations to this conference have been concerned with the learning and retention of replicative knowledge, or knowing *that*. It may be worthwhile to dwell upon that fact for a moment. Viewed as an educational outcome, knowing that means being able to state, in terms that communicate propositional meaning, the contents of a passage of verbal discourse.

Now, do we actually think this is a valuable goal of schooling? Is this what we expect students to be able to do as a result of exposure to an educational program? Be able to tell someone else about the events of American history, or the plot of *As You Like It*? Notice that, even if we think this may be *one* reasonable outcome of several, the study of this phenomenon is not likely in itself to tell us much about applicative knowledge, knowing *how*. We may learn how a student of physics can recount the events of Isaac Newton's life, but not how he can learn to put Newton's second law to use in designing a pendulum. It is a good idea, I think, to keep reminding ourselves about the nature of the ultimate performance we are studying.

This question is reflected in the chapter by Bransford, Nitsch, and Franks, who draw a distinction between "knowing" as making contact with a representation and "knowing" as using a representation. They suggest that the latter requires not simply the recall and stating of verbal information, but revising and shaping it, going beyond the current state of knowing. Knowing what to do is accomplished by using knowledge to deal with a variety of examples. What is being questioned here, though, is the prototype that conceives of this process as a matter of accumulating additional pieces. Instead, what is proposed is a process of reshaping knowledge in the direction of greater abstractness.

Regarding the learning and retention of verbal knowledge, there are many examples among these papers of the rejection of older prototypes. I need hardly mention theories of associative learning, simple or complex, which by now appear mainly to be ignored. As Meyer points out, it is simply not possible to study the learning and retention of prose passages with concepts that ignore its organizational structure, as applied, for example, to the learning of word lists or pairs. As her work shows, the structure of prose is an important variable in determining what is remembered.

Rumelhart and Ortony have provided us with an account of memory organization in terms of schemata, generalized concepts formed by networks of interrelations among represented objects, events, and situations. They see the purpose of instruction as one of communicating these schemata from teacher to student. If such communication fails, it may be because the student (1) lacks the prerequisite experience; (2) does not have sufficient clues to find the right schema; or (3) engages an entirely different (and inappropriate) schema. In general, what is being questioned by these remarks is the notion that memory is organized in terms of collections of specific facts.

Rand Spiro also calls into question the "trace retrieval" theory of remembering information from text, and presents evidence for the "active reconstruction" theory. The contrasting theories, of course, are familiar, and have been distinctively described by Royer. What is questioned by Spiro's contribution is the generalization of findings about a "high-integrity" set of discourse (which stands by itself) to "low integrity" discourse (having many relations with external information). The recall of high-integrity discourse constitutes a special case, exhibiting few reconstructive errors, whereas recall of low-integrity discourse is greatly influenced by extrinsic knowledge. The question raised, then, is should there really be two theories, or are we actually dealing with a particular type of variation when reconstruction is not found? Is reconstruction, after all, the more typical general case?

David Olson considers knowledge to be a picture of reality appropriate for the regulation of action. He draws a sharp distinction between language of the "commonsense" variety, and the specialized form of language used for description and explanation. The child comes to school with facility in the mother tongue, but then is faced with the problem of learning by means of formalized written prose. Prose texts represent translations of the mother tongue — translations that present only a particular view of reality to the learner, and that may make some knowledge inaccessible to those who have not acquired the required literary skills.

Allan Collins proposes that a Socratic method of questioning can be used to teach students information about some topic, a larger context of meaning which includes causal dependencies, and some reasoning skills such as forming and testing hypotheses. It is not clear whether this tutorial method is to supplement other methods of teaching or to supplant them. If the latter, then this surely questions the current prototype of teaching information by means of an organized set of propositions, with perhaps only occasionally interspersed questions. If the method is proposed as a supplementary form of teaching, with emphasis on establishing reasoning skills, then it is not so different from what is advocated by many people who study school instruction. They too emphasize the desirability of reasoning practice. Whether skilled reasoners can actually be produced in this way becomes a matter of testing the method's effectiveness.

In Katherine Nelson's presentation we hear the questioning of the usefulness of the assimilation—accommodation view of human conceptual development, at least insofar as it fails to provide detailed specifications of what happens in the transition from one state of development to the next. But more importantly, what is questioned by Nelson's work is the concept of the concept as a named object having certain relevant and nonrelevant attributes; and the idea that new concepts are learned by the child by a process of trial-and-error followed by suitably contingent reinforcements. The notion of hypothesis testing and rejection applied to relevant attributes is found to be no more adequate to account for concept learning. The new prototype suggested emphasizes the actions of the child in relation to objects, events, and the prediction of recurrent events. Concepts arise, in other words, from the actions of the child with familiar objects, and are represented internally as *event structures, scripts*, and ultimately as *categories.*

The consideration given to individual differences in information processing by Hunt reminds us that there are many unsolved problems in understanding what is meant by intelligence. The fact that predictions of academic accomplishments can still be best made by measures of word knowledge should be a starting point for investigation, Hunt suggests, rather than a final conclusion. Particularly, it should give rise to questions about how displayed information is encoded and recoded into "progressively more complex, meaningful units," and how it is that different learners can acquire different strategies for carrying out such processes. In particular, Hunt proposes a search for the causal factors in intelligence, as illustrated by his findings about the time of memory search and access processes.

From Wyer's discussion of attitudes, we gain some new ideas about the ways in which verbal communications affect beliefs, and how beliefs about an object may be seen to influence the acquisition of information about that object. The various characteristics of the source of the communication as factors which affect attitude change are reviewed. Attitudes are an important kind of outcome in schooling, I am inclined to think. Young children must learn a number of attitudes toward themselves and toward other people — attitudes like those of kindness, helpfulness, sympathy, responsibility. Later on, schools are often encouraged and even required by law to instill attitudes of love of country, care for the natural environment, safety in driving, avoidance of harmful drugs. Since the effectiveness of such programs seems questionable, one might hope to see in contemporary thought an even more basic questioning as to what an attitude really is. Carolyn Sherif reminds us that, first, attitudes and attitude change must be understood in terms of personal involvement, and that beliefs, after all, may be studied that have such a low degree of personal involvement that they reveal virtually nothing about attitudes.

From Berliner and Rosenshine we are reminded that translations of research findings into practical classroom techniques do not always make a difference. If we change the curriculum, we may get the learning of different knowledge, but not better learning. If we change the methods of presenting information, as by using discussion rather than lecturing, no great changes occur in the outcomes of schooling. In other words, the soup is never as hot when it reaches the table as it is when it leaves the kitchen. But the methods of direct instruction, which include goal setting, the allocation of time, and adult monitoring, do seem to produce greater achievements on the part of students. Rather than a questioning of old familiar methods, this evidence provides new reasons for a "return to basics." These methods may not all be so clearly derivable from learning theory, but they have demonstrated value for schooling.

Now a lot of different ideas emerge from these presentations. If there is anything in common, it is perhaps the notion of the *schema* as the important unit of what is learned and stored. Some might prefer a different term, but there seems to be a good deal of agreement that as we try to come to grips with how school learning occurs, we must deal with the formation and use of schemata. These are what are being learned and modified by schooling. A schema is not a single word, a single fact, a single idea, but rather a complex organization having many tentacles of contact with surrounding or associated stored entities. It is particularly notable, however, that it seems impossible to reduce the characteristics of the schemata which have been described to a single set. Instead, it appears that the different purposes served by schemata imply different types, and different organizations – they are not all the same. At least we have heard of types that have the purposes I shall identify as follows:

1. A schema whose purpose is the storage and retrieval, in accurate form, of knowledge that can be communicated in propositional form. We detect the presence of such a schema when the student can *state* certain propositions.

2. A schema whose purpose is the initiation and control of action in a regular, or rule-governed manner. In other words, this kind of schema deals with the *application of rules* to specific instances.

3. A schema which influences or modulates the choices the individual makes of his own personal actions (an attitude). We detect this sort of schema when we note regular patterns of personal commitment to certain *personal action choices.*

4. A schema which makes possible reflective thought, having the purpose of generalizing and clarifying the ideas it contains, and *interpreting* them in original ways. We assess the presence of such a schema in a variety of ways, as in metaphor, analogy, and original invention.

SOME REFLECTIONS ON LEARNING AND SCHOOLING

It is thus apparent that this conference has raised a number of questions about older prototypes of human learning, and particularly about what students *should* be learning in school. Some of the suggestions about what the learning outcomes of schooling should be are quite novel, while others are more in the nature of reformulations of familiar goals for the acquisition of knowledge.

If we set aside, for the moment, our concerns with the question of how people learn and look simply at the *outcomes of schooling*, what do we see? Are students acquiring enough knowledge, or the right kind of "knowledge"? Or, in a more nearly ultimate sense, are they becoming more competent, more able to adjust to and cope with living in our complex society, more capable of practical problem solving, increasingly able to find a satisfying quality to their lives? And what do the answers to these questions imply about what should be learned in school?

In attempting to estimate the answers to such questions as these, there is one important source of bias that must be kept firmly in mind. It is the tendency to think that all students are like ourselves, in the sense of being products of university and graduate education, and also in the sense of being adult learners. But this is definitely not the case. One has only to make some superficial observations of, say, the events in a fifth-grade classroom to realize that what may seem the simplest of intellectual operations to us is being struggled over mightily by at least 80% of these children. The encoding and recoding of information is by no means something that they have learned to do with facility. Yet if knowledge is to have the practical importance and applicability we think it has, these are the kinds of capabilities these students must acquire.

This leads me to the remark that I am skeptical of the need to abandon what are seen as the traditional goals of school learning – learning *that* and learning *how*. As for the first of these, it seems to me that many items of knowledge (or facts) are needed for normal living in our society, including social communication. Each person needs to know how to communicate to himself and others what and where Champaign, Illinois is, who was elected President in 1928, and what the First Amendment says. Presumably, it is also useful to him to have a great deal of additional organized knowledge, if he is going to be able to think about it, elaborate upon it, or interpret it in the sense of knowing *with*. It may be true that the school's interest in the latter category of knowledge is not that it be simply recalled, or accurately revived in any ultimate sense. Nevertheless, there is a practical problem here. It is the problem of assessment in the *proximal* sense. If the schools need to know at the end of each course of study what knowledge the student has learned and remembered, I do not see a better approach than to attempt to assess the accurate reinstatement of that knowledge, in the sense of stating its syntactically transformed propositional meaning. Construction and reconstruction may indeed be of interest – but these are additional ways of assessing, not simply substitute ways.

Learning *how*, it seems to me, is of equal if not greater importance as a school outcome. It is my supposition that learning *how* is not distinguished from learning *that* simply for convenience, or to amuse philosophers. By learning *how* I mean the intellectual skills involved in such activities as looking up a number in a telephone book, subtracting the amount of a check to find a cash balance, or determining the cost per ounce of a package of crunchy granola. I also mean the skills of using language, in the sense of using a verb where a verb belongs and using a noun where a noun belongs. My initial hypothesis would be that the organization of memory for intellectual skills is entirely different from that involved in the recall of propositional information.

Notice that the account of Rumelhart and Ortony suggests that knowledge schemata are initially organized by the intellectual skill of using an agent, a word denoting action, and an object of the action. This implies that knowledge schemata depend upon the use of syntactic skills, and thus, I would suppose, on the prior learning of these skills. While it is reasonable to assume their presence in accounting for comprehension of a prose passage, we also need to have a theory of how they got there in the first place, how they are stored and retrieved.

Many of the presentations here have dealt with the questions of how we learn from reading, or listening to, organized sets of propositions characterized by the syntactic structure familiar in our language; or alternatively, how we learn from displays of information which must be transformed into such syntactic forms in order to be stored for later use. In addressing such problems, we are dealing with questions of knowing *that*, and possibly to some degree with knowing *with*, or the contexts of knowledge.

Knowledge acquisition, in the sense that most investigators have conceived of it in this conference, is a matter of *learning by using language*. This is quite appropriate, and indeed it is important to emphasize that human beings do learn by using language. It should be noted, however, that this conception implies the assumption that students know how to use language – to comprehend it, in other words. Yet we should note, I think, that there is mounting evidence that school students are *not* learning to comprehend language. One of the best studies of reading literacy I have seen in recent years (Hasen & Hesse, 1974) shows that the proportion of graduating high school seniors in Madison, Wisconsin, who can gain information from printed texts is not more than 70%. In other words, 30% of these students cannot, in some carefully defined sense, gain information from reading their own language. Furthermore, an additional 18% can do this only with difficulty, and with serious inadequacy. I suspect strongly that these deficiencies are not confined to reading printed texts, but that they extend to other modes of communication (like television) as well. This is, of course, only one study, but there are many other sources of such evidence. What is implied, I believe, is that a great deal of attention needs to be paid to the schooling outcome of knowing how to use language.

My inclination, therefore, is to see the problem of knowledge acquisition as one that must deal with prerequisites. The prerequisites of acquiring and using knowledge consist primarily of *learning how* to comprehend and use language. A student cannot acquire knowledge until he can encode, recode, tune, construct, or otherwise manipulate language. Furthermore, learning how to use language is not something that can readily be conveyed by communicating "knowledge about language." Using language must be represented in human memory as a set of intellectual skills. We who already have these skills can of course use them to describe language (as is done in describing syntactical forms of propositions, for example). But that kind of exercise does not tell us how the skills of language are learned. As the systematic investigation of knowledge acquisition is pursued further, I believe we shall be led increasingly to examine this question of how language usage is learned. It is a high priority for today's schools.

REFERENCE

Hansen, L. H., & Hesse, K. D. *An assessment of student reading literacy.* Madison, Wisconsin: Madison Public Schools, 1974.

The Notion of Schemata and the Educational Enterprise: General Discussion of the Conference

Richard C. Anderson

University of Illinois at Urbana-Champaign

Ten years after I wrote [*The Golden Notebook*], I can get, in one week, three letters about it. . . . One letter is entirely about the sex war, about man's inhumanity to woman, and woman's inhumanity to man, and the writer has produced pages and pages all about nothing else, for she — but not always a she — can't see anything else in the book.

The second is about politics, probably from an old Red like myself, and he or she writes many pages about politics, and never mentions any other theme.

These two letters used, when the book was as it were young, to be the most common.

The third letter, once rare but now catching up on the others, is written by a man or a woman who can see nothing in it but the theme of mental illness.

But it is the same book.

And naturally these incidents bring up again questions of what people see when they read a book, and why one person sees one pattern and nothing at all of another pattern, and how odd it is to have, as author, such a clear picture of a book, that is seen so very differently by its readers.

DORIS LESSING
Introduction to 1973 edition of
The Golden Notebook, p. xxi.

The principal concept developed at this conference was that of *schema,* an idea whose time has finally come. Only two papers, the one by Spiro and the one by Rumelhart and Ortony, dealt expressly with schemata, but the notion was at least implicit in virtually every paper and formal discussion presented here. Broudy's concept of *knowning with* surely involves schemata. To paraphrase him, one of the important benefits of schooling may be to equip the student with knowledge, often not directly reproducible in sentences, which provides him or her with a framework or context for interpreting new experience. Very similar is the position of Bransford, Nitsch, and Franks (Chapter 2) who persuade one that existing knowledge *tunes* a person to *see* things and events in certain ways. Nelson's concept of a *script* as an event sequence that characterizes "the interaction of a number of different concepts – people, places and things – organized around a goal" is clearly a subspecies of schemata. The structures by which an author gives a high level organization to a text – which Meyer has made considerable progress in explicating – are schemata, as are the complementary ones by which readers detect this organization and use it as ideational scaffolding for detailed information.

My chief purpose in this discussion is to reflect on the implications of the concept of schema for education. My remarks are not intended to edify cognitive psychologists or the artificial intelligentsia, though I would be pleased if any of them find what I have to say interesting. Nor is my intended audience practicing teachers, though I would be delighted if any of them see these remarks as interesting and rapturous if they believed them to be useful. I aim to speak to the professional educationist – the educational researcher, the teacher of teachers, those who think about and attempt to improve curricula and teaching methods. I am operating on he assumption that many educationists have not been in a position to keep abreast of current developments in cognitive psychology and related fields; I believe, therefore, that this audience may find useful a fairly elementary synthesis – and occasionally somewhat speculative extension – of the ideas presented here.

Why are persons in the emerging discipline of "cognitive science" so excited about the concept of schema? Is the concept of schema necessary, anyway? Both questions can be answered simultaneously. A large number of American social scientists fairly recently have become convinced that the presuppositions of their traditional world view were fundamentally wrong. They have been empiricists in the philosophical as well as methodological sense of this term.[1] That is, they have regarded the human organism as driven by sensory imputs. In traditional psychology it is said that stimuli "evoke" or even "control" responses. It was always supposed that higher-order structures, processes, and

---

[1] I am contrasting empiricism with rationalism; however, I am not taking any position on whether categories are innate or learned, an issue often in the forefront of discussions of empiricism and rationalism. Also, for the purposes of this paper, I will blur distinctions which might be made between behaviorism and associationism.

patterns of behavior could be understood as concatenations of simple units, but not much progress was made in reaching this end of the agenda. Chomsky (1957) struck a heavy blow against behaviorism, by demonstrating that it is logically impossible to account for language proficiency in terms of stimulus–response chains. Meanwhile, computer scientists were trying to program computers to do such things as perceive simple objects, translate from one language to another, and play chess. Simplifying, somewhat, these early efforts also had an empiricist bias; the programs involved "bottom up" analysis; they were "data driven"; they attempted to get close-to-surface representations. Progress was slow. It became clear that a data driven approach could not possibly work for any but the most simple and trivial of problems. It proved necessary to provide computers with rather elaborate knowledge of the world even to get them to recognize simple objects.

It now appears that, like computer programs, when humans successfully recognize an object, an hypothesis is developed based on a few perceptual cues. This hypothesis guides other perceptual checks. There is no reasonable sense in which the mental representation which finally results could be said to be veridical with the sensory givens. For instance, people have no trouble visualizing that an object is a cube even though several of its faces are not in view. The schema which accounts for what is directly perceivable entails expectations about unseen features (see Kuipers, 1975). "Expectations" is too weak a word. Ordinarily, our conviction about unseen elements will be as strong as our belief in the elements directly accessible to the eye. As Rumelhart and Ortony (Chapter 4, this volume) have explained and argued at length, the implication of schema theory is that in every domain of human experience perception, comprehension, and interpretation involve an interaction of input with existing knowledge. There is the "top-down" imposition of schemata (the rationalist part) as well as the "bottom-up" thrust of data (the empiricist part).

These ideas are not new. European psychologists have always been more attuned to rationalism than their American counterparts. Figures such as Max Wertheimer and Sir Fredric Bartlett developed schema theories which have much in common with current formulations and, of course, Jean Piaget is still the preeminent schema theorist. Schema notions are not new on the American scene, either. Witness psychologist–educators such as Bruner (e.g., 1960) and Ausubel (1963). However, just a few short years ago they were largely voices in the wilderness, out of the mainstream, ignored by many, abused by a few. To use Wyer's (Chapter 8, this volume) concept, those of us with a different world view were able to "counterargue," successfully we thought at the time.

Like American psychologists, American educators have been and still are in large measure, I believe, empiricists. The same intellectual and social milieu which gave birth to the excesses of logical positivism and the crudities of radical behaviorism could not help but influence educational thinking. No doubt there was also direct influence from the Thorndikes and the Skinners; educators have always looked to psychology as the discipline which ought to rationalize educational practice. Later I will argue that changing a high-level schema (for example, a world view, ideology, or theory) is not a simple matter. It very likely involves being forced to confront difficulties in one's current schema and coming to appreciate the power of an alternative schema to resolve these difficulties. I have given an historical sketch, an outline of the reasons for a changing perspective among cognitive scientists, and an intuitively clear case (recognition of a cube) in the hope of causing educationists with an empiricist bias to pause for reflection. Other contributions to this volume contain further and more detailed arguments and additional clear cases.

A FUNDAMENTAL CHARACTERISTIC OF SCHEMATA

It is possible to use a word such as "schema" as a mere notational convenience, as a shorthand expression for what would otherwise be a tediously long list of more primitive elements — response components, perceptual features, semantic features, functional attributes, and the like. Shorthand expressions do serve a valuable function. They expedite conversations. They permit text to be written which does not flounder in details. But if the term "schema" is nothing more than a notational convenience, it is vacuous. Schema is an interesting concept only if there are structures which are more than aggregations of primitive elements. A simple analogy: a house is not adequately characterized as a heap of bricks, mortar, lumber, glass, metal, and plastic. Another analogy: no doubt part of the progress of chemistry and physics can be attributed to the identification of the fundamental units of matter, but at least equally important is the analysis of the relationship among the units, the rules of composition and decomposition. The force of the concept of schema is to direct attention to the patterning of elements. What the elements are and how they interrelate cannot profitably be addressed as separate issues.

Returning to the arena of interest to educators and psychologists, the implication of schema theory is that the mental representations which are used during perception and comprehension, and which evolve as a result of these processes, have a holistic character which cannot be understood as simple functions of their constituents. This issue is currently the subject of vigorous debate and active experimental investigation. For instance, J. Anderson and Bower (1973) have presented a model called HAM which states that sentences are coded into propositions which consist of associative links among the concepts that underlie the words in the sentences. Since the propositions are attributed no special cohesiveness, fragmentary recall of sentences is predicted. Several experiments showing fragmentary recall have been reported; however, I have repeatedly found (see R. Anderson, 1974) that when protocols are scored for substance, subjects almost always recall whole sentences if they recall anything. Only when one insists that subjects reproduce the exact wording of the original sentences and then scores the protocols verbatim is fragmentary recall apparent.

Other subtle predictions from HAM seemed at first to be confirmed only to fail upon replication and further analysis (J. Anderson, 1975; Foss & Harwood, 1975). It would be wrong to imply that the issues in sentence memory research have been resolved in favor of a holistic theory, but in my opinion associationists are now fighting a rear guard action. Probably, though, as J. Anderson (1975) has suggested, the issues are too broad in scope to be decided on the basis of direct experimental investigation. Whichever side one takes, an ingenious person faced with recalcitrant data can tinker with the model to save the theory.

The point being made in this section is the one eloquently argued by Gestalt psychologists decades ago. To use their slogan, "the whole is more than the sum of its parts." In the next sections, I consider two questions: (1) How are schemata used?; and (2) How do schemata change? Following Piaget, I shall call schema usage "assimilation" and schema change "accommodation." While I do not cite Piaget directly, the reasons for employing his terms go beyond deference to historical precedent; his analyses of these processes are among the most insightful to date.

ASSIMILATION:
THE USE OF SCHEMATA
IN PERCEPTION AND COMPREHENSION

To perceive something is to place a construction upon it that plausibly accounts for the sensory input. To comprehend a message is to discover a formulation which coherently explains its contents. Mundane acts of perception and comprehension proceed so smoothly that we are unaware of the processes of formulation and checking. This is why schema theorists are so fond of materials that cannot be comprehended readily because there is difficulty in "placing the right construction upon them." Gestalt psychologists provided many interesting cases. In recent years, the stock of examples has been enriched by Bransford and his colleagues. Here is one from Bransford and Johnson (1972):

> If the balloons popped the sound wouldn't be able to carry since everything would be too far away from the correct floor. A closed window would also prevent the sound from carrying, since most buildings tend to be well insulated. Since the whole operation depends on a steady flow of electricity, a break in the middle of the wire would also cause problems. Of course, the fellow could shout, but the human voice is not loud enough to carry that far. An additional problem is that a string could break on the instrument. Then there could be no accompaniment to the message. It is clear that the best situation would involve less distance. Then there would be fewer potential problems. With face to face contact, the least number of things could go wrong. (p. 719).

Notice that the words in this passage are familiar. No violence is done to English syntax in the individual sentences. Yet the passage does not make sense.

Now look at Fig. 1. When you see that the passage is about a modern day Romeo with technical difficulties in communicating with his Juliet, it does make sense; the pieces fit into place. It is intuitively clear that getting the passage to make sense was a matter of finding a coherent formulation.

Bransford and Johnson obtained evidence that people were able to learn and remember the sentences in this and other passages when they were shown

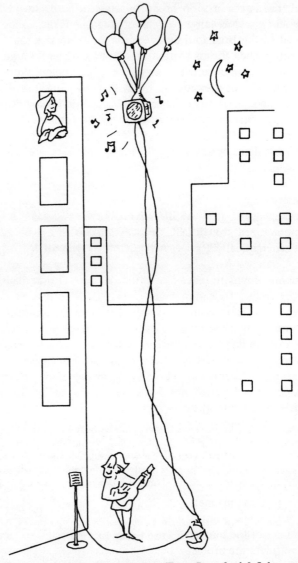

FIG. 1. A modern-day Romeo scene. (From Bransford & Johnson, 1972.)

pictures beforehand which integrated the objects in a manner consistent with the passages. Subjects who did not see pictures did very badly. So did subjects who saw pictures containing the very same objects interrelated in ways which did not give rise to sensible interpretations of the sentences. The patterning of the objects was crucial. The study suggests that comprehension and, therefore, learning and memory, depend upon bringing to bear appropriate schemata.

An adequate theory must explain how people cope with novelty. It could not be that people have stored a schema for every conceivable scene, event sequence, and message. It would be absurd to suppose, for instance, that people came ready equipped to the Bransford and Johnson experiment with a "modern day Romeo" schema, which the picture and passage somehow elicited. Even what I referred to above as mundane acts of perception and comprehension involve novelty. Few episodes are identical. Even if the nominal stimuli in two situations were the same, people change. They come to similar situations with different perspectives and different intentions; they play different roles. It follows that people do not function by selecting the right template from a great mental warehouse of templates abstracted from prior experience. The process must be more dynamic. The conclusion is that even the assimilative use of schemata must involve *constructing* interpretations, for every situation contains at least some novel characteristics.

The contributions to this volume (see Bransford, Nitsch, & Franks) have repeatedly emphasized the primacy of the abstract. It is by virtue of being abstract that schemata allow us to make sense of a range of situations. But there is an apparent paradox here. The broader the range of situations a schema can potentially cover, the more loosely it will fit any one situation in all of its rich particularity.

Determining how the abstract and the particular relate is especially important in understanding language comprehension. The fact that people are facile at using and understanding a given word in indefinitely many sentences in indefinitely many contexts has been taken to imply that words have abstract, context-independent meanings. However, a closer analysis will show that a word will have a somewhat different sense in each use. Anderson and Ortony (1975) analyzed the verb *eat,* noting that phrases such as *eat a steak, eat soup,* and *eat an apple* suggest different utensils and different actions of the lips, tongue, and teeth. Further variations in sense appear when possible agents are considered. Observe what happens to *eat,* and also *steak,* in *The executive ate the steak, The baby ate the steak,* and *The dog ate the steak.* Anderson and Ortony (1975) conclude: "Each of these sentences gives rise to different suppositions about location, circumstance, manner, instrumentality, and antecedent and consequent conditions. The general point is that a word could have different meanings in a very large number of the sentences in which it might appear . . ." (p. 169).

Let us recapitulate the problem. In order to explain the generality of language, it must be supposed that people have a highly abstract understanding of the concepts signified by words. Nonetheless, in particular cases fine gradations in meaning are easily appreciated, indeed, are probably necessary for comprehension. If linguistic understanding is abstract and, therefore, impoverished of situationally specific detail, how is it that the representations we get into our heads when we comprehend sentences are so rich? This is a troublesome question only when it is assumed that words and sentences "have" meanings. The meaning is not in the message. A message is a cryptic recipe that can guide a person in *constructing* a representation. The representation which accounts for a message will usually include elements that are not explicitly contained in the message. These imported elements will be the ones required to maintain consistency with the schemata from which the representation is built, in just the same sense that recognition of a cube requires one to assume faces that cannot be seen.

That language comprehension does involve inferential elaboration has been shown a number of times. Bransford, Barclay, and Franks (1972) presented sentences such as

(1) Three turtles rested *on* a floating log, and a fish swam beneath them. (emphasis added),

which allows the inference that the fish also swam beneath the log, or the following sentence, which does not permit this inference,

(2) Three turtles rested *beside* a floating log, and a fish swam beneath them.

On a subsequent recognition test subjects who had seen the former sentence incorrectly identified a sentence stating that the fish swam under the log as one they had actually seen. Those who saw the second sentence did not make this identification. The experiment indicated that knowledge of spatial relations was spontaneously integrated into the representations built up as the sentences were comprehended.

Schweller, Brewer, and Dahl (1976) compared recall of sentences such as

(3) *The truck driver told the waitress he'd like to have some coffee.*

with

(4) *The truck driver told the waitress he'd like to have a new job.*

As predicted, the first sentence was often recalled, *The truck driver asked the waitress for some coffee,* whereas *asked* was not substituted in the second case. It is one of a waitress' functions to serve coffee, so it is natural to interpret the first sentence as a request. The second sentence was not interpreted as a request, because a declaration can have the force of a request only if the speaker believes the hearer would be able to do what is requested. It is not likely that a truck driver would believe that a waitress could actually give him a new job. The interpretation of the two sentences hinged on knowledge about the job functions and economic influence of waitresses. Again, world knowledge was spontaneously incorporated to produce a more coherent and richly detailed representation.

The schemata brought to bear in the effort after meaning are abstract, but the representation which results as a product of their interplay is elaborated and instantiated (Anderson & McGaw, 1973). Certainly in the case of language comprehension, and probably in perception and in the interpretation of experience generally, the final representation will include elements that are not among the givens. How the process works is still a matter of conjecture. Spiro (this volume) has provided a plausible account of reconstructive processes in memory, and Rumelhart and Ortony (Chapter 4, this volume) a plausible account of constructive processes in comprehension.

The views set forth in this section can be summarized in a single statement: abstract schemata program individuals to generate concrete scenarios. Where in this view is the locus of understanding? In the schemata? The generative process (see Craik & Lockhart, 1972)? Or, the scenario (see Paivio, 1971)? My answer is that the question is poorly framed; every component is necessary; none is sufficient; the whole system understands.

The foregoing picture of language and language comprehension stands in stark contrast to the one which Olson (Chapter 3, this volume) tells us predominates in the schools. It is, he says, a naive view, which "assumes that the effects of experience can be considered as knowledge, that knowledge is conscious, and that knowledge can be translated into words. Symmetrically, words can be translated into knowledge, hence, one can learn, that is, acquire knowledge, by being told." For reasons important in the history of Western culture and important for sustaining a technological society, this naive view is embodied in written text. Text is supposed to be completely explicit, maintain a fixed meaning in any context, and stand autonomous without the need for special interpreters nor, presumably, for an interpretive framework.

While the idea of autonomous text has considerable social utility, it would appear to be wrong or, at least, to have maladaptive side effects. Text is gobbledygook unless the reader possesses an interpretive framework to breathe meaning into it. To borrow Spiro's (Chapter 5, this volume) phrase, a "minimum plausible semantic representation" is required for anything to be learned. On the naive view that the text contains the meaning, the words themselves are valuable. The student's capacity to recognize or reproduce them accurately is evidence that he or she possesses "the knowledge the text conveys." Special devices probably have to be learned to cope with the demand for a veridical reproduction. These devices permit an assimilation which, again in Spiro's terms, preserves the "particular identity" of the message. Too thoroughgoing an assimilation and the student will selectively process aspects of the text. He might, as a consequence, fail to learn some of "the facts it contains." if the student's purpose is to update his or her knowledge, instead of to reproduce the text, the text will be read in a manner which seriously engages schemata incorporating his or her knowledge and belief about the world. Read in this fashion, a reproduction of the text will be less faithful to the original, since the reader will be making deeper and broader inferences. The text is likely to be modified. New elements are likely to be introduced. It is the teacher's role to count many of these changes as errors since they distort "the true meaning of the text." Thus, it would appear that schools, in their reliance upon supposedly autonomous text, may conspire to minimize serious interaction with existing schemata.

It is generally believed that as people grow older they become more capable of abstract thinking and more capable, therefore, of coping with abstract, decontextualized language. Nelson (Chapter 7, this volume) warns that there are well-formed senses in which even very young children must possess abstract knowledge. I would like to raise the possibility that the part of the proposition that applies to adults is also misleading. The problem is with the implication that since the language of text is abstract, the thinking that goes on with respect to this language is primarily abstract as well. Centrally involved in comprehending text, I suggested earlier, is the development of instantiated representations consistent with the message. All of the ingredients needed for concretization are not in the message itself. Therefore, more of the picture has to be drawn unaided by the reader; the detail has to be generated based on what is stored in memory. If text is decontextualized, then one might think of the process of comprehending it as *recontextualization*.

ACCOMMODATION: GROWTH AND CHANGE OF SCHEMATA

No doubt schemata change by gradual extension, articulation, and refinement. Rumelhart and Ortony (Chapter 4, this volume) have suggested how modification of this order might occur. I shall be concerned with larger changes. A paradigm shift on the part of a scientist or a religious or political conversion are examples of big changes. So are the stage-to-stage shifts generally presumed to characterize cognitive development. The process by which schemata change is poorly understood. Nelson (Chapter 7, this volume) indicates, for instance, that "it must be conceded that the most complete theory of development yet proposed is still a theory of stage progression and not yet a theory of transformations" and that "attempts to specify development in information-processing models are also still at the level of description of stages." It is obvious, therefore, that the remarks that follow are speculative.

I have chosen to emphasize large shifts in perspective and conceptual framework because such changes are interesting and important, a fact not widely appreciated by the current generation of educational psychologists. Science educators, on the other hand, influenced by 30 years of active work in the history and philosophy of science, readily accept the importance of a conceptual framework. They resonate to Piaget (Driver & Easley, 1969) and tend to regard behaviorism and associationism as simplistic (Hawkins, 1966). The history of science does provide many examples of figures who apparently made significant progress because they looked at the world differently from their compatriots. According to Conant (1950), Lavoisier, the father of modern chemistry, may have been enamored with quantitative methods because he was an accountant by profession. It is interesting that in 1789 Lavoisier believed that "we must lay it down as an incontestable axiom, that in all the operations of art and nature, nothing is created; an equal quantity of matter exists both before and after the experiment. . ." (cited in Conant, 1950, p. 30), even though the methods of the day were too crude to have permitted empirical verification of this proposition. His conviction may simply have reflected the principle of the balance sheet.

Brown (Chapter 7, this volume) has reviewed evidence, particularly cross-cultural evidence, which shows that exposure to formal schooling is correlated with important changes in cognitive functioning. How schooling brings about changes in schemata is a difficult question, however. Let us first ponder the possible effects of didactic, or expository, instruction. By these terms is meant instruction in which the teacher or teacher surrogate (that is, book, movie) describes, explains, and demonstrates; then there may be practice followed by feedback. Berliner and Rosenshine (Chapter 11, this volume) appear to have mainly this style in mind when they use the term "direct" instruction; however, their term does not suit my purpose since I wish to contrast didactic instruction with other styles, such as Socratic teaching, which are also direct.

Can didactic instruction cause a person to modify a world view, ideology, or theory? The answer is assuredly "yes." Throughout this contribution I have stressed the subjectivity and relativity of language comprehension. This seems like a good place to admit the virtues of an objective view of language. To the extent that people can and do follow the rules of literate discourse, they open themselves to persuasion. We are enjoined constantly from primary school through graduate school to be open minded, to honor consistent arguments, to weigh the evidence. It would be surprising, therefore, if reasoned prose did not sometimes cause us to change our minds.

If the arguments of the preceding section are correct, however, didactic instruction will often fail to have a profound influence on high-level schemata. The more fully developed a schema the less likely it will be to change. Wyer (Chapter 8, this volume) has summarized social psychological research bearing on this point, indicating that it is "likely that the implications of new information will be resisted if its acceptance would require a major cognitive reorganization, that is, if it would require a change in a large number of other logically related beliefs in order to maintain consistency among them." Apparent inconsistencies and counterexamples often are easily assimilated into the schemata to which a person is committed. For example, the Cold Warrior (Abelson, 1973) can interpret even the most innocent of political events in terms of the machination of the international Communist conspiracy, whereas the fanatical Marxist has an equal facility for seeing everything as a capitalist–imperialist plot.

Students come to class with schemata which allow them to understand and cope with events and to which they are committed in various degrees. These schemata will not necessarily be changed merely by laying on a new set of propositions. Sometimes students may appear to have changed when in fact the new propositions have been assimilated into old schemata, a fact which it would be easy to miss if one assesses "achievement" according to the students' ability to reproduce segments of the textbook in close-to-surface form. That this may be so is illustrated in an experiment recently completed in my laboratory.[2] The following is a passage which most people interpret as being about a convict planning his escape from prison.

> Rocky slowly got up from the mat, planning his escape. He hesitated a moment and thought. Things were not going well. What bothered him most was being held, especially since the charge against him had been weak. He considered his present situation. The lock that held him was strong but he he thought he could break it. He knew, however, that his timing would have to be perfect. Rocky was aware that it was because of his early roughness that he had been penalized so severely – much too severely from his point of view. The situation was becoming frustrating; the pressure had been grinding on him for too long. He was being ridden unmercifully. Rocky was getting angry now. He felt he was ready to make his move. He knew that his success or failure would depend on what he did in the next few seconds.

This passage also can be interpreted as the momentary reflections of a wrestler trying to break the hold of an opponent. A second passage is usually interpreted as about a group of people coming together to play cards, though it can be viewed as about a rehearsal of a woodwind ensemble. The two passages were studied by students in a physical education class, who were either wrestlers or familiar with wrestling, and by students enrolled in a music education class. Multiple choice tests designed to disambiguate the interpretations given to the passages indicated that physical education students gave a wrestling interpretation of the passage included above 64% of the time. Music students gave this interpretation 28% of the time. The other passage was given a woodwind rehearsal interpretation 29% of the time by the physical education students and 71% of the time by the music education students. When answers to an interest inventory and autobiographical questionnaire (Do you have a close relative who is a law enforcement officer? Have you ever attended a wrestling match?) were considered, a high proportion of the variance was accounted for. Yet there was little difference in the free recall protocols of the two groups. Whichever interpretation was given to the passages, the number of idea units recalled was the same. Only about half of the protocols contained as many as one disambiguation.

---

[2] My collaborators in this research are Ralph Reynolds, Diane Schallert, and Ernest Goetz.

Of course, the passages that have just been described were contrived so that two different underlying themes could have the same surface realization. The prose from which students are expected to learn in school would seldom permit of such tidy alternative renderings. Still, I suspect that it is easy for us to be fooled by the student who can repeat pregnant aspects of the text or lecture. The teacher has his/her schemata, too. The easy assimilation is that errors and gaps are blemishes rather than signs of what is possibly a wholly different point of view.

Driver and Easley (1969) and Driver (1973) have done Piagetian studies which support this analysis. Their subjects were gifted high school physics students. Interviews were conducted regarding the movement of balls, launched by a spring plunger, along a horizontal track. Many of the students manifested "an Aristotelian notion that constant force is required to produce constant motion. . . . [While they] used the language of Newtonian mechanics, such as 'force,' 'momentum,' 'impulse,' etc., this in itself means very little. . . ." The general conclusion was

> that the student, not being a blank slate, has already developed many concepts from his experience with the physical world, which influence ·his understanding of the new evidence and new arguments. When faced with propositions from teachers, textbooks, or even experiments, which are not in keeping with his own conceptual framework, he either has to modify his own view or construct another conceptual framework, separate from the one generated from his earlier experiences, but which is required for the purpose of "playing the game of school". . . (Driver & Easley, 1969, p. 1).

A person "playing the game of school," it was suggested earlier, attempts to minimize the interaction of existing schemata with that to which the teacher exposes him or her. If a separate identity for the new material can be maintained, the student generally will be able to answer the teacher's questions satisfactorily, whereas the student who permits him- or herself to reason from already formed schemata is likely to err (see Spiro, Chapter 5, this volume). If these are the typical demand characteristics of school, schema change is made less likely. According to Wyer (Chapter 8, this volume), beliefs which are logically related, but "cognitively segregated," will have little effect on one another.

My conjecture is that the likelihood of schema change is maximized when a person recognizes a difficulty in his current position and comes to see that the difficulty can be handled within a different schema. Note the parallel between this formulation and the Problem → Solution structure which Meyer (Chapter 6, this volume) found provided an especially efficacious high level organization of text. There is also a parallel, one would suppose, with the traditional gambit of the evangelist: before a person can be saved, he/she must come to know that he or she is a sinner. The evangelist, therefore, gives equal time to sin and to salvation.

The suggestion is that schema change on a large scale is a dialectical process. Riegel (1973) has argued that dialectics is the transformational key to stage progression in cognitive development, and that the thinking of adults as well as children is dialectical in character. Fundamental aspects of education can also be viewed in dialectical terms. The Socratic teaching methods that Collins (Chapter 10, this volume) has analyzed can certainly be looked at in this way. The teacher plays the Devil's Advocate, resisting moves by the student to assimilate arguments and evidence into his or her current schemata. Soft spots are probed using such techniques as invidious generalization (Rules 5, 7) and counterexample (Rules, 6, 8, 9).

People attempt to preserve cognitive consistency (Wyer, Chapter 8, this volume). However, the last thing a person will do is make a fundamental change in schemata. The first lines of defense are to counterargue within the current framework, as the students in some of Collins' dialogues clearly did; to treat anomalies as the exceptions which prove the rule; or to keep incompatible systems of belief separated. Driver (1973) concluded on the basis of her studies with high school physics students that "The belief system they use in school to pass examinations and staisfy the teacher . . . may never be related to that which is used in everyday experiences" (pp. 423–424).

Socratic teaching would appear to force students to deal with counterexamples and face contradictions. Notice, too, that unlike didactic instruction, in Socratic instruction it is the student who forges the conceptual system. The teacher is guided by an understanding of the accepted system and continuously updated diagnoses of the current status of the student's schema, but the teacher does not "lay on" the accepted theory. Rather, the teacher keeps the student working until he or she has constructed a framework that will stand to criticism. The Socratic teacher is aggressive and adversarial (see Oliver & Shaver, 1966). This is clearly a dialectical method to engage what may turn out to be an inherently dialectical process. Whether Socratic teaching, and related though gentler methods such as discovery teaching (Davis, 1966), actually promotes important cognitive change remains to be seen. Applied educational research has never been very good at answering such questions, as Berliner and Rosenshine (this volume) have explained at length. But there is here at least the virtue of a fresh perspective.

I must end with a word of caution. Mine is explicitly a relativistic view of language and language comprehension. Relativism is at least implicit in the thinking of most social scientists. But there is a danger in relativism and subjectivism (see Popper, 1968). It is a foundation stone of Western culture that a sentence has a "literal meaning" not merely a conveyed import, that a proposition can be "true" instead of merely believable, that an argument can be "correct" not just persuasive. There could be serious consequences if well-meaning technocrats caused a generation of American school teachers and children to believe that any sincere interpretation of a message were as good as another. Tentatively, I take a conventionalist approach to these issues. That is, I think it will be possible to conceive notions such as literal meaning, truth, and validity as concepts which make sense within a "paradigm" (Kuhn, 1970) developed and nurtured over several thousand years of human history.

SUMMARY

Social scientists in several areas have converged on the concept of *schema* as the building block of theory. The concept appears necessary to explain why and how people go beyond the givens in acts of perception and comprehension, that is, impose an order which cannot reasonably be said to exist in the sensory input. Schema formulations emphasize the patterning of elements rather than elements themselves. Following Piaget, schema *use* can be thought of as assimilation and schema *change* as accommodation. Both processes are important in the enterprise of schooling.

Without some schema into which it can be assimilated, an experience is incomprehensible and, therefore, little can be learned from it. But the schemata by which students assimilate their lessons may not be the ones certified by some discipline or other. This fact can easily escape detection since the student will often be able to repeat segments of the text and lecture even though he/she understands them in terms of an incorrect, incomplete, or inconsistent framework. Indeed, students may develop specialized frameworks for maintaining the particular identity of lesson material in order to cope with the demand for veridical reproduction.

Schema use must be a dynamic, constructive process, for it could not be the case that people have stored a schema to fit every conceivable situation. That this is so helps dissolve the seeming paradox between abstract linguistic competence, on the one hand, and the rich particularity of the mental representation which arises from any specific instance of language comprehension, on the other. To repeat the claim made earlier, abstract schemata program individuals to generate concrete scenarios. The implication is that decontextualized prose, the principal vehicle of formal schooling, is understood in a process of recontextualization.

Schema change is the sine qua non of the acquisition of knowledge as opposed to the mere aggregation of information. I speculated that large-scale accommodation may be a dialectical process which entails a confrontation with difficulties in one's current schema and coming to appreciate the power of an alternative. People resist change in high-level schemata. In the first place, well-developed schemata have great assimilative power. What is supposed to be a new view may be assimilated by the old. Again, it is probably difficult for teachers to distinguish between assimilation and accommodation. People whose important beliefs are threatened will attempt to defend their positions, dismiss objections, ignore counterexamples, keep segregated logically incompatible schemata. If this is a reasonable account, then a forthrightly dialectical method such as Socratic teaching is a plausible candidate as a deliberate instrument for causing students to change schemata.

ACKNOWLEDGMENTS

The preparation of this paper was supported by the Navy Personnel Research and Development Center and Advanced Research Projects Agency under Contract N61339-73-C-0078, and also by the National Institute of Education under Contract HEW NIE-G-74-0007.

REFERENCES

Abelson, R. P. The structure of belief systems. In R. C. Schank & K. M. Colby (Eds.), *Computer models of thought and language.* San Francisco: Freeman, 1973.

Anderson, J. R. Configural effects in sentence memory: A reexamination. Paper presented at the annual meeting of the Psychonomic Society, November, 1975.

Anderson, J. R., & Bower, G. H. *Human associative memory.* Washington, D.C.: Winston, 1973.

Anderson, R. C. Substance recall of sentences. *Quarterly Journal of Experimental Psychology,* 1974, **26**, 530–541.

Anderson, R. C., & McGaw, B. On the representation of the meanings of general terms. *Journal of Experimental Psychology,* 1973, **101**, 301–306.

Anderson, R. C., & Ortony, A. On putting apples into bottles: A problem of polysemy. *Cognitive Psychology,* 1975, 7, 167–180.

Ausubel, D. P. *The psychology of meaningful verbal learning.* New York: Grune & Stratton, 1963.

Bransford, J. D., Barclay, J. R., & Franks, J. J. Sentence memory: A constructive versus interpretive approach. *Cognitive Psychology,* 1972, 3, 193–209.

Bransford, J. D., & Johnson, M. K. Contextual prerequisites for understanding. Some investigations of comprehension and recall. *Journal of Verbal Learning and Verbal Behavior,* 1972, **11**, 717–726.

Bruner, J. S. *The process of education.* Cambridge, Mass.: Harvard University Press, 1960.

Chomsky, N. *Syntactic structures.* The Hague: Mouton, 1957.

Conant, J. B. *The overthrow of the phlogiston theory.* Cambridge, Mass.: Harvard University Press, 1950.

Craik, F. I. M., & Lockhart, R, S. Levels of processing: A framework for memory research. *Journal of Verbal Learning and Verbal Behavior,* 1972, **11**, 671–684.

Davis, R. B. Discovery in the teaching of mathematics. In L. S. Shulman & E. R. Keislar (Eds.), *Learning by discovery.* Chicago: Rand McNally, 1966.

Driver, R. P. The representation of conceptual frameworks in young adolescent physics students. Unpublished Ph.D. dissertation, University of Illinois, 1973.

Driver, R., & Easley, J. A. Autonomous dynamical thinking of young adolescent physics students. In J. A. Easley, *The uses of mathematics in science teaching.* Final report on Project UMIST, NSF Contract GW-2252. Urbana, Illinois: University of Illinois, 1969.

Foss, D. J., & Harwood, D. A. Memory for sentences: Implications for human associative memory. *Journal of Verbal Learning and Verbal Behavior,* 1975, **14**, 1–17.

Hawkins, D. Learning the unteachable. In L. S. Shulman & E. R. Keislar (Eds.), *Learning by discovery.* Chicago: Rand McNally, 1966.

Kuhn, T. S. *The structure of scientific revolutions.* Chicago: University of Chicago Press, 1970.

Kuipers, B. J. Representing knowledge for recognition. In D. G. Bobrow & A. Collins (Eds.), *Representation and understanding.* New York: Academic Press, 1975.

Lessing, D. *The golden notebook.* New York: Bantam Books, 1973.

Oliver, D. W., & Shaver, J. P. *Teaching public issues in the high school.* Boston: Houghton Mifflin, 1966.

Paivio, A. *Imagery and verbal processes.* New York: Holt, Rinehart & Winston, 1971.

Popper, K. R. *Conjectures and refutations: The growth of scientific knowledge.* New York: Harper & Row, 1968.

Riegel, K. F. Dialectic operations: The final period of cognitive development. *Human Development,* 1973, **16,** 346–370.

Schweller, K. G., Brewer, W. F., & Dahl, D. A. Memory for illocutionary forces and perlocutionary effects of utterances. *Journal of Verbal Learning and Verbal Behavior,* 1976, in press.

Author Index

Subject Index